SEARCHING FOR ETERNITY

Also by Dr. Don Morse

Non-Fiction

Clinical Endodontology
Stress and Relaxation
        (with M. Lawrence Furst)
Stress for Success
        (with M. Lawrence Furst)
Women Under Stress
        (with M. Lawrence Furst)
The Women's World
        (with M. Lawrence Furst)
Nutrition, Stress, and Aging
        (with Robert Pollack)
The Stress-Free, Anti-Aging Diet
        (with Robert Pollack)
Electronic Pharmacy of the Mind

Fiction

Deadly Reaction
Eye To Eye
Lethal Penetration

SEARCHING FOR ETERNITY:
A SCIENTIST'S SPIRITUAL JOURNEY TO OVERCOME DEATH ANXIETY

by Dr. Don Morse

Eagle Wing Books, Inc.
Memphis

SEARCHING FOR ETERNITY:
A Scientist's Spiritual Journey To Overcome Death Anxiety

© 2000 by Don Morse

Published in the United States by Eagle Wing Books, Inc.

Address inquiries to:
Eagle Wing Books, Inc.
Post Office Box 9972
Memphis, TN 38190

email: **ewibooks@aol.com**
web address: **www.eaglewingbooks.com**

ISBN: 0-940829-27-4

LCN: Pending

Retail Price: $19.95

First U.S.A. Printing: February 2000

DEDICATION

This book is dedicated to Diane:
my soul-mate, advisor, best friend, and eternal wife.

Searching for Eternity. *Photo* — Dr. Carlos Koloffon

ABOUT THE AUTHOR

Dr. Don Morse is Professor Emeritus at Temple University in Philadelphia. He has graduate degrees in dentistry, endodontics (root canal therapy), microbiology, clinical psychology, and clinical nutrition. Dr. Morse has been the principal investigator in many research projects involving hypnosis, meditation, acupuncture, and brain wave synchronizers (BWS).

Dr. Morse has written over 200 scientific articles and twelve books, including 9 non-fiction books — 7 of which are on stress and its management. His latest is *Electronic Pharmacy of the Mind: Use of Brain Wave Synchronizers and Other Relaxation Methods to Control Stress.* He has

also written three medical mystery novels (*Deadly Reaction, Eye to Eye and Lethal Penetration*).

In addition to *Searching for Eternity: A Scientist's Spiritual Journey to Overcome Death Anxiety*, two other books are currently being completed by Dr. Morse: *It's A Zoo Out There* is a humorous, illustrated animal saying book (with Dr. Marvin Herring). A fourth medical mystery novel, *Malpractice*, is about to be submitted for publication.

Dr. Morse was President of the *Philadelphia Society for Clinical Hypnosis* for two years and was Editor-in-Chief of *The International Journal of Psychosomatics* for ten years. He is presently Editor-in-Chief of *The Journal of Religion and Psychical Research*. Dr. Morse has given courses in hypnosis, meditation, BWS, relaxation therapy, stress management, and dealing with death anxiety throughout the United States and in 28 other countries.

He is happily married to Diane (for 43 years), has three children, Andrew, Brian and Caryn and four grandchildren, Danielle, Justin, Geoffrey and Monica. Dr. Morse and Diane live in beautiful Southern New Jersey.

He can be reached through the publisher by mail or email: ewibooks@aol.com.

TABLE OF CONTENTS

ACKNOWLEDGEMENTS

This book was made possible by the support of the following people: Dr. Paul Rosch, Editor of *Stress Medicine*, who encouraged me to write the article, "Confronting Existential Anxiety," which became the stimulus for the present book; Dr. Raymond Moody, for his enthusiastic praise for that article and subsequent inspiration for the current book; Dr. Berthold Schwarz, for his friendship throughout the years and information on psi phenomena; Dr. Simcha Paull Raphael, for information about the afterlife; Rabbis Richard Simon and Mordechai Rhine, for input on Kabballah and spirituality; Dr. Rabia Lynn Clark and Boyce Batey, for information on past life regressions and reincarnation; Dr. Marvin Herring, for his insightful cartoons; Dr. Carlos Koloffon, for the inspirational photograph on the next page, and Gary Tomchuk and Mike Bortnicker for their helpful suggestions. Special thanks to: Carol Hupping, for her excellent editorial help and input; Dr. Edwin Castillo, for his support through trying times, my agent, Bob Silverstein, for his relentless pursuit of excellence, and Dr. Greg Little, for his input on many aspects of psi phenomena and spirituality.

About The Illustrations

Most of the figures in this book are numbered and have identifying information. Many illustrations come from stock art services and copyright-free books. Illustrations without identifying information come from a variety of art sources including DigitalVision®, Corel Mega Gallery®, Art Explosion®, Softkey®, Print Artist®, Art Mania®, the Dover series of copyright-free illustrations, and others.

WHAT DR. MORSE'S CONTEMPORARIES HAVE SAID ABOUT SEARCHING FOR ETERNITY: A SCIENTIST'S SPIRITUAL JOURNEY TO OVERCOME DEATH ANXIETY

"Searching for Eternity: A Scientist's Spiritual Journey to Overcome Death Anxiety" is an inspiring, clearly focused compendium of encyclopedic sweep. Dr. Morse, ever the great teacher, scholar and positive thinker, tackles the core anxiety — what happens after death — by exploring the emotionally blockbusting near-death experiences and relevant scientific aspects and data bases of the great religions. His voyage into the Unknown is totally absorbing and like a great detective story, it weaves its tale that can leave the reader breathless until the last pages. A profound synthesis that doesn't dodge touchy issues but offers comfort and hope, and points out many leads for future investigations. To be read, and reread, to be savored and thought about. Engagingly presented, "Searching for Eternity" is a book that will be with us for a long time. Dr. Morse has come close to achieving the impossible, and the reader should be richly rewarded."

— Berthold E. Schwarz, M.D., renowned psychiatrist and paranormal phenomena researcher, author of *Psychic Nexus*, *UFO Dynamics*, and *Psychiatric and Paranormal Aspects of UFOLOGY*.

• • •

"People view death in very different ways, usually as a result of religious or sociocultural beliefs about such things as Heaven and Hell, reincarnation, or some other aspect of the nature of our existence in the hereafter. In some instances, our state of mental and physical health, or compelling near-death experiences become modifying influences. Some welcome death because it offers the promise of eternal bliss as a reward for having adhered to their religious or moral beliefs, or relief from persistent pain or distress. But for most, death remains the *mysterium tremendum et fascinans*, a mysterious and alluring transformation that has components of awfulness, dread, and the sense of being overpowered by the unseen gaze of a majestic and inaccessible higher power.

In this unusually comprehensive work, Dr. Morse reviews numerous cultural and religious concepts of death and the hereafter. Man is probably the only creature that contemplates death, and for some, the anticipation of death can prove to be a source of stress that severely impairs the quality of life. The author explains how his own near death encounter led to an appreciation that existence in the hereafter can be a joyous experience, in which our souls are sustained and nourished by some higher presence, and cites similar experiences by others. He also takes on the Herculean task of assembling scientific support for these interpretations, and is to be congratulated for presenting such a convincing argument.

A panoramic panoply of relevant ancient and modern reports of apparitions, visions, dreams, séances, reincarnation, past life regressions are thoroughly reviewed and critically examined. In essence, all of these tend to reinforce the belief in a Supreme Being that governs the Universe, rather than the notion that God is essentially man's creation. More importantly, the author's account of his own spiritual journey and quest should convince many that there is nothing to be gained by worrying about death. His message is that the hereafter will provide eternal peace and pleasure, if we conduct our lives in an ethical, moral, and humane fashion, and that such conduct should provide the same rewards while we are still mortal."

— Paul Rosch, M.D. F.A.C.P., world's foremost stress authority, President of "The American Institute of Stress," Editor, *Stress Medicine*, and Clinical Professor of Medicine and Psychiatry, New York Medical College.

• • •

"In 'Searching for Eternity,' Dr. Don Morse has made a remarkable contribution to the contemporary needs of society. As I have traveled the world these past 50 years, it has become more and more evident to me that the Western World has chosen to ignore the challenges, the problems and the inescapable facts of death. Indeed it is almost as if children, in recent decades, have been artificially 'immunized' from facing the truth about death to the point of being told that it either doesn't exist or people have simply gone to sleep. As Dr. Morse's book so eloquently communicates, with the longer and more widespread length of life, it is becoming more and more apparent that unprepared people are suddenly having to face the fact that life, at least on Earth, is not permanent and cannot be ignored. We are long overdue for rediscovery of the facts of life and death, and Dr. Morse has brilliantly examined the panorama not only from a religious or a philosophical viewpoint, but from a scientist's perspective as well. It is a brilliant blending of both areas of thoughts, a blending which, at one time, was simply considered impossible.

I have known some brilliant physical scientists who have comfortably and deeply believed in the survival of the soul and then the extension of another life after what we understand to be death. It is a joy to read the crystallized and vivid thoughts of Dr. Morse's in expanding upon the facts of life and of death that surround us. He brings us to the inevitable conclusion that there is much more to life than our last day on Earth, and in so doing, he enriches our purpose for life and the positive anticipation of the future. I found this to be a rare and remarkably inspiring read."

— Kreskin, the world's foremost mentalist, psychic researcher, internationally acclaimed lecturer and author, whose current book is *Predictions for the New Millennium*.

• • •

" 'SEARCHING FOR ETERNITY' is anything but a dull scientist's tome. The book is deeply personal and involves the reader in its search to mine from the collective whole of the human family all that it can about the survival of human consciousness after death. And it does so splendidly. I congratulate Dr. Morse on his singular achievement. His compassion and caring shine through every page; his scholarship, equally so."

— P. M. H. Atwater, Lh.D., author of *Coming Back to Life*; *Beyond the Light*; *Children of the New Millennium*; and *Future Memory*.

"DEADLY" QUOTATIONS

"If a man die, may he live again?"
(Job 14:14).

"We have shown that amid much deception and self-deception, fraud and illusion, veritable manifestations do reach us from beyond the grave."
(F.W.H. Myers, *Human Personality and its Survival of Bodily Death*,
\abridged edition. Pilgrim Books, Norwich, England, 1992 [original, 1903], p. xiii).

"Death is not a word to fear, any more than birth is. We change our state at birth, and come into the world of air and sense and myriad existence; we change our state at death and enter a region of — what? Of ether, I think, and still more myriad existence; a region in which communion is more akin to what we call telepathy, and where intercourse is not conducted by the accustomed indirect physical processes; but a region in which beauty and knowledge are as vivid as they are here: a region in which progress is possible, and in which 'admiration, hope and love' are even more real and dominant."
(Lodge, O. *Raymond or Life and Death*. George H. Doran Co., NY, 1916, p. 296).

"Only if we are convinced that it (human personality) extends beyond the limits of its atomic consciousness and reaches out, potentially, to that for which the ordinary name is God, can the future of human society be secure....From the nature of the personality of man springs the possibility of the mystical divine union, the promise of a limitless inheritance, and the hope that in literal truth 'this mortal shall put on immortality.' "
(Tyrrell, G.N.M. *The Personality of Man*. Pelican, London, 1946, p. 284).

"We cannot begin to live fully until we come to terms with the reality of death. We cannot know true courage until we look death in the face and see that it is not a voracious monster with yawning jaws that will eventually gobble up everything we hold precious, but instead a thing of beauty and wonder and great adventure. We will never be free to love fully and without fear until we know deep in our hearts the truth that love never dies, but lives on, along with those we have loved, forever."
(Fairchilde, L. *Voices From the Afterlife*. St. Martin's, Griffin, NY, 1997, p. xviii).

"The tomb is not a blind alley; it is a thorofare. It closes on the twilight and opens on the dawn. You say the soul is nothing but the resultant of bodily powers: why, then is my soul more luminous when my bodily powers begin to fail? The earth gives me its generous sap, but heaven lights me with the reflection of unknown worlds. The nearer I approach the end, the plainer I hear around me the immortal symphonies of the worlds which invite me. When I go down to the grave, I cannot say 'I have finished my life.' My day's work will begin again the next morning."

(Victor Hugo, as quoted in *Spiritual Frontiers*, Winter/Spring 1998. p.39).

If belief in life after death enriches life, then it has fulfilled a great task. There is everything to live for and nothing to lose."

(Haddow, A.H. Life After Death: Psi Evidence and Religious Belief. *Journal of Religion and Psychical Research*, Oct. 1998).

"Life after death is the most profound unsolved mystery of them all."

(*Unsolved Mysteries*, Lifetime TV Channel, July 16, 1998).

"Life after death is the coming thing. Immortality is becoming popular and respectable."

(Martin Ebon, as quoted in *Spiritual Frontiers*, Winter/Spring 1998 p.62).

"I am standing on the seashore. A ship at my side spreads her white sails to the morning breeze and starts for the blue ocean. She is an object of beauty and strength, and I stand and watch her until at length she is a speck of white cloud just where the sea and sky come to mingle with each other. Then someone at my side says, "There! She's gone!" Gone where? Gone from my sight, that is all. She is just as large in mass and hull and spar as she was when she left my side, and she is just as able to bear her load of living weight to her destined harbor. Her diminished size is in me, not in her. And just at the moment when someone at my side says, "There! She's gone!" there are other eyes watching her coming, and other voices ready to take up the glad shout, "Here she comes!" And that is dying.

(Anonymous, quoted in: Meek, G.W. *Enjoy Your Own Funeral*. Galde Press, Lakeville, MN, 1999, p. 108).

FOREWORD

by **Raymond A. Moody**, Ph.D., M.D.
World's Foremost Authority on Near-Death Experiences
Author of
Life After Life (1988),
Reunions: Visionary Encounters With Departed Loved Ones (1994),
Discovering the Soul (1997),
The Last Laugh (1999), *The Light Beyond* (1989),
and many more books.

Dr. Don Morse has long experience in the field of psychosomatic medicine, and it is a good thing indeed that he has applied his field to the problems of death anxiety. Death anxiety is becoming an increasing problem in the United States as tens of millions of Baby Boomers are reaching the time of life that forces them to confront their own mortality. As their parents die in large numbers, Baby Boomers now face grief and mourning that, due to medical advances, many have escaped until mid-life.

Raymond A. Moody. Photo— G. Little

Dr. Morse skillfully integrates an amazing amount of biological and physiological knowledge with a body of research concerning near-death experiences, apparitions, and other spiritual experiences relating to the perennial human concerns about the possibilities of a life after physical death.

This is a timely book providing helpful guidelines for those grieving about the loss of loved ones, and for those who are for the first time seriously wondering about the ultimate nature of the dying process and how to care for the terminally ill.

PREFACE

by Peter Novak

Author of

The Division of Consciousness: The Secret Afterlife of the Human Psyche

Don Morse devoted his entire life to science, accumulating graduate degrees in dentistry, psychology, endodontology, microbiology,
nutrition, and immunology, and eventually retiring Professor Emeritus
at Temple University. Along the way, he wrote hundreds of scientific
articles and twelve books, seven of which were on stress management.
But in his mid-60's, he found himself up against something for which all
his scientific training had left him unprepared — Death. Caught off
guard by the unexpected deaths of a number of close friends and
relatives, and haunted by long-repressed memories of his own Near-
Death Experience, Morse developed a stress disorder — a nearly para-
lyzing and obsessive fear of death, which left him unable to concentrate,
sleep, or eat, and suffering from stress-induced physical symptoms such
as abdominal cramps and headaches.

For a man who had devoted much of his professional life to
writing and lecturing on stress management, this anxiety was all the
more disconcerting. Morse found that his most favorite, tried-and-true
stress management tools, such as exercise and meditation, were no
longer effective. Nor were methods such as avoidance and distractions
able to help him keep from thinking about the inevitable. The only way
to counter his incapacitating apprehensions about death, he realized,
was to confront them head on.

Morse put his lifetime of scientific training to good use, dispas-
sionately examining humanity's vast collection of reports about death
and the afterlife. He was resolved to determine what, if anything, awaits
us after death. The sweep and breadth of this work is unparalleled. Morse
starts off his journey by exploring the wide spectrum of afterlife phenomena being reported today, providing us with a remarkably detailed,
comprehensive, and up-to-date study of NDEs (Near-Death Experiences), OBEs (Out-of-Body Experiences), ADCs (After Death Communi-

cations), PLRs (Past-Life Regressions), as well as ghosts and apparitions, deathbed visions, dreams, afterlife teachings of the major world religions, including those of ancient Egypt and Greece, Hinduism, Zoroastrianism, Buddhism and Tibetan Buddhism, Judaism, Kabbalah, Gnostic Christianity, Modern Christianity, Islam, Sufism, Sikhism, and Bahai'ism. Morse then goes on to explore more modern theories on death and the afterlife, such as the teachings of the Seventh-Day Adventists, the Jehovah's Witnesses, the Christadelphians, the Unitarian Universalists, the Rosicrucians, the Freemasons, the Golden Dawn, Theosophy, Swedenborgianism, Religious Science, Eckankar, Urantia, Seth, and Scientology, while also considering the afterlife teachings of William Blake, Allan Kardec, Duncan MacDougal, Bô Yin Râ, Edgar Cayce, E.W. Dykes, Roel van de Meulen, Bruce Moen, Greg Little, Fred Alan Wolf, Simcha Paull Raphael and my own "Division Theory" research into the binary soul doctrine.

As I was reading this opus, I became more and more proud to have a discussion of my own work included within it, and more and more incredulous than no one had ever compiled such a thorough and fascinating study of mankind's thoughts upon the afterlife before. This book is a resource that should be on the shelf of anyone studying any facet of any set of afterlife teaching, for Morse catalogues the entire rainbow of humanity's afterlife teachings, revealing both the dignity and limitations of each, while also showing us, in the process, the true meaning of scientific integrity. He does not preemptively assume that any of these reports, teachings, or theories are true or false, nor does he dismiss or rationalize any away. Instead, he assesses each on its own merits, logically, insightfully, brilliantly, all the while showing where and how they agree and disagree — one with the other.

Finally, Morse presents his own personal theory of the afterlife, integrating the many different faces of death into an intriguing new vision of the journey that awaits us all. Through the eyes of a dedicated scientist, he examined humanity's many reports about death and the afterlife, and concluded there is indeed ample reason to believe in the soul's survival of death and the possibility of a positive afterlife. It seems that, whether it be "matter and antimatter," "male and female" or "science and religion," whenever two opposing natures successfully come together, the most powerful forces of the universe are unleashed, and magic happens. This book is one such example.

INTRODUCTION

"They come and they go and they trot and they dance, and never a word about death. All well and good. Yet when death does come — to them, their wives, their children, their friends — catching them unawares and unprepared, then what storms of passion overwhelm them, what cries, what fury, what despair!"
(deMontaigne, M. *The Complete Essays*. Penguin Books, NY, 1987, p. 95).

"It is well-known that we cannot imagine ourselves not existing. We can imagine ourselves being out of the body and looking down upon a world without us; we can imagine being at our own funerals, or reading our own obituaries. But imagining that we have ceased to exist — it's something we are just incapable of doing."
(Perry, Michael. The Soul and Its Immortality, *The Academy of Religion and Psychical Research*, Bloomfield, CT, 1995, p. 24).

I knew I was dying, but I wasn't afraid. The light was incredibly beautiful, and I felt wonderfully calm and secure with a benevolent presence beside me. My life rapidly flashed before me; then I saw my funeral and read my obituary...

It all started in June, 1983 when I took a six-month sabbatical from Temple University to do research on the effects of stress and relaxation on the salivary glands. Aside from a bout with colitis when I was ten years old and childhood and young adult attacks of asthma, I had been quite healthy. I had been eating well and exercising regularly. So it was quite a shock when on a sunny June day, I came down with a severe disease with the intriguing name of *giardiasis*. It was caused by an intestinal parasite, *Giardia llambia*. The symptoms were severe — unrelenting abdominal cramps, alternating constipation and diarrhea but mainly the former. The medications, quinacrine and Flagyl®, helped temporarily but then the cramping returned with a vengeance. I became very anxious and had to be hospitalized. Unfortunately, my bed was next to a patient dying from colon cancer and unlike the situation when my father was dying from cancer (he had been told nothing about his disease), this patient's doctor was giving him a vivid description of his cancer and its ultimate outcome. This only added to *my* anxiety as I recalled my father's agonizing death and was convinced that my unrelenting pain was related to cancer. In addition to the anxiety created by my roommate's condition, I had a bizarre psychological reaction to quinacrine.

The doctors considered that I had recovered from giardiasis and that I now had developed a mental condition that had to be treated in a psychiatric hospital. So I was transferred to a large facility in Philadelphia that looked like a country estate with several buildings and beautiful lawns and gardens.

On a bright Tuesday morning, I went outside. I walked around the grounds. Then I decided to jog. After a few moments, the world started to spin around, and suddenly I fell down. Darkness enveloped me and then I saw the light.......

I didn't die. I was taken inside and revived. It took a few months of treatment with antianxiety and antidepressant medications, but I recovered just in time to go back to teaching. I wondered about my near-death experience (NDE) with the wonderful light, blissful feelings, benevolent presence, life review, and out-of-body experience (OBE) in which I read my obituary and saw my funeral. But I put all of that on hold. For the next twelve years, I was busy teaching, doing research, writing, practicing, and enjoying life. Then in 1995, all hell broke loose.

After having retired from Temple University two years previously, none of my secondary career plans had been realized. Several friends, relatives, and family members in their 60's died. My cousin, Ernie, died of throat cancer; my cousin, Edith, died of uterine cancer. Divorces and separations cropped up. Several friends of my wife, Diane, and myself and/or their spouses who lived in the area, died. And worst of all, my beloved sister, Ruth, passed away at the age of 62 from a heart attack. I couldn't believe it. Ruth had a fine figure, exercised, meditated regularly, had a decent diet, and had a good outlook on life.

This combination of life stress events was enough to throw me into a turmoil. I developed "General Anxiety Disorder," and I started to think about death — a subject that I had been able to avoid for twelve years (since my bout with giardiasis). I couldn't meditate; I couldn't concentrate; I couldn't sleep well; I couldn't exercise; food didn't taste well; and worst of all, I developed two alternating symptoms: severe abdominal cramps (just like I had back in 1983 when I suffered from the aftermath of giardiasis); and neuralgic-like headaches.

Knowing all about stress management doesn't insulate a person from coming down with a stress-related disorder. If the life stressors are numerous and severe, no one is immune. So I saw a psychiatrist. With a combination of cognitive therapy and a low dose of an antianxiety agent and antidepressant, I recovered. I confronted the fear of death by recalling my NDE and busied myself with watercolor painting (see *Figure 1*), regular workouts at the gym, working as an endodontist one day a week, and taking vacations. I also read everything I could find about death anxiety. I subsequently had two articles published about it. But I still was not certain about the reality of the soul, the afterlife and God.

I began my search for eternity by reflecting upon my NDE. I then interviewed many people (scientists, religious leaders, teachers, health care practitioners, authors, near-death survivors, holocaust victims, and psychics). I also read many books and cruised the internet for information about religion, mysticism, cosmology, NDEs, OBEs, apparitions, visions, dreams, past life regression, séances, mediums, and related subjects. As a result, I learned a great deal more about death anxiety and how to cope with it. Although no one can claim absolute knowledge about the future, I no longer have lingering doubts. Considering this, I felt obliged to share my spiritual journey here.

Come with me on my journey as we start in Chapter 1 with a look at death anxiety and learn methods to deal with it both early in life and then later in life. We find that as we get older and the reality of death approaches, the previously learned methods are no longer sufficient. It is then that in order to overcome death anxiety, it is necessary to determine if there is life after death.

This book is unlike any other that tries to prove the reality of the three components of life after death: the surviving soul, the positive afterlife and God. In other books, only one viewpoint is given. For example, books about NDEs use personal experience as the alleged proof. The same is true for books about OBEs, reincarnation and visions. Scientific books try to prove the existence of God or the soul by using findings from cosmology, quantum physics and evolution.

In this book, a holistic, integrative approach is used. To do this, we take a spiritual journey to document the possibility of God, the surviving soul and the afterlife. Our journey starts in Chapter 2 in which my unusual NDE is presented. In the remaining chapters, our journey passes through NDEs, OBEs, apparitions, dreams, medium reports, past life regressions, immortality, God, the origin of the universe, the origin of life, and religious, organizational, and individual viewpoints of the soul, God, and the afterlife. The last stop in our spiritual journey is a personal concept of the afterlife based on all the previous steps.

The book is written for you to follow in my footsteps as I use a scientifically-based approach to look at the evidence. In other words, the support for a surviving soul, the afterlife, and God is not taken on faith alone. When stops on our spiritual journey are taken on paths such as NDEs, OBEs, apparitions, past life regressions, immortality, religions, and recent afterlife concepts, you become involved in each of these in a personal way.

Figure 1
Copy of a watercolor painting, "Spirit Island, Canada"
by Don Morse, June, 1995.

CHAPTER ONE

DEATH ANXIETY

"Life is eternal; and love is immortal; and death is only a horizon;
and a horizon is nothing save the limit of our sight."
— R. W. Raymond

Who in life at one time or another has not feared death? Can you recall flying at 35,000 feet on a 757? You're relaxed while reading a Sue Grafton novel. Your spouse is engrossed in the newest James Bond movie. The guy on the opposite aisle is drinking a scotch on the rocks. Others are sleeping, reading magazines or listening to music. The flight has been long but smooth. You stop reading for a moment and think about the wonders of the concluding 20th century, especially to be able to fly across the country in a few hours. Then it happens — a sudden strong jolt. The plane rapidly sinks. Is it an air pocket? Or is it something more serious?

The announcement echoes forth: "Please return to your seat and make sure your seat beats are fastened. We have encountered some turbulence. We'll bring the plane to a new altitude and try to find some smoother air. It should only be a few minutes, but meanwhile, remain in your seats with the belts securely fastened."

You look at the nearest flight attendant. She looks anxious. Would she be anxious if it were only an air pocket? Is the captain telling us the truth? Are we going to crash? Am I going to die? You haven't thought about death and dying for a long time. Not since years ago when a loved one suddenly died. But now you're face to face with the possibility of death.

You were brought up in an organized religion. You went to services on occasion but it was merely lip service. Suddenly you're flooded with unanswerable questions. Is there a God? Do we have a soul that outlasts the physical body? Is there an afterlife? A heaven? A hell?

You are very frightened. You wish you had more faith. But now it's too late. What will happen?

Before you can finish the last question, the plane eases into a new altitude. The bumps are gone. The ride is once again smooth. You wipe the sweat off your brow and say: "Thank God!"

Every one of us, including myself, wants answers to those unanswerable questions about what comes next. As mentioned in the Introduction, I had a near-death experience in 1983 that gave me a glimpse of the afterlife, and I suffered general anxiety disorder in 1995. The latter propelled me into an investigation of why we develop an overwhelming fear of death and how we can overcome it. The answers I received greatly reduced my anxiety and led to my writing this spiritual journey to overcome death anxiety. It has been an enlightening and reassuring experience for me, and I hope will be meaningful to you, as well.

Before we begin our actual journey, there are certain things that we must do. First of all, I've been throwing around the words fear and anxiety as if they were interchangeable. They are close in meaning, but definite differences do exist. So, let's briefly examine these differences. Following this, we'll consider how each of us deals with death anxiety at different stages of our lives. When we find that those coping techniques are no longer effective and the only thing that will help us is answering the unanswerable questions about God, the soul, and the afterlife, we'll begin our spiritual journey. I hope that it culminates with assurances that we can overcome death anxiety.

Fear And Anxiety: What Do They Look Like?

I'm sure that you have some experience with both fear and anxiety, but examining a few situations can help clarify the differences between them. *Fear is a normal response that includes feelings of disquiet or alarm elicited by the realistic expectation of pain, danger or disaster.* For example, a man enters your apartment brandishing a pistol and demands that you give him all your jewelry and money or else he'll kill you. You start to tremble and shake. Your heart is beating rapidly. Beads of sweat appear on your forehead; your hands are clammy. Your mouth is so dry. You start to speak. The words come out quietly, without force, barely intelligible: "Please, mister, I'll give you whatever you want but don't hurt me." Suddenly, you urinate. Now, not only are you scared to death, you're embarrassed. You see yourself in the mirror. It's almost like looking at an apparition: the ghostly looking face, the shaking body. You've got a sinking feeling in your gut. And now you've got a pounding headache. You feel faint.

These bodily reactions that are brought on by fear are the same as those that occur with anxiety. The principal difference between fear and anxiety is that *anxiety is an irrational or overwhelming fear.* Anxiety can be brought on by some external occurrence, but it is more often based on the person's subjective, distorted view of the circumstance. The individual with anxiety has intense fear or dread, but there is usually no realistic object or occurrence that engenders the anxious feelings. That is, the anxiety is often based on an irrational belief. For example, you drive your car through one of the Pennsylvania mountain tunnels. Even though there is absolutely no evidence that anything bad will happen (the tunnel is well lit, there are only a few cars on the road), you're extremely fearful that the car will crash and you will be killed. You slow down to 25 miles per hour and stay as far to the right as possible. You don't want to hit any oncoming car, but now you're worried that you'll crash into the side wall. This makes you even more nervous. A loud horn blast adds to your fright. It's coming from the car behind you. You realize that you're driving too slow. With trepidation, you accelerate to 35 miles per hour. Now, you're worried that you're driving too fast. No matter what you do, your nervousness intensifies. You are caught in a cycle of recurrent anxiety.

Freud stated that, at its core all anxiety is separation anxiety, with the overwhelming fear being derived from the separation from one's mother at birth. Going beyond Freud's concept, it could be considered that this core separation anxiety is *an overwhelming fear of being separated from life.* Looking at the concept from another vantage point, the separation anxiety is an overwhelming fear that one will be separated from his/her maker (that is, God). The concept here is that the person (as a soul) was once united with God, then was separated from the Lord at birth, and then his/her soul will be reunited with God in the afterlife. The anxiety comes from the dual fear: (1) Is there a God? and (2) If there is a God, will the way I lived my life have justified that my soul will be reunited with the Heavenly Presence? Consideration of various aspects of the soul, afterlife and God are discussed during our spiritual journey. But first, let us look into what is meant by death anxiety.

Death Anxiety

"We who are about to die demand a miracle."
(W.H. Auden).

As humans, we are the only species that is aware of its impending death. It could be argued that some other animals, such as chimpanzees, who witness fellow chimps dying, might understand, that they, too, will undergo a similar fate. However, there is no reason to believe that they have any concept of a soul, immortality, an afterlife, and how one's actions while alive could affect an afterlife (if there is an afterlife). The knowledge of impending death and one's thoughts and actions while alive can lead to death anxiety. *Death anxiety is defined as an overwhelming fear of death and/or dying and usually involves an all-encompassing fear about whether or not one will continue to exist in some form or fashion after physical death.* It includes unrelenting fear of dying and anxiety about the unknown. As will be discussed in the forthcoming sections, death anxiety is so overwhelming and all pervasive that all of us go to extreme lengths to avoid the anxiety. But there are major differences in how we handle death anxiety in our younger years and then later in life. Let's consider these differences beginning with death anxiety early in life.

Dealing With Death Anxiety: The Early Years

As youngsters and teenagers, most of us are so enthralled with activities, learning, and the wonders of the world that we feel immortal. As a teenager, you probably never feared that you could crash and die if a roller coaster went out of control. As you got into your twenties, thirties and forties and became involved with relationships and careers, you were so busy trying to cement relationships and achieve goals that you had little or no time to consider death. Of course, death was encountered every day: in traffic accidents; newspaper reports; radio news; on the TV screen; in movies; and occasionally with family, friends, and acquaintances. But you unconsciously rationalized that death happens to others, and in some way you still believed yourself to be immortal. Freud put it like this: "Our own death is indeed unimaginable, and whenever we make the attempt to imagine it we can perceive that we really survive as spectators.....at the bottom no one believes in his own death, or to put the same thing in another way, in the unconscious, every one of us is convinced of his own immortality."

If we are fortunate enough to live into our fifties in relatively good health, blinders are often used to avoid thinking about death. How is this done? How do we put on these blinders to the reality of our own death? The answer is that we use both negative and positive stress control techniques.

Negative Dealing

A close relative of mine pops a Valium® whenever she is highly anxious (drug addict). I have a friend who confronts anxiety by smoking like a chimney (nicotine addict). Another drinks like a fish (alcoholic). A third, stuffs her mouth with any fatty snack that's available (junk food addict). A fifth drinks coffee like its going out of style (caffeine addict). One buddy rushes off to Atlantic City, where he plays craps for hours (gambling addict).

I knew a guy who used the method of evasion to deal with his anxiety. He was a heavy smoker. He was aware of smoking and its association with diseases such as lung cancer and heart disease. But he was in his mid-30s and only suffered from a hacking cough. He used to tell me, "Death, that's something in the distant future. I'm not going to worry about that now." But twenty years later, I visited him in the hospital, with all sorts of tubes coming out of his body. He had to face death then, but having no faith and no afterlife knowledge, he died angry and without a clue about his destiny. Years ago, I, too, found a way to cope. I buried myself in work. I was a workaholic. Sure, my workaholism blocked out thoughts of death, but I also alienated myself from my family.

With all of these negative stress control techniques, there is a short-term gain that can temporarily block out anxiety, including thoughts of death. The problem is that all of the negative coping techniques have dangerous health-related outcomes. The eventual problems with all of the addictions and evasive methods we use to avoid reality should be obvious.

Positive Dealing

Avoidance is a method of coping with anxiety by not coping with anxiety. In other words, one way to manage anxiety is to avoid it. With regard to death anxiety, we can avoid it by blocking out thoughts of death or only think about death at isolated moments. For example, cemeteries are usually placed in out-of-the-way areas so that we only have to consider death when we occasionally visit our deceased loved ones.

Diversions are another way to sidestep anxiety. With diversions, we can leave the area or distract our mind. We know that we must eventually deal with death, but by getting involved with a diversion, we can become so occupied that thoughts of death are either ignored or put on hold. Diversions are of many kinds and forms and include hobbies, going to movies, shows, and concerts; watching television (if not excessive); using the computer and browsing the internet; playing sports; and going on vacations.

I always found that going on a foreign vacation was an excellent way to block out thoughts of death. I would get involved with examining historical sights, visiting castles and cathedrals (see *Figure 2*), learning local customs, and just basking in the sun. I especially avoided reading newspapers, watching TV, listening to the radio, or being in telephone contact (unless it was absolutely necessary). I realize that not everyone can afford a foreign vacation, but even taking a trip to an unusual close-by place can be stimulating.

Some other diversions that we can use to block out thoughts of death include cosmetic surgery, accumulating material possessions, having affairs with younger people, and overexercising. These could be temporarily beneficial but only postpone the inevitable.

Relaxation techniques can help keep us in balance, and a well-balanced person can stay busy and active and keep thoughts of death at bay. Several excellent relaxation techniques are available including meditation, self-hypnosis, brain wave synchronizers (photostimulating goggles, see *Figure 3*), progressive relaxation and autogenic training. I have used all of these. I found the most effective ways for me to maintain my equilibrium were meditation and brain wave synchronizers. They are also the simplest to do.

Proper nutrition also helps keep us in balance. A daily well-balanced diet supplemented with antioxidant vitamins and minerals such as vitamin C, vitamin E, mixed carotenes, and selenium is recommended. I have used this combination for over 25 years and have found it to be quite effective. The combination of the following three nutrients has been shown by others to have some antianxiety effect: GABA (gamma-amino-butyric acid), inositol (a B vitamin), and niacinamide (another B vitamin). Certain foods, (e.g., chocolate) and herbal preparations (e.g., chamomile and lavender teas, Kava Kava, and evening primrose) can also reduce anxiety.

Exercise is the third component to help keep us in balance. Exercise has many benefits including strength building, endurance, disease prevention, companionship (when done with another), improved thinking (relative to increased circulation to the brain), and pleasure (from the release of endorphins during enjoyable aerobic exercise). Exercise can also act as a diversion. The principal danger is trying to recapture youthful abilities and appearance with the unrealistic aim of preventing aging. Exercise can delay, but not prevent, aging.

Figure 2
Copy of a watercolor painting, "Stadtkirche, Badan-Badan, Germany," by Don Morse, July, 1998.

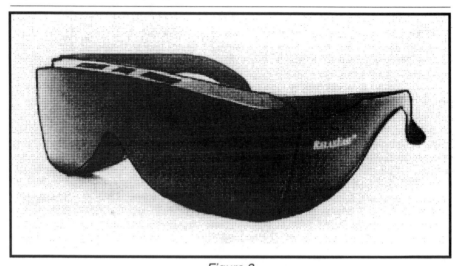

Figure 3
The Relaxease™ Brain Wave Synchronizer Goggles (Mark 2000 Corp.,
1240 Johnson Ferry Place, Suite E-30, Marietta, GA 30068; 1-888-627-5200).

With relaxation techniques, proper nutrition and regular exercise, we can look and feel our best. Being healthy, it becomes difficult to even imagine death.

Mental preparation is an excellent method for dealing with anxiety. If you are prepared, you can face the consequences. In the hypothetical example of sudden turbulence during a plane ride (given at the beginning of this chapter), if you had no anxiety about death, for example, as a result of having read this book (being mentally prepared), you would not have suffered anxiety about the possibility of dying in a plane crash.

Having a positive mental attitude is another excellent method to deal with anxiety. See the glass as half full rather than half empty. With that same flying example, you would look at the situation and consider that air turbulence is a common occurrence, and that the captain would not lie. You might still have some fear, but you wouldn't have serious thoughts of death.

After I have a good workout, I usually take a steam bath, sauna, whirlpool, and sometimes, a massage. These techniques do not directly deal with death anxiety, but they make me feel so good that it's as if I'm floating on air. And when I come down to earth, I'm prepared to go home, kiss my wife, go out for a fancy dinner and see a show. Involved with all of that, death is the farthest thing on my mind. If these facilities are available to you, I recommend them highly.

As happens with the negative methods, using these positive techniques produces a short-term gain that can temporarily block out thoughts of death or better prepare ourselves to deal with death. However, unlike the negative methods, these positive methods do not have dangerous health-related consequences.

Negative Or Positive Dealing

There is one stress management technique that can either be negative or positive. It is one of the defense mechanisms. Defense mechanisms are unconscious or semi-conscious methods of dealing with stressful situations. They involve behavior that is rigid and automatized and are considered to be neurotic methods of managing conflict and frustration. The use of defense mechanisms is a common reaction to stress that is shared by normal and disturbed people. These defenses are advantageous in preserving self-esteem, averting personality disorganization and restoring a degree of equilibrium. Usually the more intense the stressors, the greater the use of defenses. In time, these defenses become more persistent, less appropriate in relation to our experience, less controlled and more severe, disturbing, and incapacitating. Common defense mechanisms include rationalization (the use of illogical or incorrect reasoning to discount failures) and denial.

Denial is perceptual blindness that temporarily protects us from the necessity of facing intolerable stressors. When overused, it can be life threatening (for example, denying the seriousness of a breast lump that turns out to be breast cancer). Nevertheless, with respect to death, almost everyone uses denial to some extent. Until we get older or very sick, we usually just don't deal with the concept of death; we act as if it doesn't exist. This can be beneficial at times. For example, if you didn't use denial every day, you would constantly worry about things such as nuclear warfare, getting AIDS, being killed in an airplane crash, and being invaded by aliens.

As reported on the television show "Dateline," researchers at the University of Pennsylvania have shown that humans have a brain mechanism that permits suspension of reality. People can then act as if death can be denied and immortality could be possible. Nevertheless, as we get into our 60s, this mechanism starts to falter.

Other Positive Dealing Methods

Regardless of age, if you become preoccupied with death, it is important that you have a serious discussion with another person about it. Sometimes, it is only necessary to get involved with a family member, a friend, a priest, minister or rabbi to be able to get over the temporary intrusion of Father Time. If that is not beneficial, it might be wise to see a psychologist or psychiatrist. If the anxiety is severe enough, then medication is needed.

There are various drugs that can be used to quell anxiety including antihistamines (an example is Benadryl®), buspirone (Buspar®), beta-blockers (an example is Inderal®) and some antidepressants (examples are Paxil® and Serzone®). However, the most effective are the benzodiazepines. Examples are Valium®, Xanax®, and Ativan®. Although they are remarkably safe drugs, they can have some problems. First of all, they interact with other depressant drugs such as alcohol, codeine and other narcotic analgesics (pain relievers), antihistamines and anticonvulsants. Therefore, if a benzodiazepine is mixed with any of these other drugs, serious and even fatal reactions can occur. When benzodiazepines are used by themselves, in low doses, and infrequently, they are quite safe. When they are used long-term and in high doses, both physical addiction and psychological addiction (habituation) can occur. I have used a very small dose of Ativan® (1 mg a day) when I've been in highly stressful situations. I found it to be effective when I was so anxious that I couldn't meditate or exercise. It was also beneficial as a temporary means to deal with death anxiety. But using benzodiazepines regularly is a band aid approach and should not be depended upon.

Dealing with Death Anxiety:
The Later Years

Do not stand by my grave and weep.
I am not there. I do not sleep
I am a thousand winds that blow.
I am a diamond glint on snow,
I am the sunlight on ripened grain.

I am the gentle autumn rain.

When you awake in the morning hush
I am the swift uplifting rush.

The quiet birds in circular flight.
I am the soft starshine at night

Do not stand by my grave and cry.
I am not there......I did not die
(Anonymous).

It has been shown that the closer we get to the source of our anxiety, the more intense the anxiety becomes. For example, if you have a snake phobia, just the thought of a snake elicits slight anxiety. Seeing a snake at a distance causes increased anxiety. If the snake is brought closer to you, the anxiety is much greater. Bringing the snake to your face causes overwhelming anxiety. Relating this to death anxiety, as we get into our 60s, the feared object — death — gets closer. Let's consider an example.

Face To Face With Death Anxiety

You're 65 and have been welcomed into the era of Social Security and Medicare. You don't feel that old, but you can't deny the reality. You come home from playing tennis, and you get a call from a friend. You chat for a while and then he springs this news upon you. A guy you played tennis with last week went home yesterday after playing a vigorous game of singles tennis. He took a shower and dropped dead at the age of 66. He was thin and in great shape but was an intense businessman. (Was it stress that killed him?) That was just the start. Within weeks, two family members die from heart attacks and another two close friends die from cancer — all in their 60s. The next week, you attend a college reunion and find that several classmates have passed on. It used to be that you went to many weddings, bar mitzvahs and communions. Now, you're attending many funerals. The culmination: you wake up several days later with severe pain in your chest. All at once Goethe's words, "Death is, to a certain extent, an impossibility which suddenly becomes a reality," ring true. Formerly, your brain mechanism was able to use stress management strategies such as exercise, travel and relaxation to cope with death anxiety. But now, at the age of 65, you feel closer to death and it becomes more difficult to block out thoughts of death and dying. Considering this, how can you now cope?

Coping With Death Anxiety

First of all, you immediately go to your physician and find out if you had a heart attack or merely indigestion. Fortunately for you, this time it wasn't serious. But still you have to face the reality of death. Is death something to fear? Let's face it, no one knows what is on the other side. The unknown is generally a great source of stress, but it doesn't have to be negative and frightening. It is indeterminable whether there is life after death. We don't know for sure if there is life as we know it after death — but why assume the worst? The afterlife could be beautiful. Be an optimist and think the best.

If there is something beyond this life, is it merely a memory-less soul that is part of some infinite consciousness or is it a soul with the memories of the previous physical existence? Again, we can't answer this, but as optimists, we go for the latter.

A third question is: What about the infant who dies and has no memories, the person who dies very young, the individual with permanent amnesia, the mentally handicapped person, and the older person who passes on after losing all memories to Alzheimer's disease? If you believe in an omnipotent, omniscient, omnipresent and eternal God

(God is considered more fully in later chapters), then anything is possible. Again, the optimistic path would be that the soul would retain the previous memories for the Alzheimer's and amnesia victims. The infant, youngster, and mentally handicapped person would still have a soul that would get a second chance on life. (Reincarnation is examined in Chapters 6, 11 and 12.)

This leads to the next question: Could the entity that survives death be reincarnated, and, if so, would it have memories of its previous existence? This is also an indeterminable concept, but as an optimist, you would chose the second option. In Chapter 6, we examine past life regressions and the many similar world-wide religious beliefs in reincarnation that have persisted for centuries in religions such as: Ancient Egyptian, Greek, and Roman religions; North American Indian tribal religions; Hinduism; Buddhism; early Christianity; Hasidic and kabbalistic Judaism; and more currently, the Theosophists and the Rosicrucian Order (discussed further in Chapters 11 and 12).

Studies have shown that people who have a belief in a Supreme Being and an afterlife have significantly less death anxiety than those without such beliefs. During our spiritual journey in the remaining chapters, evidence will be presented to help support the concept of a surviving soul, God and an afterlife.

Summarizing Death Anxiety And Methods To Deal With It

Death anxiety is virtually unknown in infancy and childhood. In the teenage and young adulthood years, the many aspects of day-to-day life serve to block out thoughts of death. In the thirties, forties, and fifties, we generally deal with death anxiety by using various stress management strategies such as relaxation therapy, exercise, proper nutrition, diversions, and denial. However, in the mid-60s and older, with the death of family members and friends and possible personal sicknesses, Father Time with his scythe of death approaches. We then have to face the overwhelming fear of death and dying. We wonder about the afterlife, the soul, loss of memory, and reincarnation. Religious people who believe in God and an afterlife have less death anxiety as compared to those people who are non-religious.

Therefore, we should take the optimistic approach. The optimistic approach is not handed to us on a silver platter. In the search for eternity, we must take our spiritual journey through several avenues in order to come to the conclusion that death is not a finality, that there is a God, a surviving soul, and a joyous afterlife. In the next chapter, we begin our spiritual journey by examining my near-death experience.

CHAPTER TWO

MY NEAR-DEATH EXPERIENCE

"Man always dies before he's fully born" (Anonymous).

A person does not have to be near death to have a near-death experience (NDE). My spiritual journey to conquer the fear of death started with my NDE in 1983. At the time, I was certain that I was dying, but later found out that I had been nowhere near death. Yet the experience was so profound that it affected me for the rest of my life. In essence, I was reborn.

This is what I remember. I felt myself spinning around and around in ever widening circles. Then the sounds of the world became more and more quiet. Voices of people and songs of birds began to slow down. It seems that the faster I spun, the slower and less distinct the outside sounds became. Then I heard my heartbeat. First, it was very rapid and loud. Then, when it was beating so fast that I thought it would burst through my chest, it began to slow down. Slower and slower my heart pulsated, and then I could feel it no longer. I quickly fell to the ground, and my heart stopped beating. At least, I no longer heard it. Was I dead? I had no idea, but instead of seeing nothingness, I first saw pitch darkness and then an incredibly bright, white light. It enveloped me so that I could see nothing but this light. I was not afraid. I felt secure, warm, and serene. No one came to greet me but I felt a loving presence around me.

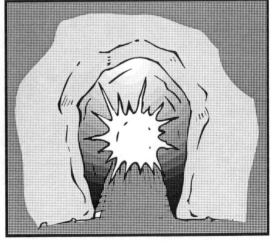

Then, in rapid succession, I saw my whole life flash before me: the temper tantrums of my childhood, my winning a dart-throwing contest, my hospital bout with colitis, the asthma attacks, the family visits to Stamford, Connecticut, throwing an opposing player out at home plate, shooting a winning basket, crying when the New York Giants lost a baseball game, seeing my father die an agonizing death from lung cancer, getting married on a cloudy day in Brooklyn, honeymooning in Bermuda, seeing each one of my three children being born, watching a developing rainbow in Las Vegas with my wife and children, vacationing with my wife in Rome, doing a surgical procedure on the day John Kennedy was killed, watching my mother wither away from Alzheimer's disease, getting the Temple University research award, falling out of a canoe and later contracting giardiasis, going out for a jog on the hospital grounds, spinning around, and falling to the ground.

Then the review abruptly ended. I left my body, flew above the clouds and arrived at the Mt. Eden Cemetery in Valhalla, New York — the same cemetery where my mother and father were buried. At this point, everything was vague. I knew I was being buried, but I couldn't

really see it. I just had the feeling it was happening. Just as quickly as I had arrived there, I was gone. Suddenly it was another day. I was reading the obituary column of the *Philadelphia Inquirer*. I could not discern what was written about me, but I was certain that I saw my name. Strangely, perceiving my funeral and reading my obituary were not frightening. Was it because I had been enveloped by that wonderful light and had felt a caring presence? I don't know, because the next thing I knew, I was back inside the hospital, and felt the sharp pain of an injection.

The injection had revived me and brought me to life, so to speak. Had I experienced another plane or was it merely an hallucination? At the time I wasn't sure. Subsequently, I found out that the experiences of observing my funeral and reading my obituary were different than other people's NDEs. However, the darkness followed by the glorious light, the life review, the blissful feelings, and the loving presence surrounding me, were similar to many other NDEs. Most importantly, that NDE set the stage for my journey to overcome death anxiety. (See *Figure 4* for

Figure 4
Copy of a watercolor painting, "A View from Cooper River Park, Cherry Hill, New Jersey, showing a glimpse of Philadelphia," by Don Morse, May, 1997.

another example of one of the methods I used to help overcome my death anxiety.)

After this incredible experience, it was important to find out whether or not I had conquered death anxiety. To do that, I had to continue the spiritual journey. There would be several paths on the journey and since I had a near-death experience of sorts myself, I decided that the first path to explore would be NDEs.

CHAPTER THREE

NEAR-DEATH EXPERIENCES

"It is impossible to convey the beauty and intensity of emotion during
these visions. They were the most tremendous things I have ever
experienced — I can describe the experience as only ecstasy of a
contemporal state in which the present, past, and future are one"
(Jung, C. *Memories, Dreams, Reflections.* Pantheon Books,
New York, 1963, pp. 295-296).

"I can hardly find words for it — the most beautiful experience of my life.
I had the most peaceful, contented feeling — but I wish there were
different words available to describe it. If you called it peaceful to the
10th power — that would be getting close to it. When they jolted me
out of that, I was really mad. The experience changed my whole outlook
on death. I think very different of it now — I'm not afraid at all. As a matter
of fact, I sometimes tell my kids that dying is the most beautiful experience
you can have but they look at me as if I'm some kind of nut.
So far as death is concerned, I can recommend it to anybody"
(Currie, I. *Visions of Immortality.* Element Books,
Victoria, British Columbia, Canada, 1990, p. 202).

The first quotation by Carl Jung describes visions he experienced while suffering a near-fatal heart attack. Dr. Elisabeth Kübler-Ross has mentioned similar experiences in her best seller, *On Death and Dying*. From her work, she stated that death is a "transition — a peaceful and benign experience to all cultures" in which the physical body is "shed....as a butterfly comes out of a cocoon." However, it was Dr. Raymond Moody who coined the term near-death experience (NDE) and did the first monumental study about it. His book, *Life After Life* (1975) became a world-wide best seller and inspired many other researchers to investigate NDEs. Since Moody's pioneering work, NDEs have been shown to be a world-wide occurrence in people of all religions, those with no religion, including both genders and all ages. *A 1992 Gallop poll estimated that there are about 13 million NDErs in the U.S. alone.* NDEs have also been recognized historically. Many articles and over 100 books have been written about them.

Four years after the publication of Moody's first book, a cardiologist, Dr. Fred Schoonmaker, reported on the results of his interviews of 2,300 survivors of acute life-threatening situations since 1961. He found that 60% of them had NDEs. Dr. P.M.H. Atwater (see *Figure 5*), who had three NDEs in 1977, was stimulated to research the field (interviews with 3,000 adult and 277 child NDErs) and subsequently wrote seven NDE books (see Notes and References).

The second quotation given above is by John Van Luyk following his NDE (as reported by Ian Currie). Although using contemporary language, Van Luyk's description of his NDE is just as powerful as Carl Jung's.

You might ask, "Why are NDEs so important in our quest for a surviving soul, a positive afterlife and the reality of God?" The answer is that, until Moody's book, the only evidence in the search for eternity had been religious faith and anecdotal and non-reproducible medium reports and accounts of phenomena such as apparitions and vivid dreams. Those of us with a scientific viewpoint could not accept religious accounts and anecdotal reports. But the NDE evidence changed all of that: NDEs are not completely anecdotal

Figure 5
Photograph of P.M.H. Atwater. Permission granted for use by Dr. P.M.H. Atwater.

— they often have witnesses who relate verifiable information. In addition, NDEs show consistency across cultural, age groups, and historical spans. That is why NDE evidence is so important.

Although the people never met, their NDEs had several features in common. Nevertheless, as Atwater has found, there appears to be four types of NDEs. However, as an introduction, here is an example of a full-blown composite NDE (based primarily on Moody's and Atwater's research).

Your Near-Death Experience

After a strenuous day, you come home from work. Suddenly, you have unbearable chest pains — a massive heart attack. Your heart stops and you have a flat EEG (brain death). You soon are on a hospital operating room table and, for all intents and purposes, you are dead. But the doctors do not give up. They inject various drugs and use electroshock therapy to try and revive you. Nevertheless, there are still no signs of life. What do you feel?

You sense you are dead but hear a buzzing or ringing noise. You then feel as if part of you (perhaps, it's your soul and spiritual body) is separating from your physical body. You then float upward, while feeling weightless, to an elevated position. (This is known as an out-of-body experience and is discussed further in the next chapter.) From this position, you can clearly observe the doctors working on you with their paddles and needles. You feel strangely detached and unemotionally involved with your body as well as the people you left behind and the world in general. Now, you no longer look at the doctors working on your body. You suddenly feel yourself being sucked up through a narrow, dark tunnel. After passing through the tunnel, an extremely bright–but harmless–light is seen at the end (remindful of the expression, "I could see the light at the end of the tunnel"). Indescribably beautiful music is heard. As you enter this golden, or vividly colored light, you no longer feel the excruciating heart pain that you had felt before you "died." Rather you feel comforted and permeated with an ineffable sense of quiet, joy, peace and love. This light now permeates your entire being, and you begin to see other people who have passed away. You can make out family members, relatives, friends and other loved ones. They appear to be vigorously alive and in the prime of their lives.

You then arrive at a wall that appears to demarcate ordinary life from a realm that lies beyond your perceived notion of life. It is sensed as a point of no return. You soon become aware of a luminous, loving, forgiving, nonjudgmental God-like presence. As a Catholic, the heavenly presence appears to you as Jesus. Without actually speaking, Jesus conducts you through an extraordinary panoramic, non-linear, extremely rapid life review. Each instant in your life is reviewed — not just the major happenings. You experience some life events from both your own viewpoint and that of the other person's perspective. After the review is finished, you learn that the most important things in life are love, service to others and knowledge.

You are feeling so peaceful, so calm, so joyous, and so infused with love that you have no desire to return to the life you just left. Nevertheless, Jesus informs you that you must return in order to attend to unfinished business. Suddenly, you feel a sharp, painful jolt and you are back in your body. You have the feeling that time has passed but you have no idea how long you were away. It could have been seconds — or an eternity. You open your eyes and the entire staff gives you a big smile. You can see the monitors showing a renewed heart beat and an active alert EEG pattern. You have come back to life.

Upon returning, you are a changed person. Before your NDE, you had been extremely anxious about death and dying. In fact, you had to see a psychiatrist and were taking antidepressants and antianxiety agents. Now, you no longer fear death and only see the psychiatrist occasionally. You are well on your way to complete recovery. (*Note:* Atwater has reported that sometimes after their experience, many NDErs become temporarily depressed. It seems that they find it difficult to fit their newly learned ideas into their current lifestyles.)

Before the experience, you rarely attended mass. Now you definitely believe in God, a surviving soul, and a wonderful afterlife. (According to Atwater's research, 1/3 of the NDErs continue in a traditional religious setting.) You go to church more regularly but what is said in church is less important to you than the spirituality that you received from your NDE. The other 2/3, if they have a religious affiliation, cast it aside and shift to a one-on-one relationship with God. (Interestingly, most of those who leave the traditional religious affiliation, after about ten years, return to some type of church setting — either New Thought, Eastern types, Shamanistic, or as I have found for some Jewish NDErs, an interest in *Kabbalah* [see Chapter 12]. If they had no religious affiliation, they move toward a spiritual path where they can also enter into a personal, intimate relationship with God.)

You formerly were pretty much of a stoic, rarely showing feelings. If you did display feelings, they were usually limited to anger and anxiety. Now, you are more curious, much kinder and more considerate; you serve others, not just yourself. You rarely lose your temper or get nervous. And most of all, you express love to your family, friends and God. Before, you were never much of a student, but now you have a strong desire to learn; you become more creative. In the past, you were never certain about your business plans and the direction you wanted to take in life. Now, you are feeling much more in control of your life. Before, you had been reckless, taking all sorts of chances. You drove too fast; you smoked pot; you drank too much; and you cheated on your spouse. Now you no longer take reckless risks. You have developed a profound appreciation of life. Before you debunked the message of interconnectedness of all life as taught by Carl Jung ("cosmic consciousness") and visualized by James Redfield (in *The Celestine Prophecy*). Now you believe in the interconnectedness of all life and possibly even with inanimate objects throughout the world and universe. You also have some physiological changes such as greater sensitivity to light, sound and electricity; energy surges; lower blood pressure; increased allergies; tendency toward eating vegetables and grains (less meat); and physically, looking younger.

Even though your life has changed so much for the better, when you think back about your NDE, you feel as if the best time of your life was when you had almost died. This reminded philosopher and near-death researcher, Michael Grosso, of the ancient philosopher Euripides' intriguing statement; "How do we know that the living are not dead and the dead living?"

What Others Experience

The Silver Cord And The Golden Bowl

"Also when they shall be afraid of that which is high, And terrors shall be in the way; And the almond-tree shall blossom, And the grasshopper shall drag itself along, And the caperberry shall fail; Because man goeth to his long home (Heaven*), And the mourners go about the streets; Before the silver cord is snapped asunder, And the golden bowl is shattered, And the pitcher is broken at the fountain, And the wheel falleth shattered into the pit; And the dust (physical body*) returneth to the earth as it was, And the spirit returneth unto God who gave it.

(Ecclesiastes 12: 5-7). — *Author's insertion

Research by the Steigers (1999) has shown that many individuals who have NDEs reported observing their spirit body being connected to their physical body by a "silver cord." Others have seen themselves as "golden bowls" or balloon-like globular spheres. Amazingly, as shown above, the Bible reported similar findings.

Psychic Abilities

Research by Atwater and others have verified that following NDEs, most people are psychic. If they were psychic before, they become even more so afterwards. If they weren't psychic, they become so afterwards. Atwater call this psychic ability *faculty extensions*. These include the following. A few of the individuals see futuristic events (*precognition*). Related to brain shifts (apparent changes in brain physiology and morphology), these people have "future memory" (an ability to remember happenings that have not yet occurred; discussed in Atwater's book, *Future Memory* [1999]). As reported in Raymond Moody's *The Light Beyond*, one woman had a NDE in 1971 and was told that, in the future when the time was right, she would meet Raymond Moody and describe her experience to him. In 1975, Dr. Moody's wife Louise took their children trick-or-treating. They arrived at one house where this same woman, whose house it was, asked the children their names. The oldest replied: "Raymond Avery Moody." Whereupon the woman spoke to Mrs. Moody and told her she had to speak to Dr. Moody. They subsequently met and the woman described her NDE to him.

A few people have been able to describe details of events that have occurred at distant locations that are beyond the reach of the normal senses (*clairvoyance*). Some verified cases have been described by Cook and her co-workers in a 1998 publication. Others can hear without the presence of sound (*clairaudience*). Some can effect an object or feel it without touching (*psychokinesis*); some can taste without using taste buds (*clairgustation*); others can smell without the use of the nose (*clairolfaction*); and still others can be aware of something or someone in advance of or without recognition (*clairsentience*). Most post-NDErs often find unrelated things come together by themselves in purposeful ways and with a strange sense of timing (*synchronicity*). As Atwater stated in "The Vital Signs Newsletter," "...leaving them with a sense that almost nothing happens by accident and that there is a grander scheme of things we can align with if we choose" (found on internet at: http://www.cinemind.comatwater/col3.html).

The Tunnel

Rather than going through a tunnel, some people go through a door or staircase: others report a rapid rise into the sky, where they see the Earth from the perspective of an astronaut. Relative to the tunnel experience, it is not that common. A Gallup poll taken in 1982 found only 9% experienced it; Atwater reported 30%.

Light And Dark

Almost everyone talks about the "light experience" and how marvelous it is, but according to Atwater's research, some NDErs experienced a "dark light experience." As with those who experienced the "light experience," certain patterns occur. Atwater found the following:

1. Both adults and children can have "dark light experiences."

2. The vast majority of those who had a "dark light experience described it as a safe, comfortable place that was loving, peaceful; a state of goodness and positive expectancy.

3. The few who described the "dark experience" negatively also encountered hellish or fearful scenarios of distressing or unpleasant episodes.

4. There were three kinds of "light experiences" regardless of the age of the individual.

A. Primary light, which is colorless. It is experienced as a pulsating luminosity or presence that is generally perceived as a piercing power, fearfully awesome; the beginning of all beginnings.

B. Dark light, which is pure black but can have dark purple tinges. It is experienced as a shimmering peaceful depth that is generally perceived as a source of knowing and strength; creation's womb.

C. Bright light, which has variations of yellow-gold white. It is experienced as a brilliant radiance that is generally perceived as a nearly blinding glow that gives off unconditional love, a warm intelligence, a feeling of union; the essence of truth.

Atwater also found that the NDErs interpretation of the occurrence is especially important over the rest of their lives. Most interpret the light as beneficial, and the experience sustains them throughout their life, but occasionally some experience it as negative and their lives are not fulfilling. There are even times when a brilliant, "heavenly" experience is interpreted negatively with detrimental fallout for the rest of the experiencer's life unless he/she receives counseling.

Heaven And Hell

Usually, there are no visions of heaven or hell, as NDEs are generally only involved with the early stages of the afterlife trip. However, the Steigers (1999), among others, have reported a few people who described heavenly scenes where they see angels. Others, including the Steigers, have reported hellish scenes or experiences. As to the lack of visions of heaven or hell for most people, in religious descriptions of the afterlife, it is only in the latter stages of the afterlife trip that heaven, hell, purgatory, or their equivalents are encountered.

The Wall

Not all NDErs reach a wall. Some reach a fence; others come to a stream or other limit.

Heavenly Presence

Catholics tend to see the heavenly presence as Jesus and also Mary, Peter, Paul, an angel or one of the saints. A Jew might see either God, Abraham, Moses, Daniel, Rachel or Ruth. A Muslim might see Allah or Mohammed; a Hindu might see any of many gods; and a Buddhist might see Buddha or a bright indescribable friendly, loving presence. An agnostic or atheist might see a warm, glowing, friendly being. The physician, George G. Ritchie, who had a NDE in 1943, described his encounter with Jesus thusly: "For now I saw that it was not light but a Man made out of light, though this seemed no more possible to my mind than the incredible intensity of the brightness that made up His form." (Ritchie, G.G. and Sherrill, E. *My Glimpse of Eternity*. Guideposts, Carmel, New York, 1978, pp. 48-49).

Life Review

The life review could also show occurrences from the other person's viewpoint. For example, in Sidney Saylor Farr's book, *What Tom Sawyer Learned from Dying*, an interesting case was reported by Tom Sawyer, a Rochester, New York resident who had a NDE in 1978. During his life review, he recalled reliving an encounter when he was 19 years old between himself and a pedestrian. The pedestrian said some provoking remark and Sawyer experienced the verbal attack from *both his own and the victim's viewpoint.* He described the pedestrian's viewpoint thusly: "...fist come directly into my face. And I felt the indignation, the rage, the embarrassment, the frustration, the physical pain. I felt my teeth going through my lower lip — in other words I was in that man's eyes. I was in that man's body..." (Farr, S.S. *What Tom Sawyer Learned From Dying*. Hampton Roads Publ. Co., Norfolk, Virginia, 1988, p. 33).

Barbara Rommer (1999) found two types of NDEs. She termed the NDE occurring in terminally ill patients a **"Nearing Death Awareness"** (NDA). The NDA usually occurs without any dramatic changes in vital signs. After the NDE, the people are usually prepared to die peacefully, and there is rarely a life review. In contrast, the NDE occurring in an acutely ill person prepares the individual for continuing life and is frequently the impetus for living more spiritually. These people often have a life review, which can show them the consequences of their previous actions with specific attention to the effects on other individuals.

Not All Pleasant

Maurice Rawlings, a well-known researcher who has been involved in resuscitations coupled with NDEs, contends that the reason there are many less reports of unpleasant NDEs is that people who have had them tend to suppress the memories because they were so disturbing. That might be one reason why not everyone who is near death reports a NDE. Nevertheless as previously mentioned, some unpleasant NDEs do occur and it is important for us who are looking for a pleasant afterlife as a means to overcome our death anxiety to try and understand why distressful NDEs occur. In order to do this, let us examine some of the reported cases of unpleasant NDEs.

A host of books and NDE reports indicate that individuals who attempted suicide and had NDEs found the experiences to be decidedly unpleasant. Such cases are reported in by Reverend Louis Richard Batzler, Maurice Rawlings in his book *Beyond Death's Door*, Raymond Moody in his books, *Life After Life*, *Reflections on Life After Life*, and *The Light Beyond*, and Angie Fenimore in her book, *Beyond the Darkness*. Raymond Moody discussed a case reported by Michael Grosso of an attempted suicide's NDE. The person described images of horrendous beings clawing and clutching at him. It was a claustrophobic, hostile, nightmarish experience. He felt that it was like descending into Dante's inferno. Mally Cox-Chapman, in her book found that some people who attempted suicide had mixed NDEs — part frightening and part enjoyable, while others had mainly pleasant experiences. Tony Lawrence found some individuals with negative NDEs experienced a void—a feeling of nothingness. Others felt themselves being dragged down into a pit with demon-like figures. Lawrence did not find a correlation between evil people and negative NDEs. Bruce Greyson and Nancy Evans Bush found negative NDEs in three categories: similar to regular NDEs but interpreted as unpleasant; a sense of void or nonexistence; and graphic hellish landscapes and entities.

In the 1990 movie, *Flatliners*, medical students brought themselves to near-death with a flat EEG in order to examine the afterlife. Their experiences were partly pleasant and partly hellish. This could be interpreted that the students' try at simulating death was similar to attempted suicides. In the recent movie (October 1998), *What Dreams May Come*, the afterlife fate of a suicide is hell. Melvin Morse in his book, *Parting Visions*, reported a case of a criminal who had performed many evil deeds. He had a NDE that was extremely hellish, seeing himself being pulled out of his body while it burst into flames. Instead of seeing God, he saw the faces of individuals known to him that had died. They were all crying in pain. Nevertheless, recent findings by Atwater and others have shown that criminals don't have hellish NDEs more often than ordinary people and more often than not, people who attempt suicide have a positive experience.

NEAR DEATH EXPERIENCES / 45

NDEs Changed Their Lives

What can we conclude from all of this? It was found that those individuals who had been evil and those who had attempted suicide, regardless of whether their NDEs were pleasant or unpleasant, *were given a second chance*. They recovered and interestingly all of them reported that their lives had changed for the better. The suicide attempters swore that they would never attempt suicide again. Although not completely supported by the latest NDE findings, for the best chance of having a pleasant afterlife, we should live a moral life, control our negative emotions, and regardless of whether the NDE will be pleasant or not, we should never attempt suicide. I realize that the viewpoints expressed here about morality and suicide are based on considerations other than NDEs that the reader has not yet come across, but these viewpoints will be supported in Chapters 11-15.

Four Types of NDEs

From her research with 3,000 adult and 277 child NDErs, Atwater described four types of NDEs.

1. *"Non-Experience" or "Initial Experience."* This includes elements such as: a living darkness; a loving nothingness; a friendly voice; and a transient out-of-body experience. This type of NDE usually occurs to those who require the least evidence for the reality of the afterlife, or who require the least amount of change in their lifestyle. Frequency: 76% children; 20% of adults.

2. *"Hell-Like Experience" or "Unpleasant Experience."* This includes either: scenes of an unexpected or startling difference; hauntings from one's past; or encounters with a stark limbo, a hellish purgatory or a threatening void. This type NDE usually occurs to those who have deeply repressed or suppressed angers, fears, and guilts or who expect some type of discomfort or punishment after death. Frequency: 3% children; 15% adults. Rommer (1999) found that 17.7% of NDEs are less than positive (elicits feelings of despair, terror, guilt and/or severe loneliness).

3. *"Heaven-Like Experience" or "Pleasant Experience."* This includes: reassuring religious figures or beings of light; heaven-like scenarios; loving family reunions with those who had previously died; inspiring and affirmative dialogue; and validation that life counts. This type NDE usually occurs to those who need to know how important life is, how loved they are, and how every effort has a meaning in the ultimate scheme of things. Frequency: 19% children; 47% adults.

4. *"Transcendent Experience."* This includes: scenes beyond the individual's frame of reference; exposure to otherworldly dimensions; and revelations of greater truths that are seldom personal in nature. This type of NDE usually occurs to those who are more inclined to use (to whatever degree) the truths that are revealed to them and/or those who are ready for a enriching challenge. Frequency: 2% children; 18% adults.

Atwater found that usually each type occurred but once to a person. However, sometimes, all four types occurred during the same experience for the same individual. Other times the types were spread out over a series of NDEs for a particular person; and still other times, the types occurred in varying combinations.

Scientific Studies Of NDEs

There have been scientific studies by well-known researchers who compared people with and without NDEs who were close to death. The researchers wanted to see if the NDE subjects changed in a different way than those who did not have NDEs. Kenneth Ring, author of the books, *Life at Death* and *Heading Toward Omega*, compared people who were close to death and didn't have NDEs with individuals having positive NDEs. The results showed that those who didn't have NDEs did not lose their fear of death.

Bruce Greyson, author of the book, *The Near-Death Experience*, compared people who were close to death without a NDE with people who were close to death with a positive NDE. The NDErs changed more profoundly and in a different way than those who didn't have a NDE. Justine Owens and her co-workers found that patients who were close to death were more likely to report NDE features than those who were not near death.

Overall, these findings are important for us if we want to use the results of NDEs as proof for the survival of the soul, a positive afterlife, and God. However, before we conclude that the phenomena found in NDEs are genuine and meaningful, we must look for alternative explanations.

Alternative Explanations For NDEs

Even though these phenomena have occurred in millions of people throughout the world irrespective of their age, gender, or religious beliefs, could there be scientific or religious explanations? One religious explanation is that offered by some fundamentalists. They consider the God-like presence of the NDE as being the work of the devil. However, most religionists consider that the NDE phenomenon could be a true encounter with God, Jesus, angels, saints, or holy people.

Some scientists wonder if NDE phenomena are products of brain activity? Many scientists have examined NDEs, and they have come up with a variety of possible explanations. Let's briefly consider all of these explanations and try to see if they have merit.

1. The Dying Brain Theory Of NDEs

The Concept

Almost all who have NDEs follow a similar path to the light. This experience is proposed to be the result of a dying brain. The neurotransmitters in the brain are shutting down and creating the same beautiful illusions for all who are near death.

The Rebuttal

If The Dying Brain Theory is true and no afterlife exists, and the NDE is merely the last vestiges of a dying brain, what is the purpose in it all? Why would the brain bother giving us this fanciful illusion if we were going to wind up as nothing more than ashes? In addition, not all who are near death receive these images. Why doesn't everyone who experiences near death have the experience? And why are there different types of NDEs? Those who attempt suicide or who are evil people can have dark and gloomy visions, and others (especially children) can see the "dark." Yet, many criminals who have NDEs experience positive NDEs. How does The Dying Brain Theory account for these differences? It really can't.

2. NDEs Are The Result Of Drugs Such As LSD

The Concept

Drugs such as LSD can give beautiful visions. In addition, some anesthetics can produce hallucinations.

The Rebuttal

The visions produced by hallucinogenics are not the same as those displayed by NDErs. There are also detrimental side effects from LSD, which are never reported by NDErs. In additional, many who have had NDEs have not taken any drugs.

3. The Hallucination Theory

The Concept

Some contend that the dying individual secretes endorphins (a brain and body transmitter substance) that create feelings of elation and pain relief. Another theory proposed by Karl Jansen, is that a powerful anesthetic named ketamine is released by the body at the time of the NDE and reproduces many of the features of the NDE as hallucinations.

The Rebuttal

Endorphins are not hallucinogens and cannot create most of the components of the NDE. However, the release of both endorphins and a ketamine-like substance at the time of death (or near death) is merely hypothetical. The pain relief during the NDE only lasts for the short amount of time during the experience. Endorphins typically give prolonged pain relief. If endorphins actually create NDE-like experiences, why aren't NDE experiences reported by people who are known to have high levels of endorphins? For example, during childbirth, mothers have a level of endorphins ten times higher than normal. While birthing mothers sometimes experience a soothing relief of pain, NDEs are not experienced. (Reported in G. L. Little's textbook, *Psychopharmacology* [1996]).

In addition, no matter what drug or chemical induces hallucinations, the hallucinations almost always occur while the person is conscious. **NDEs occur when an individual is unconscious** and even shows no detectable brain wave patterns on an EEG. Descriptions given of hallucinations are hazy and contain **distortions of reality**, while NDE descriptions are usually **normally ordered and lifelike**. Hallucinations are often accompanied by anxiety feelings, while NDEs are generally calm and peaceful. Hallucinations afterwards rarely cause life-changing occurrences as do NDEs. Finally, if it were merely an hallucination, how could a person see the objects described previously while in an elevated state?

4. Mental Illnesses And Organic Brain Syndromes

The Concept

People with schizophrenia and organic brain syndromes can have beautiful mental images.

The Rebuttal

These disorders do not produce the normal type of responses seen in NDEs. In addition, many people without mental illnesses and organic brain syndromes have NDEs.

5. The Lack Of Oxygen Or Excessive Carbon Dioxide Theory

The Concept

Brains lacking oxygen or with excessive carbon dioxide produce hallucinations.

The Rebuttal

Various studies have actually found that the brain lacking oxygen or with excess carbon dioxide produces chaotic hallucinations that abound with disorientation, confusion and fear (as with mountain climbers or fighter pilots). This contrasts with the NDEs in which calmness, tranquillity and a sense of order predominate. In addition, cardiologist Michael Sabom has reported on a patient who had a NDE and had his blood evaluated during the experience. It revealed **high** oxygen and **low** carbon dioxide. This is probably why most people who come out of their NDE are able to give complete and cogent reports of their findings. With many accident victims, there is no oxygen-depletion and yet they have had NDEs.

6. The Temporal Lobe Theory

The Concept

Certain features of the NDE occur in a type of epilepsy associated with damage to the right temporal lobe of the brain. In addition, researchers have found that by electrically stimulating this lobe, some elements of the NDE can be mimicked. These include: life memories flashing past; leaving oneself behind; feeling a union with the universe and God; and a sudden sense of enlightenment.

The Rebuttal

The usual emotions that result from temporal lobe stimulation are sadness, fear and loneliness as contrasted with the calmness and love resulting from an NDE. During NDEs, odors can be detected (not involved with the temporal lobe), and temporal lobe stimulation cannot explain the sightings and accurate details people have reported when they are out-of-body. It should also be noted that experiments on the temporal lobe produce a wide range of experiences varying greatly from the core experiences seen in NDEs.

7. General Anesthesia Theory

The Concept

Some people who go under general anesthesia can have some of the features of the NDE.

The Rebuttal

This experience occurs infrequently with anesthesia. When it does occur, the individual typically reports only hearing what is said in the operating room — not seeing it or floating out of the room. Most importantly, many people who had a NDE were not under general anesthesia.

8. The Birth Memory Theory

The Concept

The late Carl Sagan proposed that the NDE is a memory of birth. As a child is being born, it goes down a tunnel toward a light, and it encounters love and warmth. Therefore, what happens at death is merely a stored memory of the birth. The celestial being of light is the midwife or doctor who delivers the child. (Sagan, C. *Broca's Brain: Reflections on the Romance of Science*. Random House, New York, 1979, pp. 301-312.)

The Rebuttal

A typical NDE shows rapid travel through a tunnel, not the buffeting along with the mother's contractions that occur during delivery. The theory does not explain meeting deceased relatives and friends. In addition, it is known that infant's nervous systems — especially brain areas responsible for storing memory — are not sufficiently developed to assimilate and store memories of the birthing process. In addition, the infant's eyesight is too poor to perceive the birth canal. Another glaring problem with the theory is that, unlike the birth process, NDEs are blissful, painless, and pleasant. How many newborns are crying and wailing upon birth? The birth process causes head distortions and certainly cannot be considered pleasant.

9. Wish Fulfillment Theory

The Concept

Some people believe that wonderful NDEs are experienced simply because that is what we want to (or wish to) feel at death.

The Rebuttal

Many atheists — with no concept or hopes for a pleasant afterlife — have had blissful NDEs. In addition, young children with little or no ideas about death, report the same elements in NDEs as do adults.

10. The Depersonalization Theory

The Concept

The idea of depersonalization is similar to "Wish Fulfillment." When people are faced with the unpleasant reality of death, they attempt to "depersonalize" it by producing pleasant fantasies in order to protect themselves. They "depersonalize" by removing themselves from their own bodies. That is the explanation the theory gives for the experience of floating away from one's own body.

The Rebuttal

Many of the NDE features are ignored or unexplained by the theory. People in NDEs tend to have increased alertness and awareness as well as strong mystical and spiritual feelings. Nor does the theory explain how during the floating experience the "spirit body" can observe and describe verifiable events. Finally, if the experience results from depersonalization, why would the individual undergoing the experience encounter people who were close relatives and friends?

11. Darwin's Theory

The Concept

The NDE is a deliberate ploy of the human race to help those left behind by death to better adapt to the inevitable ending of their lives. In simplified form, Darwin's theory of the survival of the fittest means that every species struggles in order to increase its hold on Earth and guarantee the survival of its descendants. That is the foremost primary urge. Hence, the theory holds that the dying are merely generating propaganda asserting that death is not the end.

The Rebuttal

If Darwin's theory were true, why is it that with the advent of modern resuscitation methods there are so many more NDEs? Although NDEs undoubtedly occurred previously, they were little known. More NDEs occur today because of improved emergency medical procedures. What ensured the survival of the species in previous generations? In addition, the idea simply discounts the verifiable events and facts associated with NDEs. It denies the reality of the experiences of thousands of people and seems to assert, "if it hasn't happened to me, it can't be real."

12. Dr. Susan Blackmore's Viewpoints

The Concept

Dr. Blackmore is a brilliant senior lecturer in psychology at the University of the West of England, who has often appeared on television. She considers that NDEs are caused by physiological and psychological reactions that are initiated by disturbed brain function either at the point of death or under great stress.

The Rebuttal

This does not explain out-of-body experiences in which the *dead* person can observe sights that could only be seen from an elevated view.

The Concept

Dr. Blackmore claims that the tunnel is caused by oxygen starvation, which results in certain inhibitory brain cells to die first; the excitatory cells take longer to die.

The Rebuttal

As discussed previously, many NDErs do not show oxygen deprivation, and Dr. Sabon has shown that a person can have high oxygen and low carbon dioxide and still experience a NDE.

The Concept

Dr. Blackmore claims the similarity of NDEs is because brains behave similarly when they die.

The Rebuttal

As stated before under the *dying brain theory*, why would the brain bother giving us this fanciful illusion if we were going to wind up as nothing more than ashes? And how does this explain the disturbing NDEs of some suicide attempters and evil people and the dark images of many children and some adults?

The Concept

Dr. Blackmore says that people use the evidence from NDE to bolster their belief in an afterlife.

The Rebuttal

As mentioned before under *wish fulfillment theory*, there have been atheists who had no concept of an enjoyable afterlife who still had blissful NDEs.

The Concept

People are transformed by the NDE, according to Dr. Blackmore, because the very experience of being near death, with or without a NDE, is sufficient to make individuals less selfish and more concerned for others.

The Rebuttal

As discussed previously, Dr. Bruce Greyson of the University of Connecticut compared people who were close to death without a NDE with people who were close to death with a NDE. He found that the NDErs changed more profoundly and in a different way than those who did not have a NDE. In a similar vein, Dr. Kenneth Ring, examined the same types of individuals. He found that the NDErs lost their fear of death, but this was not true for those who were close to death without having had a NDE.

More Compelling Evidence For The Reality & Significance of NDEs

People with various religious backgrounds (or none at all) in different parts of the world have reported similar NDEs. People in combat have reported NDEs. (Atheists aren't found on the battle-field.) Melvin Morse described in his book, *Closer to the Light: Learning From Children's Near-Death Experiences*, his many detailed investigations of NDEs in young children (who haven't had the religious background of adults) and observed similar findings (e.g., dark tunnel, bright light, angelic being). The Steigers in their book, *Children of the Light* and Atwater, in her book, *Children of the New Millennium*, have given additional input on children's NDEs.

It certainly seems that the scientific arguments put forth against NDEs do not hold weight, and it definitely appears that NDEs are real and meaningful. In fact, NDEs are the best evidence for the existence of a surviving soul, a positive afterlife (for moral people), and God. Let us now examine a few interesting cases.

Intriguing Cases Of NDEs

As a scientist, I cannot give a rational explanation for any of these cases, but they certainly bolster the case for NDEs being exceptional evidence of a surviving soul and a positive afterlife.

The Red Shoe

Mally Cox-Chapman, in her book, *The Case for Heaven*, and Kenneth Ring and Evelyn Elsaesser Valarino, in their book, *Lessons from the Light*, discussed a NDE case report by Madelaine Lawrence. The patient floated up and viewed the resuscitation efforts being performed on her body. She then felt herself being elevated until she found herself outside the hospital viewing a ledge on the third floor, where she saw a **red tennis shoe**. The patient was then "sucked up a blackened hole" and continued her NDE. When she returned to her body, she described the shoe in detail to a skeptical social worker. He checked it out and found the shoe in the very place the patient mentioned and having the exact features she had described.

The Resuscitation Scene

In her book, Mally Cox-Chapman also described the experiment of cardiologist Michael Sabom. He asked an experimental group of 32 patients — all whom claimed to have had an elevated view of the resuscitation scene during their NDE — to explain in detail what they observed during the resuscitation effort. He also asked a control group of 25 "seasoned" cardiac patients — all of whom did **not** have an elevated view of the resuscitation effort — to attempt the same kind of descriptions of the resuscitation effort. The backgrounds of the two groups were similar.

In the control group, 20 out of the 25 patients made a major error in their description of the resuscitation scene. In the experimental group of 32 patients, **no errors** were found in the reported descriptions. The descriptions given by 26 of the experimental patients correlated in a general way with the known facts of the resuscitation efforts. Very specific aspects of the resuscitation were reported by 6 of the 32. They described details of gurneys, shape of the paddles used, and which family members were awaiting them down the hall.

Alzheimer's And The Light

Mally Cox-Chapman described a hospice nurse's report about a patient with severe Alzheimer's disease who was unable to recognize family members. The day before her death, she suddenly regained the ability to talk clearly. She spoke to her niece and told her about the light she saw, and she described the deceased family members by name and relationship to her.

Grandma And Grandson

In his book, *The Light Beyond*, Raymond Moody described a case of cardiologist Michael Sabon. A six-year old boy was dying and had a vision of telepathically contacting his grandmother who had been bedridden for several years with severe arthritis. The boy reported the vision at 4 A.M. At the same moment, the grandmother awakened and insisted that she be taken to the child's bedside at the hospital. She arrived and the child died soon after.

The Baby With Heart Disease

In *The Light Beyond*, Moody also described a case reported by Kenneth Ring. A woman was in childbirth when she had a NDE. She heard a voice that told her that her newborn would develop heart trouble that would be corrected in time. Upon returning to her body, she informed the doctor. Amazingly her child developed heart disease which was eventually cured.

The Blind Woman's Trip

Rabbi Laibl Wolf described a totally blind woman's NDE. The blind woman reported leaving the death scene to go to an adjoining room. She then described the people present there. She included the color of their clothes and other objects present in the room. All facts were subsequently verified as being completely accurate. Barbara Rommer has also reported cases of blind people's visions that were later independently verified.

The Child With A Birthmark

Noted psychic researcher and parapsychologist, Frank Tribbe, reported the case of Elizabeth Hoffman giving birth to her fifth child. The infant died almost immediately, and Elizabeth's physician wouldn't tell her if it had been a boy or girl in the hope that she would get over the distress quicker. Three years later, Elizabeth was in the same hospital with double-pneumonia. She almost died and had a fairly typical NDE in which she went through a tunnel, saw a brilliant light, and found herself in an exquisite garden. There she met her father who had died when she was fourteen. He took her to a playground where he stopped a child on a swing. He told Elizabeth that the child was her daughter. Her father then showed Elizabeth a comma-shaped, strawberry-colored birthmark under the child's chin. Next, he told her that she must return, and her father and daughter disappeared. While convalescing, Elizabeth asked her physician about her deceased child. Reluctantly, the physician verified the gender and the birthmark of the child.

NDEs Throughout History

NDEs appear to be a recent phenomenon, but it is not reasonable to think that they have only occurred in the late 20th century. It is only because of the resuscitative techniques of modern medicine that many more NDEs now occur. In fact, there are some indications that they have been found throughout history. However, none of these historical NDEs can be verified, but there is reason to believe that at least some of them took place. Let's look at some evidence.

Plato's Tale

In *Plato's Republic* (4th century B.C.), which may be either fact or fiction, a soldier died and rose upwards. There he met a panel of judges who took him on a trip where he saw souls leaving Earth and Heaven. The heavenly souls told him of unbelievable beauty.

Deloks

Deloks were near-death visionaries from Tibet. They would apparently die and enter Earth. The deloks then would visit a bardo version of hell, receive life judgments, and would often be given views of a bardo version of heaven. (Bardo is considered further in Chapter 11.) The deloks were usually accompanied by a protective deity who gave them messages for the living.

Hellish NDEs

During the Middle Ages, NDEs occurred but probably because of the emphasis on hell in religion, art and literature, the visions were primarily hellish. The NDErs would leave their bodies and be given tours of hell with scenes of torment such as demons clawing at their clothes. Later, they would be given glimpses of a blissful heaven. Nevertheless, there is an amazing painting by the 16th century Flemish painter, Hieronymus Bosch, entitled *The Ascent into Empyrean* in which a heavenly journey is portrayed showing a dark tunnel and a brilliant light at its end (see *Figure 6*.)

Paul's Visions

Saint Paul probably had NDEs. One possibly happened when, as Saul, he was stoned and left for dead in Lystra. Another time was when, as Saul, he fell down on the road to Damascus and had his great revelation about Jesus: ".....he came near Damascus: and suddenly there shined round about him, a light from heaven" (Acts 9:3).

Figure 6
The Ascent into the Empyrean by Hieronymus Bosch. Original on display at Doges Palace in Venice, Italy.

More Recent NDEs

Black Elk, the Native American spiritual leader, supposedly had a NDE. Joseph Smith, the Mormons' founder, and George Fox, the founder of the Quakers, apparently had NDEs. The American Congregationalist, Jonathan Edwards also apparently had a NDE. In the 1940s, the well-known medium, Arthur Ford, had a comprehensive NDE (see *An Arthur Ford Anthology*).

Experiencing Another's NDE

In his latest book, *The Last Laugh*, Raymond Moody has reported that there are empathetic NDEs, shared NDEs, conjoint NDEs, and mutual NDEs. What these all have in common is that someone at the bedside of a dying person participates empathetically in the dying experience of the person. Dozens of trustworthy people have related to Moody that, as a loved one apparently died, they themselves lifted out of their own bodies and accompanied their dying loved one upward toward a magnificent and loving light, or they perceived deceased relatives greeting dying loved ones. Those in proximity at the bedside frequently are convinced that they are participating simultaneously, intimately, and intuitively in the on-going NDEs of the dying individuals.

Moody had been informed that in these shared NDEs, the same message had been received as was the case in the individual NDEs — the message being *the overwhelming importance of love*. It had been observed that having a close personal association to the dying individual increased the chances of a shared NDE with that individual. However, that was not a necessary condition. Many physicians and nurses had described to Moody that at the point of death, they perceived their patients' spirits leaving their bodies. Not only that, some of these helping professionals, as well as psychologists and hospice counselors who happened to be at the bedsides of these dying victims, have themselves had these conjoint or mutual NDEs. Several other well-known authorities in the field have informed Moody that in their own professional practices, they have observed these conjoint NDEs. It might be that there is some kind of telepathic communication that allows caring individuals to get a glimpse of the afterlife along with the dying or near-dying person.

NDEs Of People Whom I
Have Personally Interviewed

Since my NDE only showed five of the components of a typical positive NDE (bright light, serene feeling, life review, presence of caring being, and out-of-body experience), in order to bolster my belief in the soul and a positive afterlife, I felt that I had to speak firsthand to individuals who had experienced more complete NDEs. Each of the eight people that I interviewed appeared to be honest and forthright. As they told of their experiences, there was no hesitancy. The words just flowed from their memory banks. I had no doubt that they were telling the truth as they remembered it. Their NDEs were exceptional.

David's Double Disaster

David M. is a 74-year old man of the Jewish faith who lives in Southern New Jersey. Before his NDE, David was not a very religious man, but as he is now sorting out his life, he believes that God is watching over him. In World War II, he took part in the invasion of the Philippines and escaped unscathed. In 1973, he had a massive heart attack with major damage to his left ventricle. His physicians gave him five years to live. David didn't believe their prediction and used several coping techniques including denial, a low-fat diet, megavitamins, exercise (jogging), and maintaining a positive outlook. He was well for awhile but then major stressors occurred. Three years after his heart attack, his wife died, and his daughter became involved with drugs. Nevertheless, David kept up his optimistic outlook and busied himself in his work. He began a part-time job in administration for the New Jersey Department of Environmental Protection. He worked his way up to a full-time position as an environmental/pesticide specialist in the compliance and enforcement program. In 1987, David fell head first down a flight of steps but suffered only minor bruises. By 1995, he had been alive 17 years longer than his physicians had predicted. Early that year, David felt weak and short-winded. He went to his cardiologist and was told that he had heart failure and didn't have long to live. By the summer of 1995, David was on anticoagulants, aspirin, and other drugs.

On a clear night in December of 1995, he was eating at a restaurant. As David was chewing into a piece of bread with margarine, he felt terrible. His lungs seemed to be waterlogged. He was rushed to Cooper Hospital in Camden, New Jersey, wheeled into surgery and put on a table in the operating room. David felt a surge of pressure in his lungs. He heard a team member say that his blood pressure was falling rapidly. He then blacked out. Within a few seconds, David had separated from his body and rose up from the table. He looked down and saw himself lying semi-inclined on the table with several people around him. David saw them placing tubes down his throat and attaching a respirator. He watched them frantically working on him. Immediately, he was back in his body. David's hands were lying below his chest and he saw the doctor using a defibrillator. He thought that this was going to be painful, but it wasn't. Suddenly he saw his hands go out to his sides. Surrounding his arms and extending out for a short distance, David observed a purplish aura. The aura appeared to then outline his entire body. Soon, he blacked out again. Fortunately, he recovered.

About three weeks later, he spoke to the physician who had worked on him. David was told that he had apparently died, but the staff didn't give up and defibrillated him four times. Finally after the fourth attempt, they brought him back. A short time later, David had quadruple bypass surgery and valve repair. Nevertheless, he still had heart failure and was not given long to live. This time David became even more enthusiastic in his quest to prove his physicians' prognosis to be flawed. He emphatically followed Dr. Dean Ornish's strict program, which included a very low fat diet, aerobic exercise and meditation. As I write this (October 1999), it is about four years after David's NDE. Although still sick, David exercises regularly, maintains his job efficiently and enjoys his life. When I asked him how his NDE had affected him, David said that he believes in God, is not afraid of death, and knows that there is an afterlife. Of special interest, David told me that when he has a deep meditation, he sees that same purple light that was present with him during his NDE. Meditating on that light gives him a wonderful feeling of peace.

John And The Walloping Waves

John S. is a 46-year old man of the Roman Catholic faith who lives in Southern New Jersey. He had a normal childhood, worked as an business man, got married at age 20, and was divorced at age 42. At age 44, he married Darlene. John had been a religious person, but within the last three years he began to show an interest in spirituality. His health was fine until 3 and $1/2$ years ago when he hit his head on a basement window. Damage occurred to a few neck vertebrae, but he recovered and returned to his regular activities.

In mid-July of 1995, he was on vacation with Darlene at Wildwood, New Jersey (a shore community). John and Darlene were bathing in the ocean. The surf was rough. A particularly strong wave knocked them down, and Darlene said that she had enough. She began to walk back to the beach. John told her that he would ride one more wave and then would also come out. Her back was to him as he went into the water, which at that point was only a couple of feet deep. He saw a large wave coming in and turned on his back to ride it. However, rather than just being one wave, it was a double wave. As the first wave picked him up, the second wave went under his legs. John felt a strong undertow. He was up in the air for a couple of seconds and then was knocked down and hit the top of his head on the hard sand. The water broke all around him. Before he fell, John heard a voice in his subconscious that told him to put his hands down, but he was afraid that he would break his back if he put his hands down. While he was deliberating, he hit his head. John's first thought was, "It wasn't too bad, I'm OK." His next thought was, "Move, put your arms down and move." He tried to stand up and move. He couldn't; he felt paralyzed. John couldn't move his arms, legs, or anything. Suddenly, another wave started to take him out into the ocean. He closed his mouth and held his breath. John opened his eyes and tried to move again. As the wave was taking him out, he felt helpless. Meanwhile, his wife had her back away from him as she was casually walking on the sand toward their section of the beach. She was completely unaware of any problem.

John's next thought was to try to roll over so he could get his head out of the water in order to breathe. At this moment, he was still holding his breath but couldn't move. About 10-15 seconds had passed from the time he hit his head in the sand. It was at this moment that John spoke to God: "You can't do this to me. I'm in deep trouble. I've got a new wife, only married seven months. I've got three older sons, stepsons, a business, a new home." Although he couldn't see God, John felt His presence and was certain that he was communicating directly with Him.

Just then, as he was being pulled out further into the ocean by the wave, he saw right in front of his face, a huge, white, intense light. It was almost like a tornado. The inside was tunnel shaped; it was dark but not black. Outside of the tunnel-shaped interior was an vibrant bright light that was also circular in shape. John's first thought was that it was the sun. Again, he tried to get his head above the water and get a breath of air, but it was to no avail. He thought: "This isn't the sun. This is the light you see when you die. If I continue to look into it, then I'm going to die."

John looked away from the light and prayed. But he couldn't avoid the light. It was all around him. The light was real — not in his imagination — as real as anything he had ever seen. Then he was back to the reality of the situation. From the middle of his neck upwards, he could feel sensations. From that point down, he was completely numb. He next thought, "Darlene will turn around, see me drowning, and come to my rescue." Nothing happened. John again spoke to God: "God, You can do this, You have all the power. If this is what you want of me, then so be it."

At that point, all of his pressing responsibilities were taken away. They didn't concern him anymore. John was feeling the most perfect peace that he had ever experienced. All of his present state of affairs were unimportant. He felt a wonderful bliss. John looked directly at the light. Time stood still; he had absolutely no sense of time. John knew that he couldn't hold his breath any longer, but it didn't matter. In the past, he had occasionally taken marijuana, but it was nothing like the present feelings. He had also been hypnotized, but that didn't even come close to approaching these sensations. Now, nothing mattered. He had no earthly pressures. John was at total peace. Then, all of a sudden, he saw an arm around him. It was his wife's arm. She then placed both her arms under his arms and pulled him up. Although John thought that his face was up and he was looking upward into the light, when Darlene saw him, he was floating on the water with his face down into the water. She picked him up and turned him over. He coughed out water and began to breathe. He moved his head but was totally paralyzed from the neck down.

Darlene later reported that after she had almost reached the edge where the water and the beach met, she decided to take a look around to see if John was coming back. It was then that she saw him with his head in the water, apparently lifeless. She ran to get to him.

A female physician with emergency room experience quickly came over to help. She stabilized John's head, but his lower body was still in the water. No one else touched him. He began to talk to his wife, but his body felt to him as if it were a jellyfish. Even though before his rescue, he had been feeling unbelievable bliss, he now thought: "Thank God I'm alive." He realized that he would have to go to the hospital. A lifeguard called for an ambulance, and soon he was on his way to the hospital. John looked down at his stomach; it was blown up. He felt very sick. Although he had thought that while in the water he had kept his mouth closed, he was wrong. The first thing they did in the ambulance was to pump the seawater out of his stomach and lungs. John felt pain — as if his whole body was on fire. Because of the seriousness of the case, the ambulance went to the airport, and they transported John and Darlene to the trauma center of the Atlantic City Medical Center. John realized that although he was in agony from the pain, the paralysis was not complete. Nevertheless, he still couldn't move anything from his neck down. After he was treated for the acute condition , he was taken to a local spinal cord center where they found that he had not severed the spinal cord.

Now, in October 1999, it is four years after the accident. John is still in pain, but is gradually recovering. The long-term prognosis is good. When I asked him how his NDE affected him, John said that he believes in God, is not afraid of death, and believes in an afterlife. He ended by saying that the experience was more peaceful than anything he could ever imagine.

Marjorie's Sexual Surprise

Marjorie D. is a 41-year-old woman who was brought up as a religious Roman Catholic but now is a born-again Christian. She lives alone in Southern New Jersey. Marjorie had a normal childhood, went to college, became a mental health worker and artist, and got married at age 20. When she was 21-years old, her head hair was blonde. She went to a party with her husband, Jim, given by her girlfriend, Arlene. She came early in order to help Arlene set up. Marjorie just got her menstrual period and was not feeling well. She asked Arlene for a couple of Mydols® to ease the cramps. Arlene gave them to her. Just as Marjorie was about to take them, she had an uncanny thought: "I'll die if I take these." She couldn't understand that premonition because she never had a problem with Mydol before. Marjorie had premonitions before in her life and was invariably right when she had those hunches. Hence, she couldn't understand this one. Nevertheless, she took the pills. Meanwhile the party guests began to arrive.

After awhile, Marjorie began to feel strange. She thought; "Is there something wrong?" She laid down on a sofa thinking, "What if my hunch were true? But it can't be true. You can't die from Mydol." Strangely, she felt peaceful — not afraid. Her husband Jim came over and asked her if there was anything wrong. She didn't want to upset him and said that it was just her time of the month, and she was a little tired. Jim left her. The room was now filled with people. They were drinking and smoking. Everyone ignored Marjorie. They probably thought that she just had one too many.

Suddenly Marjorie felt a tingling sensation. She floated upward and saw herself lying on the sofa completely immobile. At first she was scared, but soon that feeling disappeared. Marjorie moved out of the room. She ducked her head to avoid a door, but amazingly she was able to go through the door. She then went through the walls into other rooms in the house while observing the wild happenings. Finally, she arrived at a bedroom and was shocked. On the bed she saw Jim and Arlene having sexual intercourse. Marjorie was furious and screamed at them to stop. They did not hear her and went on with their lovemaking. She left the bedroom, moved around for what appeared to be a few minutes, and then returned to the room in which she was lying immobile on the couch. By now, Jim, Arlene, and others were hovering over her. She saw them carry her into a car and heard someone say they were going to the hospital.

The next thing Marjorie knew, she was being sucked up like into a vacuum cleaner. Higher and higher she went and entered stark darkness. In the distance, she saw a light. As she was brought closer, it became brighter, a wonderful golden color — like the brightest sun. Marjorie looked out of the corner of her eye and saw strange entities. She then observed herself; she was a tiny fleck of light. "Am I dead?" she asked.

An answer came to her from out of the light: "You are not dead."

"Who are you?" Marjorie asked.

The reply came: "I am. I am that which you term God. I am."

Marjorie then glanced to the left and heard inhuman screaming. She started to look. God said: "Don't look at that! It's the pit." He
then inquired: "Is there anything you want to see?"

Marjorie replied: "Show me when I was little." She then saw
herself as a six-year old making a peanut butter and jelly sandwich.
Her mother and her sister (holding a stuffed toy) were there. By this
time, Marjorie was feeling wonderful. There was love, peace, and
euphoria — incredibly bliss — and she did not want to return. God
told her that she could stay if she wanted to, but she should return as
He had a job for her. She was to teach truth, justice, and enlightenment. Marjorie was still reluctant to return. God then told her to look
at this. She saw an unknown, dark-haired woman living in an
unknown house. There was a 3-year-old boy playing with a plastic
toy that he was about to swallow. The woman rushed in and saved
him. Next, the same woman was watching another little boy on a
monkey bar fall into a pool. She rushed in and saved him. Finally, the
same woman saw an infant who was about to put a screwdriver into
his eye. The woman saved him. God then asked her: "Would you
have saved them?"

Marjorie exclaimed: "Of course!" Still reluctant to return,
God told her that she had been dead for 27 minutes and had to return.
He then let her hear her husband's voice. Jim was frantically crying
out for her. In spite of everything, Marjorie felt compassion for Jim.

Instantaneously, she was back in her body. She awoke and
asked Jim to take her home. Marjorie then told him what she had
seen. Although not understanding how she knew, he admitted to the
affair. She then confronted Arlene, who at first denied everything,
but then admitted to the affair. She then told Marjorie that she gave
her a narcotic because it had always worked for her cramps. Obvi-
ously, Marjorie had a life-threatening reaction to the narcotic. Marjorie
divorced Jim soon afterwards. Amazingly, the vision of the house
and the woman in dark hair saving the three children came true.
Marjorie dyed her hair black and saved her three nephews (who
hadn't yet been born when she had her NDE) in the same house and
in the same manner as had occurred in the vision. With the NDE, she
had expected to see St. Peter and the "pearly gates," and hence,
became disillusioned with Catholicism. She believes in God and an
afterlife and now has no fear of death.

Carol Meets Grandpop

Carol C. is a 17-year-old high school student of the Jewish faith who lives in Mineola, New York. When she was 7-years old, she developed a cerebral hemorrhage that left her in a coma. Carol was taken to Mineola hospital and given a CAT scan that showed the presence of an arterial-venous malformation. The medical staff attempted to stabilize her, but she apparently died as her pupils became fixed and dilated. Fortunately, they were able to resuscitate her. The surgery was then successfully performed. Carol remained in a coma for one week. When she came out of it, she spoke to her mother. Carol told her that she had gone through a tunnel and then saw a very bright light near an entrance. She then said enthusiastically: "I saw grandpa and he spoke to me. He said, 'Don't come in. It's not your time. You've got to go back.' "

Carol's grandfather had died two years previously. He was the only family member that Carol had known to have died. She hadn't even started religious school, and had no knowledge of NDEs. Carol completely recovered. Since then, she believes in God and an afterlife and has no fear of death.

Frank's Open-Heart Experience

Frank R. is a 62-year-old Roman Catholic, ex-marine, and present artist, who currently lives in Philadelphia. He "died" in 1976 while undergoing open-heart surgery. Frank saw the dark tunnel and brilliant light; he met deceased friends and his grandfather. He noticed that two close friends who had committed suicide some years before were nowhere to be seen. Frank felt marvelous; he knew answers to everything. The place was incredible and peaceful, and he would have loved to stay. However, he struggled against the force that was pulling him in, thinking that he wasn't ready to leave; his work was too important.

In 1976, Frank had no previous knowledge of NDEs. He now believes in an afterlife, some sort of God, and has no fear of death. Frank said he had died and returned to life in order to tell the story of death. After getting divorced, he remarried a Jewish woman artist, Ruth S., who used a material known as Homosote in her work. He learned the technique and also was made aware of the horrors of the Holocaust from his mother-in-law Sadie S. After she died, he decided to do work in Homosote commemorating the Holocaust. The result was a fantastic series of three-dimensional works depicting aspects of the Holocaust. (See "Notes and References".)

Roy Goes Down For The Count Three Times

Roy T. is a 56-year-old non-observant Protestant, who lives in Southern New Jersey. For most of his life, he lived in California. Roy had three NDEs. At the age of 11, he nearly drowned and recalled leaving his body and observing his own near-death taking place. In times of need, he always felt the presence of a guardian angel. As an adult, he went through many stressful times, and to deal with the stress, Roy turned to alcohol and drugs such as Valium® and Percodan®. In 1983, although he had that experience as an 11-year-old, Roy was unaware of NDEs. He had developed joint problems and was on two drugs — one to be taken upon arising and the other at noon. On this particular day, Roy forgot to take his first drug. While at work in the supermarket, at noon he took both drugs together. Shortly thereafter, he felt flushed and overheated. He went into the freezer to cool down. It didn't help. Roy returned to the back of the main room and fell down, hitting a shopping cart.

The next thing he knew, with a sudden surge, he was lifted up while simultaneously he saw his body crashing to the floor. He felt nothing as he floated up feet first toward the ceiling and then through the roof. Two entities assisted him to stand erect as he went through a tunnel. His guardian angel was also there. In the distance, Roy saw a brilliant light. To his right was the universe in all its brilliance. To his left, it was dark, but thousands of people of indefinite shape and size were there. As they approached the light, the people appeared to blend in with it. Although many of the people were unknown to Roy, he recognized some deceased family members and friends. They told him not to worry and enjoy the experience. Roy asked the guardian angel many questions, but couldn't recall the answers. As Roy approached the light, he was told that there was a purpose to all of this. Roy thought that the brilliant light would be God. The angel told him that there are no judges, and that he was to judge himself. Just then, his observed a review of his life. He had enough time to review and judge his actions. Although it could have been stressful, Roy felt perfectly safe, at peace, and full of love. He felt that if he was going to die, it would be fine.

After the review was completed, Roy knew he would be going into the light, and the light was God. Previously, he had been afraid of authority figures, but now, in front of the greatest authority of all, he had absolutely no fear. Roy was unaware of his body; he had no sensations of movement; no pain or discomfort of any kind. As soon as he stepped into the light, he was blown into millions of pieces. Incredibly, the pieces soon reassembled and he was once again whole. Although he didn't actually talk to God, he was told many things. It was a fantastic learning experience. Roy felt as if he had absorbed all the knowledge of the universe. He then felt vibrations as he explored the universe at incredible speed. Roy saw stars and planets as dots of lights. He went through portals (like black holes) and came out into other universes with brilliant colors. He heard heavenly music being played. It was if he had orchestrated the tunes and conducted the stars and planets in the playing of it. Roy then experienced the beginnings of the universe. By now, he was not aware of his body — only of his vibrations. Roy observed the evolution of the stars and planets. There were incredible color changes as the Earth emerged. And then, all of a sudden, he was back in the light with his guardian angel and the two other entities.

Roy didn't want to ever leave. He had no thoughts of returning to his wife and 13-year-old son. His marriage had been "on the rocks," and his son was quite independent. Roy didn't want to return, but his guardian angel and the two entities told him he couldn't stay. He still had a purpose, and it had to be fulfilled. Roy begged them to let him stay. It was to no avail. Immediately, he was back in his body and a police officer was yelling at him. He had been out for about 17 minutes. With his wife at his side, they took him in an ambulance to the hospital. The diagnosis had been anaphylactic shock from the drug combination. Roy now knew that there was a God and an afterlife, and he had no fear of dying.

Roy stopped drinking, reduced his smoking and felt calm for the first time in his life. For awhile, he told no one about his experience. When he did describe it, they thought he had been back on drugs and alcohol. This so angered Roy that he went back to drinking. In 1985, he joined AA and sobered up. In 1987, his wife — who also had been a drinker — sobered up and left town with her AA sponsor. Later that year, Roy was out on a date with a woman. They had seen a couple of movies and returned to his place. During sexual intercourse, he suffered severe chest pains. Just as he was about to have an ejaculation, the pain intensified. With the arrival of the orgasm, he collapsed on the floor into a fetal position. The next thing Roy knew he was back up in the light with the two entities and his guardian angel. He told them: "This is it!"

They replied, "It all depends; the decision is up to you."

Another life review passed by. Although there was some repetition, most of the events were from 1983 to the present. He observed that he had been losing financial and emotional security; and he had a high-pressure, unsecured job. But there was one bright spot. He had been helping other people with their recovery from alcoholism. Was his life over? Would he go back? He had mixed feelings. He needed someone to help him make up his mind. Roy wanted to go into the light and ask God. He was told that he had to decide first. Roy chose to go on living. He then entered the light, was immediately blown apart and rapidly reunified. Roy then became part of the light. He became a oneness with God. He felt "God's hugs" and was back in his body. After awakening, he went home. A few days later, Roy had a double angioplasty. He remarried in 1992, moved to Southern New Jersey, and started an alternative healing bookstore. Roy is now solid in his belief in God, the soul and an afterlife, and he has absolutely no fear of death.

Brett Meets The Angels And "God"

Brett J. is a 44-year-old special education teacher who lives in Daytona Beach, Florida. His father was a Christian Scientist; his mother was a Baptist. Brett was brought up with no particular religion and was ambivalent about life after death. He "died" in 1975 while undergoing cancer surgery. At that time, he had absolutely no knowledge of NDEs. Dr. Moody's book had not yet been published. Five years earlier, when Brett was 15-years old, he was diagnosed with reticulum cell sarcoma and non Hodgkin's lymphoma. For five years, he was treated by surgical and radiation treatments. In 1975, at the age of 20, Brett was being operated on for the removal of his spleen, lymph nodes and appendix. While under general anesthesia, he suddenly felt weird sensations. His "body" came alive, and he rose out of the body that was on the operating room table. For awhile, Brett hovered over the operating table. He saw the various operating room pieces of equipment, the surgeons, the anesthesiologist and the nurses. He heard someone say, "We're losing him." Then he saw one of the doctors applying defibrillators to his chest.

Suddenly, Brett was sucked up out of the hospital. He was in a field of multicolored, wonderfully-smelling flowers. The colors of the flowers were extremely vivid and appeared three-dimensional. He especially recalled the intense blue-colored ones. The wind was blowing the flowers, and he felt the warm breezes on his spiritual body. Out of nowhere, Brett then saw deceased relatives from both sides of his family. These were people he had only known from pictures — never having seen them in the flesh. However, he could recognize all of them even though they appeared as if in the prime of their lives. Brett remembered being very surprised to see them. They didn't actually speak to him, but he had telepathic communication with them. They told him that everything was wonderful.

Then Brett was whisked high into the sky. He noticed that his body became ball-like, but that didn't bother him. He was now in a sea of clouds with smoke and fog also present. Brett saw an angelic creature peek out from behind a cloud and then put its head back into the cloud. The angel then peeked out again — rabbit-like — but this time it stayed out. He recalled that the creature looked like an angel or gnome. Soon, many angels came out of the clouds and lifted him up. Brett felt as if he was a sail or spirit. The angels didn't speak, but Brett felt happy — even overjoyed. He kept on rising, and as he did, the temperature changed. First it was cold, then warm, and then even warmer. Brett was being carried higher and higher. Then he saw it. It was a huge, extremely bright light. He was brought closer to this light. In front of the light, someone (something) began to communicate with him. Brett didn't know who he was talking to, but he felt that he was talking to a supreme being. The complete two-sided conversation was telepathic. Brett asked, "What am I doing here?"

Then Brett was inside of the light, when he was told, "You know why you're here."

Brett asked, "Can I enter?"

The response was, "You are not ready. You still have work to do."

Brett then inquired, "Can I come again?"

The reply was, "Do your work on Earth and you'll be received here."

Brett then said, "Okay." Immediately, he slowly descended and before he knew it, Brett was back inside his body.

When he awakened, the operation was over. Brett was in his hospital bed in the recovery room. No one said anything specifically about the operation until four days later, when his surgeon spoke to him. Brett told his surgeon about what he thought was "the weirdest dream he had ever had." In his "dream," he thought he had died and gone to heaven. The surgeon thought that Brett's experience was related to the general anesthesia, but he did admit that they almost "lost him." One of the surgeons cut into the abdomen. The bleeding couldn't be controlled; Brett's heart stopped and his brain flat-lined. They estimated that he was clinically dead for 3-4 minutes. They finally got the bleeding under control, and with the use of defibrillators, they were able to shock his heart back into beating. The surgeon apologized profusely for the surgical mishap, but assured Brett that everything went well. The spleen, appendix and lymph nodes were removed. The lymph nodes had no cancer cells. Afterwards, he received cobalt radiation treatments and chemotherapy. Brett has now been cancer-free for 24 years. The NDE didn't make Brett ultra-religious, but seven years after its occurrence, he became baptized. He believes in God and has no fear of death. Brett believes that part of the reason he has remained cancer-free is that God told him that he still had work to do on Earth. He is certain that there is life after death. However, he feels that people are supposed to do good deeds on Earth; and if they are performed, they will "be rewarded in some way, form or shape." Brett now has a new outlook on life. He thoroughly enjoys gardens, music and the simpler things in life.

Lucy And The Follow-Up To Her Childbirth Experience

Lucy M. is a 33-year-old art director and editor who lives in Orlando, Florida. She was born a Catholic but before her NDE, she had no strong religious feelings or beliefs one way or another about death. Her mother, who was not religious, died from metastatic colon cancer when Lucy was 16. Lucy has been married for seven years to an architect. Over four years ago (July 27, 1995), when she was living in New Haven, Connecticut, Lucy had her first child. She had been taking birthing classes and as a result of the preparation, the birth was problem-free. She delivered a healthy baby boy. Then one week later, she experienced a sharp abdominal pain that progressed to waves of pain. The pain lasted for four days. It was discovered that one of her ovaries was enlarged, twisted and necrotic. Under general anesthesia, the ovary was removed and biopsied. It was found to have a specific type of cancer known as choriocarcinoma from a molar pregnancy. Her husband's sperm resulted in a healthy baby, but another of his sperm killed a second egg and made malignant tissue. Tumor metastases then went to her brain, lungs, and liver. This was all detected one week later. The uterus was tumor-free, but the pain was caused by the twisted, necrotic ovary. For the metastatic tumors, Lucy received brain radiation and chemotherapy. After five months of chemotherapy, she became very sick, losing her hair and having severe side effects. She stayed home during the one or two days of therapy every other week. At home, Lucy was attended to by a home health aide and a visiting nurse. A relative took care of the baby.

One morning in late December, Lucy had a feeling that something wasn't right. She began to cry and then lay down on a guest room bed. Lucy was very upset. Why was this happening to her? Why was she getting all of these bad experiences? She was 30 years old, had never smoked, didn't drink, had been in excellent health, and then look what happened. Lucy felt jealous of the aide, the nurses. She felt angry and had bad energy. The home health aide saw her on the bed and called over the nurse. The nurse took Lucy's temperature. She had a very high fever. The nurse believed that Lucy might have a brain infection and wanted her to be hospitalized immediately. Lucy didn't want to leave her baby, but she was in no position to resist.

Suddenly, the room began changing colors: from white to pale-yellow to yellow to purple. The transitions were gradual and were beautiful. Lucy knew that something strange was going on, but she didn't know what it was. An ambulance came and Lucy was on her way to the hospital. Then she was "out of it." She heard a sound — a whooshing noise. Lucy felt herself being pulled out of the whole situation. She felt overwhelming euphoria and love. She was surrounded by loving feelings. She sensed that this was the way it was supposed to be. All of a sudden, there was a brilliant, blinding bright light. Lucy couldn't see if she had a body or not. All she knew was that she was surrounded by euphoria, love, and joy. Lucy then looked to her left. She saw a tiny, dark spot — like the size of the head of a pin. She looked into it and saw her whole life. Then she saw her son, and his future life unfolded in front of her. He had his own path, and it was perfect, but she was still in this indescribable place. Lucy felt overwhelming joy and euphoria. The only comparison she could think of was the joyful sensation she had felt while in the Swiss Alps, but this was one million times better. No one said it directly to her, but telepathically she sensed that she was not going to stay here. Immediately, Lucy was back into her life again. She began to cry, but this time it was because she was so happy. Lucy had no way of knowing if she had died and returned to life, because by the time she "returned," she was in a hospital bed. The doctors and nurses never told her anything about her state when she was brought in. Lucy was treated for the infection and recovered completely. She never said anything about her experience to the aide, the home nurse or anyone at the hospital. Lucy had no previous knowledge about NDEs, and until she finally told a friend knowledgeable about NDEs of her experience, she wasn't aware that she had a NDE.

Her family moved to Orlando, where she became involved in a new occupation — an art director and editor. For about six months following the NDE, Lucy felt fine, except that she had changed. She became psychic. She could "hear" people's thoughts. She found out that often people say one thing and mean something else. Lucy found this ability to be very disturbing. To prevent its occurrence, when talking to others, she avoided eye contact . Fortunately, after two months, the ability waned. However, Lucy still had telepathic communications. For example, one day while driving to work, she suddenly remembered the complete words to a school play song that she sang with a fellow student named John S. That incident took place 27 years before. She hadn't thought of that song or John since her public school days. When she got to her office, she received a telephone call from a friend in New Haven. The friend told her that John S. had just been killed in a traffic accident. Aside from that unfortunate occurrence, Lucy frequently receives intrusive thoughts or messages that guide her in a positive direction.

It is now over three years since her NDE. Lucy feels fine; she goes for a checkup every six months. Her physicians have told her that she is cured. In retrospect, Lucy feels that during her NDE, she met God even though He never directly spoke to her. In that special place, she got the sense that she was completely loved, and she was one with the love and joy. However, the occurrence was impossible to comprehend and describe. She said it's like trying to explain nuclear physics to a house cat.

Liz has become a Methodist, but she doesn't adhere to any specific religious belief. She believes that her NDE gave her positive energy and taught her tolerance for all religions. She now believes that we have to be giving to each other. Practicing what she preaches, Liz donates 10% of her salary to charitable organizations. Finally, Liz now has no fear of death.

A Fictional Case: What Goes Around Comes Around

The final case is a fictional one courtesy of Mike Rogers. It's included here because of the morals involved.

Mrs. Eileen Brown, a well-to-do, middle-aged woman had a severe heart attack and was taken in an ambulance to a hospital. After stabilization, she was scheduled for cardiac surgery. During the operation, Eileen's heart stopped and the EEG went flat. Although she was clinically dead, the surgeons worked frantically to bring her back. While they were working on her body, Eileen left it and had a NDE. She saw the brilliant light and met God. Eileen asked God, "Is this it? Am I dead?"

God replied, "No. Eileen, you are not dead. In fact, you have another 30 years to live."

Reassured, Eileen left the heavenly scene and returned to her body. The doctors were thrilled with her recovery and they brought the operation to a successful conclusion.

Eileen was so thrilled with her miraculous recovery and God's prognosis that she decided to remain in the hospital and fix herself up. So she had a face lift, blue contacts inserted, liposuction, breast augmentation and a "tummy tuck." For good measure, she had a beautician come to the hospital and dye her hair red. After complete recovery and pleased as a peacock, Eillen left the hospital. Walking out of the building, her head was in the clouds. She crossed the street without looking and was hit and immediately killed by an ambulance bringing a heart attack victim to the hospital.

Eileen's soul and spiritual body went up to heaven. She again met God and was in a complaining mood. "God," she said, "I thought you said that I had another 30 years to live."

God replied, "I'm sorry, Eileen, but I didn't recognize you."

The morals are twofold.

1. Be pleased with your new lease on life but don't be overly concerned with your physical appearance. Love yourself as you are and give love and help to others.

2. Look where you're going.

From NDEs To OBEs

The consistencies in my NDE, the interviews with other experiencers, and extensive research reveal that the NDE and the shared NDE are very strong evidence for the existence of a soul that survives the death of the physical body and a positive afterlife — at least for people who are not evil and who do not attempt suicide. There is also indirect proof of the existence of God, since most of the individuals interviewed by me and others felt that they had contacted God either directly or indirectly.

Although we found that NDEs give excellent support to the possibility of a surviving soul, a positive afterlife, and God, it is important, using a scientifically-based viewpoint, to find evidence from other sources. Since I had an out-of-body experience, and others who have had them came away from the experience with a belief in a surviving soul, a positive afterlife and God, the next stop on our spiritual journey to overcome death anxiety is along the path of out-of-body-experiences (OBEs).

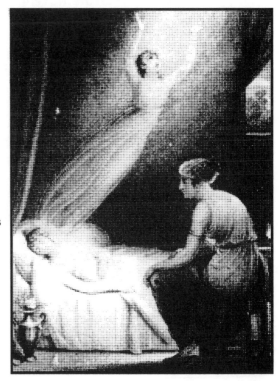

Figure 7
1829 engraving by
Corbould showing the
"astral body" that survives
death and can account
for OBEs.

CHAPTER FOUR

OUT-OF-BODY EXPERIENCES

"Now it came to pass in the thirtieth year, in the fourth month, in the fifth day of the month, as I (Ezekiel) was among the captives by the river Chebar that the heavens were opened, and I saw visions of God......And I looked, and behold, a stormy wind came out of the north, a great cloud, with a fire flashing up, so that a brightness was round about it....And out of the midst thereof came the likeness of four living creatures...... And the living creatures ran and returned as the appearance of a flash of lightning....And above the firmament that was over their heads was the likeness of a throne, as the appearance of a sapphire stone; and upon the likeness of the throne was a likeness as the appearance of a man upon it above."
(Ezekiel 1: 1,4, 5, 14, 26).

According to Robert Monroe in his book, *Ultimate Journey*, an out-of-body experience (OBE) is defined as "a state of consciousness where you perceive yourself as distinct and separate from your physical body. This separateness can be two inches or two thousand miles, or more." (Ezekiel's above description, being Biblical in origin, can only be accepted on faith, but according to his own account, he went all the way up to heaven.) If you had an afterlife visit-type OBE, here is an example of what could occur.

Your Out-Of-Body Experience

It is 11:30 P.M. You go to bed and soon you are fast asleep. In the past, when you have dreamed, the images were hazy and what occurred was often bizarre. Now, everything is extremely vivid. You are certain that you are awake. You think, perceive, and act similarly to the way you would in a normal physical awake state — with a few exceptions.

You suddenly float out of your physical body which remains on the bed. From this raised up viewpoint, you glance at your elevated self and it looks the same as it always does. Then something strange occurs. Your body changes to a more fluid shape until it finally becomes a blob. When you observe that, you find it to be disturbing. So you concentrate on it and, miraculously, your elevated body retains its original shape.

You now ignore your physical body lying on the bed. You feel free as a bird, not bounded by ordinary space-time. Yet in some way, you still feel attached to your physical body. It is sort of like a balloon or a kite on a tether. Your consciousness is different than it is in the awake state. Everything appears to be "up front" and out in the open. You are unaware of a subconscious or unconscious constraint. It does not appear possible to be devious or deceitful.

Now, it is time to take a trip. You don't choose the destination but with a surge you are pulled through a dark tunnel. Soon, you find yourself being enveloped by a glorious, bright light. You feel calm, serene, extremely happy, and full of love. You look in the distance and see people. At first, they appear to be hazy — as if covered by a soft mist. But as they get closer, they become sharper and more life-like. You recognize several of them: your dear brother, Dick, who died in a fiery car crash, your Uncle Joe, who died of a stroke, your cousin Phyllis who passed on from a heart attack. They look wonderful, just as they did in the prime of their lives. You talk to each of them and the conversions are marvelous. The next thing you know is that you feel a heavenly presence. You know that it is God but you can't actually see Him. Are you dead?

In some way, God communicates to you that you are still alive, but have been given a glimpse of the afterlife. Pleased at that, you decide to look around. You see a beautiful emerald green meadow. A bright, lavender light surrounds the meadow. Ahead of you is a park containing a picturesque garden with many gorgeously-colored flowers of all kinds. The grass and trees are of a brilliant green color. Within the park is a stream with clear, pure water. Ducks are waddling and birds are singing delightful melodies that seem to be accompanied by rapturous music. Gorgeously colored butterflies are out in full force. You are so happy because running up to you is your long-gone loving poodle, Gypsy.

The sky is a vibrant blue. The weather is ideal, not too hot, not too cool, low humidity. Everything is extremely clear, crisp and bright. The colors are so vivid that they defy description. In the distance, you observe large crystal buildings. You have seen enough. It is time to head home. Within a twinkling of an eye, you are back in your physical body.

In the morning when you wake up, you remember everything in exquisite detail. You are certain that it was not a dream. Moreover, although before as a research scientist you had been an agnostic and skeptical of all psi phenomena, you are now a firm believer. There is a surviving soul, a wonderful afterlife and a God. You know that there is life after death and you no longer fear dying.

Leaving The Body With Or Without NDEs

There are other occurrences with OBEs. According to Monroe, people in the out-of-body state can travel not only within the present time frame but can travel to the past and the future. As discussed in the last chapter, an OBE can occur as an integral component of the NDE, as it occurred with me. In the 1982 Gallup poll in which it was found that 8 million Americans had been involved in a NDE, 26 percent of them had an OBE. These individuals reported that they felt themselves rising up and viewing their body down below. When that occurs, as Monroe stated, they are not just a spot of consciousness. They remain in some kind of body even though they are out of their physical bodies. According to Raymond Moody, in his book, *The Light Beyond*, these people feel that the spiritual body has a form that is unlike the physical body. Although it has arms and legs, the people have great difficulty in describing the appearance of the spiritual body. Some individuals even describe it as an energy field or a cloud of colors. One NDEr told Dr. Moody that his hands appeared to be composed of light-containing tiny structures. He could see the delicate whorls of his fingerprints and tubes of light flashed up his arms.

According to the Guggenheims in their book *Hello From Heaven*, some people's concept of their spiritual body is different than the previous descriptions. Rather than being a physical body with a state of consciousness that can leave it (but still be attached to it) a person is a spiritual being inhabiting a physical body during his/her lifetime. Therefore, an individual (the spirit being) can temporarily leave the body and travel anywhere — as far away as the distant stars. In rare circumstances, the spiritual person can even take a heavenly journey, as did Ezekiel.

As was discussed in the last chapter, with an OBE, some people (as described in the Bible in Ecclesiastes 12:5-7) see themselves as a spiritual body attached to their physical body by a silver cord. Batey (1999) has an excellent discussion on OBEs and cites an ancient Chinese drawing that shows the astral (spiritual) body above the physical body attached to each other by a cord. From his research, it is concluded that the silver cord extends from the spiritual body's medulla oblongata (on the lower back of the head) to the middle of the forehead of the physical body.

In the last chapter, a case was presented of a blind person having an OBE during a NDE and describing events that were "seen." Dr. Kenneth Ring (1980; 1984) has performed research on individuals who are congenitally blind and blind following birth and observed that during OBEs, these people are able to see and later describe events and objects.

An OBE can occur during other happenings aside from the NDE. It can take place just before a person dies. As in our opening description, many OBEs have occurred during dreams. Dreams are usually hazy with an unreal quality. However, people who have OBEs report that their dreams are lucid. Everything appears as sharp as it would be in normal awake consciousness. Aside from the NDE during surgery, some individuals report having an OBE when they are under general anesthesia while undergoing surgery — which is not life-threatening. In other words, when they see themselves on the table, they do not observe a dead person. Other individuals have an OBE during a traumatic experience such as: anticipating an accident; during an accident; during childbirth; when in a coma; under intense pain; and when in shock. OBEs can occur during a hypnotic trance, while listening to musical sounds (for example, Monroe's tapes), and during deep meditation. James Redfield (*The Celestine Prophecy* and *The Tenth Insight*) and the Steigers (1999) describe people getting into an OBE from deep meditation. This has happened to me occasionally during profound meditation. Finally, some people can spontaneously get into an OBE while wide awake.

OBEs are not something unique to this century. They have been reported: in the Egyptian religion with the concept of *ka* and the immortality of the soul (discussed more fully in Chapter 11); in the Hebrew Bible with Ezekiel and other prophets; in the New Testament with the possible ascendancy of Christ to heaven; with Native American shamans escaping their bodies and existing in a spirit form during healing rituals; and during the ancient Yoga practice of Kundalini. Since those days, many accounts of OBEs have been reported in books and articles. Based on their research, the Guggenheims have estimated that 20 million living Americans have experienced an OBE. Whether these are real occurrences or a figment of the peoples' imagination is difficult to determine. OBEs are not as strong evidence for an afterlife as are the NDEs, because the latter have shown a unique number of characteristics that are shared by many of the experiencers . For the OBErs, the experiences vary and can occur under many different circumstances. Nevertheless, just as was the case for the NDErs, the OBErs were convinced that the experience was real, and it confirmed their belief in God and an afterlife. They also reported no longer having a fear of death.

According to Robert Monroe, in his book, *Ultimate Journey*, when a person is in an OBE, he/she can actively seek out and find a deceased family member, friend, acquaintance, or business associate. This is very similar to what some NDErs have reported. Perhaps, this is another glimpse into the afterlife — one that can occur while the individual is alive and not close to death as with the NDErs.

Possible Physiological Changes During An OBE

Charles Tart investigated subjects who were having an OBE (not during an NDE) that occurred while they were in a deep state of relaxation, such as meditation. They showed physiological indications of relaxation such as slightly decreased galvanic skin response, heart rate, and respiratory rate. One particular subject showed low alpha brain wave patterns (one to one and a half cycles per second slower than normal) while she had an OBE. In 1998, Jedd reported that at the Monroe Institute it was found that theta waves (indicative of deep relaxation) and delta waves (indicative of sleep) increased during OBEs. Nevertheless, a study by Morris and his co-workers showed that physiological states varied among individuals having an OBE. Hence, it is not definitely known whether or not an OBE is related to a person's physiological state.

After Death Communications

The Guggenheims interviewed 2,000 people throughout the United States and Canada in their study of after-death communications (ADCs). Results were published in their book, *Hello From Heaven*. An ADC is a direct one-on-one experience of a spiritual communication between a deceased family member or friend and a living person. It is initiated by the deceased and occurs spontaneously. The ADCs are divided into many types. Most of these are of the apparition and visionary type and will be discussed in the next chapter. For now, the relevant type ADC is *OBE ADC*: **an out-of-body experience in which the individual contacts the deceased.**

In some descriptions of OBE ADCs, certain findings are similar to the NDE. These have been described in many ways: floating up out of the body; going through a tunnel; being enveloped by a bright light; meeting loved ones; and encountering a heavenly presence. Some OBErs have reported seeing either an angelic presence (see *Figures 8* and *9*), Jesus, Mary or God. Mary has been described as wearing a glowing, bright robe and exuding warmth

Figure 8
"Sistine Madonna" by Raphael Sanzio. Original on display at Gemaldegalerie, Dresden, Germany.

Figure 9
19th Century engraving
of angelic and
Marian experience.
From — *Harter's
Ultimate Angel Book.*

and love. Frequently, the appearance of God is more like a presence who speaks to them inside their own head. The visions of angels is more pictorial with descriptions such as wearing an illuminated, glowing white robe. Descriptions of Jesus varied from detailed artistic viewpoints to more glimmering appearances.

Intriguing Cases Of OBEs

Hitching To See Jesus

An interesting OBE case of a person visiting Jesus was reported by noted psychic researcher, Frank Tribbe. This is an example of an OBE hitch-hiking case. The New Orleans' Reverend Jack Wise, used hypnosis to "send" a willing lady parishioner to first century Palestine to observe Jesus' ministry, and give a report upon her return. This was done every week for several months. The following year, the lady parishioner was greeted very warmly on a Canal street corner by two strange ladies. Speaking for the two of them, one of the ladies explained to the lady parishioner, that living in rural Mississippi, they had learned OBE from a correspondence course. However, they had been bored because they didn't know what to do in order to go to a specific place. Then they saw her, Palestine-bound, and hitched a ride. Thereafter, sensing her regular schedule, they went along for the ride for several weeks. The spokesperson then told the lady parishioner that they were very grateful to her for allowing them to have the wonderful experience.

Other Realms

Some individuals who explored heaven also found other realms. They extended from the heavenly one previously described in our opening story down to regions that were grayer and darker. When they reached the lowest realm it was devoid of emotional warmth, light and love. This might be a concept of hell. However, the feeling these experiencers had that nothing was permanent. Even those who inhabited the lowest realm felt that if they changed for the better, they could move upward and achieve serenity.

Being In Two Places At Once: Alabama And Los Angeles

Raymond Moody, who initiated NDE studies (see the last chapter), has also done extensive work with producing apparitions and visions (discussed in the next chapter). In one session, he was working with the renowned television talk-show host, Joan Rivers. Toward the end of her session, Ms. Rivers suddenly had an OBE and described traveling from Alabama to Los Angeles. When she arrived there, she went to her daughter's house and sat in the living room. She reported that she could hear her daughter taking a shower. After Ms. Rivers came back to normal consciousness, she telephoned her daughter. The telephone rang several times. Just as Joan was about to hang up, her daughter picked up the receiver. She told her mother that she had been in the shower.

Being In Two Places At Once: Brazil And Italy

There is a related phenomenon known as *bilocation*. It also involves being in two places at the same time. Psychic researcher and parapsychologist, Frank Tribbe, reported the following case. A Capuchin monk, who was a healer and stigmatist, bilocated several times. In one incident, he sat for three days at the deathbed of a longtime friend in Sao Paulo, Brazil. At the same time, he had been in Italy speaking to his Abbot. Both incidences were independently verified by people who had no knowledge of the other incident.

Sandy's Hellish Hypnotic OBE Trip

Not every OBE is pleasant as I found out during a recent two-day course on stress and stress management that I had given in Mexico (October, 1998). I was doing group hypnosis with twenty health care professionals. Most of the individuals had no prior experience with hypnosis, but a few had been hypnotized before and three had previously used meditation. As far as I knew, none of the participants had any history of psychiatric problems. During the entire course, even though most of the individuals understood English, simultaneous translation (from English to Spanish) was done. However, during the hypnotic induction in English, I noticed that the translator was not translating. Instead, he appeared to be getting deeply into a trance. I had been speaking very slowly and from the response of the audience (all appeared to be getting into a trance), I assumed that they understood enough English to follow my words. I was using a standard induction technique with a meditative technique for induction. For deepening the trance, I employed progressive relaxation and taking the people on an imaginary trip from the top of a mountain down to its base, and then to a beautiful lake to each person's "special place." During the induction and deepening, the words were carefully chosen so that everything said should result in tranquillity. I used words such as safe, warm, pleasant, calm, relax, tranquil, peaceful, beautiful and euphoric. Not a negative or threatening word was spoken. By the time the people had reached their special place, everyone appeared to be completely relaxed. Not a sound was heard. Suddenly, the silence was shattered by a piercing scream following by loud crying and sobbing from a young woman in the front row (Sandy). I quickly calmed her with gentle stroking and relaxing words. Two Spanish colleagues assisted me by saying relaxing words in Spanish. In a few minutes, I brought everyone else out of their trances (those who hadn't already been awakened by the screams and moans) and reassured them.

After everyone was back to normal, including Sandy, my Spanish colleagues interviewed her and the following is what they told me and the audience.

First of all, Sandy had a few previous unpleasant experiences while meditating — during which she went out of her body. Then, she said that she didn't understand a single word that I had spoken. Hence, it was only the monotonous sound of my voice, along with her use of a meditation mantra, that got her into this deep trance. So, all the relaxing words and descriptions I had employed had no effect on her.

Sandy's trip started out very well. She became extremely relaxed and got out of her body. However, Sandy soon traveled through darkness to an unpleasant hellish-type place. She saw people being beaten up; she saw knives and blood. Sandy couldn't stand it and quickly left the hellish region. She wanted to get back into her body. But she was too small and couldn't fit into her body. That's when Sandy started to scream and cry. Finally, with our gentle stroking and words, she was able to get back into her body. The only after-effect was a slight stomachache. She apologized for her outburst. Later, I found out that she had psychological problems of which no one in the room had been previously informed.

The bottom line here is that hypnosis and meditation are not for everyone. If a person has psychological or psychiatric problems, before using hypnosis and meditation, he/she should have professional consultations and treatment. Fortunately, nothing like that had ever happened to me in twenty-five years of using hypnosis, and it wouldn't have happened this time if Sandy had understood English, and she had informed me ahead of time about her previous negative reactions with meditation. This case also shows that, as with NDEs, hellish kinds of responses can occur with OBEs for certain individuals. I do not believe Sandy's hellish trip occurred because she was an evil person but rather the reaction was related to some unresolved psychological conflicts.

The Soul Lives On

Even though OBEs are impossible to prove, the fact that so many people have had them and that they include components similar to the NDE (for example, floating, tunnel, bright light, rapturous feelings, leaving the physical body, contact with deceased loved ones and heavenly presences) gives added support to the belief that there is a soul that is not tied down to a physical body, a God, and an afterlife, and that death is nothing to fear. For example, during my OBE (described in Chapter 2), I was enveloped by a bright light and the serene feelings persisted even though I was watching my own funeral and reading my own obituary.

The next path on our spiritual journey in the quest for a surviving soul, a positive afterlife, and God is through the phenomena of apparitions, visions, dreams, séances and medium reports.

Figure 10
"Healing the Soul" by Marvin Herring, June 5, 1998
— a humorous look at a Rabbi's soul.

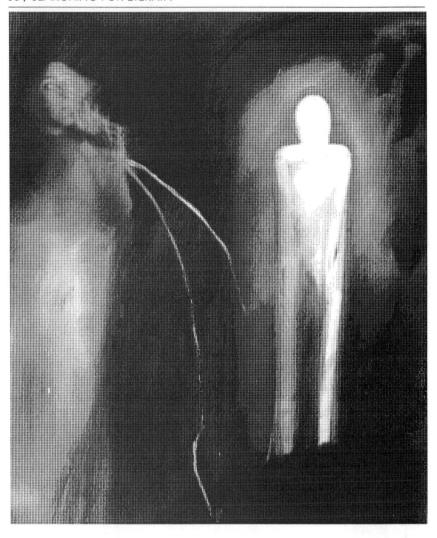

CHAPTER FIVE

APPARITIONS, VISIONS, DREAMS, SÉANCES AND MEDIUM REPORTS

"So a spirit lifted me up, and took me away; and I went in bitterness, in the heat
of my spirit, and the hand of the Lord was strong upon me....And it came to pass
at the end of seven days, that the word of the Lord came unto me.."
(Ezekiel 3: 14, 16).

"I know a man in Christ who fourteen years ago was caught up into
the third heaven — whether in the body or out of the body, I do not
know. And I know that this man was caught up into Paradise —
whether in the body or out of the body I do not know. God knows —
and he heard things that cannot be told, which man may not utter"
(2 Corinthians 12: 1-4).

Although NDEs give excellent support to the possibility of a
surviving soul, a positive afterlife, and God, and OBEs further add to
this, it is still important, using a scientifically-based viewpoint, to
find support from other sources. Therefore, the next stop on our
spiritual journey to overcome death anxiety is along the path of
apparitions, visions, dreams, electronic voice phenomena (communication), séances and medium reports.

Defining Visions, Apparitions, And Dreams

"...., he struggled in that black sack into which he was being forced by
an unseen, invincible power. He fought as a man condemned to death

fights in the hands of the executioner, knowing that he cannot save himself. And every moment he felt that, notwithstanding all his struggles, he was drawing nearer and nearer to what terrified him. He felt that his agony was due both to his being thrust into that black hole and, still more, to his not being able to get right into it. What hindered him from getting into it was his claim that his life had been good. That very justification of his life held him fast and prevented him from advancing, and caused him more agony than everything else. Suddenly some force smote him in the chest and side, making it still harder to breathe; he sank through the hole and there at the bottom was a light.......It was at this very same moment that Ivan Ilyich had fallen through the hole and caught sight of the light, and it was revealed to him that his life had not been what it ought to have been but that it was still possible to put it right.....And all at once it became clear to him that what had been oppressing him and would not go away was suddenly dropping away on one side, on two sides, on ten sides, on all sides....

'And death? Where is it?' He searched for his former habitual fear of death and did not find it. 'Where is it? What death?' There was no fear because there was no death either. In place of death there was light. 'So that's what it is!' he suddenly exclaimed aloud. 'What joy.' To him all this happened in a single instant, and the meaning of that instant suffered no change thereafter. For those present, his agony lasted another two hours. There was a rattle in his throat, a twitching of his wasted body. Then the gasping and the rattle came at longer and longer intervals. 'It's all over,' said someone near him. He caught the words and repeated them in his soul. 'Death is over,' he said to himself. 'It is no more.' He drew in a breath, stopped in the midst of a sigh, stretched out and died [25 March 1886]" (Tolstoy, L. *The Death of Ivan Ilyich and Other Stories* Penguin Books, New York, 1960, pp. 159-161).

This remarkable description by Leo Tolstoy of Ivan Ilyich's dying vision antedated much of what we have described about NDEs and OBE's, especially the dark tunnel, the blissful light, the life review and how a vision can overcome the fear of death. But what exactly is a vision and how does it differ from an apparition?

A dictionary definition of a vision is: "something seen in a dream, trance, or ecstasy; specifically a supernatural appearance that conveys a revelation; an object of imagination; a manifestation to the senses of something immaterial; direct mystical awareness of the supernatural usually in visible form; an apparition; a phantom."

A dictionary definition of an apparition is: "an unusual, unexpected, or eerie sight; a phenomenon; a ghostly figure; a specter; a phantom; a visible spirit." As you can see, this definition is similar to that of the vision.

Dreams occur while we sleep. The beta brain wave patterns of dreams are the same brain pattern we have during the alert, waking state. However, in a normal dream, the perceptions are hazy, colors may or may not be present, and the sequence of events is often illogical. In contrast, those people who have visions with an after death contact (ADC) during dreams report that the visions are **extremely life-like**. They also describe sights and sounds that are superimposed over ordinary reality (such as mists and heavenly presences next to ordinary people).

Most dreams are quickly forgotten. Visionary dreams have a long-lasting quality. The information revealed in a visionary dream is usually meaningful for the dreamer and others as well. Frequently, there is a brilliant white light present and a heavenly presence. Many doctors and scientists consider that apparitions and visions are hallucinations and have no relationship to any real occurrence. A dictionary definition of a hallucination is: "a perception of objects with no reality usually arising from a disorder of the nervous system or in response to drugs (such as LSD); a delusion." Nevertheless, investigations of these ADC visions show that the vast majority of the people involved are healthy and are not taking drugs or alcohol.

Visions And Apparitions

Just as with NDEs, it has been considered that visions occur because of overactivity of the right temporal lobe of the brain. However, rather than merely being the cause of the vision, the temporal lobe could be a site in the brain where input is received from beyond the body. If these visions are contacts from the deceased or heavenly presences, the communication could be made via the temporal lobe. At any rate, no firm conclusions have been made on either possibility.

Raymond Moody, in his book, *Reunions*, has investigated the phenomenon of apparitions of the deceased and the means of communication with deceased loved ones. Studies have revealed that 66% of widows experience apparitions of their deceased husbands. Moody has also reported that 75% of parents who have had a child die have some type of an apparition within a year of the loss. Dianne Arcangel, in a 1997 article in the *American Journal of Psychic Research* has corroborated Moody's findings. She found that 84% of the people in her study encountered apparitions of departed loved ones.

Beginning in 1967, the Steigers sent out a questionnaire related to mystical experiences. In their 1999 book, *Touched by Heaven's Light*, they reported that their questionnaire was distributed to almost 30,000 people. The results showed that:

(1) during a NDE (from an accident, serious illness, surgical procedure or other major occurrence), (a): 76% reported that their soul left their body; (b) 57% claimed to have gone to a heavenly dimension or realm; and (c) 60% stated that they received an inspirational communication from a Higher intelligence;

(2) as a result of a NDE, OBE, apparition, vision or dream, (a) 50% reported that they had been aware of a guardian angel or guide; (b) 35% described having been blessed by the appearance of a holy figure; (c) 58% reported having an intense religious experience; (d) 72% affirmed that they had an illumination experience, and (e) 44% claimed to have communicated with the spirit of a departed loved one.

Although most of these experiences were visual, some were auditory or sensory resulting from some form of mediumistic intervention or electronic voice communication. In their book, the Steigers present many fascinating case reports that seem to corroborate: (1) the presence of a surviving soul; (2) the probability of a blissful afterlife; and (3) the reality of God.

Ancient Methods To Induce Apparitions

Ancient methods used to bring forth apparitions included: gazing into crystal balls, cauldrons, bowls, basins, cups, and other vessels filled with liquid; staring into lakes (and other bodies of water); and peering into mirrors. Apparitions have been described in all kinds of cultures since the dawn of history. Biblical prophets such as Ezekiel and the apostle Paul have had apparitions. Native American cultures, and aboriginal cultures in Africa, India, Nepal and the

Figure 11
19th century engraving depicting religious apparition appearing in mirror.
From — *Harter's Ultimate Angel Book.*

West Indies have beliefs in apparitions from the deceased. Within these cultures, ghosts are apparitions of the deceased that are believed to hover around particular sites. They either choose to stay or cannot move on to the spirit world. Shinto and other religions also have a belief in apparitions of the dead.

Moody developed a technique of mirror gazing based on the ancient Greek *psychomanteum* (an apparition chamber in which a mirror was used in order to bring forth visions of the dead). Dianne Arcangel used a similar chamber and called it an oracle. Recently, the Synergy Center was opened in Overton, Texas by The Reiki practitioner and Essene minister, Tom Dodd. Among other components, it features a psychomanteum (they can be reached on the internet at http://www.synergycenter.com/). If you experienced an afterlife mirror apparition, the following is an example of what could occur.

Your Afterlife Mirror Apparition

Six months ago, you lost your beloved younger brother, Richie. Although still sad, you are no longer actively grieving. You read in either Dr. Moody's book, *Reunions*, Dianne Arcangel's article, or the Synergy Center web site that it might be possible to have a reunion with Richie. So you decide to visit a psychomanteum (oracle) center. When you enter the room, you meet the facilitator. In answer to her question, you tell the facilitator that you have come here in order to have a reunion with your deceased brother. She replies that the oracle chamber is a place for acquiring wisdom. It is not necessarily a place where you will meet your deceased brother, but that could happen. You reply, "That's fine."

You are then told that you can enter the oracle and should remain there for at least 30 minutes. If you want, you can stay as long as 90 minutes. You go inside. It is a six-foot long by three-foot wide space that is enclosed on all four sides by a black velveteen curtain with a black ceiling and black floor. At one end, a mirror is hung. It hangs just above your head. At the other end is a chair that appears to be comfortable. Behind the chair is a seven-watt light. You are told it is used for indirect lighting. Nevertheless, the room is quite dark. You have brought a memento of Richie's. It is his watch. Holding it in your left hand, you sit down. The chair is comfortable. You try to relax as you look into the mirror.

At first, nothing happened. Then, very gradually, a fine mist appears. It begins to clear up and a shape takes form — a human shape. It's your brother, Richie. He had been killed in a car crash and his body was mutilated, but now he is his old physical self. As he steps out of the mirror, the mist dissipates and he appears as real as anything else. You call to him. He answers you as he approaches. You get up and the two of you have a warm embrace. You feel Richie's body; you can even smell his distinct body odor. It is unbelievable. For the next 45-minutes, you have an animated conversation. Then, Richie tells you that he has to leave, but not to worry. Death is nothing to fear. He leaves you and reenters the mirror. The mist returns and then clears up.

You leave the oracle after having been inside the small room for about fifty minutes. You tell the facilitator of your wonderful experience. Although you belong to an organized church, your beliefs about God, the soul and the afterlife had been tenuous at best. Now, as you head home your belief system has changed 180 degrees. You have no doubt that your experience was real and that there is a surviving soul and a positive afterlife.

Other Mirror Apparition Experiences

Not everyone who enters a psychomanteum or oracle receives such a wonderful experience. Moody and Arcangel's findings were that many individuals did receive life-like visions of deceased loved ones. However, some people saw visions of other deceased individuals, while some people saw symbolic visions. For example, one woman saw a peacock, then a black person, then a bell and finally, Jesus Christ. (The introductory Biblical quotations from Ezekiel and Corinthians in which heavenly visions occurred can only be accepted on faith.)

The characteristics of these apparitions varied. As in our story, for some, the reunions were perceived as being real. With some people, the apparitions were confined to the mirror. With other cases, the viewer entered the mirror. As in our story, actual conversations took place in about fifty percent of the cases. In some cases, the apparitions didn't occur until *after* the person seeking a vision left the psychomanteum. (For example, apparitions have been reported to occur in the person's car as they drove home as well as at home.)

As in our story, the after-effects made the person less fearful of death — other people feel kinder and more understanding.

Figure 12
In 1908, the *Strand Magazine* published this picture with an account reported by Leigh Hunt in 1884. Ms. Hunt lived in Hyde Park Place (London) and stated that she had followed a "housemaid" up the stairs when the maid suddenly vanished. The picture attempted to reproduce the ghostly apparition seen by the witness.

Possible Physical And Physiological Causes Of Apparitions

Of course, whether or not apparitions are figments of the persons' imaginations or are real encounters is not known. Some physiological and physical changes have been proposed for apparitions. Neuroscientist Michael Persinger found that apparitions were more prevalent when the Earth's magnetic activity was high following periods of magnetic stability. This can, in turn, inhibit melatonin production by the pineal gland and could lead to visual hallucinations (proposed by Persinger and parapsychologist Sérena Roney-Dougal).

Emotional experiences can affect the limbic system and temporal brain regions and also induce visual images. Some investigators have found that in areas of earth where apparitions have consistently appeared there were increases in electromagnetism and radiation levels (especially gamma rays) and decreases in temperature and negative ions. Nevertheless, the physical and physiological changes could be the result rather than the cause of the apparitions. Now, let us consider three particularly interesting cases of apparitions.

Abe's Apparition

On the night of the 1860 presidential election, Abraham Lincoln looked into a nearby mirror and saw a strange double image of himself. The first image was a realistic image. The second image was of a pale and ghostly Abraham Lincoln. Lincoln told his wife and she interpreted it for him. She told him that he would be elected to a second term but would die in office. Unfortunately, the apparition and Mrs. Lincoln's interpretation were absolutely correct.

Grandma's Return

Dr. Moody was sitting alone in a room when a woman walked in. After a little hesitation, he realized that she was his paternal grandmother who had died some years before. She did not appear "ghostly" or transparent but was surrounded by a light or indentation in space. Even though during her life, she and Dr. Moody had their differences, he now felt warmth, love, empathy and understanding between himself and his grandmother. They had a pleasant conversation. The meeting ended with Dr. Moody saying "Good-bye." He then walked out of the room. When he returned, his grandmother was gone.

Mary And Elisabeth

The psychic researcher, Frank Tribbe, reported his encounter with Dr. Elisabeth Kübler-Ross in which she told him the story of Mary Swartz, who had been one of her special patients and had recently died (Tribbe, F.G. "The Breadth of Psychical Research Establishes Survival." In: *1995 Annual Conference Proceedings: Personal Survival of Bodily Death.* Acad. Religion. Psychical Research, Bloomfield, Connecticut, pp, 102-103,1995).

Along with a young minister, Elisabeth had been conducting "death and dying" seminars for interns and nurses for over a year at a Chicago hospital. She became fatigued and had decided that at the conclusion of the current seminar, she would not start a new series. Dejectedly, Elisabeth walked to the elevator when a woman cut off her approach and said, "Dr. Ross, I must talk with you urgently. Can we go to your office?"

Reluctantly, Elisabeth walked silently with the woman to her office. While walking, she glanced sideways, trying to recall the woman's face. Suddenly, she was aware that this woman was Mary Swartz, the patient who had died a few months previously. Elisabeth suddenly realized that she was a scientist and was not going to be "taken in." She stopped one stride from her door.

Without hesitation, Mary opened the door and allowed Elizabeth to enter. Elisabeth then sat behind her desk, and Mary sat in front of it, and began to talk: "Dr. Ross, you must not stop your seminars! No matter what the interns and nurses might say, your seminars are too important for the patients, and the staff needs all the orientation you can give them. Please promise that you will continue."

With slight hesitation, Elisabeth agreed.

Then Mary said, "And will you convey my thanks to the Reverend for the help he gives in the seminar."

Again, acting as a scientist, Elisabeth pushed a note pad across the desk and said, "Why don't you write him your thanks."

Unhesitatingly, Mary wrote and signed a short note. She then arose, thanked Elisabeth, opened the door, left the room and closed the door behind her. Elisabeth then rushed to the door, opened it and looked in both directions. No one was to be seen, but later the note was delivered.

The Many Forms
Of After Death Contacts

As I mentioned in Chapter 4, in the Guggenheims' book, *Hello From Heaven,* descriptions were given of the ADCs of 2,000 people. Many of these individuals had apparitions and visions of deceased loved ones and friends that were always initiated by the deceased. Some also had visions of heavenly presences and heaven and rarely, hell.

With a *sentient* (feeling) ADC, the person senses the presence of the deceased person without actually hearing or seeing him/her. Related to this is the *physical phenomena* ADC in which the person observes phenomena taking place that are considered to be the work of the deceased. These include: lights being turned on; electrical devices being turned on; mechanical objects being activated; and pictures and objects being moved. Also related to sentient ADC is the *symbolic* ADC in which the deceased are believed to leave signs and symbols of their presence. These manifestations are supposed to be things that the deceased were strongly associated with and include: rainbows; butterflies; flowers; birds and other animals; and a variety of inanimate objects.

Somewhat related to this is *spirit art*. Frank Tribbe, the noted psychic researcher, reported the case of Carol Polge, who is a clairvoyant artist from London. She appears regularly at public sessions where another clairvoyant gives a reading from a deceased loved one to a member of the audience (the subject). At the same time, Carol draws a sketch of that particular spirit as it apparently hovers near the subject. Within a few minutes, both the clairvoyant and Carol are finished. Carol then hands the picture to the subject. Frequently, the subject will return the following day with a before-death photograph of the deceased that dramatically matches the artist's sketch.

Also somewhat similar is *spirit photography* (pictures of deceased people who appear on normal film — often near the images of the live individual who was photographed). An example of this was reported by Frank Tribbe. An amateur photographer from Paris named Baraduc lost his wife and son within a few months of each

other. He observed a mist forming over each of their corpses. The mists were roughly the size and shape of the deceased's bodies. He then took several pictures of the spirit forms for more than an hour (until they had dissipated). These dramatic photographs have been circulated among researchers for almost a century.

With *auditory ADC*, the individual hears the deceased without actually seeing him/her. Related to this is the *telephone ADC* in which the individual receives an actual telephone call from the deceased. Another related communication is *electronic voice phenomena* (communication) in which the voice of the deceased can be heard either during a tape recorder playback or from a radio, telephone answering machine or computer. Pictures of a deceased individual have also been apparently seen on a television screen. Extensive work with these techniques has been done and reported by George Meek in his book, *Enjoy Your Own Funeral* (1999) and the Steigers in their book, *Touched by Heaven's Light* (1999).

After Death Contacts have involved virtually all of the senses. With *tactile ADC*, the person feels the touch of the deceased without actually seeing or hearing him/her. In *olfactory ADC*, the person smells a fragrance that the deceased either used or was very familiar with. Again, the deceased is neither seen nor heard. With *visual ADC*, which Haraldsson reported to be the most prevalent type, there are two variations. In one, only a partial appearance of the deceased or a heavenly presence (e.g., an angel) is seen. In the other, there is a complete visualization of the deceased or heavenly presence. Sometimes the deceased or heavenly presence is silent. In other apparitions or visions, the deceased or heavenly presence speaks.

Jasper Swain, A South African magistrate, regularly communicates with his deceased son, Mike. Mike once told him: "As I said, thought is all-powerful here. For example, if I want to own a brand new Jaguar, all I have to do is visualize the car in my mind, and it is created right there before my eyes, out of the energy of this world" (Swain, J. *On the Death of My Son: An Account of Life After Death.* Turnerstone Books, London, 1974).

With *sleep-state ADC*, the after death communication occurs while the person is asleep. Usually, the deceased or heavenly presence can be seen and frequently speaks to the person. Some people have a *telephone ADC* while in the dream state. Related to the sleep-state ADC is the *twilight ADC* in which the person has a vision when just falling asleep or just awakening.

In *ADC visions*, the individual has a glimpse of the afterlife, seeing heaven-like scenes, and in rare cases, observing hellish scenes.

A host of other ADC descriptive categories exist. With *pre-death ADC*, the person is contacted by the deceased before the person was aware that the other person had died. Another category is termed *years later ADC*. While most visionary encounters occur during the first year of the person's death, in *years later ADC*, the contact occurs five years or more after the person's death. *Evidential ADC* derives its name from a form of proof (evidence) disclosed to the person by the deceased: it is typically some fact that was not known or could not have been known ahead of time. *Protection ADC* also involves the disclosing of information: a warning from the deceased is given that subsequently protects the individual from a disaster such as: an accident; harm from a criminal; a house or business establishment fire; a health problem; and an emergency involving a child. Related to this is the *suicide intervention ADC* in which the deceased says something to the individual so that he/she does not commit a planned suicide.

Shared ADC is more rare. In shared ADC, two people have the same ADC simultaneously. As described in Chapter 3, this is similar to people having shared NDEs.

Tyrrel (reported by Harvey Irwin) described two other types of apparitions: the *crisis apparition* (wraith) that is seen by individuals connected to the person in crisis (who is often dying and in some way projects his image); and the *recurrent apparition* (ghost) that can be seen by various people.

A Special Pre-Death ADC

Melvin Morse, a well-known pediatrician and researcher of near-death studies in children, in his book, *Parting Visions*, described many of the same ADCs as did the Guggenheims. Of special interest is his description of a *pre-death* ADC. In this case, a nurse's mother who was dying of stomach cancer was on the nurse's own ward. While in the laundry room, the nurse heard her mother whisper to her: "Good-bye, thank you."

She immediately rushed down the hall to her mother's bedside and found that her mother had died (Morse, M. *Parting Visions: Uses and Meanings of Pre-Death, Psychic and Spiritual Experiences.* Villard Books, New York, 1994, p. 31).

Shared Visions

Dr. Morse also described three shared visions (similar to the Guggenheims' Shared ADCs and Moody's Shared NDEs).

A Hearty OBE Vision

An older woman had received a heart transplant. Most of her family members were present except for her son-in-law. An unexpected complication occurred and the patient became very sick, but fortunately she recovered. The patient's daughter called to inform her husband of the good news. The patient's son-in-law answered that he already knew since his mother-in-law had come to him in a vision at 2:15 A.M. to inform him that she would be fine. Upon awakening in the morning, the patient told her family members that during the surgery (which took place in the middle of the night), she had an out-of-body experience in which she traveled miles away to the home of her daughter and son-in-law and told him that she would be fine.

Mother And Daughter's Shared Special Trip

A woman who had a 6-year-old daughter was about to give birth to a second daughter. Complications set in and the baby died. Later, when the woman went to the grave site by herself she had a vision. She saw a tunnel that ended in a bright light. She then saw adults playing with children including her deceased daughter. When the woman returned home, her six-year-old daughter told her mother that she had gone with her to see baby sister. She knew that the baby was dead and asked her mother to hug her the next time.

Arthritis And The Heavenly Vision

A 50-year-old woman had terrible arthritis. One January morning, she and her husband awakened and saw two men standing at the foot of their bed. They were dressed in white with a white halo. They said nothing and stayed about five minutes. The same vision happened the next night. Five days later, they both saw a ball of light that hovered over their bed. Afterwards, the woman's arthritis disappeared never to return again.

Additional Visions: Dying Experiences

Dr. Morse reported some additional types of visions. One is termed *dying experiences*. The latest estimates are that at least 13 million Americans have had NDEs, but by their very nature, fewer people have had dying experiences of the afterlife. The reason is to confirm a dying experience, it is necessary to have a witness. Here are five cases.

Death During Birth

In 1927, Sir William Barrett, a renowned physicist and President of the English Society for Psychical Research, wrote a book, *Death-Bed Visions*. In it, he described the deathbed vision of a woman who died during childbirth. Just before she expired, she described a lovely brightness, wonderful beings and her deceased father. She also said that her father had her sister with him. The sister had died three weeks earlier. However, the dying woman was not told of her sister's death because of her own delicate condition.

Sandy and Chrissy

More recently, two young hospitalized cancer patients (Sandra and Chrissy) were both dying. Sandra was sent home to die, hundreds of miles away from Chrissy. As she was dying, Sandra said that she went to heaven — described as a beautiful white light — and Chrissy was there to help her. It was only after Sandra had died that her parents found out that Chrissy had died several weeks before their daughter.

A Car Accident And A Heart Attack

In her book, *On Life After Death*, Dr. Kübler-Ross told of a case in which a man witnessed a hit-and-run accident and offered help to the injured woman. She told him that nothing could be done except for him to tell her mother that she was all right and happy now because she was with her father. The woman then died.

The man was so affected that he drove 700 miles to the Native American reservation where the deceased woman's mother lived. He repeated the dying woman's words but was amazed to find out that the woman's father had died from a heart attack about an hour before the woman's fatal car accident. There was absolutely no way she could have known about her father's death unless there was a dying telepathic communication from the father to the daughter.

The Return From Leukemia

A woman's daughter had apparently died of leukemia. After the resuscitation team had left the room, the mother was alone with her daughter. Suddenly the girl sat up, and told her mother not to worry because she would now be okay. She then died.

AIDS And The Tunnel

A patient was dying of AIDS. As the hospital staff watched, the man told them about a bright light that had entered the room. He went on to describe a tunnel with a man inside who was standing next to a gate. He then told them that the gate was opening, and he was entering it. He immediately died.

Additional Visions: Deathbed Visions

Sir William Barrett described instances of the spirit leaving the body; the experience of the dying hearing music; and the dying person seeing someone who was already deceased. In some cases, the dying person saw someone who was dead but that fact was unknown to him at the time. To determine whether death-bed visions were real or products of brain activity, Karlis Osis, the Director of Research at the American Society for Psychical Research, and E. Haraldson sent out questionnaires to 2,000 physicians and 2,000 nurses requesting information about patients who had died in their care (e.g., treatment, cause of death, religious beliefs, and an account of any visions experienced). An additional 704 medical personnel in India, received similar questionnaires. The results given in the classic report, "Deathbed Observations by Physicians and Nurses" were: 753 patients experienced an elevated mood during their last hours; 888 reported visions, such as seeing heaven or a beautiful scene (only 2 patients described hellish scenes); 1,370 reported apparitions (mainly of deceased relatives or friends); the mood, visions, and apparitions were not influenced by the cause of death, drug effects, or being American or Indian; and the only difference between the heavenly or hellish visions were related to the religious beliefs of the individuals.

Dr. Morse's Descriptions Of Deathbed Visions

Dr. Morse reported on patients' deathbed visions that showed striking similarity to the Guggenheims' Pre-Death ADC, in which a person is contacted by the deceased before the person was aware that the other person had died. However, there are cases where the person is contacted by a "heavenly presence" to inform them about the death of a close family member or friend. For example, a woman's father had just had a medical checkup for indigestion. Later, the woman was awakened from a deep sleep at 3 A.M. by an opaque white light and a soothing voice saying that the heavenly presence was going to take him. A little later, the woman received a telephone call from her mother telling her that her father had unexpectedly died at 3:15 A.M.

Additional Visions: Pre-Death Visions

Dr. Morse studied women who had babies that later died of Sudden Infant Death Syndrome (SIDS). In many of these cases, the mothers had pre-death visions of their children dying.

A Spirit's Floor-To-Ceiling Trip

Psychic researcher, Frank Tribbe, reported a case of a pre-death vision. A woman in Washington, D.C. had been nursing her dying husband for several weeks. One morning, the physician told her to go upstairs and take a nap while he sat with her husband. In the room just above the sickbed, the woman lay down. She had not closed her eyes when the apparent spirit of her husband came up through the floor, and smiled and nodded to her as he passed on through the ceiling. The woman ran to the stairs as the physician was coming up. He told her that her husband had died. The woman answered that she already knew.

Additional Visions: Angelic Visions

Another type of vision observed by Dr. Morse are Angelic Visions. Related to the Guggenheims' ADC visions in which the person has visions of heaven and heavenly presences as well as rarer visions of hell, are the visions of angels. Angels are seen in some NDEs, OBEs, and in apparitions and visions by people while awake, dreaming, under general anesthesia or during a deep meditation.

At least 50% of Dr. Morse's children patients who have had NDEs reported seeing "guardian angels." A *Time Magazine* poll showed that 69% of Americans believe in angels (see *Figure 13*).

Historical Angels

Historically, angelic visions have been seen by religious leaders and saints. Abraham saw an angel who told him to spare Isaac. An angel spared Daniel from the lion. Paul frequently encountered angels in his visions, and Mohammed had three angels cleanse him.

Additional Visions: Precognition Visions

An additional type of vision observed by Dr. Morse is *precognition vision*. These are related to Guggenheims' *protection ADC* and *suicidal intervention ADC*. In the former, the deceased tells the individual about a disaster that is going to happen and how to avoid it. With the suicidal intervention ADC, the disclosure is such that it prevents the suicide from taking place. With the precognition vision, rather than it being a deceased individual giving the warning, it is a heavenly presence that foretells the future to help the individual. Here are two examples.

Surviving Sarcoma

One of Morse's patients was undergoing surgery for Ewing's sarcoma, which is usually a fatal tumor. While under anesthesia, she had a vision. A light filled her and a voice said that she would live at

Figure 13
The idea of guardian angels standing by to give us comfort and aid in times of need is an ancient one. This 19th century engraving depicts what the recent movie, *City of Angels*, concerned: the role of angels in death and crisis.

least forty-five more years. She recovered and is well on her way to fulfilling the prediction.

Surviving A Brain Tumor

Another of Morse's patients was being transported to her hospital room prior to brain surgery for a tumor removal. She was certain that she would die when she suddenly felt a wonderful presence and heard a voice telling her not to cry because everything would be all right. She had the surgery and recovered completely.

Personal Interviews

Although the previous reports describing apparitions and visions are also strongly supportive about the enduring soul, a positive afterlife, and God, I wanted to interview people who had these visions to investigate the reliability of their reports. The following vision cases came from two people who I consider to be honest and reliable. Their reports added credence to the concept that people's visions can, at times, allow for contact with deceased individuals.

Marlene, Roberta And The Halo

The first person I interviewed is a 42-year-old single woman named Marlene S. She is of the Methodist faith, is religious and spiritual, and resides in Southern New Jersey. She seemed to be an honest, reliable person, and her story came out without hesitancy. Marlene informed me that she had a normal upbringing, but soon became aware of having certain psychic abilities such as precognition and telepathy. Nevertheless, none of her talents were ever exploited. Marlene never had a complete vision until a particular day in 1994. Prior to this day, she had contacted a severe case of Lyme disease. This made her anxious, and in addition to the antibiotic therapy, she was given a small dose of Xanax®. As a result of her condition, she had a nurse's aide, named Roberta T., assigned to her. They soon became good friends.

Marlene learned that Roberta was a widow, but she didn't know any details about her deceased husband (for example, his name, his appearance, how long ago he died). One week before, she had seen Roberta and noticed a strange halo above Roberta's shoulders. She wasn't certain, but it vaguely resembled a face. The image soon disappeared. She told Roberta about it. Roberta thought Marlene was acting strange, but Roberta did admit that she had felt the presence of something on her shoulders recently, but hadn't attached much importance to it.

Several times during the week, Marlene had heard a voice say "Robbie." She just ignored it. At about 7 PM on that fateful evening, Marlene sat down on the couch, having just finished eating pudding. She turned on the television and, after watching it for a few minutes, she turned to the side. There was a man in front of her! He seemed to be middle-aged, and he was wearing an old army uniform. The man appeared to be real, but Marlene noticed that he was partially transparent. There was also an aura around him.

Marlene was immediately certain that he was a spirit, and she wanted no part of him. Being religious and spiritual, she tried to get rid of him by invoking the name of Jesus Christ. The man laughed, but then became serious and said that he was there to protect her and would also like a favor from her.

Marlene then thought: "Maybe he's an angel." So she asked him: "If you're an angel, where are your wings?" The man didn't answer but pointed to an insignia on his lapel. Marlene looked at it, and it appeared to be some sort of design with wings. Figuring she had nothing to lose, she asked him to identify himself.

He replied: "I'm Frank, Robbie's husband."

Marlene didn't know the name of Roberta's husband or anything about him and she had never heard anyone call her friend (Roberta) Robbie. Then she remembered hearing a voice saying Robbie to her several times during the week. Still, she said to the man: "I don't believe you. I don't know any Robbie."

The man replied: "Her real name is Roberta; I call her Robbie."

By now, Marlene was starting to believe him. "What do you want me to do?" she asked.

He replied: "I tried to contact her and you before, but was unable to reach her. Please call my wife and tell her that you saw me. Ask her if she remembers this scene?" He then showed her a hotel room in which Frank and Roberta were sitting on the bed. They were much younger. Frank looked into Roberta's eyes and said: "I will never leave you. I'll always love you."

Marlene said to him: "If I do this, will you leave?" He said he would. Marlene made the call. Roberta listened and began to cry hysterically. Her husband's name was Frank. He always called her Robbie, and he had been an army paratrooper. The wings on his lapel were his paratrooper's wings. The scene she described was the hotel room on their wedding night. That was the first time Frank had said: "I will never leave you. I'll always love you."

Roberta subsequently had a few after-death contacts with her husband. She often felt his presence; she could feel his touch on her shoulders; and occasionally she heard his voice. Roberta also had a dream in which he came to her (reported in the next section). She was very thankful for Marlene's contact. Previously, Roberta had been a non-practicing Methodist; now she had a firm belief in God and the afterlife. She also said that she no longer feared dying.

For the skeptics, there has never been reported a hallucination-producing side effect from taking Xanax®. In addition, I spoke to Roberta and she confirmed everything that Marlene had reported.

Marjorie Meets The Spirit

The second case involves Marjorie D., the same woman who had the NDE in which she saw her husband having an illicit affair and later spoke to God (presented in Chapter 3). It was now five years after her NDE. She was in a New Jersey hospital suffering from a severe form of bacterial pneumonia. Marjorie was being treated with antibiotics but had not received any mind-altering drugs. She was in her bed when suddenly, she saw a man standing in front of her. His appearance was not well defined, and Marjorie surmised that he might be a spirit. The man said: "Excuse me, I was told you can help me find the light."

She asked him what made him think that she could guide him to the light?

He replied: "A voice told me that you could help me find the light." Marjorie was surprised but figured that after her NDE, anything was possible. She asked him his name. He replied: "James." Marjorie felt that maybe God wanted her to help this person. So she said: "I want you to concentrate. Do you believe in God?"

James answered: "Yes." She continued; "Do you believe in Jesus?"

Again, he said: "Yes."

Marjorie than said to him: "Say out loud: Lord Jesus, show me the light." James repeated those words. Just then Marjorie saw the beautiful light, the same light she had seen with her NDE.

James cried out: "I see it!"

"Now go towards it," Marjorie said. James spoke: "Before I do, could you do me a favor?"

Marjorie was reluctant but said: "What?"

He answered: "My wife and daughter are alive. They know I'm dying, but my wife can't handle it. She is holding everything in. She refuses to cry. I always wanted a son, and my daughter thinks that I don't love her because she came instead of a boy. I love her. Please tell her that. Tell my wife that it's all right to cry. Let her know that there is a life beyond this one. Please let them know you saw me and tell them what I said."

Marjorie gave him her word. She saw him step into the light and then the light and the man disappeared.

Suddenly, she heard loud screaming: "It's a code blue." Marjorie got out of her bed. The commotion was coming from the next room. A man who had terminal cancer had just died. Marjorie looked inside. Around the bed were two women, one middle-aged, one young. They were both crying. Marjorie heard the older woman cry out: "Oh, my James, my James!" Now Marjorie knew that the vision she had seen was that of James' spirit. At first, she didn't want to speak to his wife and daughter, but finally felt that she must. Marjorie prayed and asked God to give her the right words to use. She entered the room, approached the two women, and said, "Excuse me. I'm so sorry about your loss. I happen to be psychic. When I was in bed, I was praying and a vision came to me." Addressing the older woman, she said, "I saw your husband. He told me his name was James, and he said to me that I should tell you that you shouldn't be afraid to cry. He's going to be with God, and he will come to see you in a dream."

Marjorie then spoke to the younger woman, "Your father told me that he once wanted to have a son, but when you came, he loved you. He wanted you to know how much he loves you." The two women burst out crying, but they appeared happy. They embraced Marjorie and thanked her very much.

Later she told them about her experience with the light when she had her NDE five years before. Marjorie then relayed James' experience with the light. She then went back to her room feeling that she had done the right thing. Marjorie lay down in bed and began to sweat. She heard God speaking to her telling her that she was now fine. Marjorie's fever broke and in one hour she was discharged from the hospital.

Dream Visions

"And he (Jacob) dreamed, and behold a ladder set up on the earth, and the top of it reached to heaven; and behold the angels of God ascending and descending on it. And behold, The Lord stood beside him, and said: "I am the Lord, the God of Abraham thy father, and the God of Isaac. The land whereon thy liest, to thee will I give it, and to thy seed.

And thy seed shall be as the dust of the earth, and thou shalt spread abroad to the west, and to the east, and to the north, and to the south. And in thee and thy seed shall all the families of the earth be blessed."

(Genesis 28: 12-14).

"...and he took one of the stones of the place, and put it under his head, and lay down in that place to sleep. And he dreamed, and behold a ladder set up on the earth, and the top of it reached to heaven; and behold the angels of God ascending and descending on it."

(Genesis 28: 11,12).

Many people have extremely vivid visions while dreaming of departed loved ones or friends, of heavenly presences, of heaven and occasionally of hell. Dream visions have occurred frequently in the Bible. The above example is one that Jacob had of a ladder to heaven (see *Figure 14*). As has been discussed with other introductory Biblical quotations, these can only be taken on faith.

As mentioned previously, the Guggenheims discussed: sleep-state ADC in which visions of departed loved ones or heavenly presences occur while dreaming; telephone ADC, in which the person receives a telephone call from a deceased loved one while dreaming; and twilight ADC in which the person has contact with a deceased loved one or a heavenly presence in the period just before awakening or just before falling asleep.

The Dream Of David

Brian Weiss, in his book, *Only Love is Real*, discussed an interesting dream vision. In this case, a woman knew that she would have a child named David. When she got married, she had two daughters. When she was in her mid-thirties, she had a vivid dream in which an angel came to her and informed her that she would have a son named David but he could only stay for 19 and $^1/_2$ years. A few months later, she became pregnant, and in the ninth month, David was delivered.

He died at the age of 19 and $^1/_2$ years from a rare type of brain cancer. One month after David died, she had another vivid dream. This time the angel reappeared and David was there as well. He told his mother that she shouldn't grieve because he loved her and chose her, not the reverse.

Figure 14
Copy of watercolor painting, Jacob's Ladder
by Don Morse, April 20, 1999.

The Brother

In Melvin Morse's book, *Parting Visions,* interesting cases of dream visions are presented. In one case, a man had a vivid dream about his brother. His brother was sitting in the living room and told him that he shouldn't worry because there was nothing to worry about. The man then asked his brother if he were dead. The brother didn't reply. The next morning, the man received a telephone call from his sister-in-law telling him that his brother was killed in a car crash.

The Father

In 1988, Dr. Morse had a dream in which his father came to him and told him to call his answering service. He called his answering service and was told that his mother had been trying to reach him to tell him that his father had died.

Abe's Dream

In the section on apparitions, it was shown that Abraham Lincoln had seen a mirror apparition that his wife interpreted as him dying in office. Similarly, Lincoln dreamed of his death just a few days before he was assassinated.

Roberta's Dream

In the first personally interviewed vision case (discussed earlier), Marlene had seen Roberta's deceased husband, Frank, and told her about the vision. As a result of that, Roberta had non-visual contacts with Frank. She also had a dream visual contact. Roberta told me that Frank had received a war injury which made it difficult for him to dance. However, he loved to dance but usually had to have a couple of drinks to loosen up. This is what she dreamed.

The dream was very clear. They were in a dance hall. Frank was younger and had no physical problems. He was completely sober. They were dancing and having a wonderful time. Roberta looked into Frank's eyes, which were the same vivid blue that she had known and loved. The band was playing their favorite song, "You Make My Brown Eyes Blue." As he whirled her around effortlessly, looking into her brown eyes, he said: "I love you. I'll never leave you. I'll always be there for you." Roberta is certain that she will be reunited with her wonderful Frank.

My Special Dream

I dream almost every night. However, my dreams are usually confusing with an unreal quality. Only once have I had a vivid dream in which I was in contact with a deceased individual. In 1995, my cousin, Ernie, died of throat cancer. He was two years older than me, and although we didn't see each other too often, when we did, we got along quite well. I liked him very much. Unfortunately, I never told him.

His death deeply affected me and contributed to my becoming afflicted with general anxiety disorder. Since Ernie had died, I hadn't thought about him too much. But a few months ago, I had the most vivid dream that I had ever experienced. I was sleeping next to my wife Diane, and in the middle of the night, I got out of bed, put on my coat and went to the home of my cousin, Ernie, and his wife, Elaine. While there, we had a very animated conversation, especially between Ernie and myself. It was pleasant, warm and wonderful, and never for a moment did I imagine that I was conversing with a dead person.

When I returned to my house, I threw my coat on the floor and got into bed. That caused Diane to awaken. It was then that I realized that Ernie had died and yet, I saw him as real as anyone I had seen while awake. I told Diane, and she told me that it must have been just a dream. With those words, I **really** awoke and so did Diane.

I immediately told Diane my vivid dream. Had I visited my cousin Ernie in my dream or was it nothing more than a vivid dream stimulated by all the research that I have been doing on the afterlife? No one knows, but in some small measure I feel better about having had such a wonderful renewed relationship with my cousin Ernie.

With The Help Of Séances And Mediums

"A man also or a woman that divineth by a ghost or a familiar spirit, shall surely be put to death; they shall stone them with stones; their blood shall be upon them."
(Leviticus 20: 27).

"Then said Saul unto his servants: Seek me a woman that divineth by a ghost, that I may go to her. And his servants said to him: Behold, there is a woman that divineth by a ghost at En-dor. And Saul disguised himself, and put on other raiment, and went, he and two men with him, and they came to the woman by night; and he said: Divine unto me, I pray thee, by a ghost, and bring me up whomsoever I shall name unto thee."

(First Samuel 28: 7).

With apparitions, visions, and dreams, the individual has the vision either by him/her self or with the aid of a mirror or similar object. With séances, a medium is needed to induce the presence (either visual, auditory, tactile, olfactory, or some combination of those) of a deceased person or persons. A dictionary definition of a séance is: "a spiritualist meeting to receive spirit communications." A dictionary definition of a medium is: "an individual held to be a channel of communication between the earthly world and the world of spirits."

Unfortunately, there are charlatan mediums who conduct séances while using devices such as phonograph records, tapes and discs, and artificially induced mists and ectoplasm to produce sounds and sights that simulate ADCs. If telepathy is possible, the medium could "read" the mind of the person seeking to contact a deceased loved one and know in advance certain characteristics of the deceased. Therefore, before anyone seeks the service of a medium, thoroughly check out the credentials and reputation of the medium. Nevertheless, there appear to be ethical mediums, and some evidence exists that a person can contact a deceased loved one or a heavenly presence during a séance.

Historical Mediums

As can be observed in the biblical quotations in the beginning of this section, the Bible had mixed feelings about using a medium to call up spirits of the deceased. Although the first quotation said that it was forbidden by God, the second quotation showed that King Saul used a medium to summon up a spirit. In this case, it was the spirit of the prophet, Samuel. Again, I must emphasize that biblical quotations are only used as interesting introductions to particular subjects. They cannot be considered as reliable and can only be taken on faith.

Mediums and séances began before biblical times. Mediumistic practices have existed among all of the world's cultures since the earliest of times. They were in existence even before humans knew how to farm or write. Mediumship and séances were very popular as an aftermath of World War I, when many widows wanted to communicate with their deceased military men. With the advent of scientific reasoning, mediumship and séances were considered to be charlatanism by most people. Yet some well educated writers such as Sir Arthur Conan Doyle (author of the Sherlock Holmes books and *The New Revelation*) and Victor Hugo (author of *The Hunchback of Notre Dame* and *Les Miserables*) were firm believes in the reality of medium contacts with the spiritual world (see *Conversations with Eternity: The Forgotten Masterpiece of Victor Hugo*).

Current Cultures With Mediums

There are still many cultures throughout the world which practice a form of mediumship. These include: the Inuit (Eskimos) of the Arctic, who practice *Irinjelo*; the Haitians who practice *Voodoo*; the Brazilians who practice *Umbanda* and *Candomblé*; the Trinidads who practice *Shango*; and the Jamaicans who practice *Obeayisne*. Early medium pioneers were Margaret Cameron, Darbey & Joan, Stewart Edward White, and Arthur Ford (see *An Arthur Ford Anthology*).

With the current interest in spiritualism and New Age phenomena, the findings from NDEs, OBEs, apparitions, visions and dreams, and the development of ethical mediums, interest in mediumship has resurfaced.

Medium Functions

According to Leo Gough in his book, *Mediumship: A Beginner's Guide*, mediums make predictions, get information, solve problems, and heal people mentally, physically and spiritually. In the West, a medium's main task is to contact the deceased by various means. These include the following:

The deceased's voice speaks through the medium without the medium being aware of saying anything.

The medium "sees" the spirit of the deceased individual(s) and describes their appearance.

The medium enters a trance, which allows her/him to contact the spirit of the deceased, ask and answer questions, and report the results to the observer.

The medium's intervention can yield physical phenomena related to the deceased such as moving objects, noises and images. As discussed before, artist, Coral Polge, makes illustrations of contacted deceased, which often are amazingly similar to photographs of the same deceased.

Mediums also can practice channeling (the method through which a medium receives teaching and assistance for humans from heavenly presences such as angels). However, Reverend Angus Haddow recently discussed the difference between mediumship and religious concepts of the afterlife. The medium's contact with spirits (spiritualism) is more concerned with survival than with God. In spiritualism, the afterlife is primarily viewed as an extension of this life's experience, not immortality or eternal life. Most religions' afterlife is concerned with God, immortality and eternal life.

Of all the subjects covered in this and the last few chapters (NDEs, OBEs, apparitions, visions, and dreams), the one with the least scientific documentation is mediumship. Nevertheless, because many of the same phenomena have been elicited by mediums as have occurred with the other phenomena, it is possible that mediums can contact deceased loved ones and heavenly presences. However, one must realize that charlatan mediums have always practiced and are still around. (See Ruth Brandon's book, *The Spiritualists*.)

Well-Known Mediums

Stephen O'Brien, a well-known British medium, in his books, *Visions of Another World* and *Voices From Heaven*, discusses the sessions he held with several hundred people in a large hall during which he exchanged information with their dead relatives and friends with him acting as the medium. One popular spiritualist medium is James Van Praagh, whose best-selling book, *Talking to Heaven*, details his experiences in contacting the deceased. As displayed on some 1998 and 1999 television shows (such as *Larry King Live*), while in an altered state of consciousness, but still alert, he was able to talk to people via the telephone, get the deceased's name, and give details about the deceased to the living relative. Some things he revealed about the spirits are that they: have spiritual bodies and can do things similar to real life (but they don't eat); develop mentally but don't age physically; can contact the living in dreams; can go to various "heavenly realms;" can contact God who is everywhere; and can reincarnate (but only after about 200 Earth years). Skeptics (e.g., Michael Schermer, author of *Why People Believe Weird Things*), consider Van Praagh to be only a clever mentalist.

Van Praagh is not the only well-known medium who has displayed his capabilities on television. Recently (Oct. 3, 1998), Brian Hurst showed uncanny ability to apparently contact the deceased on the program *Hard Copy* (CBS, 5:30 P.M., East Coast U.S.A.). John Edward gave a similar performance on *Larry King Live* (Oct. 30, 1998, CNN, 9-10 P.M., East Coast U.S.A.).

Cross-Correspondence:
An Interesting Medium Phenomenon

As discussed by the renowned psychic researcher, Frank Tribbe, in the early 20th century eight mediums (in different areas of the world) received a series of communications ostensibly coming from the spirit of the renowned psychic researcher, F.W.H. Myers. Most of the mediums were unknown to each other. The message fragment that each medium received referred to classical literature that by itself made no sense. Of the eight mediums, only Mrs. Verral had any knowledge of classical literature. Under the auspices of the Society for Psychical Research (S.P.R.), months after the communications ceased, the fragments were connected and integrated. It was then found that a full pattern of complete messages emerged. This cross-correspondence has been considered to be firm evidence of life after death.

A Vision Of Jesus As A Result Of
Channeling By A Clairvoyant

As a result of channeling by the British clairvoyant Margaret Flavell Twaddell, Alvin Mattson, a Lutheran minister, described his vision of Jesus (as described in Ruth Taylor's book, *Witness From Beyond*) in the following way: "When I first saw Him, the light and the glory and the surging power was so tremendous. It was like an avalanche of feeling over me. At the present time, I just don't feel that I have a way in which to describe what it was like. ...an indescribable contentment and uplifting, a tremendous ecstasy of feeling on all planes, being completely out of yourself, an unusually vivid knowledge of the intense, sympathetic love around you the warmth of it, the light of it, something that is not external but is part of you. It's like a sunrise on a mountain that is covered with snow, when the colors come down and reflect on you a dazzling brilliance that would make you close your eyes and yet feel it in every pore of your body. This is the feeling that you have as you come toward the LIGHT." (Taylor, R. *Witness From Beyond*. Foreward Books, South Portland, ME, 1975, pp 36-39.)

A Shared-Death Experience
Between A Medium And Her Sister-In-Law

I recently interviewed Cheryl S., a 41-year-old woman of the Conservative Jewish faith. She is a physical therapist by profession and a medium by fate. She has been married for 19 years to a physician and has lived in many states. Cheryl currently lives in Moorestown, New Jersey. She first noticed her mediumistic tendencies five years ago in California when she had spiritual communication with a friend's deceased mother.

Recently, Cheryl had a shared-death experience with her sister-in-law, Dawn L. Dawn was a 48-year-old teacher, married to Cheryl's brother, Jack, and was dying from metastatic cancer. Jack and Dawn had two daughters, Phyllis (17 years-old) and Joan (20-years-old). The fateful time period occurred in September, 1998 from a Sunday through a Friday with Monday and Tuesday being Rosh Hashanah (The Jewish New Year).

Dawn was in bed at home in Boston when Cheryl came to visit her on Sunday evening. At that time, Dawn was conscious and not in extreme pain. There was no indication that she would be dying soon. Cheryl, who previously had lived in Boston, was staying with friends. Monday morning, she received a telephone call from another friend, Nancy, who often had prophetic dreams. Nancy told Cheryl that she had a dream that a woman had died, and she believed that it was Dawn. Nancy was certain that Dawn would die sometime during this week. Since Cheryl had just seen Dawn the night before and she looked fine, Cheryl told Nancy that she was wrong. Nancy still insisted Cheryl's sister-in-law would die this week.

At that very time, unknown to Cheryl or Nancy, Dawn went into the hospital for a chemotherapy treatment. Afterwards, she was in extreme pain and was admitted to the hospital. Because of a turn for the worst, Dawn's two daughters (who were attending out of town colleges) were called and told to come to Boston immediately. Other family members and friends were also notified. That afternoon, the daughters (Phyllis and Joan) and Dawn's sister, Laura, who was already in Boston, and some other family members visited Dawn in the hospital. Dawn's husband, Jack, (Cheryl's brother) was already there.

Joan called Cheryl and told her that Dawn wasn't making much sense; a physician cousin said that she sounded psychotic. Later, Laura called Cheryl and said that Dawn was now sounding spiritual and talking about nirvana.

Since it was the first day of Rosh Hashanah when it is customary to blow the shofar to herald in the New Year, the Jewish chaplain walked up ten flights of stairs to Dawn's room and blew the shofar. Dawn seemed to be appreciative of the gesture. That evening (Monday), Cheryl came to the hospital and listened to Dawn for awhile. Cheryl believed that Dawn wanted help in reaching the other side. All of the people present had come into the room with different ideas and concepts. After a discussion with Dawn, Cheryl believed that for Dawn to die peacefully and cheerfully, they all would have to come together. Dawn directed everyone to hold each other's hands. In that way, they said, "goodbye" to Dawn. The oncologist told Cheryl that for Dawn to die peacefully, she would have to require strong pain medication, then sleep more and finally go into a coma.

On Tuesday morning, everyone had returned to the room. The chaplain again came into Dawn's room and blew the shofar. Dawn smiled in recognition. A little while later, Dawn asked Cheryl for help in preparing her to die. Cheryl asked everyone except Laura (Dawn's sister) to leave the room for about a half-hour. A *Do not disturb* sign was placed outside the door. Cheryl and Laura held Dawn's hands. Cheryl again told Dawn that she would have to go to sleep and then enter a special door. Dawn said that she wanted to take the images of all the people with her when she went to the other side. Cheryl said to her, "Let go of our hands, take the images with you, and reach for your teacher guides."

Dawn stretched and reached out. She saw five guides: her deceased grandmother and four other deceased friends. Cheryl said, "Now you must stay asleep and quickly go to the peace."

Dawn went into a deep sleep. Cheryl thought it was a coma, but four hours later, Dawn awakened. She now was in severe pain and required a strong dose of a narcotic.

Wednesday morning, the chaplain came in and read the final prayer to Dawn. She joined in the recital with him. In the afternoon, Cheryl led another session to help Dawn reach the other side. This time, Jack (Dawn's husband and Cheryl's brother) joined Cheryl, and they held Dawn's hands. Cheryl said to Dawn, "Close your eyes; look for the door."

Dawn interjected, "You missed a step."

"What do you mean?" asked Cheryl. "You missed the ladder," Dawn replied.

Cheryl asked, "Where does the ladder go?"

Dawn replied, "The door is at the top of the ladder." Dawn had to climb up the ladder and then go through the door to reach heaven.

Cheryl asked Dawn, "What do you see at the top of the ladder?"

"I see God," she answered.

"Is there a book there?" asked Cheryl.

She was referring to the "Book of Life," which determines who is to live and who is to die. The Jewish belief is that the book is opened on Rosh Hashanah and closed ten days later on Yom Kippur (The Day of Atonement). If you had been a good person the previous year, then your name is written in the "Book of Life" for the next year. However, if you had not been good, or if your time was up for some unknown reason, then your name would not be in next year's "Book of Life."

Dawn replied, "Yes."

"Is your name written in it?" asked Cheryl.

Dawn answered, "No," meaning that she would have died before Yom Kippur and would not be in next year's Book of Life.

"Whose names are in it (next year's Book of Life)?" asked Cheryl.

She replied, "Jack, Jim (Dawn's other brother who was due to arrive tomorrow), Laura and Cheryl."

Cheryl said, "Call out for your guides and let them lead you to your special door."

Dawn then told the others that she took the images of her family and friends with her, met her guides and went to the door, but she wouldn't let go of her husband's hand.

Cheryl said, "You have to go with your guides through the door in order to bring your soul to the next dimension." Dawn released her husband's hand. She reached out and suddenly had a ecstatic look on her face. Dawn went into a deep sleep and was never verbal again.

A little while later, Cheryl was in the room alone with Dawn. From that time on, all communications between Dawn and Cheryl were by telepathy. Dawn said, "We two will become one."

Cheryl agreed and then Dawn told Cheryl that she would appreciate it if everyone wore red the next day. She said that would help her climb the ladder faster. Dawn then told Cheryl that she had to do a 50/50 split to leave the bed and go to the other side. She also let Cheryl know that water would help her get there. Cheryl interpreted the message as the 50/50 split meaning that one-half of her would die (the body), and the other one-half (the soul) would go to heaven. Cheryl believed that the water that would help her would be the water in her lungs.

Early Thursday morning, Cheryl was in her apartment. She received a telephone call from the hospital and was informed that (among other things), Dawn had fluid in her lungs. Cheryl then knew that Dawn would be leaving soon. Although everyone had only a few items of clean clothing left, they all had something with red in it. Coincidentally (Cheryl never mentioned Dawn's request to the others), they all had some red as part of their clothing when they arrived at Dawn's hospital bed on Thursday.

Cheryl was the first to arrive. She held Dawn's hands and telepathically told her to take her images, climb the ladder, go through the door, and meet her guides. Although it was undoubtedly with great effort because of the excessive fluid in her lungs, Cheryl had the telepathic sensation that Dawn was able to move her arms as if she was climbing. Telepathically, Cheryl climbed the ladder with her.

Suddenly, Cheryl felt Dawn's fingertips stretch apart, loosening her grip on Cheryl's hands. Then, Dawn telepathically said to Cheryl that she could go no further because God was at the top of the ladder. In the Jewish tradition, a person cannot live and see God's face. Realizing this, Dawn did not want Cheryl to climb any higher.

After a little while, God apparently left, because Dawn asked Cheryl to now continue the journey with her. Cheryl felt herself being with Dawn as they climbed the ladder, opened the door and met the guides. Dawn then went through the door with the guides, and Cheryl went back down the ladder and returned.

A little while later, the rest of the people came into the hospital room and saw that Dawn was in a coma. Jack left and went to the funeral home to make arrangements. Cheryl felt that she had to join him.

Once she arrived at the funeral home, Cheryl received telepathic communications from Dawn with a request to find out what was going to happen to her physical body. Acting as a channel for Dawn's spirit, Cheryl asked the funeral director many questions with regards to the preparation of the body, the casket, and the place and time of the burial. Dawn told Cheryl that she was satisfied. Afterwards, Cheryl returned to her apartment knowing that Dawn was on her way to heaven.

At about 2:00 A.M. Friday morning, Cheryl had a coughing fit and woke up. She felt disturbed, but with great difficulty got back to sleep. Cheryl later found out that a nurse had entered Dawn's room at 2:30 A.M. She was dead, probably having died within the last half-hour.

Saturday morning Cheryl took a shower and washed her hair. In the past, it took one or two soapy rinses to clean her hair. For some reason, this time she had to perform three rinses for her hair to be clean. Later, Cheryl found out that in the ritual bath, the deceased's hair can be rinsed two or three times, but never more than three times. When they prepared Dawn's body that evening, her hair was rinsed three times. Could Cheryl's hair washing have been a premonition?

The funeral was held that Sunday. Many people cried, but the people who had been with Cheryl at Dawn's bedside and bore witness to the sessions, were solemn but not tearful. They knew that Dawn had not died, but just left for another dimension. Leaving the cemetery, Cheryl had one more communication with Dawn, but this time it wasn't telepathically. In her right ear, she heard a clear voice. Dawn said to her, "Thank you for all your help."

The Underlying Reality Of Psi Phenomena

Apparitions and visions can occur either spontaneously, through hypnosis, meditation, and visualization techniques, with the aid of mirror gazing, in dreams, during séances with mediums or through mediums without séances. Many of the reported phenomena are similar to those occurring with NDEs and OBEs. Nevertheless, the support given to the concepts of a surviving soul, a positive afterlife, and God is not nearly as strong as with NDEs and less so than that with OBEs. However using a scientific viewpoint (as discussed before), the more supportive data that hypotheses receive, the greater is the reliability that the conclusions are valid. Therefore considering that many apparitions and visions show the same phenomena as NDEs and OBEs, it appears that there is an underlying reality in all of these psi phenomena that is supportive of the possibility of an enduring soul, God and a positive afterlife.

However it is still important, using the scientifically-based viewpoint, to find support from as many sources as possible. In the quest for further supporting data, our spiritual journey next travels through the intriguing phenomena of reincarnation and past life regressions.

A Moral Vision

A woman left her house and saw 3 strange-looking old men with long white beards sitting in her front yard. She said, "I don't know you, but you must be hungry. Please come in and have something to eat."

"Is your husband home?" they asked.

"No," she said, "he's out."

"Then we cannot come in," they replied.

When her husband returned that night, she told him what happened. Her husband stated, "Go tell them I am home and invite then in!" The woman then invited the 3 men in.

"We do not go into a house together," they replied.

"Why is that?" she asked.

One old man explained, "His name is Wealth," as pointed to one of his friends. Pointing to the other he said, "He is Success and I am Love." Then he added, "Now go in and discuss with your husband which one of us you want in your home."

The woman told her husband what was said. He was overjoyed. "How nice!" he said. "Since that is the case, let us invite Wealth!"

His wife disagreed saying, "Why don't we invite Success?"

Their daughter-in-law was listening from the other corner of the house. She said, "Would it not be better to invite Love? Our home would then be filled with love!"

"Let us heed our daughter-in-law's advice," said the husband. "Go out and invite Love to be our guest."

The woman then asked the 3 old men, "Which one of you is Love? Please come in and be our guest."

Love got up and started walking toward the house. The other 2 also got up and followed him. Surprised, the lady asked Wealth and Success: "I only invited Love, why are you coming in?"

The old men replied together: "If you had invited Wealth or Success, the other two of us would have stayed out, but since you invited Love, wherever He goes, we go with him. Wherever there is Love, there is also Wealth and Success."

Chapter Six

Reincarnation and Past Life Regressions

"One generation passeth away, and another generation cometh;
And the earth abideth forever. The sun also ariseth, and the sun
goeth down, And hasteth to its place where he ariseth. The wind
goeth toward the south, And turneth about unto the north; It
turneth about continually in its circuit, And the wind returneth
again to its circuits. All the rivers run into the sea, Yet the sea is not
full; Unto the place whither the rivers go, Thither they shall go again....
That which hath been is that which shall be, And that which hath been done is
that which shall be done; And there is nothing new under the sun."
(Ecclesiastes 1: 4-9).

"Knowledge easily acquired is that which the enduring self
had in an earlier life, so that it flows back easily."
(Plato).

A dictionary definition of reincarnation is: "a rebirth of a soul
in a new human body." However, in Hinduism, it is believed that a
soul can be reincarnated into an animal body as well as a human
body. With respect to this, let's digress a moment and consider the
following case recently reported to me.

In the last chapter, I discussed an interview concerning a
shared death experience between a medium and her sister-in-law.
The same individual, Cheryl S., a 41-year-old woman of the Conservative Jewish faith encountered a case of apparent reincarnation into
an animal.

In California, Cheryl met a young lady, Charlotte, and be-
friended her. Cheryl also met Charlotte's father, Paul.

Charlotte's mother, Amy, had recently died from cancer. During the next few months, Cheryl renewed contacts with Charlotte and her father, Paul. One day, when Cheryl was by herself, she had feelings that someone was around. She saw a "daddy long-legs spider" and immediately knew it was Amy — the deceased wife of Paul and the mother of Charlotte. Telepathically, Amy (as the spider) talked to Cheryl and told her that something that Charlotte had been looking for and wanted desperately to find would soon be found in the hall closet. Cheryl thanked Amy (the spider) and went to visit Charlotte. Cheryl told Charlotte what Amy, as a spider, had told her about the lost item. Charlotte was not completely surprised at the disclosure that her mother had reincarnated as a spider, because she said her mother had "long and spidery" arms and legs. Charlotte subsequently searched her closet and found a cherished, ornamental *Chalah* cover (Chalah is a particular kind of bread used in Jewish Friday night services and meals). Charlotte had been looking for it for months and was thrilled to have found it. She thanked Cheryl repeatedly.

This is difficult case to unravel. It is not "proof" of reincarnation, of course, but it did contain a significant point of verifiable information that served as evidence to those involved. Maybe we should be careful before we destroy insects and other small creatures (as espoused by some religions) and listen to Shakespeare's advice: "The sense of death is most in apprehension; And the poor beetle that we tread upon, In corporal sufferance finds a pang as great As when a giant dies" (*Measure for Measure,* Act 3, Scene 1).

You might recall that in the chapters on NDEs and OBEs, the people who experienced these conditions *retained their personal memories.* In other words, they were the same individuals — with the same personal identity — in both the "living state" as well as during the NDE/OBE conditions. One important aspect of reincarnation is that, under most circumstances, **people cannot recall any of their previous lives**.

This fact doesn't provide a hopeful outlook for those of us who are pleased with ourselves and would like to retain our memories and identity. Gandhi gave a reason for the non-recall of previous lives following reincarnation when he purportedly said: "It is nature's kindness that we do not remember past births. Life would be a burden if we carried such a tremendous load of memories."

Alan Wolf in his book, *The Spiritual Universe*, states that, in taking its physical form, the soul has to follow quantum physics concepts of matter and energy regarding the fetching of memory. **This means that the fetching process itself wipes out part of the prior memories.** In short, as the soul arranges a meaningful "order" between the present incarnation with its past lives, the pattern of memory is represented in various aspects of the present life — but specific memories are erased (or made inaccessible).

Nevertheless, as we'll explore in Chapter 12, in at least one religious concept, not all of us undergo reincarnation. If we've led a good, moral life, this religion tells us we do not have to be reincarnated to either make up for defects in previous lives or to evolve further spiritually.

Reincarnation Beliefs Extend Into Prehistory

The belief in reincarnation has a long history. Our prehistoric ancestors considered reincarnation a fact. Death meant a return to Mother Earth from where the person would arise once again. The Shamanic belief of 15,000 to 25,000 years ago held that animals and humans were reborn from their own bones. The essential life force was considered to reside in these bones. The Hebrew kabbalists (a mystical sect discussed in Chapter 12) interpreted the quote at the beginning of this chapter (from Ecclesiastes) to mean that a generation dies and subsequently returns by the process of reincarnation. Well before the kabbalists, the ancient Egyptians and Greeks had a sophisticated awareness of reincarnation. Plato wrote extensively about the subject. The famous Roman orator, Cicero, also was a strong believer in reincarnation. The ancient northern European inhabitants had a firm belief in the transmigration of souls. So did the ancient Druids. The first major religion that extensively described reincarnation was Hinduism.

In Hinduism, reincarnation can and does occur repeatedly to individual souls. As mentioned before, in Hinduism, the transmigration of souls can take place into animal as well as human forms. Shiva, the four-armed Hindu god of creation and destruction, signifies death and rebirth (see *Figure 15*).

Shiva is the Hindu name for the Universal Godhead, or divine creative energy. He is the God of Creation (Fertility) and Destruction. First comes death — but death is also the generator of life. Shiva is also the Lord of Dance. In *Figure 15*, Shiva is shown doing the dance of bliss which is the catalyst for the destruction of one period of time and the creation of a new cosmos.

Shiva has a vertical third eye and three horizontal stripes on his forehead. In Shiva's right hand is a *drum* — symbolic of creation — and in his left hand is *fire* — symbolic of destruction. Cobra snakes are around his neck and he wears prayer beads strung like a rosary. Shiva is trampling the dwarf — symbolizing **Ignorance**. Ignorance (being unaware) has to be eliminated in order for a believer to attain release from the eternal cycle of birth and death (reincarnations). The

Figure 15
"Dancing Shiva" by Don Morse — April 23, 1999.

ring of fire depicts the creation of the cosmos. The waters of the Ganges River are depicted as coming from Shiva's head. This is because Shiva was supposed to have helped bring the river to the Earth by catching it in his matted hair.

Buddhism took from Hinduism the belief in reincarnation. Buddha was said to have had 550 previous lives. In Taoism, the Tao symbol of unceasing cycles of coming and going signifies the nature of life. Although not an official part of Christian doctrine, reincarnation appears in certain Christian sects, such as the Christian Cathars. Certain Islamic sects also believe in reincarnation. Jewish sects of the second century A.D. such as the Gnostics, Orphics, and Manicheans believed in reincarnation. A Jewish sect of the eighth century A.D., Karaism, also spoke of reincarnation. In the 12th century A.D., the kabbalists, taught the concept of reincarnation. In almost all these tribes and religions, the idea was that **death and repeated incarnations were necessary for the attainment of spiritual purity**.

With each rebirth, the soul was supposed to evolve into a higher state of purity. Followers of the religions of Hinduism, Buddhism, Taoism and other Eastern religions, number well over one billion people (mainly Asiatics) who believe in reincarnation. Countries with a strong Buddhist population including Southwest China, Nepal, India, Sri Lanka and Tibet have a history of intriguing reincarnation cases. (The religious aspects of reincarnation will be considered further in Chapters 11-13 on the afterlife.) Interestingly, many children from infancy to four years of age have been able to recite details of a supposed past life including specific identification of their family and friends during the past incarnation. These children also showed individual characteristics of the past person such as food likes and dislikes, following that person's religion, having the past individual's methods of social contact, and having fears and anxieties attributed to the past individual. In some instances, the children show birthmarks and birth defects that correspond to war and other death-inducing injuries of the previous deceased persons.

Possible Scientific Explanations For Reincarnation

As has been stated before with Biblical quotations, all of these above beliefs in reincarnation, from a scientific viewpoint are unreliable. They must be accepted on faith alone. However, there have been some attempts to explain reincarnation on a scientific basis. One line of research has focused on birthmarks and their link to the previous wounds recalled from past lives. These birthmarks are genetically-produced. However, the birthmarks and "wounds" are usually found in living people who have no biological relationship to the persons identified as receiving the wounds in past lives. Biologist Rupert Sheldrake stated that morphogenetic fields, in which people of the same species are connected by a special type of field (often called a "species memory" which influences the person's behavior based on the past behavior of the whole species), can account for reincarnation. However, this should only be possible if there were a close relationship between the child and the past person. In addition, Sheldrake's "species memory" doesn't account for the correlation between birthmarks and wounds.

"*Super-psi*" has been offered as a possible cause of reincarnation. It proposes that past life characteristics and memories are produced between the child and the deceased person just before or upon death. However, this, too, cannot account for birthmarks. It is also considered that the child has been consciously or subconsciously been taught about the deceased person by the parents or close friends of the deceased. Nevertheless, this is often shown not to be the case, and it, too, doesn't account for birthmarks.

Reincarnation's Popularity In The United States

Reincarnation received a strong boost in the United States with the wide acceptance of the teachings of spiritualist Edgar Cayce (mainly during the years 1923-1944). In the 1940, 50s, and 60s, investigators such as Colonel de Rochas, John Bjorkhem, Alexander Cannon, Morey Bernstein, Denis Kelsey, Joan Grant, Ian Stevenson and Hemendra Banerjee used hypnotic regression techniques with thousands of individuals to uncover past lives.

Current Reincarnation

Current researchers, who have used past life regressions to uncover examples of previous incarnations and reincarnations, include the well-known psychiatrists Joel Whitton, Raymond Moody and Brian Weiss. In the United States, reincarnation now has a strong following. In a 1982 Gallup poll, 23% stated that they believed in reincarnation. The results of a follow-up *USA Today/CNN/Gallop poll* dated December 18, 1994 revealed that the number had increased to 27%.

Reincarnation can also be considered from a scientific, theoretical viewpoint. Quantum mechanics tells us that sub-atomic particles are constantly dying and being reborn. Every sub-atomic interaction involves annihilation of the original particles and creation of new ones. In every human being, cells are constantly dying and being replaced. A person is *always* dying and being reborn on a cellular scale. The same thing on a grander scale occurs in the universe with stars constantly dying and being reborn. Thus, from this advanced physics point of view, a form of reincarnation does occur.

In Defense Of Past Life Regression

Past life regression depends primarily upon the use of hypnosis. I am a member of the Philadelphia Society of Clinical Hypnosis (1975-present) and from 1983-1985, was its President. The society is a division of the American Society of Clinical Hypnosis and consists of physicians, psychologists, dentists, social workers, and other professionals who use hypnosis in their clinical practices. The prevailing attitude of the membership has been that past life regressions are parapsychology and do not belong in the realm of the practice of clinical hypnosis. One reason is that under hypnosis, the truth is not always told, and people can be manipulated by therapists. This is similar to the finding that ,while under hypnosis, some people lie (or confabulate) stories about parental sexual abuse (this is called *False Memory Syndrome*).

Until I read Brian Weiss's book, *Many Lives, Many Masters*, I concurred with the society's viewpoint regarding the unreliability of past life regression. Dr. Weiss is an esteemed psychiatrist. In his book, from the disclosures of his patient, Catherine, he presents strong evidence for the possibility of reincarnation. In his subsequent books, *Through Time Into Healing* and *Only Love is Real*, as well as in *Life Between Life* by Joel Whitton (another prominent psychiatrist) and Joe Fisher, and the eminent psychiatrist, Raymond Moody's *Coming Back*, further evidence supporting reincarnation is given. The esteemed reincarnation researcher and physician, Ian Stevenson, in his monumental new book, *Reincarnation and Biology*, has given physical evidence of reincarnation as judged by birthmarks and birth defects observed in both the present individual and his/her past life As a result, I now consider the genuine possibility of reincarnation. This idea has been reinforced because the evidence from the psychiatrists' patients disclosed certain purported events that are similar to those found in NDEs, OBEs, apparitions, visions, dreams, séances and medium reports.

Does It Have To Be Reincarnation?

Considering past life regression results, aside from the reincarnation explanation, there are other possibilities. If *telepathy* (thought transference from one to another) can occur, then a psychiatrist or any other interviewer, could transfer his/her knowledge to the hypnotized patient. Thus, even if the patient knew nothing about previous lives, that knowledge could be unconsciously transferred from the hypnotist to the patient. Of course, this assumes that telepathy is possible. If telepathy occurs, it also assumes that the hypnotist is aware, at some level, of the knowledge of the patient's past lives.

One possible response to this is in Dr. Weiss' book, *Many Lives, Many Masters*. Weiss stated that his patient, Catherine, while in a deep trance, told him private details about the lives and deaths of Weiss' infant son and father. There was no way she could have known these facts — unless — by telepathy, Dr. Weiss has somehow transmitted the details to her, and then she, in turn, spoke them aloud while in trance. A rejoinder to this would be, why would Dr. Weiss want to supply details of these very personal tragedies to his patient?

A second possibility is that the hypnotized subject would have *super ESP*. As discussed by the eminent psychical researcher, Frank Tribbe, super ESP is an unproven ability to tap into knowledge held by anyone alive, knowledge available anywhere on Earth, or information stored in either Jung's "cosmic consciousness" or Whitton's Akashic Records (the source of all knowledge, discussed by Edgar Cayce; see Chapter 14). In this case, the person undergoing past life regression would obtain the needed information about personal myths and other components of past lives. A third possibility is that the subject is remembering something that is hidden deeply in his/her memory bank (*cryptomnesia*). A fourth explanation is that the subject is entering the hypnagogic state (the twilight zone between sleep and awake, when vivid images occur).

Since some people can have distressing episodes while having past life regressions attempted, they should only go to reputable practitioners and be aware of the possible negative consequences. If you had a past life regression, here is an example of what could occur.

Your Past Life Regression

Your name is Bill. You are a 35-year old male in good health. You are neither religious nor do you know much about parapsychology. However, you have heard about past life regression and are curious about whether or not you have had past lives or could remember them. You enter the hypnotist's private office. After exchanging greetings, you tell him that you want to find out if you had any past lives. In other words, had you been reincarnated?

The hypnotist answers that he doesn't know for sure whether he can get you deep enough to have a past life regression. He also tells you that, even if you do have one or more memory, there is no certainty that it was real or a product of your imagination. Nevertheless, he is willing to try.

That is what you came here for and you agree to let him tape the session. Now, you are ready to start. You enter a clean, semi-darkened room. The temperature and humidity are pleasant. You sit semi-inclined in a comfortable, contoured chair. On the opposite wall you see a drawing. It has concentric circles radiating outward. It is a typical bullseye except for a sharp, pointed, centrally-placed object in it directly facing you.

Following the hypnotist's directions, you remove your shoes, loosen your belt, and unbutton your shirt collar. The hypnotist speaks: "Get comfortable in your chair. Now, look up at the wall hanging opposite you. See the circles. Notice the separate colors. As you concentrate, as you stare, as you focus, watch the circles move. They come out and in, in and out; they get smaller and larger, larger and smaller. Focus on the center. See the pointed stone. It is coming closer to you, moving out of the circle. Watch it move. Everything is getting blurry, distorted, altered, changed. All is moving around and around, out and in, in and out, backward and forward, forward and backward, side to side."

You have gradually become oblivious to everything except the speaker's monotonous tone and the bullseye picture. The only activity you perceive is from your own quiet, even, rhythmic breathing and your fluttering eyelids.

The hypnotist continues: "You are becoming sleepy, deeply relaxed, tired. Everything is quiet, calm, peaceful, tranquil. As your eyes close, you feel yourself in a wonderful relaxed state."

Your eyes close as your head slumps forward.

The hypnotist speaks again: "Now you are on the top of a majestic mountain. The sun is shining brightly; there's not a cloud in the sky. Birds are flying by and singing joyfully. Everywhere flowers are in bloom. You can smell the delectable scents. You start to walk down the mountain. It is a very safe mountain. A few squirrels dash about in the forest. Tall, graceful trees give you shade as you carefully and slowly descend. With each step you take, you feel yourself getting deeper and deeper into this wonderful relaxed state. You touch a flower. It feels so soothing. It smells so magnificent. Now, you are on a path approaching the bottom of the mountain. Directly in front of you is a beautiful, calm, brilliantly blue lake. And there is a sailboat right at the end of the path. Without hesitation, you step into the boat. The friendly captain is there, ready to take you to your own secret destination. He asks you where you want to go. You tell him about your special place — the wonderful place where you always go to, the destination that makes you calm and peaceful, your own private place of joy and happiness. The captain casts off. The ship is sailing. It is a wonderful ride. As the boat sails along, you feel yourself floating with it. You feel tingling and floating sensations, warm, pleasant, relaxed feelings. You are going to your own wonderful place. You are almost there. You feel so good — as wonderful as you have ever felt. Now, I will be quiet and let you enjoy this magical tranquillity all by yourself. Then in a little while, I will guide you further."

By now you are in a majestic trance, feeling as relaxed as you have ever felt.

The hypnotist takes you further: "I want you to go back in time. Now, you are twenty years old and feeling young and chipper. How do you feel?"

You reply: "I feel fine."

"Good. Now let's go further back in your life. You are six years old and in first grade. It is the first day of school. You're in the classroom. You can see the teacher and your classmates. Can you see them?"

"Yes, " you answer.

"Fine. Let's go further back. You've just come out of your mother's belly. The doctor slaps you on the backside. Did you feel it? Was it painful?"

You quickly reply: "Yeah, it hurt like hell."

By this time, the hypnotist realizes that you are a very good hypnotic subject and are ready for an attempt at a past life regression.

"Now, I want you to go further back in time. Just relax, and when you have arrived somewhere, tell me about it."

Time passes. After a minute or so, you speak: "I'm on some island. I see Black natives all around. Gee, I'm a native, too. There's some kind of ceremony going on. Drums are beating loudly. I see dancers. They are pounding the ground, and they're sticking out their backsides. Wow! This is wild. Another weird thing. On the top of each drum is a large flaming candle. If it wasn't for the light from those candles, it would be pitch black. Now, the drummers are beating even faster and the dancers, they're dancing real fast. Around these dancers and drummers are a bunch of native spectators. They're chanting something strange. And when they stop chanting, they're drinking some dark brew. Wait! Something's happening. From out of nowhere, I see a tall, dark man. He's got on a black robe and a high hat. And he just picked up a thin, jagged bone. Oh my God! He's pointing the bone at me. What is he saying? I can't stand it. The ground is shaking. I'm scared. I'm raising my hands. I'm trying to stop that evil fluid from coming into my body. I think I've seen a ghost. I feel my face getting all contorted. It's getting grotesque. I wanna scream. I can't. Nothing comes out. Thick spit is pouring out of my mouth. I'm shaking wildly. I can't stop. I'm falling. I'm gonna die. Oh, it's horrible."

By now, the hypnotist is a little upset. From what you have said, to him, this sounds like a voodoo curse taking place on a Caribbean island. He wants to get you out of there as soon as possible. He speaks: "Bill, where are you now?"

You answer: "I don't know. I feel as if I am in a void. It's real strange. Now, I feel myself going through a dark tunnel and at the end of it, I can see a magnificent light. It is all around me. Dying that way was horrible, but now I feel so calm, peaceful, and loving. I see an angelic-like person. He is telling me that I am going to be reborn in another place far from where I was. I think it will be nice."

"Okay, Bill, let it just happen and when you're ready, tell me about it."

A few minutes pass. You are somewhere else. It is entirely different than where you had been before. You look around. You're inside a packed stadium and all the people are Japanese. You look at yourself. "Oh my God!" you exclaim. "I'm Japanese, too and I'm a fat slob. I'm inside a ring. Who is that guy over there? He's coming towards me. He's fat as a hippo. Oh, now I know; he's a sumo wrestler. He's gonna fight me. I hope I know what to do. Well, here goes. Uh oh, he just lifted me up. He's twirling me around. I'm flying. Oh, that hurt like hell. I just landed outside the ring. Everyone is cheering. I guess they like him more than me. I'm not going to let him get away with this. I climb back into the ring and grab the behemoth under his arms. I fling him into the ground. He looks angry. He's coming at me again. He's leaping up in the air. He's coming down on me. Everything is going black."

"Okay, Bill, that's enough. Let's come back now." With that, the hypnotist reverses the trip taking you forward into time until you are in your present body. He takes you from your birth to your present age. The hypnotist then takes you from your special place, across the lake, down the mountain and awakens you. You feel refreshed and relaxed. You do not remember the past lives you described while under hypnosis. When the hypnotist lets you listen to the tape with the details of your past lives, you are amazed. You have absolutely no knowledge of voodoo ceremonies or sumo wrestlers, having never read anything about either of them. But you are convinced that you had past lives.

Now that you have had a hypothetical trip, let us consider some examples and other aspects of real past life regression experiences.

Catherine's Flotations, Light Encounters And Spirit Visits

In Brian Weiss's book, *Many Lives Many Masters*, Catherine, the woman who apparently had many past lives, stated that she had never read the studies on NDEs of Elisabeth Kübler-Ross, Raymond Moody or anyone else. Yet, during her regressions, she manifested certain components of the NDE. In one incarnation, she floated back into her body. Floating in and out of the body is a common aspect of the NDE and the OBE. In another incarnation, Catherine died and floated out of her body and became aware of a bright light. She described the light as being wonderful, giving her energy. In a third incarnation, she also floated out of her body. This time she also became aware of a light. Moreover, she felt herself being drawn

Figure 16
"The Empyrean" by Gustave Doré. Illustration for Dante's Divine Comedy — 1855. The illustration depicts angels surrounding the heavenly light of God.

toward the light. The light became even brighter and more luminous than was the case with the other incarnations. In a fourth incarnation, after Catherine died, she again observed a light. She then saw wonderful people coming toward her to give her help and comfort. Catherine said that the light was very brilliant with many colors. It appeared to her as if it were a magnetic, energizing, healing source. Catherine felt peace, serenity and comfort.

A wonderful bright, luminous light is another common aspect of the NDE and has also been reported with the OBE. The helpful presence of others is also common in both the NDE and OBE. The feelings of peace, serenity and comfort are additional components of a NDE and an OBE. In still another lifetime, Catherine was aware of the presence of spirits.

The Light Is Most Important

Boyce Batey (personal communication, 1999), a well-known psychic researcher, has induced hypnosis in which individuals have revealed past lives in approximately 200 cases. With 75% of these individuals, as was the case with Dr. Weiss' Catherine, while "dying" in one of the past lives they saw the light. Some of their remarks were: "I'm going into the light," "I feel the light," "The light is enveloping me." After returning to normal, almost all of the people stated that the perception of the light was more satisfying and transforming than the experience of entering a past life.

Rabia Lynn Clark, in her review book, *Past Life Therapy: The State of The Art*, found that 89% of the survey responders' subjects had an experience of inner light, 97% found the light experience to be useful in healing, and 86% remembered realms of light.

Other Similarities Between Past Life Regressions, NDEs And OBEs

The presence of angels or heavenly spirits has also been reported with NDEs and OBEs. In the periods between incarnations (known as bardo in Hinduism and Buddhism and the interlife by Whitton), Master Spirits were evoked who spoke of the importance of love and learning. In both the NDE and OBE, the importance of love and learning are stressed. Other findings similar to those of the NDErs and OBErs is that the past life regressions experiencers, following the hypnotic regressions, invariably state that they believe in God, in an afterlife, and have no fear of death.

In Weiss's other books, *Through Time into Healing* and *Only Love is Real*, in Whitton and Fisher's book, *Life Between Life*, and Moody's book, *Coming Back*, similar examples are given of patients having past life regressions showing components of both NDEs and OBEs. An even more remarkable aspect of past life regressions is when they are shared.

Shared Past Life Regressions

In Brian Weiss's latest book, *Only Love is Real*, he reports on the amazing situation of a man and a woman who were total strangers in this life. However, while under hypnosis, they independently divulged very similar past life experiences during which they were lovers. In the normal waking state, they had absolutely no knowledge of each other. Furthermore, they came from completely different cultures and were never seen by Dr. Weiss at the same time. In fact, they were seen on different days and never met until Dr. Weiss brought them together and told them about the remarkable "coincidences." They subsequently fell in love and believed they were eternal "soul-mates." (Soul-mates who reincarnated were depicted in the recent [October, 1998] afterlife movie, "*What Dreams May Come.*")

One thing seems certain in this case. The two people involved couldn't have telepathically transmitted the knowledge of past lives from one to the other because they were never even close to each other — nor knew each other. Of course, if one believes the extreme concept that telepathy can occur at great distances, then they could have transmitted thoughts to each other.

Another rather remote possibility is that Dr. Weiss, for some unclear reason, would unconsciously telepathically transmit the same past live histories to two different patients. However, in order for Dr. Weiss to have telepathically transmitted all the knowledge spewed back to him in the thousands of cases of past life regression that he had performed, he would have to be the most brilliant person imaginable to have accumulated such a vast wealth of information from such a wide diversity of fields. The truth of competing scientific hypotheses is always considered to be the one that can be explained in the most simple terms. (This is known as the *Law of Parsimony* or *Occam's Razor*.) An incredibly brilliant therapist who unconsciously uses thought transference on a variety of patients is a much harder pill to swallow than the possibility of reincarnation. Of course, neither telepathy nor reincarnation can be proven, but reincarnation has a much longer history and is believed by many more people than is the case for this extreme form of telepathy.

Others have also described shared past lives. Reider, in the 1993 book, *Mission to Millboro*, reports on more than 30 individuals who remembered themselves together in Millboro during the Civil War. Cunningham, in the 1994 book, *A Tribe Returned*, relates the story of 25 people who remembered their massacre as Native American tribe members.

Celestial Sanctum To Facilitate Past Life Regressions

Past life regressions can be induced without the use of hypnosis. Dr. Whitton favors a visualization technique in which one envisions a huge and magnificent celestial sanctum. It could be a cathedral, temple, mosque, or synagogue. In one's mind's eye, it would be seen floating far above the Earth. Inside it is a huge library that contains the Akashic Records. These records purportedly contain an imprint of all that has happened in the lives and interlives of every soul that has ever existed. Let us consider an example of such a past life regression.

Your Celestial Sanctum-Induced Past Life Regression

After preliminary visualizations, you go to a quiet place, wash your hands in clean water and dry them well (this symbolizes a cleansing of the body). You then spend several minutes in complete relaxation while trying to eliminate negative thoughts and concentrate on positive thoughts. After this, you lie down, breathe deeply, and become gently relaxed. As you get deep into the meditation, visualization is done of a great celestial sanctum high in the sky. Mentally, you climb the steps and push open the doors. As you advance inside, you observe everything. Finally, a small door handle is seen. You go through the doorway and walk down a narrow stone stairway. At the bottom, you meet an old man, who is the guardian of the records. You then explain your request for the record of your last interlife. The old man grants your request and guides you into the library to the book containing your most recent past life. The guardian gives it to you. You now open the book and examine any aspect of it that you desire. All the time you need to examine the book is given to you. When you finish, you hand the book back to the guardian, who then redirects you back home. In a few seconds, you awaken from the trance.

Is It Telepathy?

The technique of self-induced past life regressions can be successfully practiced by many people. A wide diversity of past lives are typically discovered in which the individual has no possible means of knowing the information. In addition, the information found in the regressions can be, and often is, verified by outside sources. These facts show that telepathy **cannot** be the cause of past life occurrences. Telepathy can be the source of these events only if the original hypnotist (who trained the person in this meditation/ visualization technique) somehow used telepathy at a distance to implant the past lives that were apparently acquired during the celestine sanctum technique. This latter possibility appears to be extremely unlikely. In addition, telepathy could not account for the person who facilitated past life memories by learning and employing the celestine sanctum technique on his or her own.

Other Facilitators For Past Life Regressions

Another way to enhance recall of past lives is for you to keep a diary of dreams and personal intuitions and use them when making successive visits to the celestial sanctum. Dr. Morse also suggests keeping a dream journal, because some dreams convey literal past life memories.

In Dr. Weiss's second book, *Through Time Into Healing*, he described several other methods, aside from hypnosis and dreams, to facilitate past life regressions. The first is one that had occurred to him while he was undergoing *shiastu* therapy and using meditation.

When he was in a deep state, Weiss spontaneously entered a past life. In this ancient life, Dr. Weiss was a priest.

Meditation is an excellent deep relaxation technique during which, on occasion, past life memories can spontaneously surface. Recently, it has come to my attention that brain wave synchronizers (photostimulating goggles) can also be used to facilitate past life regressions.

Another method to facilitate past life regressions is to use self-observation. For example, if you have a specific fear whose origin you can't account for, you can use dreaming and visualization to see if a source of it could be found in a past lifetime.

"Play" techniques, such as free-association of words and phrases that come into your mind, might also help you access past lives. Therapists use a similar technique called the *affect bridge*. With the affect bridge, phrases, emotions, or sensations are used to evoke a person's past life. Examining other peoples' faces is another "play" technique that can help facilitate past life regressions.

Sometimes a reputable psychic can give you a reading that can provide clues to a past life. Body work, such as acupressure massage, reflexology, and kinesiology, in which key areas of the body are stimulated, is a final method to help you experience flashes from previous lives. Dr. Moody, in his book, *Coming Back*, describes the techniques of self-hypnosis and scrying (crystal ball gazing) to help people explore past lives. Nevertheless, as mentioned before, some of us have distressing experiences while having past life regression attempted for them. Hence, you should go to a reputable practitioner and be cautious.

Past Life Regression Characteristics

From analyzing the commonalties from about 200 regressed patient's reports, Dr. Moody found twelve core past-life regression traits: (1) they are usually visual; (2) they have a life of their own; (3) the imagery has an uncanny feeling of familiarity; (4) the subject identifies with one particular character; (5) past-life emotions can be experienced; (6) events can be viewed from both the first and third person; (7) the past-life experience often mirrors present issues; (8) following the regressions, improvement can occur in mental health; (9) following the regression, improvement can occur in physical health; (10) the past-life regressions develop according to important personal meanings and issues rather than as a chronological personal history; (11) past-life regressions become easier with repetition; and (12) most past lives are mundane. That is, most past life memories are of rather common lives rather than the more sensational — and often highly publicized reports — of lives as famous people.

Sisters Share A Past Life

As with NDEs, OBEs and apparitions, to strengthen my belief in the reality of similar phenomena reported in past live regressions, I felt it important to personally interview reputable people who had

a past life regression. The individuals whom I interviewed had a partially-shared past life regression.

The woman, Mary R. and her sister, Phyllis, R. were both in their mid-30s. They were of the Presbyterian faith and were spiritually minded. They went to a group hypnosis session for people who wanted to attempt to return to a significant past life. Mary and Phyllis sat inclined in chairs next to each other, but they weren't touching. The hypnotist used a standard induction technique and had them go on a railroad train to go back into a significant past life. In Mary's vision, she saw herself on the train where sitting next to her was Phyllis. Mary saw Phyllis remain on the train, but she got off and was in an ancient Indian village. She was a 17-year-old Native Indian girl and many other Indians were around. She observed many thatched huts. Mary was weaving, and she saw many children playing in the lake. When she walked over to the lake, she looked at two of the children. She could tell that they were her cousins in her present life. Mary then found the village elder. He was her great-grandfather and was very wise and he helped her in her life activities. Mary looked

into his eyes and recognized him as the art teacher in her present life — a man who had been very helpful to her in pursuing an art career. She looked for her boyfriend, whom she had loved greatly. Mary was told that he was away fishing. Just then the villagers were attacked by another tribe. Everyone was killed. Mary felt a spear go through her gut, and she screamed and died.

Next, it was the early 1800s; Mary was a young girl back in the train. She was then let off the train in a western town and saw twelve young girls dressed in long, frilly dresses. Mary went to them and was surprised to see that her sister, Phyllis, was one of them. They then played together.

Soon, Mary came out of her trance and was back in her present life. Later, Mary and Phyllis compared notes and amazingly their experiences in the western town were almost exactly the same.

Reincarnation *Is* Possible

"I hold that when a person dies, His soul returns again to earth;
Arrayed in some new flesh disguise, Another mother gives him birth.
With sturdier limbs and brighter brain. The old soul takes the road
again."

(*A Creed*, John Masefield).

So, what can be concluded from all this information from past life regressions? There is evidence from reputable sources indicating that, at the very least, the possibility of reincarnation exists. The primary method to elicit past lives is to use hypnosis, although Whitton claims that with the use of the meditation/visualization technique of a celestial sanctum, a person can visit past lives without the aid of a second individual. Weiss, Moody, and Clark give several other self techniques for inducing past life regressions. There is also evidence that shared past lives can occur, thus increasing the strength of evidence showing that reincarnation could be genuine.

Despite my initial skepticism, I am now inclined to believe that reincarnation is *possible*. In my opinion, the greatest support for reincarnation is that several of the manifestations of past life regressions are also found with NDEs and OBEs. These include: (1) floating in and out of the body; (2) going through a dark tunnel; (3) observing a brilliant light; (4) visiting deceased loved ones; (5) sensing or seeing a heavenly presence; (6) observing a heavenly scene; (7) feeling in a rapturous, blissful state; and (8) subsequently believing in an underlying soul, God, the afterlife, and having no fear of death. Nevertheless, since few of the people who had undergone past life regression had any memory of their previous lives while awake, the concept of reincarnation without previous memories is not the kind of afterlife that would reduce death anxiety.

In Chapters 11-15, we consider religious and other concepts of the afterlife. It will be seen that in at least some religions, reincarnation does not necessarily have to occur, and, if it does occur, it might be possible to retain memories of previous existences. However, since religions are a matter of faith, religious viewpoints, by themselves, are not sufficient to those of us with a scientific viewpoint to help overcome death anxiety.

In the next chapter, our spiritual journey in the search of a surviving soul, a positive afterlife and God pauses as we take into consideration the concept of immortality.

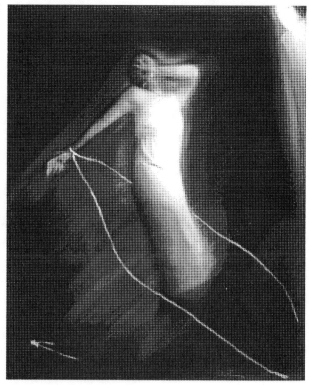

CHAPTER SEVEN

IMMORTALITY

"The dead look so terribly dead when they're dead."
(W. Somerset Maughn, *The Razor's Edge*, as stated by
fictional character, Larry Darrell).

"I'm well aware that immortality is simply an illusion
we carry with us to keep ourselves functional from day to day."
(Grafton, S.G., 'G' is for Gumshoe, as stated by
fictional Private Eye, Kinsey Millhone).

"If you want to destroy in mankind the belief in immortality, not only love but every
living force maintaining the life of the world would at once be dried up."
(Dostoevsky).

We now pause in our spiritual journey to look into the concept of immortality. Do we remain "terribly dead" or can we become immortal? If so, would it be worthwhile? Can we help overcome death anxiety if we were to become immortals?

Tipler's Immortality

Frank Tipler, in his book, *The Physics of Immortality: Modern Cosmology, God and the Resurrection of the Dead*, considers how humans could become immortal. In his description of the Omega point theory, he gives a concept of God and the resurrection of the dead. It is a computer-simulation kind of immortality in which every human who ever lived will be resurrected as a **simulation in a computer** beyond the edge of space and time. The concept is that the constant increase of computer intelligence shall permit future computers not only to equal human accomplishments, but to recreate in perfect detail all humans who have ever lived including their thoughts and memories. Tipler's God is a universal computer intelligence. Although the book contains a well-thought out concept of immortality based on general relativity, quantum physics, other aspects of cosmology and computer intelligence, by its very nature, Tipler's immortality would not help in overcoming death anxiety.

Frozen Immortality

One concept that might appeal to some is *cryogenics* (the freezing the body after death). Cryogenics (cryonics) is the process of freezing humans after death in the hope that medical science might be able to revive them in the future. Researchers in the field are divided over whether the reanimation would be a true restoration of an individual's being or simply a reanimation of a physical body. Rather than freezing the whole body, another technique is to sever the head and freeze it in liquid nitrogen. This process is based on the concept that future scientists would be able to attach the head to a new body. However, if the person were brain dead (a flat EEG) when the severing occurred, how would it be possible to restore brain function including memories? In some instances, barbiturates are injected prior to the severance of the head in the hope that this will preserve the brain. No one knows if that will have the desired effect.

Aside from the tremendous expense involved (about $50,000 per head, $100,000 per whole body), there is no scientific proof that a frozen dead body could be revived. And if it could be revived, it is a quantum leap to believe that the future would come up with the techniques that could reanimate the person while still retaining the brain function and the unique personality. (Or that future people would want to do so.) Another possibility is that the person could be revived and function, but because of the extreme damage caused by the death, the freezing process, and the reanimation, the person would have developed amnesia. In that case, is the revived person still the same person, or an entirely new person? So, in my opinion, you should save your money. The cryonic path to immortality appears to be a dead end and would in no way alleviate death anxiety.

Cloning For Immortality

With the uproar that has accompanied the cloning of sheep in Scotland, there has been a great deal of interest in the possibility of cloning humans. Some people have thought that this might be a way that a person could become immortal. His/her identical genetic makeup could be passed on and on with repeated clonings. However, it has been learned from the study of identical twins, that no matter how identical they are physically, they do not have the same personality. Hence, even if you could clone yourself, the cloned you would be different from the original you. So, cloning should be considered another futile attempt to achieve immortality and does nothing in the quest to overcome death anxiety.

Has It Been Done Before?

Alan F. Alford has an interesting concept that is described in his 1998 book, *Gods of the New Millennium*. It is best described using the author's own words, "Personally, it gives me a lot of hope for immortality knowing that it has been achieved before! I do not believe that the 'gods' evolved life spans of thousands of years through the natural forces of evolution. I think they must have started with something similar to our life spans today and used gene therapy to enhance their genes in the right places. It ought to be possible for us to follow in their 'gene-steps' (to coin a new expression)" (quoted in: Books about Physical Immortality on the internet on pp. 3-4 at: http://www.powersurgepub.com/books/pi.html).

This is quite an interesting idea, but first we have to believe that the Egyptian, Greek, Roman, Persian, and Hindu gods really lived. That is not an easy step to take.

Interplanetary Immortality

Another unique possibility is to become immortal by escaping Earth. A concept espoused by Alfred Schickentanz is that we could conceivably become immortal if we left Earth and lived in potentially infinite orbital space. There is no theoretical limit to the "terrain" in orbital space as there is on Earth. Schickentanz states that each organism's life span is determined by the environment to which it has adapted. He believes that we should be able to disable the genes that dictate the termination of the human lifespan.

This is a fascinating concept, but it is based on several unprovable assumptions. First of all, most humans enjoy life on Earth. It remains to be seen if most of us would enjoy life in orbital space. Second, it has not been proven that a species lifespan is determined solely by environment. Environment is certainly a factor, but there appears to be a genetic limit to the lifespan of each species regardless of the type of environment. Finally, while we have performed amazing genetic innovations, to be able to completely turn off the genes that determine lifespan appears to be extremely difficult if not impossible nor do we know what the ramifications of this could be to other life-sustaining functions. At any rate, time will tell.

An Immortal Future

Aside from Tipler's computer concept and the field of cryogenics, if science ever advanced to the point that it could make people immortal with their own personalities (albeit in new or altered bodies), would it be a feasible choice? Would it be desirable? If an individual could do anything he/she desired, how long would it take before boredom set in? If one had all the time imaginable, would tasks ever be accomplished? Books written or read? Trips taken? Or would things constantly be put off until tomorrow? Most great scientific and artistic achievements were done by individuals working against the constraints of time. Consider Mozart, Schubert and Gershwin as examples. They all died young but made monumental contributions to music. In the USA, as another example, it is the hectic, bustling, stressful cities such as New York, Philadelphia, Boston and Washington in which many scientific, art, music and political accomplishments have occurred. Down south, where life is slower and more leisurely, in general, less seems to be accomplished. Nevertheless, the trade-off is that Southerners usually live longer than Northeasterners.

With respect to boredom, some existentialists have applied George Bernard Shaw's saying, "But a lifetime of happiness! No man alive could bear it: it would be hell on earth" to the afterlife, claiming that the blissful heavenly life would be so boring that it would be hell itself. Nevertheless, from the assertions of almost all of those who have had a NDE, at least the first stages of the afterlife are described as indescribably joyful and euphoric. We will return to afterlife considerations in Chapters 11-15. For now, let us further consider the life of an immortal human.

You As An Immortal Human

The year is 2150. You happen to be an extremely wealthy man. It cost you 100 million dollars to have the intricate medical and surgical procedures required to have an immortal body. But now you have it and it feels wonderful. You eat at the fanciest restaurants; you see all the best shows; you take trips all over the world and even travel to the moon and Mars. You make love to many women, and your potency never slackens. You do anything your heart desires. And best of all, you keep on doing these things for many years. However, you are one of the few people who could afford these expensive procedures. It greatly saddens you when those less wealthy than you begin to die off. Loved ones, friends and acquaintances, being mere mortals, fall by the wayside. For awhile, you overcome their deaths by having new families and making new friends and acquaintances. But they, too, die off. You're still undaunted and start over again. However, in time, the thrill is gone. You begin to get bored. You realize you have to do other things.

As there is no logical association between immortality and a sense of morality, you begin to have evil thoughts. These soon turn into evil actions. First it's only robbery. Then you become a rapist. Even that is not enough. You turn to killing. You start off with what you consider to be the dregs of society: criminals and bums. Then you get rid of the disabled. But the thrill of these killings soon dissipates. You decide to take on people who can defend themselves — you seek a challenge. Some give you a good fight, but you're an immortal, and they are no match for you. Although you can't die, you can still be apprehended. The police finally catch up with you. You go to trial and are found guilty of murder in the first degree. And then the truly ironical aspect occurs: you are sent to prison for life.

Can anyone imagine eternity being spent locked up in a prison cell? I definitely wouldn't want immortality on Earth in this fashion. Would you? In fact, it appears an immortal life on Earth is the worst of all the ways we have considered to overcome death anxiety.

Immortality Through Creation

Let's assume that science will never devise a method to allow us to **live forever** on Earth. Does that imply an end? Not really, because immortality can be looked at in other ways. A person can achieve a certain degree of immortality by having children and grandchildren who incorporate part of his/her genetic makeup. So in a way, part of the

Figure 17
Copy of a watercolor painting, "Martigues, Provence, France"
by Don Morse, July, 1997.

original person lives on past his/her death. One can also pass on accomplishments to future generations. It could be a book, a painting (see *Figure 17*) or other work of art, an architectural masterpiece, a musical piece, or merely teaching one's children, grandchildren, other family members or friends the moral way to live in a stressful society. Hence, in this way the immortal component of the person is his/her name and all that it represents. This is fine in itself, but it will not alleviate our death anxiety.

An Immortal Soul

At the present time, the best we can hope for as far as our physical body is concerned is that we could live to be 100 years old or more with a good quality of life. If medicine continues to advance as dramatically as it has done in the last fifty years, there is a good probability that a high quality life could be extended to age 200 or more. Although there are theoretical possibilities for humans to live forever on this planet, at the present, anything beyond age 200 or slightly more is in the realm of fantasy or science fiction.

However, there is another way in which humans could become immortal. That is by having an immortal soul and/or to be reincarnated or resurrected at the end-of-days. To investigate this possibility, we have to turn to religion and also examine cosmology and evolution. This is our concern in the next eight chapters, where the soul, the afterlife, God, the origin of the universe, and the origin of mankind is discussed. In the next chapter, our spiritual journey takes us face-to face with God.

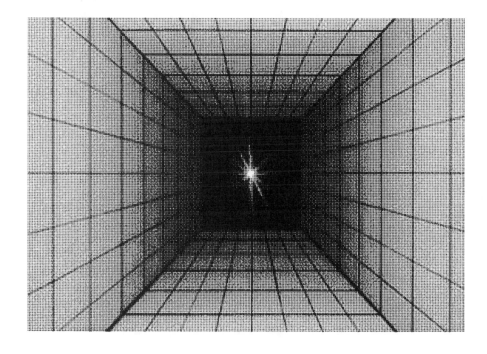

CHAPTER EIGHT

GOD

"O Lord God, Thou hast begun to show Thy servant Thy greatness,
and Thy strong hand; for what god is there in heaven or on earth, that
can do according to Thy works, and according to Thy mighty acts."
(Deuteronomy 24).

Our spiritual journey now continues as we look into the most unknowable subject of them all: God. You might ask: "Why are we interested in God? And if we are interested, as a scientifically-based inquiry, how can we determine the presence of God?" First, some spiritualists believe that there can be surviving souls and a positive afterlife **without** the presence of God. This does not appear to be a justifiable position as judged by the recently investigated psi phenomena. Most of the millions of people who had a NDE, OBE, apparition, or past life regression encountered a Godly presence. Therefore, from a scientific viewpoint, it would be helpful to examine the religious concept of God to determine whether or not it correlates with those individuals' experience of God.

The answer to the second question — How can we determine God's presence? — is that the reality of God is indeterminable. The only way we can even hope to determine the existence of God is indirectly. Therefore, we want to examine whatever indirect proof exists for the reality of God. If there is something beyond the grave, the first step in our inquiry is to evaluate if it is related to religion and the belief in God.

Pascal's Wager

Blaise Pascal, the famous 17th century mathematician and philosopher, offered an interesting hypothetical bet. He stated that life could be considered a wager. If one believes and acts as an atheist, and it turns out that there is a God and a heaven for the good souls and a hell for the bad souls, then that atheist would lose the gamble and would wind up in eternal torment. In contrast, if there is a God and a hereafter, and, acting on that assumption one chooses to be a faithful religious believer and acts morally, then that person would go to heaven. But if he/she were wrong and this is the only life, nothing was really lost.

In either case (atheist or religious believer), one would cease to exist on Earth at the point of death. But by acting morally, the believer would have helped others live a better life. Of course, the argument could still be given that, by acting according to the religious faith of that time, one would have had to sacrifice many of the passions and pleasures that the Church frowned on and considered as sinful. Nevertheless, according to most modern religious beliefs (discussed in Chapters 11 - 14), it is possible to have an enjoyable life and still be moral and religious. However, an individual can still be moral without being religious. In that case, the person would not be looking for a heavenly reward (and have no ulterior motive), and conceivably could have a better afterlife (if there was one).

A Scientist's Outlook

I am a scientist and researcher. I have graduate degrees in dentistry, endodontics (root canal therapy), genetics, microbiology and immunology, clinical nutrition, and clinical psychology. I have had training in ecology, evolution, comparative anatomy, and physics. In addition, I have done extensive reading in astronomy and cosmology. As a scientist, I had accepted the current concept that mind and body are one and that all our thoughts, emotions, behaviors, dreams, and personality (basically, the mind and the "soul") are nothing more than neural connections in the brain, limbic system, and other nervous system structures. Furthermore, the solid-appearing human body, when analyzed at a quantum level, is nothing more than quarks and other sub-atomic particles. The body is over 99% energy. Considering this, a logical belief is that when an individual dies, the circuitry is shut off, and the quarks, other sub-atomic particles, and energy flow out of the body into the endless cosmos. If that is the case, it appears that the soul cannot survive outside the physical body.

Divergent Biblical Viewpoints

The dying soul seems to be corroborated in the Bible when God said to Adam (after he ate the forbidden fruit):

"In the sweat of thy face shalt thou eat bread, till thou return unto the ground; for out of it wast thou taken; for dust thou art, and unto dust shalt thou return."

(Genesis 3:19-20).

Nevertheless, there are numerous other sections in the Bible in which the soul and some sort of afterlife is implied or mentioned. Here are a few of them:

"And Enoch walked with God, and he was not; for God took him."
(Genesis 5: 24).

"But God will redeem my soul from the power of the netherworld; For He shall receive me."

(Psalms 50: 16).

"The cords of death compassed me, And the straits of the netherworld got hold upon me; I found trouble and sorrow. But I called upon the name of the Lord; 'I beseech Thee, O Lord, deliver my soul.' Gracious is the Lord, and righteous; Yea our God is compassionate; The Lord preserveth the simple; I was brought low, and He saved me."

(Psalms 116: 3-6).

"Then a spirit lifted me up, and brought me into the east gate of the Lord's house."

(Ezekiel 11:1).

"The Lord will not suffer the soul of the righteous to famish; But He thrusteth away the desire of the wicked."
(Proverbs 10: 3).

"And when after my skin this is destroyed, Then without my flesh shall I see God."

(Job 20: 26).

"And it came to pass, as they still went on, and talked that, behold, there appeared a chariot of fire, and horses of fire, which parted them both asunder; and Elijah went up by a whirlwind into heaven."

(Second Kings 2: 11).

"Thy dead shall live, my dead bodies shall arise — Awake and sing, ye that dwell in the dust — For Thy dew is as the dew of light, and the earth shall bring to life the shades"

(Isaiah 26: 19).

"Yea though I walk through the valley of the shadow of death, I will fear no evil; for Thou art with me....And I shall dwell in the house of the Lord for ever"

(Psalms 23: 4-6).

The Scientist's Dilemma

With all of my scientific background, I was still faced with a scientific dilemma. How did the universe begin? Was it purely by chance? How did we get here in the first place? Was it merely evolution? Was some sort of God or Creator not involved in starting the universe? Before we can answer these questions, let us look at my changing concept of God and the afterlife.

A Changing Concept Of God And The Afterlife

I was brought up in the Bronx, New York and attended an orthodox Jewish synagogue. I went there every Friday evening and Saturday morning. I went to Hebrew School and got bar mitzvahed when I was 13 years of age. Later in life, I joined a conservative Jewish temple. Nevertheless, with all my training and in all the services that I attended, I never heard the mention of a surviving soul, and a positive afterlife. Of course, some of the above Biblical excerpts were included in the prayer services, but no elaborations were given. It was instilled in me that Judaism is a religion of this life, and we shouldn't be concerned with the soul and the afterlife. God's purpose was to give the Jews a better life, but heaven and hell were never mentioned.

Combined with my scientific background and Judaism's de-emphasis on a surviving soul and a positive afterlife, I led most of my life as an agnostic. As the result of my spiritual journey through NDEs, OBEs, apparitions, past life regressions and related psi phenomena (which I have shared with you), my viewpoint has changed to the belief in the strong possibility of a surviving soul and a positive afterlife. That viewpoint was reinforced after studying Kabbalah (Jewish mysticism). I have learned that there is a rich Judaic belief system in the surviving soul and a positive afterlife. (We will come to this in Chapter 12.) Now, let us consider other concepts of God.

The One God

The concept of one solitary God began in ancient Israel. Other ancient peoples such as the Canaanites, Assyrians, Egyptians, Babylonians, Greeks, Romans, Persians, Chinese, Japanese, Hindus, Aztecs, Native Americans and other aborigines had many gods. One exception was the ancient Filipinos. They believed in one supreme God, whom they called *Bathala*. Their society was the only ancient monotheistic society in Asia. Although they believed in Bathala, they considered that He was far removed from the affairs of humans. Hence, they needed intermediaries to petition Bathala on their behalf. This led to a "split-level theology" in which animism and monotheism were reconciled. (An excellent discussion of the Filipino religion is given in Howard Martin's book, *The Secret Teachings of the Espiritistas*.) Aside from the ancient Filipinos, with all of these ancient peoples, their gods interacted with each other, with mankind, and with the Earth and the stars.

The ancient Native Americans believed in the Great Spirit, which is the basic equivalent of the Western God. Specific ancient American Indians had somewhat different concepts of "the Creator." The Cheyennes believed that humans live in the middle zone of a 7-layered universe. *Maheo*, the creator, lives in the world above (*Otatavoom*). The ancient Crows believed in "First Worker" known as *Eehtreshbohedish*, which translates to "Starter of All Things." The Crows considered that First Worker started as "vapory elements that existed before the world was formed by him."

The ancient Egyptians had many gods, but one, Osiris, was believed to be supreme and the "Being of Light." (Further discussion of the Cheyennes' *Maheo* can be found in Dr. Greg Little's book, *People of the Web*. More complete discussion of the Crows' *Eehtreshbohedish* and the "Light of Osiris" can be found in Dr. Greg Little's book, *Grand Illusions*.) Another of the Egyptian gods, who flourished for a short time, was the monotheistic Aton (Atum). He was a creator god, depicted as the solar disk, bestowing life on all living things. In one viewpoint, Moses adopted Aton for the Hebrews. However, this gives no credence to the monotheism of Abraham and his descendants. Most authorities consider that God, as shown in the Hebrew Bible, was different from all the others because He was alone with no other Gods with which to interact. After the creation of the world, His only interaction was with mankind. The concept that most people have of God is a deity who is: (1) omniscient (all knowing); (2) omnipotent (all powerful); (3) omnipresent (able to be in all places); (4) beyond time and space; (5) eternal; (6) without predecessors; and (7) without a successor. Yet, if one reads the Hebrew Bible in the order it was inscribed, it can be seen that God is a paradox in some ways. He seems to act many times as if He were not omniscient, omnipotent and beyond time and space. God also appears to have **evolved**. With regard to this, the concept of God has also evolved. In Chapters 11 - 14, we'll explore the more esoteric concepts of God. In this chapter, the traditional concept of God is examined.

In the beginning, God was outside of time and space as he created the universe. He seemed to be pleased with the results of His creation:

> " And there was light. And God saw the light, that it was good,'....."And God called the dry land Earth, and the gathering together of the waters called He Seas; and God saw that it was good"...."And the earth brought forth grass; herb yielding seed after its kind, and tree bearing fruit, wherein is the seed thereof, after its kind; and God saw that it was good"...."And God set them in the firmament of the heaven to give light upon the earth, and to rule over the day and the night, and to divide the light from the darkness; and God saw that it was good"...."And God made the beast of the earth after it kind, and the cattle after their kind..... and God saw that it was good"...."And God said: 'Let us make man in our image, after our likeness; and let them have dominion over the fish of the sea, and over the fowl of the air, and over the cattle, and over all the earth, and over every creeping thing that creepeth upon the earth. ....And God saw everything that He had made, and behold, it was very good"
>
> (Genesis 1:4-33).

It appears from this opening section of Genesis that God's original purpose in creating the universe was to create a place for mankind, since man has dominion over all plants and animals as well as the Earth itself. It also seems that since God created man in His image (see *Figure 18*), a second purpose would be for God to have mankind be God-like, which would give God an opportunity to interact with compatible humans. However if this were true, God, being omniscient, should have known that mankind would frequently not act in a Godly manner.

Then another strange thing occurred. Omnipotent God apparently became tired, because He rested.

Figure 18
"Head of God" by Michelangelo. Detail from the fresco, "The Creation of Adam." Original on display on the ceiling of the Sistine Chapel, Rome, Italy.

"And on the seventh day God finished His work which He had made; and He rested on the seventh day from all His work which He had made. And God blessed the seventh day, and hallowed it; because that in it He rested from all His work which God in creating had made." (Genesis 2: 1-4).

Once God created Adam and Eve (from Adam's rib), he no longer was beyond time and space, for He now directly interacted with mankind. God gave Adam and Eve dominion over all the Earth. He also gave them free will. This became their downfall because after they ate from the tree of knowledge, they acquired the knowledge of good and evil. It seems strange that if they were given dominion over all the Earth that

Figure 19
God forms Eve from Adam's rib — *Nuremberg bible* — 1483.

they would be forbidden to eat the fruit of the tree of knowledge. If God is omniscient, would He not know that Adam and Eve would eat the forbidden fruit? Could it be that God's omniscience is tempered by the granting of free will to mankind?

In the New Testament, God's pronouncements are mainly through Jesus. And in the New Testament, God, who showed some interest in the poor and the meek in the Hebrew Bible, now primarily dealt with the downtrodden. An additional change is that God, again through Jesus' words, became a God of love. A few other changes are prominent in the New Testament. With the establishment of a new covenant, God's covenant with the Israelites was finished. Therefore, it was no longer correct to be circumcised, worship the Sabbath, or follow the Kashruth rules of the Hebrew Bible. The path to God now had to go through Jesus, who was considered to be of the seed of David (although He supposedly came from a virgin birth). The *Qur'an* (*Koran*) accepts the

Hebrew God and the prophets and Jesus (also considered to be a prophet), but Mohammed is the final and greatest prophet and is the one to lead the followers of Islam to God (*Allah*). The god, *Ahura Mazda* (Zoroastrianism), was originally monotheistic but soon had other associated gods. *Brahma* (Hinduism) was the omnipresent creator but also had other gods. The Divine Father-Mother (Tibetan Buddhism) was the supreme deity, but other gods were also present. Sikhism blends Hinduism and Islam but retains the monotheistic God of Islam. These other concepts of God are examined further in Chapters 11 - 14.

A Summary Of God

God began outside of time and space as a creator of the universe. He became tired and rested on the seventh day. God created man in His image to have humanity with which to interact. Hence, He was now inside of time and space. God was considered as omniscient, omnipotent and omnipresent. God evolved further in the New Testament, becoming a God of Love who cares for the meek and the poor, but only through the interaction of Jesus Christ. In the *Qur'an* (Koran), all the prophets (including Jesus) are worshipped as such. God (Allah) is considered as the Great Forgiver. With the other previously discussed religions, God is not alone.

My Current Viewpoint Of God

My current viewpoint is based on everything we have observed so far during our spiritual journey. Although this is a personal concept, hopefully, you can go along with my reasoning and accept most, if not all, of what I now present. The Hebrew Bible is literate as far as the scribes who wrote it believed their interpretations of the unfolding events. However, since they did not have access to scientific understanding of certain apparently miraculous events, they interpreted them as the works of God. In the next two chapters, indirect proof is presented for the existence of God. This, along with the indirect proof from NDErs, OBErs, visionaries, past life regressors and related others, plus the findings from religion and others (considered in Chapters 11 - 14) **has given me enough proof to believe in the reality of God.** With this in mind, I believe that God could have intervened at certain times (not all of the miracles have scientific explanations), and He could have changed His methods to fit the unfolding times. During the developing times of Judaism, miracles, such as what occurred at Sinai, were needed to establish the belief in one God. Currently with monotheistic religions firmly established, either God doesn't intervene as He did in Biblical times, or else His interventions are on a much smaller or more individualistic scale.

Judging the Hebrew Bible as being part true and part embellishment, I consider that God's actions are beyond our understanding. Therefore, I believe that God is omniscient, omnipresent, omnipotent, beyond time and place and eternal. The omniscience, however, is not complete because of the granting of free will. With this in mind, is it not conceivable that God started the process of the evolution of the universe (which had to be exact as is discussed in the next chapter) that had to lead to the development of man (which also had to be exact as is discussed in Chapter 10)? Is it not possible that having given mankind free will, God let humans evolve and only performed some major interventions in the early stages of their spiritual evolution (as with the splitting of the Red Sea)? Then, when mankind had reached a certain stage of development, He selectively intervened but basically let humans fend for themselves.

God could be pictured as putting information into a computer (mankind), activating it, selectively giving inputs, but generally letting the computer work on its own. Is it also not possible that God allows for the introduction of a soul at some point in each human's development

and then at the death of the physical body, God permits the soul to leave for the afterlife? And is it not possible that when the soul leaves the body, it retains its memory bank? (This is discussed further in Chapters 11-15.)

The Soul Remembers

In the Hebrew Bible, the possibility of the soul's retention of memories is mentioned.

"Then the Lord God formed man of the dust of the ground, and breathed into his nostrils the breath of life; and man became a living soul." (Genesis 2: 77).

"And the dust returneth to the earth as it was, And the spirit returneth unto God who gave it." (Ecclesiastes 12: 7).

More Evidence For God

The findings from NDEs, OBEs, apparitions, dreams, past life regressions and related psi phenomena give indirect proof to the reality

of God. The material in this chapter does not prove the existence of God because only the basic viewpoints —without elaboration — of certain religions are given. Elaboration will take place in Chapters 11-15, when we consider religious and other viewpoints of the afterlife. In those chapters, along with the definitions and pathways of the soul, the concept of God is discussed further, and the more esoteric viewpoints of God are considered, including *pantheism* (God is everywhere) and *monism* (God is one and is in everything including ourselves). To ascertain more indirect evidence for the existence of God, our spiritual journey now continues. In the next chapter, the subject matter is God and the origin of the universe, and in the following chapter, God and the origin of life is evaluated.

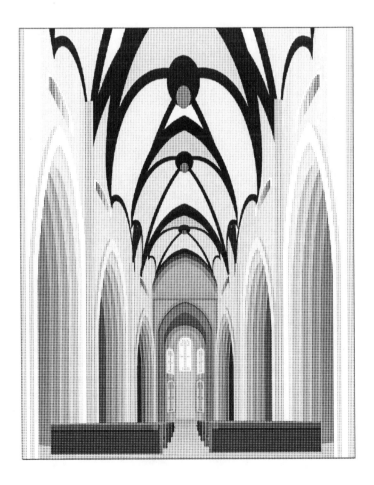

CHAPTER NINE

GOD AND THE ORIGIN
OF THE UNIVERSE

"In the beginning God created the heaven and the earth. Now the
earth was unformed and void, and darkness was upon the face of
the deep; and the spirit of God hovered over the face of the waters.
And God said: 'Let there be light.' And there was light."
(Genesis 1:1-3).

The origin of the universe is either a chance occurrence or God's
doing. Even though I had a thorough Jewish education, I never believed
in the biblical account of God creating the universe in six days (see *Figures
20, 21, & 22*).

The First Day: The Separation of Light From Darkness
The Second Day: The Creation of Heaven
The Third Day: The Creation of the Earth, the Seas and
        Vegetation
The Fourth Day: The Creation of the Stars, Moon and Sun
The Fifth Day: The Creation of Birds and Creatures of the Sea
The Sixth Day: The Creation of Animals and "Everything
        That Creeps Upon the Ground," Man and Woman
The Seventh Day: God Rests

My scientific training reinforced my earlier belief that the universe was self-created. However, within the last few years, I have read
updated information in astronomy and cosmology. As a result, I now
believe that God did create the universe. Let us look at the evidence that
brought me to this conclusion. Some of this astronomical and cosmological material is quite technical. Nevertheless, to try and prove the concept

that God created the universe, it is necessary that this material be included. I have tried to simplify it as much as possible. We begin with quantum mechanics and uncertainty.

The Randomness Of Science

When I was a graduate student, I was informed that physics is an exact science and that some day the universe would be completely deterministic. However, with the formulation of

Figure 20 - below
Gustave Dorés' depiction of "The Creation of Light" —1886.

Figure 21 - right
This is a section of an initial letter from a 13th century illuminated manuscript showing "God Creating the World in Six Days and Resting on the Seventh Day." The original is on display at the British Museum, London, England.

Heisenberg's uncertainty principle and the development of quantum mechanics, it now appears that when the most finite particles are examined (quarks [of which there are at least three], gluons, bosons, photons, and other sub-atomic particles), these particles can no longer have separate and well-defined positions and velocities. In fact, these particles behave in some way as if they were waves rather than particles. An incredible, yet scientifically verified fact about quarks, is that **our observation of them changes their position and appearance**. That is, human observation of these quantum particles effects them! This had led to the belief that without the human observer, these finite particles would not exist. This leads us to the well-known hypothetical question, "If a tree fell in a forest and there was no one there to observe it, would it really have fallen?"

This basic philosophy question — given new impetus from the research showing that subatomic particles respond to their observation

Figure 22
"Stages of Creation": Right middle to right — Separation of Light from Darkness, Earth & Water, Vegetation, Sum, Moon, & Stars. Left to middle right — Fishes & Birds, Animals & Man, Sabbath & Rest. From the *Sarajevo Haggadah* (14th Century). Reproduced from *The Jewish Encyclopedia* (1903).

— requires a rather startling assumption. That is, prior to the development of human consciousness, the literal universe could not exist because it requires observation of itself. If the physical universe did exist prior to human consciousness, then it could mean that every living creature, including a virus or a bacterium, has some form of consciousness. A religious answer to this quandary was offered by Bishop George Berkely (1685-1753) when he wrote the following limerick.

"There was once a man who said, 'God
Must think it exceedingly odd
If He finds that this tree
Continues to be
When there's no one about in the quad.' "

And the given reply was:

"Dear Sir, Your astonishment's odd:
I am always about in the quad.
And that's why the tree
Will continue to be,
Since observed by Yours faithfully, God."

It is by no means certain that quarks are the smallest particles that will ever be found. It is as if quantum reality is similar to peeling an onion with always a layer remaining yet to be uncovered. Everything about the universe today, it seems, is probability — not certainty. Quantum theory has introduced unpredictability and randomness into science. The new physics — with its unpredictability and astonishing findings — has shaken some of our fundamental scientific assumptions to their core. For example, after the establishment and general acceptance of Newtonian physics, many scientists assumed there was no need for "God" or a "creator." The static, predictable physics of Newton could lead us to understand creation itself. Almost everyone believed that science would eventually provide all the answers. But that doesn't seem to be the case now.

Physics has generally accepted the so-called "Big Bang" theory as the most probable explanation for the universe's creation. With new insights from quantum physics, this theory is less tenable. Before looking at some other possible explanations, let us consider the "Big Bang" theory.

The Big Bang And Before

"It seems as though science will never be able to raise the curtain on the mystery of creation. For the scientist who has lived by his faith in the power of reason, the story ends like a bad dream. He has scaled the mountains of ignorance; he is about to conquer the highest peak; as he pulls himself over the final rock, he is greeted by a band of theologians who have been sitting there for centuries." (Astronomer Robert Jastrow, as quoted in, Smoot, G. and Davidson, K. *Wrinkles in Time.* Wm. Morrow, New York, 1993, p. 291).

The strong possibility that science will not provide us with all the answers to creation is shown in cosmology's main concept: the big bang theory. Most cosmologists believe that at the start of the universe, there was a single point of *infinite density* and *infinite curvature* of space-time. This dense compaction of **everything** into the smallest space imaginable — possibly smaller than a quark — has long served cosmologists as the theoretical beginning point for the universe. It has been proposed that the **infinite density created infinite heat** leading to the "big bang." From this explosive start, the universe expanded in every direction (at first very rapidly in an inflationary, explosive episode, and then, more slowly as it cooled and began to "feel" the gravitational pull back toward the hypothetical "center"). Just prior to the big bang, the theory stresses that nothing existed but this infinite density (called a *singularity* by most cosmologists). In addition, big bang theorists have been in agreement about the laws of physics prior to the big bang: there weren't any. All conceived laws of science break down at that point. In other words, most cosmologists have no real theoretical explanation for how the big bang initiated the universe or where the point of singularity originated.

Quantum Gravity

In contrast, Stephen Hawking, one of the world's leading cosmologists, disagreed with Robert Jastrow's quotation at the beginning of this section. Hawking utilized concepts of imaginary time and imaginary values to state that quantum gravity existed prior to the big bang.

Hence, according to Hawking, there was no actual start to the universe. **It just always existed and always will.**

According to Hawking, since the universe is self-contained, having no boundary or edge, it would have neither a beginning nor an end. In that case, he stated: "What place, then, for a creator?" Hawking did add something to that, which could possibly leave room for a creator. He stated; "What is it that breathes fire into the equations and makes a universe for them to describe?..... Why does the universe go to all the bother of existing? Is the unified theory so compelling that it brings about its own existence? Or does it need a creator, and if so, does he have any other effect on the universe? And who created him?" (Hawking, S. *A Brief History of Time: From The Big Bang to Black Holes*. Bantam Books, New York, 1988, p. 174). One problem with Hawking's quantum gravity is that it can't account for its existence — if there was no creation to the universe, under what principles could quantum gravity exist?

How Will It All End?

Most cosmologists adhere to the concept of a singularity or unexplainable nothingness prior to the big bang. They envision three possible outcomes of the expanding universe, either: (1) a continually expanding universe; (2) a flat (parallel) universe; or (3) a collapsing universe (the "big crunch"). At this time, no one is certain which of the three outcomes will occur. However, recent evidence points toward the expanding universe. Nevertheless, any of the three possible outcomes proposed by cosmologists would leave the universe as a place incapable of supporting any kind of life as we know it. The universe would have either collapsed into quantum gravity (the big crunch back to a point of singularity) or the stars would have burned out or collapsed into black holes (expanding and flat universes). The "burning out" of all the stars is referred to by some theorists as the "heat death" of the universe — a perpetual darkness and absolute cold due to the total exhaustion of all the universe's energy.

If the universe ends as a big crunch, in essence, it would be like the state of affairs prior to the big bang. Some cosmologists hypothesize that there could then be a recurring cycle of big bangs, expansions, and big crunches — *ad infinitum*. This idea is sometimes called the "pulsating universe." However, even this doesn't appear to be possible. Relative to thermodynamic principles, there cannot be an infinite number of recurrent cycles of expansions and crunches because of energy exhaustion. In reference to the primary questions we are exploring in this book, none of these three theoretical outcomes have a possibility of the continued existence of life as we know it.

If the present universe were only here by chance and its eventual outcome is complete annihilation — no matter how events unfolded — Hawking's question of why the universe would even bother to exist makes sense to me. Why would it exist if it's here only to be destroyed? **To me, the eventual self-destruction of the universe is at least partial proof of the existence of God.** Would an omniscient God create a universe in which mankind could live only to have it all eventually destroyed? If God created the universe, He certainly could prevent its eventual demise, or by dint of giving mankind free will, He could allow humans the means to escape into another more compatible universe.

Either No Universe Or An Alien Universe

What is truly amazing about the origin of the present universe is that the minutest variation in certain occurrences or properties would have resulted in either no universe or a very alien universe (completely unlike what we know). This has been elaborated on by Gerald Schroeder — an astrophysicist and religious scholar — in his excellent books, *Genesis and the Big Bang* and *The Science of God*. Let us consider some of these possibile variations proposed by Schroeder.

First, if the energy of the big bang had differed by one part in 10^{120} (an enormous number), or if there was a minute difference in temperature, there would be no life anywhere in the universe.

Why does the universe have only three dimensions of space rather than four or more? It is only with three dimensions that the stars, galaxies, planets, moons and life itself could have existed?

Why are there four forces in nature (strong nuclear force, weak nuclear force, gravity, and the electromagnetic force)? Why not three or five? The strong nuclear force makes: (1) quarks into protons and neutrons; and (2) these latter particles into atomic nuclei. The chance encounters between quarks had to be exact or else atomic nuclei wouldn't have formed. The strong nuclear force acts through the formation and destruction of particles known as mesons. If the strong nuclear force had been somewhat weaker, the universe would have been composed only of the element hydrogen and it would have been cold, dark and lifeless. If the force had been somewhat stronger, hydrogen couldn't form water and the universe would have been helium-filled. Life as we know it couldn't have developed!

The force of gravity caused primordial clouds of gas to condense into stars. The chance encounters between atoms in the core of stars had to be exact or else stars could never have formed nuclear furnaces. The chance encounters between the atoms in the stars' nuclear furnaces had to be exact or there would not have been an eruption of higher elements and molecules into space that led to planets. Had gravity been too weak, matter would never have been able to come together to form galaxies, stars, our sun, planets, and life. Had the force of gravity been too strong, the universe would most likely have collapsed into a big crunch much too quickly for life to have formed.

The electromagnetic force binds: (1) electrons and nuclei to form atoms; (2) atoms to form molecules; and (3) molecules to form matter. Had the electromagnetic force been too weak, solids and liquids could not form and the universe would be filled with gas. If the electromagnetic force had been too strong, then protons would repel each other too vigorously and complex atomic nuclei (that form elements) would not exist.

The weak nuclear force is the cause of radioactive decay of heavy, unstable nuclei. It is responsible for the emission of particles called neutrinos. If the weak nuclear force had been slightly different than it was, the universe would have become either pure hydrogen or helium. In the latter case, no water and hence, no life would have formed.

The universe is composed of mass (matter) and energy, and as Einstein proved with his famous equation, $E = mc^2$, matter and energy can be converted into each other. However, physicists have proven that for every particle of matter, there is a corresponding particle of antimatter. For example, there are protons and antiprotons, neutrons and antineutrons, and electrons and antielectrons (positrons). Whenever matter is created, antimatter is always formed simultaneously. And when a particle of matter and antimatter meet each other, they are mutually annihilated and disappear with a burst of energy. However, only minute amounts of antimatter are found in the universe. This creates a difficult problem. When the universe was created, there should have been equal amounts of matter and antimatter. Knowing this, the opposite particles should have annihilated each other leaving a universe composed of nothing but energy. Physicists explain this paradox by stating that when the universe was at the very early age of 10^{-32} seconds old, certain massive X particles existed, and they decayed into particles more often than antiparticles. It is hypothesized that after the X particles disappeared, there were a billion and one particles of matter for each billion particles of antimatter. Hence after the particles and antiparticles annihilated each other, only the matter particles remained. Eventually this gave rise to the present universe. If this minute advantage of matter over antimatter hadn't occurred, no one would be here to investigate the universe.

Even the particles of matter have exacting requirements. Why does the proton have a mass that is 1837 times greater than the mass of the electron? The neutron is 0.14 percent heavier than the proton, which allows for its existence in the nucleus of atoms. If the proton was 0.1 percent heavier than the neutron, the universe would consist of little more than neutrons. Of course, under this condition, life would be inconceivable. Why are there exactly three kinds of neutrinos? The basic unit of electrical charge has a specific value with no room for variation. Why?

At a very early stage after the big bang (10^{-32} seconds), a quantum soup existed containing quarks, electrons, neutrinos, photons, and their antiparticles. Scattered throughout this soup were **irregularities**. These irregularities later gave rise to galaxies, stars, planets, and life. These irregularities could not be too small or else the 15 billion year age of the universe would have been too short a time for the development of all the cosmic structures. The irregularities could not be too large either or else the 15 billion year age of the universe would have been too long a time for the development of the cosmic structures. The COBE satellite measured the irregularities and found no irregularity larger than 0.001 percent in the fossil radiation that came from the early universe.

The early universe started from a specific, critical density and then it expanded rapidly. If the early universe was not close to that critical density, either it would have collapsed into a big crunch long before life had a chance to evolve or it would have expanded so rapidly that matter would never had the opportunity to condense into galaxies, stars, planets, and moons.

Another amazing finding is that probably between 90 and 99 percent of the universe contains unobservable dark matter. This is what lies between and beyond all the observable stars, galaxies, clusters, super-clusters and supernovae. As of now, no one is certain of what the dark matter consists. Yet, it is this dark matter that is primarily responsible for determining the critical density and whether the universe will eventually collapse or continue to expand.

As Smoot said, "Had the expansion rate of the universe one second after the big bang been smaller by one part in a hundred thousand trillion, the universe would have recollapsed long ago. An expansion more rapid by one part in a million would have excluded the formation of stars and planets" (Smoot, G. and Davidson, K. *Wrinkles in Time*. Wm. Morrow, New York, 1993, p. 293).

The two most abundant elements in the universe are hydrogen and helium. They were formed in the first few minutes of the universe's existence. At that time, and still today, the universe consists of 75 percent hydrogen and 25 percent helium. Had it been any other way, life would not have developed.

Life on Earth is based on the existence of carbon. Carbon's nucleus contains six protons and six neutrons. Carbon is an intermediate step in the formation of oxygen and other heavier elements. If enough carbon was not produced early in the universe, then very few of the subsequent elements would have formed. The existence of sufficient quantities of carbon appears to depend upon a fortunate accident. Beryllium, an element with a nucleus containing four protons and four neutrons, is a principal ingredient in the formation of carbon. The formative process works like this. Two helium nuclei (which were made from hydrogen) collide. If they manage to strike one another with just the right energy, a beryllium nucleus is formed. If the beryllium nucleus is then struck by a third helium nucleus (also with the right energy), a carbon nucleus is formed. Oxygen is formed when nuclei of carbon (twelve particles) and helium (four particles) collide at just the right energy levels. Beryllium and carbon nuclei have energy levels in exactly the right place so that sufficient carbon is created in the nuclear reactions of stars. How is it that beryllium and carbon have energy levels in just the places that are required to cause all the familiar elements to be synthesized (e.g., silicon, iron, uranium)? Did this happen only by chance, or is there another reason?

Water is rather unique among substances in that when it freezes it expands, rather than contracts. If it acted as most other substances do when they change phases, then the Earth would freeze solid, and life could not exist.

The universe is approximately 15 billion years old. Had it been much younger, then intelligent mankind would not be around to observe it. Had it been much older, then the universe would have either had the stars die out or be on the way to a big crunch. In either case, mankind would no longer be around to observe it. Is it just pure chance that the universe is just old enough for it to be observable by humanity?

The huge number of chance happenings (of which only some have been illustrated) had led the cosmologist, Brandon Carter, to formulate the anthropic principle. This basically means that the incredible sequence of coincidences that led to the present universe and the formation of life on Earth must have happened because, from the very beginning, all of the various laws of physics were so fine-tuned to expressly allow for the eventual emergence of humanity. As Princeton physicist Freeman Dyson stated it, "the universe in some sense must have known we were coming" (Quoted in Smoot, G. and Davidson, K. *Wrinkles in Time.* Wm. Morrow, New York, 1993, p. 293).

Other Universes

Although some cosmologists went along with the anthropic principle, most of them did not because of its implication that a creator would be required to effect the eventual outcome. They came up with several alternative answers to the anthropic principle. The underlying assumption for all of them was that there could be a large number of possible universes (even an infinite number), and this present universe, merely by chance, got everything right for the eventual development of humanity. There could be innumerable universes in which conditions were just *not* right for the development of life. These other universes could also operate under different physical principles. It has been hypothesized that these universes could have formed in different ways. In one theory, multiple parallel universes occurred at the same time as ours, but we are just ignorant of their existence. With the early inflationary universe, different amounts of inflation would have produced different universes — including our own. Another hypothetical concept, which is also based on inflationary theory, is the development of bubble universes. Still another type of universe could form theoretically as a baby universe. It could be reached through a black hole and then a wormhole to another universe.

On October 21, 1997 on the internet, the sponge theory was unveiled. It states that there are an infinite number of universes connected by a vast network of black holes. According to this theory, prior to the big bang, there was a star that became a supernova and was reduced to a black hole in another universe. Hence, the singularity that is at the center of a black hole is akin to the singularity that created our universe. With this theory, there are an infinite possible number of universes. This is interesting, but totally without proof. Superstring theorists are also trying to discover a ten-dimensional "theory of every-thing," and quantum cosmologists are trying to find out if multiple universes are out there. Meanwhile, relative to all of these proposals, **all is speculation and nothing is really known.**

How The Universe Began

Now let us examine the two possibilities of how the universe began: (1) the principal cosmology viewpoint of the universe beginning about 15 billion years ago with a big bang out of a singularity (nothing-ness); and (2) Hawking's viewpoint of an eternal universe with no boundary or edge that arose 15 billion years ago from quantum gravity and always was and always will be.

Big Bang From Nothing

With the concept of the universe beginning from nothing 15 billion years ago with the big bang to the incredibly complicated mixture of stars, planets, galaxies, supernovae, and on and on, it makes much more sense to me to consider that God started the universe. The prior section detailing the incredible sequence of coincidences that had to occur to create a universe with self-aware beings leads me to this conclusion. A self-starting universe, creating itself in just the correct way to result in the present variegated universe, is too coincidental.

Hawking's Concept

Hawking's concept of an eternal universe that knew exactly what it had to do to evolve to its present incredibly complicated state makes more sense to me. It permits me — and almost requires — to believe in a God that always was and always will be forming a self-perpetuating universe.

God And The Creation Of The Universe

Of course, a question that we haven't considered is the ultimate question. Who created God?

It has been said that God didn't create man, but the reverse is true: man created God out of the need for something to believe in. Nevertheless, there are many religions that don't believe in a single God but believe in some other entity, multiple gods or nature. However, that again brings us to the question: who created the universe?

My response is that it makes more sense for a God-created universe than for a self-created universe. However, if man didn't create God, then who — or what — did? Was there a pantheon of gods with God as the chosen or ultimate leader? Of course, one would have to go one step back and ask: who created the other gods ... *ad infinitum*? This is another example of the peeling onion example — it leads us nowhere.

Even if one believes that there is one God who created the universe, a logical question that could be asked is: "What did God **do** before He created the universe?" An answer attributed to Saint Augustine is: "He was preparing Hell for people who might ask such questions." This could be considered a question that humans, with their limited knowledge of God, cannot ask. In this stage of our spiritual evolution, we are just incapable of asking questions such as this, perhaps because we are incapable of grasping the answers. Therefore, it is easier for me to accept one eternal God who can decide to do anything He wants to do when He so decides. I find it more logical to accept one God — one that always was and always will be — than to try and imagine a hierarchy of gods that continues to go backwards in time endlessly with each set of gods creating the next.

Eastern Concept Of God

In Eastern religions such as Hinduism, Buddhism, Zen Buddhism, and Zoroastrianism, the concept of God is not clear. (These religions are discussed in greater detail in Chapters 11 and 12.) In Hinduism, depending upon the sect, there is theism, atheism, polytheism, and pantheism. However, it has been stated that all the gods are manifestations of the same divinity, reflecting various aspects of the infinite, omnipresent, and incomprehensible Brahman. In Buddhism, which is an offshoot of Hinduism, the deities are minimized, and the quest is to reach enlightenment. Zen is only concerned with enlightenment. Taoism has three or more gods, depending upon the sect. However, the balance of nature is of paramount importance. Zoroastrianism is also an offshoot of Hinduism. There are several gods, but one god is primary. Jainism is yet another offshoot of Hinduism. Here, too, several deities are worshipped. What appears to be common with most of these religions is the concept of the universality and interconnectedness of all of things in nature including man. Hence, God is not someone out there, but is everywhere and inside us as well (monism).

The universe was either created by a universal consciousness or it has always been and always will be. I can agree with the belief of God being omnipresent and being within us as well. But my concept of God is of an eternal being who created the universe and to whom one can communicate. A phrase embodying the concept of communicating with God is: "prayer is talking to God and meditation is listening to God."

The Creation Of The Universe: Science Versus God

As mentioned before, it is a scientific dictum that the easiest explanation of a physical occurrence is most likely the correct one (the law of parsimony — known as **Occam's razor** — *non sunt multiplicanda entia praeter necessitatem*; i.e., things are not to be multiplied beyond necessity). Bearing this in mind, it appears to be more reasonable to accept one eternal God who created the universe than to have to deal with an unending universe that, in some inexplicable way, just was, is, and always will be. It appears to be even more incredible to consider an infinite number of unobservable universes that are self-creating.

The Biblical Account Of Creation

If God created the universe, how can we correlate that with the biblical account of creation?

"Study astronomy and physics if you desire to comprehend the relation between the world and God's management of it" (Maimonides, *The Guide for the Perplexed*, 1190).

Does the Genesis account of creation have any validity? First of all, the possibility of multiple universes is not unique to modern physics. The *Midrash* and the *Talmud* are ancient books written by Israeli sages who interpreted the Hebrew Bible. In these books, it is stated that God had created other universes before this one, but they were not satisfactory. Therefore, He destroyed them. Then God created the present universe that yielded the planet Earth which was fit for men to live in. (This sounds like the anthropic principle.) Here, men could find all that would sustain them and allow them to achieve a productive and enjoyable life provided they used the abundant treasures of the Earth justly and humanely. To show that God was pleased with the present universe, He stated after the entire universe was completed, that it was "very good" for men to live in (as was shown in the last chapter).

The six days for the creation of the universe (and the Hebrew calender date for it being 5760) are difficult ideas for us to understand. An excellent account of correlating the scientific viewpoint with the Biblical concept can be found in Gerald Schroeder's excellent books, *Genesis and the Big Bang* and *The Science of God*. Schroeder concludes that, the Biblical scribes who either transcribed Genesis from what Moses delivered or wrote Genesis from the oral history, did not base their views of the universe and its laws on the critical use of empirical data. Scientific principles had not yet been discovered. The Biblical scribes had imaginative thinking, and their verbal expressions were concrete, emotional, pictorial, and poetic. In other words, they spoke in the language of their contemporaries. The Biblical scribes believed that God was beyond time and space. Completely unlike other religions that were prevalent at the time with their multitude of gods, the Hebrew God was not born, had no

182 / SEARCHING FOR ETERNITY

family, had no history, was alone, had no relations with other gods, had no use of magic, and had no life of His own. For the Biblical scribes, God's existence did not have to be explained. It was self-evident. All the other religions and societies that flourished in the Hebrew Biblical time period have long since disappeared, but the Jews, with their concept of one eternal God and a holy book (the *Torah*) given to them by God at Mount Sinai are still around.

One reason why the Jews are still around is that the revelation at Sinai was witnessed by approximately three million people. Could all of those people have been misled by an act of nature or as some have said by the observation of an interplanetary space ship? (See William Bramley's, *The Gods of Eden*.) Although conceivable, there is no evidence to prove either contention. Although there is no evidence aside from the biblical account that God spoke to the assembled Israelites, their accounts of what happened were inscribed and passed on by oral tradition as well. Today, those very words in Hebrew are still spoken throughout the world. Some have said that this is the best proof of the existence of God.

The Age Of The Universe: Correlating Science With The Bible

Using the independent techniques of radioactive dating, background radiation measurements, and Doppler shifts in starlight, it has been estimated that the universe is approximately 15 billion years old. Genesis states that it took 6 days to create the entire universe culminating with man on the 6th day.

Comparing the Biblical dating of events that took place after Adam with dates for these same events as ascertained by archeological findings, it can be determined that they match within accepted margins of error for the archeological findings. (This is discussed further in the next chapter when the origin of life is examined.) It is only the early part of the Biblical calendar which concerns the events prior to Adam's appearance that seem to contradict the results of modern scientific inquiry.

Gerald Schroeder stated in his excellent and fascinating books, *Genesis and The Big Bang* and *The Science of God*, that it is possible to integrate the pre-Adam Genesis chronology with current cosmological data. It can be done by the process of *stretching time*. This actually was mentioned in the Hebrew Bible.

"For a thousand years in Thy sight Are but as yesterday when it is past"
(Psalms 90: 4).

This alludes to the possibility that God's perception of time is different than that of mankind. The verse in Psalms is in some ways comparable to Einstein's revolutionary thought experiment in which he demonstrated that when a single occurrence is viewed from two frames of reference, a few days in one can pass for a thousand or even a billion years in the other. Prior to the appearance of man, there was no one around to record time. Therefore, the first six days of creation (prior to Adam's appearance) were not man's time but were God's time. According to Einstein's law of relativity, it is impossible in an expanding universe to describe the elapsed time happening in certain sequential events in one part of the universe in a way that will be equal to the elapsed time for these same events when viewed from a different part of the universe. Related to the differences in gravitational forces and motions among the various stars and galaxies, the absolute passage of time is a local event. This means that time varies from place to place.

Because of this, it is impossible to choose an all-encompassing time frame to describe the chain of events of the developing universe. This is because a whole host of factors effect the rate at which time passes in different areas of the universe as well as at different moments of its evolution. During creation, this included motions of intergalactic gases, forces of gravity within stars and galaxies, supernova explosions, and the mass of the Earth. Every star, galaxy, and supernova had its own speed, its own gravity, and therefore, its own space-time reference. Since it would have been impossible to describe all the events preceding mankind's appearance in a single time frame, the Genesis Biblical scribes used *their* time frame of 24-hour days to describe the happenings during the pre-Adam time period. It is only the moment when God breathed a soul into Adam that one time frame was chosen which would then be used from that moment forward.

In the last chapter, we mentioned that omnipotent God rested on the seventh day. According to Maimonides, God didn't actually rest, but He caused a repose to encompass the universe that had been created during the first six days. Following this repose, the laws of nature (including the time clock) would function in a normal manner — unlike the situation that occurred during the first six days.

In Schroeder's books, many other correlations between the Biblical scribes' description of Genesis and cosmological findings are described. Suffice it to say, that the account of creation as written by unscientific Biblical scribes is compatible with the current cosmological concepts of the creation of the universe.

> "Any scientific hypothesis of the world, such as that of a primeval atom from which the whole of the physical world derived, leaves open the problem concerning the beginning of the universe. Since science cannot by itself resolve such a question: what is needed is that human knowledge that rises above physics and astrophysics and which is called metaphysics; it needs above all, the knowledge that comes from the revelation of God."
> (Pope John Paul II. Quoted in Wilkinson, D. *Our Universes* Columbia University Press, New York, pp. 188-189).

In his excellent books, *The Fingerprint of God, Creation and Time, Beyond the Cosmos, The Creator and the Cosmos,* and *The Genesis Question,* Hugh Ross, an astronomer and religious scholar, gives added insight into the contention that the biblical and scientific accounts of the origin of the universe are compatible.

From Creation Of The Universe To The Creation Of Life

As previously discussed, our spiritual journey to overcome death anxiety requires evidence for the existence of God. From the findings of cosmology and the Biblical account of creation, it appears that there is more indirect evidence for a God-created universe than for a self-starting universe. In the next chapter, our spiritual journey continues as we look for further evidence of the existence of God by examining the origins of life from both the scientific perspective and the Genesis account.

CHAPTER TEN

GOD AND THE
ORIGIN OF LIFE

"And God created man in His own image, in the image of
God created He him; male and female created He them."
(Genesis 1:27).

E̶ven though I had an extensive Jewish background, I never
believed in the biblical account of God creating Adam, and Adam being
the first human. My training in evolution and genetics could not envision
a separately created human. I used to believe that the creationists were
scientifically ignorant, religious zealots. Now that I have thoroughly
read the latest information on evolution, I believe that there could be a
grain of truth in what the creationists state. And I am convinced that God
created not only the universe, plants, animals, and other living creatures
— but humans as well. Let us look at the evidence that brought me to this
conclusion. As in Chapter 9, the scientific material is somewhat detailed,
but I'll try again to bring it in as clear a form as possible. We begin with
the evolution of life.

The Beginning Of Life

Gerald Schroeder — the renowned astrophysicist and religious
scholar — in his superb books, *Genesis and The Big Bang* and *The Science
of God* considers the necessary occurrences for the initiation of life.

By an incredible series of fortuitous events, life began on Earth
about 3.8 billion years ago. Before that, stars had to explode and release
elements and molecules into interstellar space. Most of these molecules
contained carbon, hydrogen, oxygen, and nitrogen. These substances,

known as organic molecules, would later form more than 99 percent of the bodies of all living things. The organic molecules became integral parts of planets, and conditions were just right on planet Earth for clusters of these organic molecules to have formed into amino acids.

As discussed in the excellent new book, *God, Humanity and the Cosmos*, the formation of the moon (as a result of a massive spatial collision) was instrumental in the necessary slowing and stabilization of the Earth's orbit. It is also suggested that the action of the moon-induced tides stimulated the mixing of these organic molecules. Only Earth — of all the planets in the solar system — had an atmosphere that could protect it from the injurious effects of the sun. Earth had to be massive enough to retain that atmosphere but not so massive that the resulting atmosphere was so thick that the energy of the sun (its light) would be blocked off. If Earth rotated too rapidly, the atomic and molecular parts of its matter would be split apart. Nevertheless, Earth's rotation was just right to prevent such an occurrence.

Carried by rain, these amino acids fell to Earth and landed in the primitive oceans. Water was an ideal medium for the development of life because it could shield the harmful rays of the sun and protect against raging storms. These amino acids were able to be assembled into long-chained proteins by the interaction of deoxyribonucleic acid (DNA) and ribonucleic acid (RNA). It is unknown how the intertwined double helix

The relative sizes of the Planets and the Sun.

THE SUN

MERCURY VENUS EARTH MARS

JUPITER

SATURN

URANUS

NEPTUNE

of DNA originated, but lightning might have had a stimulating effect on the path toward life.

The DNA was able to make partial copies of itself by producing RNA. The RNA then selected specific amino acids and constructed proteins and enzymes (organic catalysts that speed up chemical reactions) that formed the physical structures and functions of living organisms.

Because the DNA strands had the unique capacity of self-replication, they were able to transmit the genetic code and form all living things. Amazingly, all forms of life: a blade of grass, a bacterium, an earthworm, a tiger, a human — every animate thing — is formed by just 20 amino acids. In spite of the fact that there are about 300 amino acids, only the same 20 amino acids are used to build life-forming proteins. Identical proteins are found in organisms as diverse as a single-celled amoeba and humans. But it is the unique blueprint for each organism — dictated by its own DNA structure — that organizes the proteins to form the incredible variations of life. There is no such equivalency to DNA in inanimate forms (for example, a stone or a piece of plastic); they may be formed from a variety of amino acids or other molecules in a multitude of ways.

Despite prevailing opinion, recent fossil evidence revealed that once water was present on Earth (about 3.8 billion years ago), life began. The first cells formed in a primordial mix of water, gases, and elements. (Each cell somehow contained millions of DNA molecules.) It was only with the development of enzymes and the formation of protective cell walls that life as we know it could have began. Without the benefit of a protective barrier formed by a cell's wall (called a "membrane"), chemical reactions took place and formed structures such as salt crystals, coal and diamonds. Life processes require a protective barrier. However, we have absolutely no knowledge about how the transition from non-living structures to living organisms took place.

Life In A Test Tube

In 1953, the American chemists, Harold Urey and Stanley Miller, reproduced Earth's primitive terrestrial atmosphere in a test tube. They had a mixture of hydrogen, ammonia, methane, and water. They subjected this mixture to electrical discharges to simulate the effects of thunderstorms that took place on Earth about 4.6 billion years ago. After

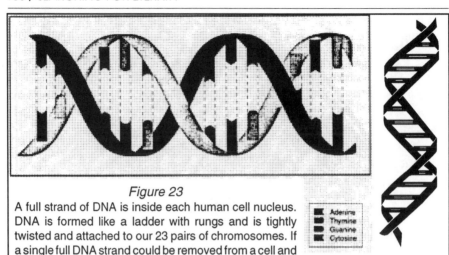

Figure 23

A full strand of DNA is inside each human cell nucleus. DNA is formed like a ladder with rungs and is tightly twisted and attached to our 23 pairs of chromosomes. If a single full DNA strand could be removed from a cell and untwisted, it would be an incredible six feet long! The rungs of the ladder (all three billion bits of them) are formed by two amino acids that lock together. Only four different amino acids can form the rungs. It is believed that between 80,000 to 100,000 of these genes are the most important. Within the next few years, the entire code is expected to be worked out by the *Human Genome Project*. Many scientists are becoming convinced that the amazing human blueprint formed by DNA cannot have formed by chance or coincidence — it is so complex that some form of creative intelligence must have been involved.

From — *Psychopharmacology* (1997) by G. L. Little; by permission.

several days, they were able to form amino acids out of their original mixture. Since that time, numerous experiments by other investigators were attempted, but no one has been able to go beyond the stage of amino acid formation. Despite the efforts of many scientists, there has been no evidence that biochemically, life can be created. An enormous gap remains between the most complex "protocell" laboratory model systems (showing how scientists think life forms under these conditions) and the reality of even the simplest life forms (such as Mycoplasma).

Harold Morowitz, a Yale University physicist, performed mathematical computations about the time required for random chemical reactions to eventually produce a single-celled bacterium. His calculations showed that the needed time for the bacterium to spontaneously develop would not only exceed the 4.5-billion year age of the Earth when life first arose, but also **the entire 15-billion year age of the universe**. Gerald Schroeder has stated: "The likelihood of random processes producing life from a primordial bath of chemicals is even less likely than that of your shaking an omelet and having the yolk and white separate back into the original form of the egg!" (Schroeder, G.L. *Genesis and the Big Bang: The Discovery of Harmony Between Modern Science and the Bible.* Bantam Books, New York, 1990, p.111). Edward Conklin, a former Professor of Biology, gave a vivid comparison of life evolving by chance. He stated that the probability of life originating accidentally is just as likely as the possibility that an unabridged dictionary would form by an explosion in a printing shop!

The Rapid Formation Of Life

Despite its apparent improbability, not too long after Earth formed, the first species of life developed in the primeval ocean. These were single-celled bacteria and blue-green algae. This amazingly fast appearance of life on Earth has caused some renowned scientists including Nobel laureates Svante Arrhenius and Frances Crick, molecular biologist Leslie Orgel, and cosmologist Fred Hoyle to consider that life might have arrived on Earth from an extraterrestrial source. However, that again is like the peeling onion metaphor we have used before to show that each explanation offered by science for an inexplicable event needs an explanation for itself! How did life originate on that extraterrestrial source? Did it come from a previous planet? We can keep asking this question *ad infinitum.* The assertion that life on Earth came from an extraterrestrial source doesn't answer where life **first** came from.

Rather than a gradual change, for 3.2 billion years only single-celled microbes existed on Earth. This changed about 650 years ago as the recently discovered globular forms known as *Edicaran fauna* have shown. Amazingly, fossil evidence indicates that 530 million years ago in the Cambrian era, an explosion of multicellular organisms appeared simultaneously in the oceans. Sponges, worms, insects, and fish all appeared at the same time. No gradual evolution was found.

About 450 million years ago, on land, plants and trees first appeared. The plants and trees absorbed water through their roots and atmospheric carbon dioxide through their leaves. As a result of the process of photosynthesis, the plants and trees utilized energy from sunlight and converted water and carbon dioxide into sugars and released oxygen into the atmosphere. Some of the oxygen combined into threes to form ozone. Eventually, enough ozone was produced so that it formed an environmental layer which effectively blocked dangerous ultraviolet rays from the sun. The formation of the ozone layer was another of those unique—but necessary—"coincidences" in nature that permitted non-aquatic animal life. Of all the planets in our solar system, Earth is the only planet that has free oxygen in the atmosphere.

With the formation of the ozone layer, the land was protected from the damaging effects of the sun and animal life then developed on the Earth. About 300 million years ago, amphibians left the water and reptiles and birds made their appearance. Almost all of these organisms (from bacteria to birds) are still around today.

About 75 million years later, dinosaurs came into the picture and ruled the planet for about 160 million years. It is believed that a cataclysmic event occurred — possibly an asteroid that crashed in Mexico near the present Yucatan — and the dinosaurs became extinct. Mammals then became the dominant animals on Earth. Of these, three groups evolved that were endowed with primary intelligence (rats, dolphins and primates). Approximately two million years ago, some type of mankind made its appearance.

It has been asked: If dinosaurs were not destroyed, would mammals have become dominant allowing for the emergence of mankind? One concept is that God granted nature "free will," which allows for disasters such as hurricanes, earthquakes, cyclones, tornadoes and asteroid and comet collisions with Earth. However, God could have bypassed nature's "free will" and intervened 65 million years ago to cause the asteroid collision that destroyed the dinosaurs. It has been argued that a caring God would not allow for the destruction of dinosaurs and other species just to ensure the evolution of humans. But we can't know whether that asteroid collision was an "act of God" or a chance occurrence. We also do not know whether humans would have evolved if the dinosaurs hadn't become extinct. It can only be concluded that **we are here**, and the "mind" of God is unknowable.

Was It Self-Organization Or God?

Is it possible that there was something beyond self-organization (evolution & natural selection) that led to life? Could it have been God's intervention at the universe's beginning (with God producing the exact combinations to produce the eventual development of life)? Or might it have been a second intervention by God to create life?

As mentioned previously, major gaps have been found in Darwin's theory of evolution. A gradual evolution of a new species from a predecessor has never been found in the fossil record. Instead, glaring gaps are found with the apparent sudden appearance of new species. In addition to those life-permitting "coincidences" discussed before, another sudden explosive appearance was that of *angiosperms* (flowering plants). Plant proliferation over the Earth provided high-energy food sources that permitted the proliferation of mammals. Darwin himself referred to the sudden appearance of the angiosperms as an "abominable mystery." Could the unexplained sudden appearance of these flowering plants and other major gaps in evolution also have been an intervention of God?

From Adam To Us

The principal chapter in evolution is the origin of mankind. As far as can be determined, among the animal kingdom, only humans have: (1) language; (2) self-consciousness; (3) the ability to think, reason, emote and make decisions; (4) an ethical sense (chimpanzees show no evidence of guilt feelings); and most importantly, (5) free will. (In *Figures 25 & 26*, Marvin Herring gives us a humorous differentiation between a human and a bird as well as God's creation of man in His image.)

As mentioned previously, only humans have the knowledge of death and the anxiety that accompanies it. Let us now examine the uniqueness of the human mind.

Figure 24
The "evolutionary chain" as some scientists would have us believe.

There is an unknown evolutionary leap from the most intelligent ape to the human with all of the aforementioned characteristics. Is it more logical to believe that the rational (at times), emoting, thinking human merely evolved by chance from an ape-like creature, or was an ape-like creature given something additional — a soul — by God, which then allowed it to become human?

Almost three million years ago, ape-like creatures stood upright and grasped objects. The tools they made were flint blades and stone cores. *Homo Sapiens*, the human species, first made its appearance about 300,000 years ago. Not much changed in human evolution until 40,000 years ago when a form of speech occurred. This allowed for the formation of harpoons, stone spear points, bone needles, and statuettes. Care of the sick seemed also to have occurred. Skeletons of pre-historic villagers have been found dated to over nine thousand years ago in areas as diverse as the Arctic, France and the Ukraine. Housing, clothes, utensils, sculptures, and drawings were also discovered. Hence, there were certainly man-like animals that predated Adam. However, Genesis does in a sense go along with the evolutionary development of man from some primordial substance.

Figure 25
"Human beings are created in the Divine image."
by Marvin Herring, October 5, 1999.

Figure 26
"The Triumph of Reason" by
Marvin Herring,
August 12, 1998.

"And out of the ground made
the Lord God to grow every
tree that is pleasant to the sight,
and good for food"
(Genesis 2; 9).

"And out of the ground the
Lord God formed every beast
of the field, and every fowl of
the air."
(Genesis 2: 19).

"Then the Lord God formed
man of the dust of the ground."
(Genesis 2: 7).

Enter The Soul

The creation of man
from "the dust of the ground"
was 5,790 years ago (as I write
in October 1999). The *Talmud*
and *Midrash* have interpreted
Genesis to the effect that God
gave every living thing a life-
giving spirit known as *nefesh* in Hebrew. Adam and all his predecessors
— upright apes and *Homo Sapiens* — also received this *nefesh*. However,
and this is the crux of the matter, it was only with the appearance of
Adam (see *Figure 29*) that an additional spirit or soul, known as *neshamah*
was placed.

"Then the Lord God formed man of the dust of the ground, and breathed into
his nostrils the breath of life; and man became a living soul."
(Genesis 2: 7).

Therefore, prior to Adam, it could be concluded that human development had reached a physical limit of evolution. Each human contains 30 billion billion inanimate (non-living) particles. Putting all these particles together doesn't create a human with consciousness, thoughts, emotions, feelings, reasoning and the ability to exercise free will. However, if one believes that the Genesis account has validity, it was only after the soul was implanted that humans were suddenly granted all of these "higher" characteristics. Once the soul was implanted, human development made a sudden physical advance and a profound spiritual leap. Therefore, that is the reason Genesis considers Adam to be the first true man. Everyone after Adam had also received *neshamah* and was therefore a complete human (physically and spiritually). From Adam's time forward, the space and time frames of God and mankind are the same. Gerald Schroeder's books, *Genesis and the Big Bang* and *The Science of Life* give several examples of direct congruence between the post-Adam Biblical account of dates and archaeological investigations. One example is given here.

Figures 27 & 28
Days 4 and 5 of creation depicted.
From *The Stream of History* (1928).

Tubal-Cain And His Tools

"And Zillah, she also bore Tubal-cain, the forger of every cutting instrument of brass and iron."
(Genesis 4: 22).

Archaeologically, this biblical time period is known as the early Bronze Age. Tubal-cain was a descendent of Cain. From Biblical records, it has been determined that he lived around 4400 in the Hebrew calendar. The first appearance of early brass tools has been dated by archaeological investigations to be about 2400 B.C., which is equal to the Hebrew calendar's 4400. Considering this and several other findings reported by Schroeder, it appears that the biblical calendar is accurate. Hugh Ross, in his excellent book, *The Genesis Question*, gives added impetus to show that the biblical account matches the scientific depiction of the creation of man.

The Hand Of God

From the material presented here, it seems that the sudden appearance of life, the major gaps in Darwin's evolutionary theory, and the uniqueness of mankind makes it difficult, if not impossible, to believe that life originated on Earth merely by a series of fortuitous occurrences. Looking at it from a scientifically-based viewpoint, it makes little sense that an incredible series of improbable chance occurrences could have been responsible for life in general and mankind specifically. It makes more sense to me, just as with the big bang start to the universe, that an omnipotent, omniscient, omnipresent, and eternal God was responsible

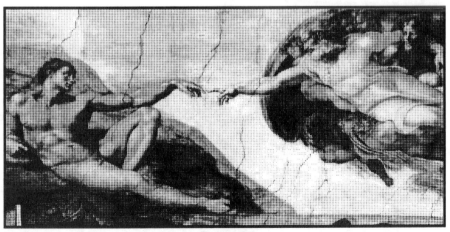

Figure 29
From the fresco, "The Creation of Adam" by Michelangelo. Original on display on the ceiling of the Sistine Chapel, Rome, Italy.

for the start of life, the sudden appearance of new species, and the presence of physical and spiritual mankind.

Considering this and the previous chapter, there appears to be sufficient indirect evidence for the existence of God. From the findings of Chapters 3-6 (NDEs, OBEs, apparitions, visions, dreams, séances and medium reports, reincarnation and past life regressions), there is ample evidence for the existence of a surviving soul and a positive afterlife. And we now have some fairly strong evidence for the existence of God.

In the next chapter, we extend our spiritual journey into the major religions that support the belief in a surviving soul, a positive afterlife, and God. Let us see if they strengthen the findings of NDEs, OBEs and related psi phenomena with respect to the reality of God and the post-death travels of the soul into the afterlife. If they do, this will give added support to the belief of the reality of a surviving soul, a positive afterlife, and God.

CHAPTER ELEVEN

THE AFTERLIFE IN RELIGIONS -
PART 1: ANCIENT EGYPTIAN, GREEK, HINDU, ZOROASTRIANISM, & BUDDHISM

"The Attuned One liveth, the Earth Bound One dieth."
The Egyptian Book of the Dead, cited in *Ancient Egyptian Mysticism*
by John Van Auken (1999) ARE Press.

In Chapter 7, we looked at the possibility of achieving immortality in this life. It was concluded that immortality in our present physical form, with the conditions of our world's affairs and the state of mental and emotional development in humans, is neither feasible nor beneficial. We temporarily abandoned the concept of immortality as we examined God in Chapters 8-10. In our continuing spiritual journey, we now reconsider immortality from a more traditional viewpoint — the religious path to immortality via the soul's continued existence after physical death.

In this chapter, we'll explore historical accounts from a few major religions that believe in an immortal soul, a positive afterlife and God. Of special interest in the quest to overcome death anxiety are those religions that give support to findings of the psi phenomena (NDEs, OBEs, apparitions, reincarnation, etc.).

The Egyptian World View

According to the *Egyptian Book of the Dead*, the sun god, *Atum*, was completely self-created. He was present at the beginning of time and will be present at the end of time. Atum was considered to be nothing with the potential to be everything. Atum apparently reversed entropy (the degradation of the matter and energy in the universe to an ultimate state of inert uniformity) by creating from a vacuum everything that now exists in the universe (sort of like Stephen Hawking's version of the big bang theory). The Egyptian God, Atum, is believed by some to have been the basis for the Hebrew God. I do not consider this to be true as I'll explain later.

For the ancient Egyptians, the soul was not in the physical world but in the vacuum world — the world that has the potential to become anything. **The soul was not a simple entity but consisted of nine souls.** These souls resided in different parts of the body.

The Nine Souls

The first soul is *aakhu* (*khu*). It resides in the blood and is the primordial life spirit (first soul, divine intelligence). It represents the inspirational aspect of life — the message of the gods. It is regarded as an ethereal being, is immortal and is able to feel emotions.

The second soul is *åb*. It resides in the heart and is the seat of wisdom, knowledge, and understanding. It links the physical body with the spiritual body.

The third soul is *ba*. It resides inside of *åb* and is defined as the heart-soul of man or that which is sublime and noble. It is believed that, at death, the *ba* flies to the sun. It can take on human form and can be material or immaterial. It can be a ghost that appears after death and flies in and out of the tomb, often in the form of a bird. (See *Figure 30*.)

Figure 30
The *ba* hovers over the body on papyrus from *The Book of the Dead of Ani*.

The fourth soul is *ka*. It resides inside our emotional center. It is considered as our emotional double and can be observed as the image one sees when he/she looks into a mirror. It comes to the fore when we express emotions such as anger or depression.

The fifth soul is *khaibut*. It is our shadow and is dark or black in the light. It can exist either inside or outside of the body. If the shadow is captured by an evil spirit, the person could die.

The sixth soul is the *khat*. While a person is alive, *khat* is associated with bodily functions such as unconscious breathing, heartbeat, elimination and other automatic nervous system (ANS) functions. It is also the physical body after the individual dies (the corpse).

The seventh soul is *sekhem*. It resides throughout the body as the incorporeal representation of the vital force of a human. *Sekhem* is the spiritual being incorporated into the body. In the body, it acts to maintain vital power (similar to Chinese *ch'i*). *Sekhem* also exists in heaven and in the place between death and rebirth. It powers and energizes to allow for reincarnation.

The eighth soul is *ren*. It is the person's name, and, as such is powerful and holy. As a person goes in the afterlife, his or her name follows — so goes his/her destiny. If the soul forgets the name, then the soul is banished either to an inferior rebirth or to a rebirth into a lower animal.

The ninth soul is the *sahu*. It is the spiritual body that springs from the material body at death. Within it, the mental and spiritual attributes of the natural body are united and given additional powers. The *sahu* has the same bodily form as the *khat*. However, it is nonmaterial and contains all the other souls within it. It is the bodily form of the soul that travels to higher worlds (heaven).

Similarities Between NDEs And Egyptian Souls

Although the Egyptians had numerous souls, two of them are similar to the common experiences uncovered by NDE research. The third soul, *ba*, is the closest thing we have to the Western definition of a soul. It is the soul that leaves the body at sleep and then returns, appears as a ghost, and apparently is present when a person has a NDE. The ninth soul, s*ahu*, is the bodily form of the soul that travels to heaven. Since some NDErs and OBErs report heavenly trips, it could be via this type soul. Although the Egyptian viewpoint of nine souls is difficult to believe, *ba* and *sahu* could be the original basis of a soul that departs a deceased's body and enters the afterlife realm.

A related ancient Egyptian belief system was the *Cult of Osiris*. It was concerned with death and spiritual existence. The Pyramid texts describe a tunnel with a light at its end, a life review and Osiris as the "Being of Light." As can be seen, these concepts are amazingly similar to NDEs. (For a more complete description of the Cult of Osiris, see Dr. Greg Little's excellent book, *Grand Illusions*.) John Van Auken's newest book, *Ancient Egyptian Mysticism* (1999, ARE Press), explains that various Egyptian tomb inscriptions and paintings depict not only the *ba* leaving the body of a deceased person, but also of the human DNA structure.

The Ancient Greek Philosophies

Although not practiced today, several ancient Greek religious concepts gave rise to several currently practiced religions. The ancient Greeks had divergent concepts: for example, Socrates and Plato's position as contrasted with that of Aristotle. Let us begin with Socrates' viewpoints.

Socrates' Statements

Socrates (*ca.* 470-399 B.C.) was Plato's (*ca.* 428-348 B.C.) teacher. Socrates said that death was the separation of the soul and the body: it was a separation of reality and illusion. By illusion, Socrates meant the world of the senses. By reality, he meant the soul.

When the soul is in the body, it is infected by bodily evils. In spite of its bodily corruption, the soul remains substantial and immortal. When a person dies, his soul survives in its pure state. Socrates stated that the soul was substance and could not vanish but merely changed form. He stated that all substances are indestructible, but

Figure 31
Socrates — From *Ridpath's History of the World* (1911)

their forms can change (this is similar to Einstein's concept of matter and energy being interchangeable). To explain this interchangeable nature, Socrates cited the example of moving from waking to sleeping and vice versa.

Socrates asserted that everything in nature operates by the law of opposites. Therefore, life leads to death and death leads to life. When people die, since their souls are of an indestructible substance, the souls will continue to exist somewhere. However, Socrates believed that the soul did not have an opposite. It can change form but not substance.

The idea of something coming from nothing was earlier rejected as a genuine possibility explaining creation (as is believed in Stephen Hawking's concept of the quantum soup that was present prior to the big bang). Hence, the ideal soul is considered to be made of substance that could change in form only. Thus, Socrates' view of the soul falls in line with ideas of an afterlife.

Plato's Platitudes

Plato perceived the world in terms of reality, art and illusion. First, there was *primary reality*. This was the original form of reality and it was created (supposedly only once) probably by God or lesser gods. From that moment on, it was copied and mimicked by nature or humans. Copies are secondary reality. Tertiary reality is illustrations of secondary reality. For example, your red pencil is a secondary reality of an *ideal* red pencil. An illustration of that pencil is a tertiary reality.

For Plato, the soul is pure, simple, unchanging, coherent, invisible and eternal. Unlike the Egyptian viewpoint, Plato's soul cannot be split into different parts. Plato's soul is logical and rational — based on reason. This is totally unlike the ideas that most Westerners hold

Figure 32
Plato — From
Ridpath's History of the World (1911)

about the soul. For them, the soul deals with emotions and feelings. Plato's soul is a cold, intellectually pure primary reality that is *ideal*. Plato disagreed somewhat with Socrates in that for him, life and death were not absolute opposite qualities but *relatively* opposite qualities. Plato believed that the soul, albeit a nonphysical substance — like any other physical substance — can never be destroyed. The soul could not vanish or die. He argued that because sleeping and waking are only **relatively** opposite each other (a person can gradually fall asleep or wake up), dying and living are also relatively opposite each other. A soul's attributes could change by taking on a particular opposite quality such as a wise soul taking on the attributes of an ignorant soul. However, a soul could not perish and disappear from the universe. Because it was substance, it had to persist in some manner.

Plato also believed in the theory of **recollection** which stated that everyone remembers ideas and events that are not in his/her immediate experience (the present life) and which are the memories of previous lives (see Chapter 6 on past life regressions). Plato considered these memories to be evidence of people having lived before; hence the soul is immortal. Memories are retained by the soul regardless of living in different bodies.

Plato said that the soul is neither created nor destroyed. Every soul has been here forever and will exist for eternity. No soul can die and no soul can be created or born. When a person dies, the soul lives on.

Socrates, Plato and many of the other ancient Greeks believed that before souls are born, they are gathered together within a transcendent region awaiting birth. Then, following death, there is a supernal sphere to which such souls return. And as mentioned before, in Plato's view, souls can be reincarnated into other bodies.

Aristotle's Attitudes

Aristotle (*ca.* 384-322 B.C.) was Plato's student, but his view of the soul was diametrically opposite to that of his mentor. For Aristotle, the soul was part of the mind/body process by which a person lives, perceives, feels, moves and understands. He said that there was no soul without a body. Aristotle's soul is a real substance, but it is immovable — it cannot be separated from the body. Yet, it has the power to determine and control the body's actions. The body is inert until it is

Figure 33
Aristotle — From
Ridpath's History of the World (1911)

made to move by the soul. **To Aristotle, the soul is a real entity even though it does not exist in space and time.** The soul has three divisions: (1) vegetative (controls physical nourishment and procreation); (2) sensory (controls movement, sense perception, and imagination); and (3) rational (controls reasoning). For Aristotle, as the soul is an intricate materialistic part of the body, when a person dies, the soul dies as well.

Summarizing The Ancient Greek Viewpoints

The ancient Greeks did not have the concept of a single all-powerful God. Although Socrates' and Plato's concepts of a soul are somewhat different from the Western viewpoint, it is an immortal soul and one that can be reincarnated. Although the necessity for reincarnation for everyone is not necessary nor helpful as a means of overcoming death anxiety (discussed later), the Socrates-Plato soul could be the basis of a soul that departs a deceased's body and enters the afterlife realm.

From what we have discovered so far in our spiritual journey, there is no evidence for the "ashes to ashes, dust to dust" concept. Hence, Aristotle's claims that the soul dies with the body should be rejected.

Hinduism: From Monotheism To Polytheism

Hinduism is the first of the presently practiced religions to be considered. It is the major religion of India. It has a complex nature with its diversified forms. Hinduism encompasses every variety of theism: atheism, polytheism, pantheism (every aspect of the natural world is filled with the energy of life and is part of God), and monism (all things are ultimately one). There are six Sanskrit sacred books and numerous gods. Later, one of the gods, *Brahma*, was conceived as the Supreme Being and believed to be infinite, absolute, impersonal, omnipresent and unimaginable. Brahma is also known as *átman*. ("world soul)." The changing world of daily living is considered to be an illusion, known as *maya*. To reach salvation is to realize absorption into the "world soul" (*átman*).

The attainment of knowledge in Hindu religion is through the neutral discipline known as *yoga* (union). Since Brahma is believed to be everywhere (a pantheistic idea) and every thing is Brahma, humans have an individual soul in which Brahma is present. To attain union with Brahma, people practice meditation, repression of activity, restraint of breath, withdrawal of the senses from their objectives, concentration and reflection, speculation and good works. Once union with Brahma is achieved, there remains no judgment of right and wrong or good and evil. This is because the person who attains union with Brahma is in a region **beyond** moral considerations. The latest Hinduistic concept is that, despite many gods existence, there is but one God who can make Himself known in a thousand different ways.

Hindu Afterlife Concepts

The primary Hindu idea of what happens at death is the following. When you die, your spirit-soul (*átman*) departs from your gross, natural body (made up of the four elements of earth, air, fire and water). There also exists a "subtle" body (consisting of mind, intelligence and the false ego). If you led a bad life, or had unpleasant thoughts at the time of death, you require purification. Therefore, your spirit-soul takes your subtle body and enters another body to be reincarnated (*samsara*). Several reincarnations could be required to end the cycle of birth-death-reincarnation. If you led a good life, learned from mistakes in your present life, learned stress management techniques to control angry and hateful thoughts, and meditated to be in a blissful state, you would discard your subtle body and be liberated from the cycle of rebirth. This liberation is known as *moksha*, which has two viewpoints.

The impersonal viewpoint concludes that we are all God, with no personal God. When *moksha* occurs, your spirit-soul is absorbed into the all — this is bliss. This blissful union is but temporary, and then the process of rebirth starts again.

The personal (the predominant viewpoint) states that, when *moksha* occurs, your spirit-soul, with its spiritual body (a seed of which is found in your soul), goes into the spirit sky (similar to heaven) to be with God forever. Your individuality always remains, but you are united in love with God and never return to the cycle of rebirth again. Love and bliss are emphasized in this heavenly existence as has been found in NDEs, OBEs, and related psi phenomena.

God Is Everywhere

The Hinduistic concept that God is everywhere including within ourselves is compatible with the concept of God that we have developed so far. So, too is the belief that your spirit-soul departs your physical body upon death. The major lessons found here are that if you lead a righteous life; act well when dealing with stressful situations; meditate when you are dying to be in a blissful state; and learn from your mistakes during life, you will not have to learn throughout many lives.

Zoroastrianism: God Versus Demons

Zoroastrianism was founded by Zoroaster in Persia toward the end of the seventh century B.C. He distanced himself from the polytheism of Hinduism, and considered that the one god was *Ahura-Mazda*. He viewed the other deities as demons. *Ahura-Mazda* is in constant struggle with evil spirits (*devas*). These *devas* are the instruments of *Ahriman*, who is the source of all wickedness in the world.

Zoroastrianism stresses the virtues of honesty, straightforwardness, hospitality toward strangers and charity. The scripture of Zoroas-

Figure 34
Ahura-Mazda —
From Harter's *Ulti-mate Angel Book.*

trianism is the *Avesta*. Zoroastrianism spread beyond Persia into Babylon (where the Jews were held captive), and it had a Greek influence from the capture of Persia by the Greeks. Although Zoroastrianism was replaced by Islam for many inhabitants (especially the laborers and artisans), it still remains in Iran (present day Persia) and has spread to India where a refinement of it is practiced by the *Parsis*.

Some consider that much of Hebrew thought concerning the afterlife, angels, the judgment at the end-of-days, and the nature of God as Light was influenced by Zoroastrianism. It is also considered that the Essenes (a mystical Hebrew sect present in Jesus' time) were influenced by Zoroastrian concepts. One example is the belief in a final battle between the Sons of Light and the Sons of Darkness. In the New Testament, in the opening verses of the Gospel of John, a similar concept is mentioned as the four horsemen of the apocalypse (see *Figure 35*).

Afterlife Concepts

The Zoroastrian viewpoint of the afterlife begins by asserting that death is a temporary victory of evil over good. Death is also a time when there is a great risk of evil spirits being present. Several rituals can prevent or limit their influence.

After you die, your soul hovers close to your physical body for three days. At dawn on the fourth day, your soul starts to travel and goes to the bridge of judgment (*Chinvat Bridge*). Before crossing the bridge, your soul meets face-to-face with the representation of its conduct, a guide known as a *daena*. If your good deeds on Earth had outweighed your bad deeds (for example, you controlled anger and hate), then your guide appears in the form of a beautiful maiden. The maiden then leads your soul across the bridge to "the best existence" (an equivalent of heaven).

Figure 35
"Four Horsemen of Apocalypse" by Albrecht Durer.
Original on display at
British Museum in London, England.
From *Harter's Ultimate Angel Book.*

In contrast, if your Earthly bad deeds outweighed your good deeds, then the *daena* appears in the form of a very ugly maiden. The maiden then leads your soul across the bridge to "the worst existence" (an equivalent of hell). If your Earthly deeds were balanced between good and bad, then a neutral *daena* takes your soul to a temporary, neutral abode known as "Hamistagan" (an equivalent of purgatory). Neither much pain or much happiness is found there. Each of these three realms has subdivisions to which your soul goes dependent upon its "vibrations." The holier a soul, the greater the frequency of its vibrations, and consequently, the better is its place in the "astral world."

God is the Being of Light. For souls to remain in "the worst existence" would be a sort of defeat for God. Therefore, one day in the future, there will be a collective final resurrection in which all are redeemed to spend eternity with God. Ultimately, good will prevail and the heavens and earth will be made new. As shown later, some of these same ideas are seen in Judaism, Christianity, Islam and other newer religions. Similarly to Zoroastrianism, most people who have had a NDE are enveloped with a brilliant loving light and a being of light is often present.

A Benevolent God

The Zoroastrian concept of a benevolent God and a soul departing the dying body are the same as the beliefs developed thus far in our spiritual journey. So, too is the concept that your soul's fate depends upon whether or not you had led a good life.

The Many Faces Of Buddhism

Buddhism is an off-shoot of Hinduism that developed in India from the teachings of Gautama Buddha in the sixth century B.C. It has two major divisions: (1) Southern Buddhism (known as *"Hinayana"* or "Small Vehicle") in India, Burma, Ceylon, Cambodia and Thailand; and (2) Northern Buddhism (known as *"Mahayana"* or "Great Vehicle") in China, Japan and Korea.

"Small Vehicle" emphasizes individual salvation, and "Great Vehicle" emphasizes universal salvation. In Tibet, there is "Lamaism" which is a mixture of "Mahayana" and the animistic Bon religion of Tibet. *Zen Buddhism*, which developed in Japan as a blend of Indian Buddhism

Figure 36
Gotama Buddha — Stone
sculpture (200 A.D.).

and Chinese Taoism, believes in salvation by contemplation, meditation and intuition.

Buddha promoted the traditional doctrine of *Kharma*, the principle stating that every deed and action has a definite moral influence which determines the nature of one's future existence. For a full life, Buddha taught the benefits of virtue, kindness, love, compassion, non injury in the broadest sense, liberality, the Golden Rule and the sense of duty.

Buddhism has an elaborate pantheon of gods dependent upon the type practiced. Various concepts of reality exist in Buddhism. In some Buddhist concepts, a soul exists; in others, there is no such thing as a soul.

The Afterlife In Tibetan Buddhism

A basic Buddhist concept of the afterlife is contained in *The Tibetan Book of the Dead*. It apparently was transcribed into writing in the early centuries when Buddhism first came to Tibet. It is a manual that is to be read near the body of a person who has just died. It gives the soul instructions on what to do in the afterlife. The purpose of the instructions is to give the soul the means to attain "liberation," meaning that it will be freed from the endless "Wheel of Death and Rebirth." (This concept of liberation was derived from Hinduism.)

The *Bardo* is an intermediate state that occurs between one incarnation and the next. The *Bardo* state is divided into three main parts,

Figure 37
Hindu Wheel.

which "dawn" upon the soul in the moments, days and weeks after death.

The First Bardo

The first bardo arrives at the exact moment of your death when there dawns the *Clear Light of the Ultimate Reality*. This is the substance and content of the state of Liberation. However, your soul must recognize it and act in the following way: You are told to be unselfish and unegotistical, showing love and compassion for all sentient beings. If you had led a good life and learned by stress management techniques (for example, meditation) how to overcome hate, anger, rage and frustration, you would be more likely to attain Liberation than if you were not so well-prepared. The second step is the realization that your mind and self is identical with the Clear Light, which implies that **you** are the Ultimate Reality, "the All-Good Buddha," who transcends time, eternity and all creation. If you recognize this while in the supreme state at the moment of death, you attain Liberation. That is, you remain in the Clear Light forever. This is known as "*dharmakaya*," which is the highest spiritual body of the Buddha.

Most souls simply are not be able to do this. They are "drawn down" by the weight of their karma into the second stage of the First Bardo. This is known as the *Secondary Clear Light* and it is seen immediately after death. At this moment, there are separate instructions to be read according to your spiritual condition while you were alive. If you were advanced in meditation and other spiritual practices, the same instructions are constantly repeated at the moment of your death. The object is to enjoin you to recognize yourself as the "*Dharmakaya*." If you were still on the student level on the spiritual path, an injunction is given to you to meditate on your "tutelary deity" — the particular god to whom, while alive, you performed devotional practices. Finally, if you had been one of the commoners, unpracticed in any spiritual disciplines, the instruction is for you to meditate upon the "Great Compassionate Lord" (an "*Avatar*"), who is worshipped by the multitude and is similar to the typical Christian's concept of Jesus.

The Second Bardo

If your soul is still not liberated at this stage, it descends into the Second Bardo, which is divided into two subparts, with one week spent in each part. In part one, your soul encounters "the Peaceful Deities." On each of the seven days of the first week, a specific Buddha-being will appear in radiance and glory along with a bevy of angelic attendants. At the same time on each day, a light will shine from one of the six worlds of the Buddhist universe, known as "*Lokas.*"

On the first day, your soul meets the Divine Father-Mother, who is the supreme deity of the universe. Your soul's next step is determined by its reaction to this God. If your life on Earth was good, you will now be in a state of purity and grace, and your soul will enter into the joy of the God and attain Liberation. If you lived an ignoble and impious life, the results of the bad karma will cause the intense radiant presence of the God to strike fear and terror in you, and your soul will be drawn into the softer light of the deity called "*Deva-Loka.*" This remains a fairly attractive fate because the *Devas* are the Gods (or angels), and their *Loka* is equivalent to the Christian heaven.

Nevertheless, the Buddhist teaching is that *Loka* is not the highest spiritual objective. It is only a temporary state in the manifest universe. Even high and pure souls can lose their footing in heaven and descend again into the cycle of death and rebirth. Liberation is considered as the only final and permanent resting-place for your soul. It is an unmanifest state beyond all existence.

On the second day, there appears to your soul, the second-highest God in the Buddhist pantheon. At the same time, a smoky light from hell dawns. Just as the Buddhist heaven ("Deva-Loka") is not a permanent, eternal state, neither is its hell. The most wicked souls will eventually work their way out of the deepest pit of hell. Once again, if your soul responds to the dazzling white light of the second God with pure joy, it will be Liberated. However, if your soul reacts with anger from having indulged in this emotion while on Earth, your soul will recoil from the light in fear and be drawn into hell. Hence, if you had led a good life and learned to control stressful emotions (for example, anger and fear) with emphasis on meditation techniques, Liberation could be reached.

The pattern is repeated on the third day. On this day, it is the response of egotism to the light of the God that will cause your soul to recoil in fear. Your soul will then be drawn into the human world, where the next incarnation will take place. On the fourth day, the God of Eternal Life appears. If your soul has a negative reaction to him because of miserliness and attachment, your soul will be drawn toward rebirth in the "Preta-Loka," which is a world of "hungry ghosts." They have huge stomachs and throats the size of pinholes, which causes them to wander about in a constant state of unsatisfied ravenous desire. On the fifth day, God arrives in the form of an Almighty Conqueror. This time your soul will be unseated by jealousy. Your soul will then travel into the "Asura-Loka," which is a world of fierce warrior-deities (demons). On the sixth day, all the deities return and dawn together along with the lights from all six Lokas. On the seventh day, the Knowledge-Holding Deities appear. These are more fierce and demonic-looking than any of the other previous gods. They are a type of transitional element to the next stage of the Second Bardo, where your soul encounters the Wrathful Deities. If, because of stupidity, your soul cannot face the Knowledge-Holding Deities, it is drawn toward the "Brute-Loka." This will cause your soul to be reborn as an Earth animal.

In the second week of the Second Bardo, your soul meets seven legions of Wrathful Deities. These are hideous, terrifying demons who advance upon your soul with sword and flame, while drinking blood from human skulls. They threaten to wreck unmerciful torture upon your soul, to maim and slay it. The natural tendency for your soul is to try and flee from these beings in stark, screaming terror. However if it occurs, all is lost. The instructions at this stage of the Bardo are for your soul to have no fear, but rather to recognize that the Wrathful Deities are really the Peaceful Deities in disguise. Their dark side has manifested only because of your soul's evil karma. Your soul is told to calmly face each demon in turn and visualize it as the deity it really is. If your soul can do this, it will merge with the being and attain the second degree of Liberation — that lesser aspect of it which is now the most that your soul can hope for here in the Second Bardo. Your soul is informed to realize that all of these fearsome creatures are not real, but are merely illusions from your soul. If your soul can recognize this, the creatures will vanish, and your soul will be Liberated. If your soul cannot, it eventually travels into the Third Bardo. The lesson of these aspects of the second bardo is for you to learn, while alive, stress control techniques that can manage fear, jealousy and stupidity in order to achieve Liberation.

The Third Bardo

Your soul encounters the Lord of Death in the Third Bardo. This is a fearsome, demonic deity who appears in fire and smoke. He subjects your soul to a judgment. If your soul protests that it has done no evil, the Lord of Death holds up before your soul, the *"Mirror of Karma."* Within it is reflected every good and evil deed you did in your lifetime. Now demons inflict punishments and torments upon your soul for its evil deeds. The instructions at this time are for your soul to recognize the Voidness of all these beings, including the Lord of Death himself. Your soul is told that the entire scene unfolding around it are its own projections. If your soul recognizes this, it can attain Liberation.

If your soul is not Liberated after the Judgment, it will now be drawn remorsely toward rebirth. The lights of the six Lokas dawn again. Into one of these worlds, your soul must be born. The light of the one that your soul is destined for will shine more brightly than the others. Your soul is still experiencing the frightening sufferings and apparitions of the Third Bardo, and it feels that it will do anything to escape from this condition. Your soul will seek shelter in what appear to be caves or hiding-places. However, they are actually entrances to wombs. Your soul is warned by the instructions not to enter them, but to meditate upon the Clear Light instead. If your soul does this, it is still possible to achieve the third degree of Liberation and avoid rebirth. Again, this supports the importance of you learning the stress management technique of meditation while alive.

Finally, a point occurs where it is no longer possible to attain Liberation. After this, your soul is given instructions on how to chose the best womb for a favorable incarnation. The basic technique is *"Non-Attachment."* That is to try and rise above both attraction to worldly pleasures and repulsion from worldly ills.

Light, Light Beings, Life Review, And Love

Here, too, it can be observed that the brilliant light, beings of light, and life review found in Hinduism are similar to that which is experienced by many NDErs. The importance of love is stressed which is also the case with the NDE.

The Hindu belief in several deities is not compatible with our current concept of God. However, the concept of a soul that departs the deceased body is compatible with what we have developed so far in our spiritual journey. The principal lessons learned here are: if you have led a good life, learned to control stressful emotions (especially anger, fear, and jealousy) with an emphasis on the use of meditation techniques, you can reach the highest state of bliss by using these stress management techniques in the bardo states of the afterlife. However, the concept of several bardo states does not enhance our developing afterlife viewpoint. As is explained in Chapter 15, in the afterlife, each of us has a stopping off place where we can learn to control our negative emotions that will allow us to escape the chain of reincarnation and go to a higher state of bliss. In the next chapter, our review of the afterlife in religions continues.

CHAPTER TWELVE

THE AFTERLIFE IN RELIGIONS - PART 2: THE JUDEO-CHRISTIAN & ISLAMIC PERSPECTIVES, SIKHISM AND BAHAI'SM

"But as for me, I know that my redeemer liveth, And that He will witness at the last upon the dust; And when after my skin this is destroyed, Then without my flesh shall I see God."
(Job 19: 25-26).

"And many of them that sleep in the dust of the earth shall awake, some to everlasting life, and some to reproaches and everlasting abhorrence."
(Daniel 12: 2).

"And shall come forth; they that have done good, unto the resurrection of life; and they that have done evil, unto the resurrection of damnation."
(The Gospel According to John 5: 29).

Since the Jewish concepts of God, the soul and its afterlife travels are closest to the findings from NDEs and related psi phenomena, and therefore are of major importance in the personal afterlife concept, these are considered in some detail. Although several sources have been used for this section (e.g., Labowitz, S., *Miraculous Living: A Guided Journey in Kabbalah Through the Ten Gates of the Tree of Life*; Aaron, D.A., *Endless Light: The Ancient Path of the Kabbalah to Love, Spiritual Growth, and Personal Power*; Gillman, N., *The Death of Death: Resurrection and Immortality in Jewish Thought* and Little, G. *Grand Illusions: The Spectral Reality Underlying Sexual UFO Abductions, Crashed Saucers, Afterlife Experiences, Sacred Ancient Sites, and Other Enigmas*) much of the following material has been derived from a careful analysis of the outstanding book, *Jewish Views of the Afterlife*, written by the eminent psychotherapist, rabbinic pastor and professor, Simcha Paull Raphael. The Jewish perspective can be divided into the early biblical period, the preexilic biblical period, the postexilic biblical period, the apocryphal period, the talmudic and midrash period, the medieval period, the kabbalistic period, the Hasidic period and the current periods.

The Early Biblical Period: Abraham To The Exodus (1800-1250 B.C.) — No Afterlife

In the beginning, Judaism was concerned exclusively with the destiny of the Israelite people as a whole. The fate of the individual Israelite after death was of no concern. In the times of the patriarchs, Moses, and the Israelite tribal confederacy the Hebrew Bible says nothing about the fate of a person after death except that death is considered to be a return to the company of the deceased's family. Although there is no mention of any individual afterlife experience, death is thought to be a gathering to one's ancestors where departed family spirits cohabited within the sacred ancestral society of the family tomb. It was also a common practice then to feed the dead with food and water. The belief was that the living would sustain the dead, and the dead would protect the living.

The Preexilic Biblical Period: Joshua To Babylonian Exile (1250-586 B.C.) — Sheol Appears

In this time period, the concept of death had a changing outlook. It was now explained as a diminution of energy. Vital energy, which was called *nefesh*, existed in each person. While the individual was alive, *nefesh* was present dynamically. When the person was sick, nefesh was in a weakened state. At death, *nefesh* had a maximum loss. *Nefesh* combines breath, life force, vital energy and spirit. The concept of the individual soul leaving the body at death was unknown since *Nefesh* is the **totality** of being. When alive, a person is considered to be a *nefesh* *hayyah:* a living *nefesh,* which is a vital psychophysical being. Once the individual dies, he/she becomes a *nefesh met* which is basically deanimated energy. The living person stayed with either family, clan, tribe, or nation in the Earthly realm.

Prior to the emergence of this belief, it was accepted that the subterranean dead dwelt in the grave in the family tomb. In this time period, something new was added to accepted thought. Now, it was believed that the graves of the family, tribe, and nation united into an underground place (a subterranean region) known as *Sheol.* Sheol was considered to be the abode of the ancestral dead. Later in this time period, the Hebrew spiritual leaders believed that the dead descended into the bowels of the Earth into Sheol. In Sheol, an existence of sorts took place, but it was a faded and weakened condition. The beings existing in Sheol were know as *rephaim* (shades, ghosts, powerless ones, weak ones). However, death was still a group process with all the deceased collec-

Figure 38
Doré's depiction of the shades.
From *The Dore Illustrations for Dante's Divine Comedy.*

tively going to Sheol. Sheol has been compared to the Christian hell as illustrated by the following:

"Therefore, the nether-world (Sheol) hath enlarged her desire,
and opened her mouth without measure."
(Isaiah 5: 14).

"Thy pomp is brought down to the nether-world, And the noise of they psalteries; The maggot is spread under thee, And the worms cover thee."
(Isaiah 14: 11).

"Yet thou shalt be brought down to the nether-world.
To the uttermost parts of the pit."
(Isaiah 14: 15).

Nevertheless, Sheol was considered to be neither good nor bad. At this point in time, God was the personal God of the Israelites, and Sheol was a realm outside of His concern. It was thought that God dwelt in the heavens, humans dwelt in the earth, and the dead dwelt in Sheol. Sheol was not a region of terror or punishment. It was simply where the deceased — rich and poor, saints and sinners — went and where the relations and customs of Earthly life were reenacted. The disembodied beings in Sheol also had the power to be aware of the Earthly realm and interact with the humans there as is shown in the following passage:

"And the woman said to Saul: I see a godlike being coming up from the earth. And he said unto her: What form is he of? And she said: An old man cometh up; and he is covered with a robe. And Saul perceived that it was Samuel, and he bowed with his face to the ground, and prostrated himself."
(First Samuel 28: 13-14).

However, the disembodied entities residing in Sheol were in a weakened and faded condition. Nor was Sheol a pleasant place judging by these descriptions:

"Before I go whence I shall not return, Even to the land of darkness and of the shadow of death; A land of thick darkness, as darkness itself; A land of the shadow of death, without any order, And where the light is as darkness."
(Job 11: 21-22).

"They shall go down to the bars of the nether-world,
When we are at rest together in the dust."
(Job 17: 16).

"Her house is the way to the nether-world,
Going down to the chambers of death."
(Proverbs 8: 27).

As mentioned before, one of the names (or descriptions) for the inhabitants of Sheol was **shades** as depicted in these passages:

"But he knoweth not that the shades are there;
That her guests are in the depths of the nether-world."
(Proverbs 10:18).

"The shades tremble Beneath the waters and the inhabitants thereof.
The nether-world is naked before Him, And Destruction hath no covering."
(Job 26: 5-6).

"The man that strayeth out of the way of understanding
Shall rest in the congregation of the shades."
(Proverbs 21:16).

The Postexilic Biblical Period: Babylon Exile To The Hellenistic Era (586-200 B.C.) — Sheol Becomes A Temporary Stop-Off Place

In this time period, the concept of God changed from being the local God of the Israelites to being the God of the entire universe. As such, He had control of everything including Sheol. This being the case, all deceased people did **not** have to go to Sheol as seen in the following:

"Like sheep they are appointed for the nether-world; Death shall be their shepherd; And the upright shall have dominion over them in the morning; And their form shall be for the nether-world to wear away, That there be no habitation for it. But God will redeem my soul from the power of the nether-world; For He shall receive me."
(Psalms 49: 15-16).

"The cords of death compassed me, And the straits of the nether-world got hold upon me; I found trouble and sorrow. But I called upon the name of the Lord; "I beseech Thee, O Lord, deliver my soul. Gracious is the Lord, and righteous; Yea our God is compassionate. The Lord preserveth the simple; I was brought low, and He saved me."
(Psalms 116: 3-6).

As previously mentioned, in the preexilic biblical period, the deceased could interact with the living, but now that could no longer occur:

"Thou hast laid me in the nether-most pit, In dark places, in the deeps. Thy wrath lieth hard upon me, And Thy waves Thou pressest down. Thou hast put mine acquaintance far from me; thou hast made me an abomination unto them; I am shut up, and I cannot come forth."
(Psalms 88: 7-9).

"Oh that Thou wouldest hide me in the nether-world, That Thou wouldest keep me secret, until Thy wrath be past."
(Job 15: 13).

In this period, Sheol also became a realm of retribution for the enemies of Israel:

"...the word of the Lord came unto me, saying: Son of man, wail for the multitude of Egypt, and cast them down, even her, with the daughters of the mighty nations, into the nether parts of the earth, with them that go down into the pit."
(Ezekiel 32: 17-18).

As Sheol became a destiny for the enemies of Israel, it became accepted belief that not every deceased Israelite had to go there. The possibility of a righteous deceased entity that could be with God after death suddenly became possible:

"And when after my skin is destroyed, Then without my flesh shall I see God."
(Job 20: 26).

However, there was a further change in the role Sheol played in the afterlife. Sheol took on the role of a temporary stop-off place following death. The righteous deceased who deserved redemption would wait for an undetermined time period in Sheol. Then, when the messiah (redeemer) came, the deceased would be resurrected from the dead (along with their bodies) and enjoy the wonderful messianic kingdom. As discussed before, a concept of a final resurrection had previously appeared in Zoroastrianism. Here during the postexilic biblical period, at first, it was described as a resurrection of all of Israel. This is shown in the following passage:

"The....Lord carried me out in a spirit, and set me down in the midst of the valley, and it was full of bones....And He said unto me: Son of man, can these bones live? And I answered: O Lord God, Thou knowest. Then he said unto me: Prophesy over these bones, and say unto them: O ye dry bones, hear the word of the Lord:... Behold, I will cause a breath to enter into you, and ye shall live. And I will lay sinews upon you, and cover you with skin, and put breath in you, and ye shall live... So I prophesied ...and the bones came together, bone to its bone. And I beheld, and, lo, there were sinews upon them, and flesh came up, and skin covered them above; but there was no breath in them. Then said He unto me: Prophesy...and say to the breath: Thus saith the Lord God: Come from the four winds, O breath,... and breathe upon these slain, that they may live." So I prophesied...and the breath came into them, and they lived, and stood up upon their feet, an exceeding great host. Then He said unto me: ...these bones are the whole house of Israel; behold they say:

Our bones are dried up, and our hope is lost; we are clean cut off. Therefore ...say unto them: Thus saith the Lord God: Behold, I will open your graves, and cause you to come up out of your graves, O My people; and I will bring you into the land of Israel. And ye shall know that I am the Lord, when I have opened your graves, and caused you to come up out of your graves, O My people. And I will put My spirit in you, and ye shall live, and I will place you in your own land; and ye shall know that I the Lord have spoken, and performed it, saith the Lord."

(Ezekiel 37: 1-14).

Figure 39
Doré's depiction of the Valley of Dry Bones—
Dante's Divine Comedy.

Later, the resurrection of deceased individual entities is addressed:

> "Thy dead shall live, my dead bodies shall arise. Awake and sing,
>   ye that dwell in the dust. For Thy dew is as the dew of light,
>   And the earth shall bring to life the shades."
>   (Isaiah 26: 19).

However, if a person had been evil, resurrection would be unfavorable as is shown here:

> "And many of them that sleep in the dust of the earth shall awake, some to
> everlasting life, and some to reproaches and everlasting abhorrence."
>   (Daniel 12: 2).

Therefore, as the biblical time periods came to a close, the Jewish disembodied being was believed to reside in Sheol as a temporary resting place. Upon the arrival of the messiah the disembodied spirit would be united with its physical body and resurrected to enjoy the messianic kingdom. However, if a person was evil during life, his future "reward" would not be blissful. In fact, it could be unpleasant. This belief set the stage for the later idea of heaven and hell as intermediate destinations of the disembodied entity before the arrival of the messianic kingdom and resurrection.

The Apocryphal Period: Heaven And Hell

The apocryphal period spans the centuries from 200 B.C. to 200 A.D. During this time, Jewish writers from inside and outside of Palestine produced a collection of literature that was not included in the Hebrew Bible. The collective texts are known as the *Apocrypha* and the *Pseudepigrapha*. One of the most complete is *3 Enoch: The Hebrew Book of Enoch*. Fifteen of the apocryphal texts are included in the Catholic Bible. The *Pseudepigrapha* are not included in either Bible. It is in this time period that the belief in an individual soul as separate from the body emerges. Enoch stated that all humans are a part of God's creation. Each person's individual soul represents a piece of God. The belief that was first brought up in the Book of Daniel was now emphasized. That is, there will be separate fates for good and evil people after death. The idea of the dualism of body and soul (with the soul surviving the dead body) is addressed in the apocryphal period literature several times:

"Evildoers will go down into Sheol...into the place of judgment
they will descend. And into the darkness of the depths
they will all be removed with a cruel death."
(Jubilees 7: 29).

"Woe to you who spread evil to your neighbors!..,
for you will be slain in Sheol."
(1 Enoch 99: 11).

"Their bones (the righteous) will rest in the earth
and their spirits will increase in joy."
(Jubilees 23: 31).

Sheol is now described as an assembly place for the deceased souls who wait for the judgment time:

"These beautiful corners are here in order that the spirits of the souls
of the dead should assemble into them they are created so that the souls
of the children of the people should gather here. They prepared these
places in order to put the souls of the people there until their day of their
judgment and the appointed time of great judgment is upon them."
(1 Enoch 22: 3-4).

In this same time period, a new term comes into use: *Gehenna*. Gehenna was used as a synonym for Sheol, and both terms represent the equivalent of hell:

"In those days, Sheol will return all the deposits which she had
received and Gehenna will give back all that which it owes. And
He shall choose the righteous and the holy ones from among the risen
dead, for the day when they shall be selected and saved has arrived."
(1 Enoch 51: 1-3).

Sheol also becomes a place of torture — a veritable hell with various punishments such as fire, burning and darkness:

"Woe unto you sinners who are dead!...You yourselves know that they
will bring your souls down to Sheol; and they shall experience evil

and great tribulation in darkness, nets, and burning flame."
(1 Enoch 103: 7).

"And with all their glory and their splendour, and in shame and in slaughter and in great destitution, their spirits shall be cast into the furnace of fire."
(1 Enoch 98: 3).

"Know that their souls will be made to descend into Sheol, and they shall be wretched in their great tribulation. And into darkness and chains and a burning flame where there is grievous judgment shall your spirits enter; and the great judgment shall be for all the generations of the world. Woe to you, for you shall have no peace."
(1 Enoch 63: 10).

During this time period, heaven made its first appearance in the apocryphal period literature. In *The Hebrew Book of Enoch*, it states that not long after Earth's creation, 200 angels fell from heaven to Earth. These fallen angels led humans astray by teaching them secrets about how the universe worked and initiated them into the practice of magic. The fallen angels taught some humans how to perform magical rituals and how other angels could be manipulated. Angels were considered to be alive, and they could appear in various shapes and forms depending upon their purpose and function.

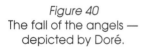

Figure 40
The fall of the angels —
depicted by Doré.

Apocryphal literature started by describing a single heaven, then four heavens, then seven heavens (which in the third heaven includes hell and paradise) and finally the garden of Eden (Gan Eden) emerged:

"Be hopeful, because formerly you have pined away through evil and toil. But now, you will shine like the lights of heaven, and you shall be seen; and the windows of heaven will be opened for you... You are about to be making a great rejoicing like the angels of heaven." (1 Enoch 104: 2, 4).

"When the Holy One, blessed be he, went out from the garden to Eden, and from Eden to the garden, from the garden to the heaven, and from heaven to the garden of Eden, all gazed at the bright image of his Shekhinah (feminine aspect of God) and were unharmed." (3 Enoch 5: 5-6).

It is also in this period that a third category of souls is designated. First are the wicked souls who go to Sheol (Gehenna) for punishment. Second are the good souls who go to heaven (paradise, Gan Eden) for bliss. The third category of souls are the intermediate souls who are partially defiled and can go through post-mortem purification and then can continue on to heaven as is shown here:

"Samkiel (one angel of destruction) is in charge of the souls of the intermediate, to support them and purify them from sin, through the abundant mercies of the Omnipresent One. Zaapiel (another angel of destruction) is appointed to bring down the souls of the wicked from the presence of the Holy One, blessed be he, from the judgment of Schechina to Sheol to punish them with fire in Gehinnom with rods of burning coal." (3 Enoch 44: 1-2).

Up to this point in time, there were two concurrently running beliefs regarding the soul. The principal one was that at the end of days when the messiah would come, all worthy souls would be reunited with their physical bodies and live in bliss. Unworthy ones would be condemned to Sheol (Gehenna). However, with the concept of the separation of the soul at death, there arrived the belief that each individual soul had to have a fate until the end-of-days. This was considered to be the plan: Immediately following the soul's emergence from the dead body, seven days would pass during which the soul reviewed and considered its various possible postmortem options. Then the individual souls, dependent upon their merit, were either assigned to abodes reserved for the wicked or the righteous. Each abode had seven realms. The souls remained there until the end-of-days with the ultimate resurrection and final assignment occurred:

> "Now, concerning death, the teaching is: When the decisive decree has gone forth from the Most High that a man will die, as the spirit leaves the body to return again to him who gave it, first of all it adores the glory of the Most High. And if one of those who have shown scorn and not kept the way of the Most High, and who have despised his Law, and who have hated those who fear God such spirits shall not enter into habitations but shall immediately wander about in torments, ever grieving and sad in seven ways..."
>
> (4 Ezra 7: 78-79).

"There shall be a judgment upon all including the righteous. And to all the righteous He will grant peace. He will preserve the elect...They will belong to God and they will prosper and the light of God will shine unto them....He will

destroy the wicked ones and censure all flesh on account of everything that they have done, that which the sinners and the wicked ones committed against him."

(1 Enoch 1: 8-9).

Hence, it can be seen in the apocryphal time period, the soul achieved a separate identity. The righteous souls would go to heaven. The wicked souls would go to Sheol (Gehennah) the equivalent of hell.

The intermediate souls would be

purged and, when purified, would go to heaven. At the end of days, when physical resurrection would take place, the souls would leave their temporary resting places for final judgment.

The Rabbinic Period: The Soul's Journey

The earlier concepts about the soul and its destiny were further elaborated during the rabbinic period of the *Talmud* and *Midrash*. This time period lasted from 70 A.D. to 800 A.D. The writings produced during this period were based on interpretations of the Hebrew Bible, the *Apocrypha* and the *Pseudepigrapha* plus additional legalistic and moralistic literature and interpretations. They are known as the *Talmud* (composed of the *Mishnah* and the *Gemara*) and the *Midrash*.

The earliest of these writings was the *Mishnah*, which was compiled in the late second century A.D. The *Gemara* was written between the third and fifth centuries A.D. Two separate Talmuds were written, one in Babylonia (the *Babylonian Talmud*) and one in Jerusalem (the *Jerusalem [Palestinian] Talmud*). The *Midrash* is primarily a compilation of interpretations of the Hebrew Bible. Within both *Talmud* and *Midrash* are found discussions of the

Figure 41
Heaven or Hell: What's Your Choice? by Marvin Herring, May 4, 1999.

soul and its journeys. The basic concept they assert is that the way a person served God and fulfilled the commandments while alive determined that individual's fate in the afterlife. The relative importance given to this life and the afterlife were sometimes contradictory as shown in the following:

"Better is one hour of bliss in the World to Come (Olam-Ha-Ba)
than the whole of life in this world (Olam Ha-Zeh)......Better is
one hour of repentance and good works in this world (Olam Ha-Zeh)
than the whole of life of the World to Come (Olam-Ha-Ba)."
(Mishnah Avot, M. Avot: 17).

Nevertheless, most often the rabbis stressed the importance of doing good deeds in this life. With regard to the afterlife, for most of the rabbis, the world to come was at the end-of-days when the messiah would arrive. However, some rabbis stressed an immediate afterlife following death as is shown here:

"But there is no basis for the assumption that the world to come will only begin after the destruction of this world. What it does imply is that when the righteous leave this world, they ascend on high...."
(Tanhuma, Vayikra 8).

There is also disagreement on whether the soul alone will be judged or whether the body and the soul will be judged together at the time of the resurrection:

"He will overlook the body and censure the soul, and when it pleads, Master of the Universe! The two of us sinned alike, so why do You overlook the body and censure me? He answers, The body comes from below where people sin; but you come from above where sin is not committed. Therefore I overlook the body and censure you."
(Leviticus Rabbah 4: 5).

'The Holy Blessed One puts the soul back into the body and judges them both as a single being. He calls on the heavens to bring forth the soul and he calls on the earth below so that he can judge the body along with it."
(Sanhedrin 91a).

The rabbis also discussed various ways that the soul departs the body — with the manner of departure reflecting the type of person involved. A righteous individual would have his soul depart similarly to drawing a hair out of milk, while an evil person would have his soul depart similarly to pulling a tangled rope out of a narrow opening:

"How does the soul depart? R. Yohanan said: "Like rushing waters
from a channel (when the sluice bars are raised)"; R. Hanina said:
"Like swirling waters from a channel;" R. Samuel said: "Like a moist
and inverted thorn tearing its way out of the throat."
(Ecclesiastes Rabbah 6: 6,1).

Interestingly, recent findings (discusssed by Dr. Joanne McMahon at the 1999 Annual Conference of "The Academy of Religion and Psychical Research") have shown that fear and anger accelerate rigor mortis. Normally, upon death, the body's muscles relax. Rigor mortis, a rigid constriction of the muscles of the body, begins between two to six hours after death. However, when people die fearfully or angrily, rigor comes on sooner and is much stronger. A rare and related phenomenon is known as cadaveric spasm. In contrast to rigor mortis, it begins immediately after death. Amazingly, it is brought on by great psychological anxiety or tension. It has been observed in some suicidal deaths. Individuals have been seen grasping branches of trees or shrubs following accidental falling. Soldiers dying on the battlefield sometimes rigidly hold onto their rifles. Could it be that not only evil people — but people who die with anger or great fear — also have their soul depart with a great deal of resistance?

At the moment of death as the soul departs, a noise is supposed to occur. (Some NDErs have reported hearing a noise as they elevated out of their bodies.) This viewpoint is shown here:

"....when the soul departs from the body, the cry goes forth from
one end of the world to another, and the voice is not heard."
(Pirke de Rabbi Eliezer, Chapter 34).

Another phenomenon that has been reported by many NDErs is a life review. This was also discussed by the rabbis:

"When a man is righteous, his righteousness is recorded; when a
righteous man arrives at the end of his days, his recording angels

Figure 42
The Angel of
Death or the
Doctor: Who
Will Win?
by
Marvin Herring,
July, 1996.

precede him into heaven singing his praise....But when a wicked man dies, a man who did not bring himself to turn in repentance to God, the Holy Blessed One, says to him: Let your soul be blasted in despair! How many times did I call upon you to repent, and you did not."
(Pesikta Rabbati 44: 8).

It is in the rabbinic literature that the Angel of Death (*malakh hamavett*) first appears. (In *Figure 42*, Marvin Herring's cartoon shows a modern interpretation of a fight between a doctor and the angel of death for a dying patient.) Accompanying the Angel of Death was a colleague of his named *Dumah*, who was the caretaker of the souls of the departed:

(After the Angel of Death takes the soul from an individual's body), "the man dies right away, but his spirit comes out and sits on the tip of his nose until the body begins to decay. As decay sets in, the spirit weeping, cries out to the Holy Blessed One, saying: Master of the universe, where am I to be taken? Immediately Dumah takes the spirit and carries it to the courtyard of the dead, to join the other spirits."
(Midrash on Psalms 11: 6).

The rabbis believed that even in the grave, one could still feel pain and communicate with both living and heavenly realms. It was in this time period that the belief emerged that, immediately after death, both body and soul went through a process of physical torment. The rabbis also stated that during the first three days after death, the soul remained close to the body:

> "For three days after death the soul hovers over the body, intending to reenter it, but as soon as it sees its appearance change, it departs."
> (Leviticus Rabbah 18: 1).

As previously discussed, this is similar to a Zoroastrian belief. In another rabbinical account, it was the first seven days during which the soul remains close to the body:

> "All the seven days of mourning the soul goes forth and returns from its former home to its sepulchral abode, and from its sepulchral abode to its former home. After the seven days of mourning, the body begins to breed worms and it decays and returns to dust as it originally was...and returns to the place whence it was given, from heaven, as it is said, And the soul returns unto God who gave it."
> [Ecclesiastes 12: 7] (Pirke de Rabbi Eliezer, Chapter 34).

The rabbis used the term Gehenna or *Gehinnon* as a place for the wicked rather than the previous Sheol. Gehenna was equivalent to hell.

However, even a person who sins and merits the punishment of Gehenna can avoid it if he/she repents and does good deeds. It was in this era that the rabbis stated that, in most cases, the time a soul remained in Gehenna was for a maximum of twelve months. However, certain evil doers who showed no sign of repentance could stay there forever. Nevertheless, for the vast majority of souls, Gehenna was a place for purging one's sins and for purification. Afterwards, the soul would go to *Gan Eden* (the heavenly garden of Eden where the righteous souls dwell).

It is stated in the *Midrash* that before the righteous can enter Gan Eden they are shown Gehenna and vice versa. (Somewhat related to this is the report of the woman whom I interviewed about her NDE. As described in Chapter 3, she said that she had seen a glimpse of hell, but God told her that it was the pit and it wasn't for her.)

In this time period, Gan Eden was usually considered a place for the righteous to go during the messianic era. However, it is also mentioned as an after-death destination:

> "...these, when they die, I lay down with great honor under the
> tree of life in Gan Eden; and I give them rest in their graves."
> (Pesikta Rabbati 50: 1).

Here, for the first time, the *Midrash* describes a place in the highest region of Gan Eden where the souls of the righteous gather. It is known as *otzar* or "divine treasury":

> "Both the souls of the righteous and those of the wicked alike ascend
> above, but those of the righteous are placed in the divine treasury,
> while those of the wicked are cast about on earth."
> (Ecclesiastes Rabbah 3: 18).

Somewhat related to the "divine treasury" is the "treasury of life," "bundle of life," or "bond of life." In Hebrew, it is known as *tzror ha-hayyim*. It was a holding place for souls in the highest spheres of Gan Eden. It is related to the ancient Greek concept (discussed previously) of the preexistence of souls in a transcendent realm. The *Midrash* also discusses a storehouse of souls where the souls stay prior to being physically embodied. This storehouse is known as "body" (*guf*). The idea was that all preexistent souls descended from the *guf* into physical incarnation. After death, righteous souls returned to *otzar* (divine treasury).

In the first century A.D., there were two major divisions in Judaism: the Sadducees and the Pharisees. The Sadducees believed that the soul totally ceased to exist at the time of physical death. Hence, their viewpoint was similar to that of Aristotle. The Sadducees, therefore, totally discounted the belief in the afterlife transit of the soul and the resurrection at the end-of-days. They denied the possibility of any post-mortem rewards and punishments. In contrast, the Pharisees believed in the afterlife transit of the soul and the end-of-days resurrection. The Pharisees' viewpoint became the predominant one and was adopted by the rabbis in the *Talmud* and the *Midrash*. Interestingly, Jesus Christ followed the Pharisees viewpoint of the end-of-days resurrection for mankind (discussed further in the Christian Viewpoints). The end-of-days resurrection of the dead was asserted for the righteous:

> "More important is a day of rain than the resurrection of the dead,
> since the Resurrection is for the righteous and not the wicked,
> whereas rain is for both the righteous and the wicked."
> (Taanit 7a).

Interestingly, it was generally considered that the end-of-days resurrection would take place in Israel. This is believed yet today by some, who, regardless of where they live, arrange to be buried in Israel. The basis for that is shown in the following passage:

> "Those who die outside the land of Israel will not live again....
> and those who die in the land of My delight will live again,
> but those who do not die there will not."
> (Ketubbot 111b).

Realizing that this interpretation would create a great problem for all Jews, another Midrash interpretation offered the following solution:

> "God will make underground passages for the righteous who, rolling
> through them like skin bottles will get to the Land of Israel, and when
> they get to the Land of Israel, God will restore their breath (soul) to them."
> (Pesikta Rabbati 1: 6).

By the end of the rabbinic period, the consensus was that, upon death, the body and soul would undergo a period of physical torment. Then the soul would go to Gehenna for twelve months where purgation of sins and purification would take place. Following this, the soul would travel to Gan Eden, where a blissful existence would take place until the end-of-days resurrection.

Medieval Judaism: The Luminous Soul, The Dark Soul

During the medieval time period from about 850 A.D. to 1450 A.D., the major Judaic concepts that hold true today were formulated. The rabbinical concept of physical torment of the body and soul upon death was elaborated upon and was known as judgment of the grave (*din ha-kever*). Various types of punishment occur. They are known as the pangs of the grave (*Hibbut Ha-Kever*). The severity of punishment depends upon whether the person had led a moral and righteous life or an immoral and evil life. Some rabbis state that the judgment in the grave is more severe than that in Gehenna.

In this time period, Gehenna becomes interpreted as hell, with all sorts of elaborate punishments depicted for those who had sinned during their lives The concept was an elaboration of the biblical passage:

> "...eye for eye, tooth for tooth, hand for hand,
> burning for burning, wound for wound, stripe for stripe."
> (Exodus 21: 24-25).

Just as Gehenna becomes hell, Gan Eden becomes heaven with elaborate descriptions of the heavenly realm. In the same way as with punishment for the wicked, the more righteous a person had been in his life, the more wonderful would be the heavenly rewards.

Medieval Jewish Philosophers Tackle The Afterlife

During this same time period, Jewish philosophical writings emerged as a result of a blending of rabbinic viewpoints with Greek, Christian and Arabic philosophies. The principal philosophers of this time were Saadia Gaon, Maimonides, Gersonides and Nahmanides.

Gaon's Immortal Soul

Saadia Gaon (882-942) believed that the soul was created in the human embryo by God and because of this, the soul is immortal. This belief is in conflict with the talmudic teachings of a preexistent storehouse of souls (*guf*). Although Plato believed in the nonmaterial nature of the soul, Saadia Gaon considered that the soul is comprised of a spiritual, transparent substance that is as pure as the heavenly spheres. This soul achieves luminosity as the result of the light it had received from God. This is somewhat related to the brilliant light people reported who have had NDEs (see Chapter 3).

Although the soul is a unity, it has a three-fold division into *nefesh* (appetive awareness), *ruah* (ability to experience emotions such as anger and courage), and *neshamah* (the ability to have cognition and reasoning). These separate manifestations of the soul occur because of its union with the physical body. At the time of death the soul exists as a unity.

People who were ethical and moral will have a bright and luminous soul. In contrast, Saadia Gaon cited a biblical passage to show that people who were immoral and evil will have a soiled, stained, and darkened soul. The cited biblical passage is the following:

> "When the wealth of his house is increased; For when he dieth he shall carry nothing away; His wealth shall not descend after him. Though while he lived he blessed his soul: Men will praise thee, when thou shalt do well to thyself, It shalt go to the generations of his fathers; They shall never see the light. Man that is in honour understandeth not; He is like the beasts that perish."
> (Psalms 49: 17-21).

The darkness of the soul is reminiscent of the few reports of evil people who had a dark and dismal NDE. Saadia Gaon also believed that while alive, a person is capable of repentance (*teshuvah*), and the tarnished soul can be purified. However, once a person died, his soul could no longer be purified. The rewards or punishments will take place at the end-of-days. The righteous would have luminescent light in Gan Eden; the wicked would have a burning fire in Gehenna. Saadia Gaon followed the rabbinical concept of a physical reunion of body and soul at the end-of-days. Hence, he did not believe the possibility of reincarnation, during which a soul would enter another body. Here too, is the luminescent light reminiscent of NDEs.

Maimonides' Separate Body And Soul

Moses ben Maimon (1135-1204) was known as Rambam or most frequently, Maimonides. For Maimonides, the body and soul were completely separate. He said that the pleasures of the spiritual world could not be understood by living people. Maimonides' concept of the soul was similar to that of Aristotle — having three divisions: (1) vegetative (controls procreation and nourishment); (2) sensory (controls imagination, sense perception and movement); and (3) rational (controls reasoning).

At the time of death, the first two aspects of the soul cease. However, the rational and intellectual aspect is retained as the portion of the soul that can understand universal truths and concepts. It is important for the living person to advance intellectually because then, he/she will be able to know the spiritual world and eventually attain immortality of the soul. For people who were moral and righteous, the third part of the soul experiences the bliss of the "World to Come" (*Olam Ha-Ba*). The World to Come is a spiritual realm that is entered by righteous souls immediately after death.

The blissful state of the soul in the World to Come is incomprehensible for a living person. Maimonides stated that there is no comparison between the bliss of the soul in the hereafter and the feelings of joy, pleasure or even euphoria that living people experience. The spiritual bliss is incomparable and unsearchable. This is also reminiscent of the reports of people who have had a NDE. Almost every one of them has stated that the bliss that they felt in the experience was beyond comprehension and impossible to adequately communicate.

Maimonides further stated that people who were evil and wicked would not receive the pleasures of the World to Come. They would be excluded from that domain and remain as isolated matter.

Maimonides, however, still followed the traditional concept that, at the end-of-days, there will be a physical resurrection of body and soul. However, he stated that this resurrection will only be for the righteous. Nevertheless, Maimonides is contradictory in his writings. Sometimes it appears that after death, the righteous soul goes immediately to the blissful World to Come. At other times, his writings stated that the World to Come is an end-of-days event. There is also some confusion about resurrection. Maimonides stated that here will be a physical resurrection of souls with their own bodies, and these resurrected beings will live a long life in the messianic era. Eventually, the resurrected dead will return to the dust. Then, the immortal souls will exit their bodies and continue to exist in a form similar to the angels.

Gersonides' Two Intellects

Levi ben Gershom (1288-1344) was known as Ralbag by the Jews and Gersonides by the Christians. He considered that each human has two intellects: a human (material) intellect; and an agent (acquired) intellect. When the person dies, the human intellect is lost. The knowledge that was acquired through the use of the human intellect remains as part of the agent intellect and is immortal. So for Gersonides, the soul is the acquired knowledge that becomes part of the agent intellect. No new knowledge can be acquired after death. Therefore, post-death intellectual enjoyment is a reflection of what the person acquired during his/her lifetime. This is similar to Maimonides' viewpoint about the importance of acquired knowledge. These concepts are reflective of the NDEs of many who have reported that they received the message that the attainment of knowledge is very important as a preparation for the afterlife.

Nahmanides' Two Edens

Moses ben Nahman (1194-1270) was known as Rambam or most frequently, Nahmanides. He believed that when an individual died, his/her deeds are evaluated and rewarded or punished. The completely righteous souls are immediately inscribed and sealed and enter Gan Eden. Nahmanides mentioned that there are two Gan Edens: a lower one; and a higher one. This concept is elaborated on by the kabbalists (discussed next).

The completely wicked are immediately sealed and sent to Gehenna for their punishment. Punishment is given in proportion to one's deeds. Most souls are in Gehenna for a maximum of twelve months. The thoroughly wicked remain there for many generations. For most souls, after twelve months, they enter Gan Eden, but their experience there is not nearly as blissful as that of the completely righteous. Those souls which are intermediate between the righteous and the wicked cry out in prayer and are sent to a place of tranquillity.

The next judgment takes place at the end-of-days when the body and soul are united during resurrection. Hence, unlike Maimonides who makes contradictory statements about the World to Come, for Nahmanides, the righteous go to Gan Eden after death, and remain there until the end-of-days when resurrection of body and soul occurs in the World to Come.

Nahmanides also introduces a new concept known as the "World of Souls" (*olam ha-neshamot*). This is the realm that the righteous soul enters immediately upon death. (Previously, Nahmanides had considered this to be Gan Eden.) His concept was that at the end-of-days, when the messianic era is ushered in and the resurrection of the dead occurs, then God will create the World to Come. In the World to Come, the bodies will exist along with their souls. The righteous souls will be in a most elevated state in their bodies, and the people will then exist for ever and ever. Nahmanides, therefore, disagreed with Maimonides, who considered the World to Come to be an immortal realm — but only for souls.

Kabbalah: The Wondrous Jewish Mysticism

"A man's good deeds done in this world draw from the celestial
resplendency of light a garment with which he may be invested when
he comes to appear before the Holy Blessed One. Appareled in that raiment,
he is in a state of bliss and feasts his eyes on the radiant effulgence."
(Zohar II, 141b).

Kabbalah (Qabala, Cabala) is the major formalized type of Jewish mysticism. It developed in Provence (formerly a separate country, now a part of France) and Spain from the thirteenth-to fifteenth centuries and in Palestine in the sixteenth century. Nevertheless, some believe that it actually originated in ancient Sumer as a religion separate and distinct from Judaism. Babylon succeeded Sumer, and the ancient teachings were then transmitted to the Hebrews who were held captive in Babylon. In this viewpoint, many elements of their ancient religion were incorporated into the Book of Genesis of the Hebrew Bible (the *Torah*). It is then believed that in the second century, the Jews added to the kabbalistic lore with a book known as the *Sepher Yetzirah*.

In the thirteenth century, the principal text of the Kabbalah was written. It is known as the *Zohar* and is a mystical commentary on the *Torah*. The *Zohar* soon came to the attention of Christian scholars and initiated an interest in the *Kabbalah* by a wide range of European occultists and mystics. Hence, the *Kabbalah* became an important component of such groups as the Rosicrucians and Freemasons. Others who later incorporated kabbalistic teachings into their teachings were the Theosophists and the Golden Dawn. Collectively, these groups were known as Anglo-Kabbalah. An essential teaching of the *Kabbalah* is that those patterns that govern the universe's operation are found in the deepest soul of a human, as well as the forces that drive those patterns.

Before considering the kabbalistic viewpoint of the afterlife journey of the soul, first it is necessary to consider the kabbalistic idea of the soul in the living person.

The Living Soul

The soul is unified, but it has three levels for most individuals (first considered by Saadia Gaon) and two higher, sublime levels of intuitive cognition that can only be within the reach of a few chosen people. The levels are:

Nefesh

This is the lowest level of the soul and is known as appetitive awareness or bioenergetic field. It is the vital energy of the physical body that animates and preserves it. *Nefesh* originates at the moment of birth.

Ruah

This is the second level of the soul and is known as emotional awareness or emotional energy field. *Ruah* is the emotional or feeling aspect of the soul.

Neshamah

This is the third or supernal level of the soul and is known as intellect, transpersonal self and higher mind. *Neshamah* is the intellectual, mental or thinking aspect. It is a bridge between human and divine levels of the soul.

Hayyah

This is a subconscious level of the soul and is known as spiritual, divine life force or universal self. *Hayyah* could be achieved by some during meditation, and it is a connection to the source of Eternal Life, God.

Yehidah

This is the highest level of the soul where all the soul's facilities are unified with God. *Yehidah* is known as essence, innermost uniqueness and transcendental field of light. It can only be achieved by few people while still alive. It would require a very deep level of meditation to possibly reach this level.

The Voyage Of Your Afterlife Soul

Now, let us consider the post-mortem fate of your soul. As you die, you are blessed with a vision of the *Shekhinah*, the female essence of God. The *Shekhinah* appears as a formless, radiant image. When your soul sees the *Shekhinah*, it goes out in joy and love to meet Her. If you had been righteous during life, your soul cleaves and attaches itself to Her. If you had not been righteous, your soul is left behind and mourns for the separation from its body. The radiance and love relationship of the *Shekhinah* is reminiscent of the NDErs seeing a celestial being of light and feeling intense love.

As you die, the *Angel of Death* also makes an appearance. If you were virtuous during life, then your soul cannot be harmed by the Angel of Death. If not, then your soul is subjected to punishment. As your soul separates from your body, it has the experience of being welcomed into the post-mortem realms by deceased family members and friends. This is a common manifestation of NDEs.

While dying, you are given a life review, an instant recall of all life occurrences. As previously discussed, this phenomena has been found in other religious traditions. This is another manifestation often observed in NDEs. Now, let us consider the fate of the five integrated components of your soul.

Nefesh

This remains closely attached to your physical body and experiences the pangs of the grave (*Hibbut Ha-Kever*). This is a 3-to-7 day process. The concept originated in the Talmudic and Midrashic period. *Nefesh* remains with your dying body.

Ruah

The process of separation of your soul from its body is considered to be painful and emotional. However, the pain can be lessened. Dumah, the guardian of the dead, appears to the departing *Ruah* and asks its name. If your soul remembers its name, that will minimize its struggle to leave your body. As previously, discussed, this name concept originated in ancient Egypt with the eighth soul (*ren*). With *Kabbalah*, Ruah next experiences the "catapult" (*kaf ha-kela*): your soul is believed to be thrown about or catapulted through the postmortem realms. This can be compared to the rapid upward movement often found in NDEs. As your soul leaves, your body decomposes and separates into four elements. This is similar to the Tibetan Hinduism concept of the body's dissolution of its elements of earth, water, fire, and air (discussed previously). Once your soul departs, it becomes enveloped by a separate field of light known as a "transparent body" (*guf ha-dak*). This again is similar to the NDErs who frequently are surrounded by a brilliant light. However, you would you receive this celestial garment only if you were righteous. If you were wicked, your soul would go naked to its fate. As previously discussed, some non-righteous individuals who had NDEs did not experience the brilliant light, but rather had a hellish experience.

Ruah next goes through the twelve-month purgations of Gehenna. However, if you were righteous during life, you wear the celestial garment and do not suffer the torments of Gehenna. In contrast, if you were wicked and never repented, you could remain in Gehenna forever.

These concepts originated in the medieval period. The severity of the purgation depends upon your lifestyle — the more wicked one was, the more severe the punishment. In essence, purgation functions as an abreaction — discharge and catharsis. It is also a time for purification and allows for progressive resolution of painful, incomplete emotions. It could be seen as similar to a prolonged, intensive psychotherapy. It is the process in which *Ruah* gets to deal with unresolved and unconscious emotional issues. Hence, it can be seen that, if you had led a relatively good life and dealt with the negative emotions such as hate, anger, fear, anxiety and frustrations, very little or any punishment would occur in Gehenna. However, if you failed to learn in life how to deal with these negative emotions, there remains an opportunity to resolve them in the afterlife at Gehenna and still be able to have a blissful afterlife, as is now shown.

From Gehenna, your purified *Ruah* moves toward healing and transformation, with its next stop being Lower Gan Eden (first mentioned by Nahmanides), which is considered to be the earthly Garden of Eden. It is here that the processes of purification and preparation for entry into *Upper Gan Eden* occurs. If all goes well, your soul goes to Upper Gan Eden.

Neshamah

If you were righteous during life, this part of your soul directly enters the sublime regions of Upper Gan Eden (also first mentioned by Nahmanides), which is the realm of heavenly delights. In these regions are schools of learning and understanding. NDErs often revealed that the importance of learning was stressed to them. In Upper Gan Eden, the light is brilliant. Immersion in the divine light source serves to further purify your soul of any lingering psychic recollections of Earthly existence. Your soul then enters the "River of Light" and becomes completely purified and is ready to come before the presence of the Master of the Universe. It is of interest that a few NDErs stated that they ascended into heaven where the light was brilliant beyond description.

Hayyah and Yehidah

If you are one of the few truly enlightened people, these two aspects of your soul would be linked, and they enter the Bundle of Life or the Bundle of the Living (*tzror ha-hayyim*), the divine region where all souls are stored. It is also known as the storehouse of souls. This concept originated in the Talmudic and Midrashic period.

If you had been an ordinary person, your soul, which had gone through the various other realms and reached Upper Gan Eden thoroughly purified, now enters the *tzror ha-hayyim*. This is the center where souls are given their assignment for subsequent incarnations. This is based on the kabbalistic doctrine of *gilgul* or reincarnation of souls.

The Voyage Of Your Afterlife Soul Continues: Reincarnation And Beyond

Reincarnation is an ancient tradition that has been incorporated into various religious traditions throughout the world. For the kabbalists, reincarnation is for the purpose of the soul's restitution for the wrongdoings of a former life and to attain further perfection. Unlike Hinduism and Tibetan Buddhism, the vast majority of kabbalists did not believe in reincarnation into the bodies of animals. For the most part, they did not believe that all souls get reincarnated only those that had some imperfections remaining or had a pressing need to return to Earth.

The idea of reincarnation most probably entered the *Kabbala* through the influence of Plato, Hinduism, Tibetan Buddhism, ancient Gnostics and the Christian Cathars (discussed later). The kabbalists embraced the widespread Jewish notion of the resurrection of the dead at the end-of-days. If your soul had gone through reincarnation, the predominant belief was that only the last body that had been firmly planted and took root would have physical resurrection.

The end-of-days resurrection is not the ultimate state. The belief is that your fully awakened soul with its spiritualized, resurrected body will have itself fully actualized. This will occur when your soul merges with the source of the Divine Being.

Because of all of the above, for the kabbalists, the idea of death was not distressful or anxiety-provoking. This is because they considered that death was not the end but rather another phase in the continuous process of coming closer to God.

Kabbalah, NDEs And Related Psi Phenomena

The kabbalistic viewpoint is very important to our discussion. The reason is that the kabbalistic afterlife journey occurrences are similar to many of the components of the NDE and associated psi phenomena. These include: the catapulted surge out of the physical body; the brilliant light; the Celestial Being of Light; meeting deceased relatives and friends; a life review; and learning that love and learning are the most important aspects. Also, that only virtuous people have this splendid afterlife. Evil people have to suffer in their afterlife journey. This is also found in certain NDEs when criminals and people who attempt suicide often have hellish episodes.

Hasidism: Mystical Judaism
With A "Righteous One"

Hasidism is a mystical Jewish movement that was founded in the mid-eighteenth century in the Ukraine by Rabbi Israel Baal Shem Tov. It emphasizes ecstatic devotion and religious fervor over scholarship and legalism. Unique to Hasidism was the concept of the righteous one (the *tzaddik*). He was considered to be an intermediary between a person and God. The *tzaddik* was the means through which a divine blessing (*shefa*) was transmitted to people. The *tzaddik* was also considered to be a spiritual redeemer of souls. The *tzaddik* was conceived as a holy man who had the powers to control life and death and to travel in the worlds beyond death in ways similar to that of shamans of many different primitive cultures. Hasidism integrated the concept of the *tzaddik* with the kabbalistic viewpoint of the journeys of the postmortem soul. Now, let us consider the current viewpoints.

Current Jewish Viewpoints

The major divisions of current Judaism are Orthodox, Conservative, Reform and Reconstructionist. The Orthodox adheres to strict biblical, talmudic and midrashic interpretations. Each successive movement is less strict in its interpretations. Each division has some concept of the afterlife, but much more attention is placed on living one's life fully in God's way. Every year from Rosh Hashanah to Yom Kippur, all are judged by God on their deeds for the preceding year, and the result determines whether they will live or die. Nevertheless, with the renewal of interest in spirituality and Kabbalah and concern with life after death, these concepts are becoming more popular in Judaism as a whole.

Kabbalah At The Forefront

Of all the Judaic concepts, for afterlife considerations, the kabbalistic viewpoint is most important. The major lesson learned from *Kabbalah* is that, you — as a virtuous person — would have the best possibility to reach a blissful afterlife. If you learned how to control your negative emotions (for example, anger, hate, fear, jealousy) by using positive stress management techniques such as meditation and psychological counseling, the need for emotional purging in the afterlife would be greatly decreased, if not eliminated. In addition, if you had stress management training while alive, you would have a shorter and less painful postmortem and would have a better chance to avoid reincarnations. As has been discussed previously, similar viewpoints had been found in a branch of Hinduism, Zoroastrianism, and a branch of Buddhism. It is also a major basis of the personal afterlife concept as is discussed in Chapter 15.

The Christian Soul
And Its Afterlife Travels

"The Christians came to believe that on the Cross of Jesus,
God and death were locked in mortal combat; and it was death, not God,
which died. What happened to Jesus was not a declaration of the inherent
immortality of the human soul, after the doctrine of Socrates, but a decisive
victory by God over the forces of death whereby resurrection was achieved.
Death can no longer isolate us from God. God has entered the realm of
death and by so doing has ensured the death of death.
(Perry, Michael, "The Soul and its Immortality," in: Batey, B.
[Ed.], *Personal Survival of Bodily Death*, The Academy of
Religion and Psychical Research, Bloomfield, CT, 1995, p. 26).

Christian viewpoints about the soul and its afterlife travels can be
divided into the early Christian mystery sect of Gnosticism, other early
Christian mystics and modern Christianity. First, let us consider how
Christianity developed from Judaism.

Jesus Christ made his appearance around the time when the Jews
lived in Israel but were kept as slaves by the Romans. As described
before, the Jews were looking forward to the arrival of the Messiah.
However, their primary concern was for a leader to come and remove
them from Roman slavery similar to how Moses had removed the
Hebrews from Egyptian slavery. Hence, for the vast majority of Jews
alive when Jesus began his mission, the idea of a Messiah who would
lead them to a heavenly kingdom was not particularly appealing. That
is probably why Jesus' message was first accepted by the poor and
downtrodden Jews who had little offered them on Earth. For them, a
Kingdom of Heaven had a great deal of appeal. Therefore, after Jesus'
death and apparent resurrection, there evolved a new religion, known as
Judeo-Christianity.

The Judeo-Christians were persecuted by the Romans and might
never have had their eventual success if it were not for the visionary
revelation to Saul (renamed Paul) which changed him from a persecutor
of the Judeo-Christians into a stalwart proponent of the cause. The
division between Peter, who believed that only the circumcised could
become Christians, and Paul, who believed anyone could become a
Christian if he/she accepted Jesus Christ as the Son of God and as the

savior, was won by Paul. This gave a strong impetus to the ability of the now-named Christians to convert many other pagan groups including the idol-worshipping, polytheistic Romans.

One of the principal concepts of Christianity that differentiated it from Judaism was the replacement of the single God of Israel (YHWH) by the Trinity of the Father, the Son, and the Holy Ghost (Spirit). Another clear distinction was Christianity's major emphasis on the afterlife as opposed to Judaism's emphasis on the present life. A third distinction is that God, as portrayed in the Hebrew Bible, is changeable and can act with anger and vengeance as well as love. God, as portrayed in the New Testament, is primarily a God of Love.

Early in the development of Christianity, a division occurred between those who strictly adhered to the accredited Gospels of the New Testament and those who emphasized mystical knowledge rather than merely faith as the road to salvation. The latter group were known as the Gnostics.

The Gnostics' Hierarchy Of Heavens And Consciousness

The early Christian mystics were called Gnostics (derived from the Greek word *gnosis*, meaning knowledge). Some Gnostics considered themselves as a new Jewish sect (not a new religion) who believed they had found the Messiah. However, most Gnostics regarded themselves as part of the organized body of Christians of the early church. Nevertheless, as the organized Church gained political control of the Roman Empire, the Gnostics were persecuted. Among the works of the Gnostics are some of the early gospels including secret gospels that were not included in the New Testament. They also included in their works five Apocalypses.

Gnostic Afterlife Concepts

The principal Apocalypse is the *Apocalypse of Paul* (discovered in 1945), which discusses the early Gnostic Christian concept of what happens after death when the soul is judged: Each soul must rise as best it can through a hierarchy of heavens and face the increasingly difficult challenges posed by the guardian angels of each heaven. The book concentrates on Paul's ascent to the tenth and highest heaven. The journey starts with Paul meeting a child on the mountain of Jericho, on the way to heaven (which is symbolized by Jerusalem). The child turns out to be the Holy Spirit, who takes Paul first to the third heaven. The Holy Spirit warns Paul to be alert, for they are about to enter the realm of principalities, where there are archangels, powers and demons. The Holy Spirit also mentions that they will pass an entity that reveals bodies to a soul-seed. That is the being that takes souls and places them in new bodies for reincarnation. For the soul who wished to ascend to the highest heaven, reincarnation was to be avoided (similar to a *Kabbalah* concept). Reincarnation was a part of Christian doctrine until 553 A.D., when it and other Gnostic doctrines were suppressed.

When Paul reached the fourth heaven, the Holy Spirit encouraged him to look down on his body which was left behind on the mountain of Jericho. Paul then witnessed the judgment and punishment of another soul. The soul had been resurrected so that it could be judged at the end-of-days (similar to Jewish concepts about resurrection at the end-of-days). The soul was accused of anger, envy and murder. The soul was cast down and went into a body which had been prepared for it, and it was reincarnated (similar to the kabbalistic viewpoint of reincarnation for souls who had not been purified). In later Christian doctrine, such a soul would have been cast into hell. Considering the negative emotions of anger and envy, if such a person had practiced stress management and learned to control negative emotions while alive, he/she would have been spared that fate.

Paul then was taken to the fifth heaven where he saw his fellow apostles and a great angel holding an iron rod in his hand. The angel and three other angels, with whips in their hands, were scourging the souls of the dead and driving them on to judgment. Paul was then taken into the sixth heaven, where he saw a strong light shining down on him from the heaven above. This is again reminiscent of the *Kabbalah*, and many other religious viewpoints in which a brilliant light is featured in the afterlife. Again, it is characteristic of the NDE. Paul then is taken through the seventh heaven where he sees an old man filled with light and wearing a white garment. His throne is brighter than the sun by seven times. Again, a celestial being in white has been described in *Kabbalah*, in other religions and in the NDE. After communicating with God, Paul enters the eighth heaven and embraces the twelve disciples. Together, they rise to the ninth heaven. Finally, Paul reaches the tenth and highest heaven, where he is transformed. (In previous Jewish descriptions of the heavens, seven heavens were described.)

The *Apocalypse of Paul* never became part of standard Christian doctrine. The early Christian fathers edited it out and declared that salvation could only be attained through the Church rituals. Salvation through a personal mystical experience apart from the organized Church was cast away.

Another important Gnostic document is the *Gospel of Thomas* (discovered in 1945). Much of the gospel has the sayings of Jesus found in the other gospels. Those found only in this gospel and relevant to the afterlife are now given. The following passage relates a belief that is also found in Kabbalah and many other religions:

> "Jesus said, If your leaders say to you, Behold, the kingdom is in the sky, then the birds in the sky will get there before you. If they say to you, It is in the sea, then the fish will get there before you. Rather, the kingdom is inside you and outside you. When you know yourselves, then you will be known, and you will understand that you are children of the living Father. But if you do not know yourselves, then you live in poverty, and embody poverty"
> (Thomas, Saying #3).

Here, too, as in *Kabbalah*, many other religions and the NDE, the concept of the light is found:

> "Jesus said, I am the light that is all over things. I am all: all came forth from me, and all attained to me. Split a piece of wood, and I am there. Pick up a stone, and you will find me there"
> (Thomas, Saying #77).

Again, there is the recurrent theme of the celestial being of light as per the following:

> "Jesus said, Images are visible to people, but the light within is hidden in the Father's image of light. He will reveal himself, but his image is hidden by his light"
> (Thomas, Saying #83).

Just as much of kabbalistic theology is mystical and difficult to understand, so, too, is Gnostic theology.

Principal Gnostic Concepts

A series of falling away from the Whole that is God occurred in eternity, which led to all that exists today. After the first fall, the divine consciousness descended to the level of the divided consciousness. Now after another fall, it has fallen even further into the depths of the unconscious, where it has been forgotten. It is now up to humans to discover the potential dimensions of human existence and face the great challenge of the ascension of consciousness through the Man-God-Spirit transformation.

Once souls fell into the lower levels of consciousness, they became infatuated with it and had a strong desire to experience the pleasures of matter. The souls then no longer desired to release themselves from these lower levels. They forgot their original habitation, their true center and eternal being. The Gnostics believed that this world of ours is thoroughly and irretrievably evil. Our souls are trapped in the prison of matter, and matter is intrinsically evil. The Gnostics believed that the creation of the cosmos occurred as the result of a tragicomic mistake, which was the fall of the Soul. However, they believed that all could be saved through the advent of Jesus Christ in the lower dimensions of consciousness. The power of reconciling the fallen souls has been given by Jesus Christ. He can rebalance the Godhead and issue in the kingdom of Light over the kingdom of matter. Through him, the divine plan of creation will be restored and all of the world will be redeemed. The Gnostics believed that when more and more people hear the wake up call of Jesus and are liberated, their souls are received back into the bosom of the Universal Divine Consciousness. To return to the divine source, each soul must pass through the various levels of consciousness (considered as seven to ten). On the one hand, they were considered as heavens, and, on the other hand, they were conceived as demonic barriers between Man and God. When the souls pass through the barriers, they shall be freed from matter, and the present world shall cease to exist. The Gnostics believed that there is nothing to be done for this world but to end it.

The Pessimistic Gnostics

These Gnostic concepts are probably the most pessimistic of all ideas that we have examined so far. For the Gnostics, the one redeeming factor is salvation through Jesus Christ. However, what about all the billions of people worldwide who do not believe in Jesus Christ as the Son of God? It is hard to reconcile this concept with all the others that present a far more optimistic outcome for both the afterlife and the present Earth. Of course, the eventual fate of the Earth isn't too good anyway according to cosmological principles, but at least, most religions consider that there is not only one way to achieve salvation.

Other Early Christian Mystics

The other early Christians mystics believed in predestination. They did not believe in free will and they quoted scripture to prove their point:

> "Man lost his free will through the fall of Adam and is a slave of the devil."
> (Rom. 6: 17-18).

> "Everything, nothing excluded, was planned by
> God before the universe was created."
> (Eph. 1: 11).

> "God planned the destiny of every person before the universe was created."
> (1 Thes. 5: 9).

> "The Holy Spirit gives faith only to those predestined by God to receive Him."
> (Rom. 8: 3).

With this outlook, nothing that anyone does with respect to prayer and good deeds can help him/her in the soul's afterlife journey unless it was predetermined by God. This concept is not believed in Judaism and most other religions — with the possible exception of the Calvinists. However, these early Christian mystics then went on to contradict themselves by stating that salvation is possible through Jesus Christ. Their idea was that once you were saved, you would always be saved:

> Jesus said: "I tell you the truth, whoever hears my word
> and believes him who sent me has eternal life and will not be
> condemned; he has crossed over from death to life."
> (John 5: 24).

Jesus said: "My sheep listen to my voice, I know them, and
they follow me. I give them eternal life, and they shall never perish,
no one can snatch them out of my hand."
(John 10: 27-28).

Strict Viewpoints Of The Other Early Christian Mystics

As stated before, these early Christian mystics either believed in predetermination or the acceptance of Jesus Christ as the savior as the only path to the afterlife. In contrast, the viewpoints of most other religions with respect to the afterlife is that every person has free will in this life to act morally or wickedly, and these actions will determine his/her fate in the afterlife.

Modern Christianity:
Heaven, Hell And Purgatory

"Better to go to heaven in rags than to hell in embroidery"
(Thomas Fuller, Gnomologia, 1732).

Modern Christianity, regardless of whether it is Roman Catholicism, Eastern Orthodox Catholicism or any of the major Protestant faiths (except for Calvinism), believes in the concept of free will. Within each branch, the more strict interpretation (as with the *Fundamentalists* or *Born Again Christians*) is that, even though Jesus Christ died for everyone, only those who accept him as the savior will go to heaven. All others will go to eternal hell. In contrast, the less strict viewpoint is that righteous people, regardless of their beliefs, will have an opportunity to be saved. Here, the Christian concept of purgatory (somewhat similar to the Jewish Gehenna) allows for purging of one's sins which would be followed by salvation. Again, the strict interpretation is that heaven, hell and purgatory exist as discreet realms. The less strict interpretation is that they are more abstract. For example, rather than being a place of torture, hell is being separated from God, love, the light and one's loved ones.

Now let us examine the afterlife in some of Jesus's own words. The following assertion (God being within us) was also considered by the Kabbalah and other religions:

"The Kingdom of God commeth not with observation: Neither
shall they say, Lo here! for, behold, the kingdom of God is within you."
(Luke 17: 20-21).

The following viewpoint is also shared by kabbalistic Judaism,
that is, Earthly good deeds allow for going to Gan Eden (heaven):

"Not every one that saith unto me, Lord, Lord, shall enter into the kingdom of
Heaven; but he that doeth the will of my Father which is in heaven."
(Matthew 7: 21).

In kabbalistic Judaism, it is considered better to live a good life
and go to Gan Eden than lead an evil life and suffer Gehenna's tortures.
However, in Judaism, Gehenna (for most people) is limited to 12 months.
In this belief, which is the most strict Christian one, **hell is an eternity**:

"And if thy hand offend thee, cut it off: it is better for thee to
enter into life maimed, than having two hands to go into hell, into
the fire that never shall be quenched....And if thy foot offend thee, cut it off:
it is better for thee to enter lame into life, than having two feet to be
cast into hell, into the fire that shall never be quenched.... And if thine
eye offend thee, pluck it out: it is better for thee to enter the kingdom
of God with one eye, than having two eyes to be cast into hell fire."
(Mark 9: 43-47).

*Figure 43
Lucifer's
abode —
by Doré,
Dante's
Inferno.*

Figure 44
Jesus giving the
Sermon on the
Mount. *Doré Bible
Illustrations.*

The following is definitely not a viewpoint of Judaism (which states that a rich person can **also** be devout and righteous). Less strict Christians would also not adhere to the concept that rich people cannot enter heaven:

> "Verily I say unto you, That a rich man shall hardly enter the kingdom of heaven. And again I say unto you, It is easier for a camel to go through the eye of a needle, than for a rich man to enter into the kingdom of God."
> (Matthew. 19: 23-24).

The Divergent Viewpoints Of Strict And Liberal Christianity

As far as strict Christianity is concerned, being a righteous individual and controlling anger, hate, fear, jealousy and other negative emotions will still not prevent you from going to hell as long as Jesus Christ is not accepted. This is a viewpoint that is not compatible with our developing afterlife concept. However, this is not the viewpoint of liberal Christianity, which states that your deeds during this life determine your fate in the afterlife. As mentioned before, this concept is followed by kabbalistic Judaism, a branch of Hinduism, Zoroastrianism, and a branch of Buddhism, and is the basis of the personal afterlife concept (discussed in Chapter 15).

Islam's Reward And Punishment

Islam began in the Near East where Judaism and Christianity had footholds. It followed the other two monotheistic religions and acknowledged the validity of both Judaism and Christianity, but it considered itself the fulfillment of those earlier religions. Muhammad (571-632 A.D.), their Prophet, is considered to be the latest and most important Prophet of the one God, Allah. Of lesser importance are the Hebrew prophets such as Moses and Isaiah and Jesus Christ, who was not considered to be a Son of God, but a prophet. Muhammad is not worshipped but is regarded as God's last and greatest messenger.

Although having a strong basis in Judaism and Christianity, evidence shows that Islam's roots went back to a primitive monotheistic belief of ancient Arabia. Although this early faith in Allah was not a complete monotheism, there was a continuous tradition among the desert peoples that maintained a belief in an Originator, a Supreme Being. This High God acted as a guardian of their flocks, sender of rain, protector of their lives and defender against the hazards of fate. The belief in one God that inspired Muhammad had a strong native foundation along with its biblical roots.

The principal holy book of Islam is the *Qur'an* (*Koran*), and its major tenet is that "Allah is great." This means greater than anything conceivable. Allah is also considered to be the merciful, compassionate ruler of the world and the entire universe. He is God of the here and the hereafter. Islam is similar

THE PROPHET MOHAMMED.

Figure 45
Muhammad
From Ridpath's *History of the World* (1911)

to Judaism in the belief in the one indivisible God. This contrasts with Christianity's Trinity of the Father, Son and Holy Ghost. The one God concept is shown in the following passage:

> "Say, He is God alone. God the Eternal. He begets not
> and is not begotten. Nor is there like unto Him anyone."
> (*Koran* 112).

In one definition, Islam is considered to be the Light that Allah sent to everyone through his final Messenger Muhammad, who is the True symbol of love, the symbol of external and internal knowledge and the symbol of mercy to everyone. Islam, like Christianity, preached love of everyone. It is of interest that the concepts of light, love and knowledge appear here and in almost all other mystic traditions (for example, *Kabbalah*) and with most NDErs.

Afterlife Concepts

As far as the afterlife is concerned, Islam has been a religion of reward and punishment. The life to come (*Al-Aakhira*) is completely shaped by one's present life. Just as Judaism and Christianity believe in a resurrection at the end-of-days with a final judgment, so, too, does Islam believe in a Day of Reckoning during which the righteous shall be rewarded in paradise, and the wicked shall go to a severe and eternal fire in hell (as is the case with the strict Christians).

However, unlike Judaism and Christianity, which believe in an interim period before the end-of-days judgment, the Muslims consider that afterlife begins at the end-of-days as is shown here:

> "...when the sun is folded up, and the stars do fall, and when the
> mountains are moved, and when the she-camels ten months' gone
> with young shall be neglected...and when the seas shall surge up,
> and when the souls shall be paired with bodies....And when
> Paradise shall be brought nigh, the soul shall know what it produced."
> (Koran 81: 1-15).

Nevertheless, as with Judaism and the less strict versions of Christianity, there are ways to avoid eternal damnation. Comparable to Gehenna (of Judaism) and purgatory (of Christianity), the *Qur'an* speaks of an intermediary realm between paradise and hell where those who were half-way between evil and good in their Earthly lives will go for a time. Those who were believers in God but whose balance of evil deeds outweighed their good deeds will only experience hell for a period of time. God can and will forgive those who repent during this time. Although not specifically stated in the *Qur'an*, in one of the traditions of the Prophet Muhammad, there is the concept that even hell might not be a permanent place. In the end, God's mercy will triumph over his justice and everyone can be saved. Allah is the Mighty, the Great Forgiver.

The End-Of-Days

It can be seen that, in Islam, the afterlife is primarily concerned with the judgment at the time of the resurrection at the end-of-days. And although your fate in the afterlife is mainly determined by what you did during life, it is still possible, if you repent, to be saved in the afterlife.

Here, too, if you are a righteous God-believing person who controlled anger, hate, jealousy and other negative emotions, you can go to paradise. There is also a second chance for those of us who did not reach the necessary standards during life. One could repent while in the intermediary realm and still go on to paradise. As mentioned before, similar viewpoints are followed by kabbalistic Judaism, a branch of Hinduism, Zoroastrianism, a branch of Buddhism, and non-strict branches of Christianity and is the basis of the personal afterlife viewpoint (discussed in Chapter 15).

Sufism — Mystical Islam

The name, *Sufism*, is derived from the Arabic term, *súf* (wool), referring to the ascetic practice of wearing wool. Sufism began in the eighth century in the Middle East as a rebellion against the intellectualism and formalism of Islam that developed from the Qur'anic emphasis on the power and arbitrary sovereignty of Allah. Sufism was influenced by the Greeks, Buddhism and Hinduism, but it takes its principal characteristics from Islam. Sufism is a response to the profound aspiration of each individual for a personal relation with God and an immediate awareness of truth. A major purpose of Sufism is to gain insight into the Divine Being. Sufi mystics practice contemplation and nocturnal meditation and experience ecstasies. Ecstasy is considered to be a means for the attainment of divine knowledge.

Sufism is known as the *Way of the Heart*, the *Way of the Pure*, and the *Mystical Path of Islam*. Sufism is a means by which you can move from the gravity of your lower self to ascend, with the assistance of a mystical guide, through the methods and practices defined by the Way you have chosen, to the state wherein the Vision of God is presented to you. There are many Ways to ascend, but the essence of the path to God is to find yourself:

"The Ways to God are as numerous as the breaths of humankind."
(Sufi tradition).

"Know thyself, know thy Lord!"
(Sufi saying).

The Sufis consider each of us as a being endowed with the Divine Light with a spiritual connection to the flow of energy that penetrates the entire universe. Again, the light concept is similar to many other religions and NDEs.

In Sufism, the mystical guides are people who (through Divine Grace) have received their Trusts from God. They move around in this world as if they were part of it. However, inside their hearts and souls is the Divine Presence. The Sufis believe that if they ask something of God, their request is accepted. They look at other people who are less fortunate than themselves with the eye of mercy. These mystical guides are known as the Friends of God (*Awliya*). These special people help others to show them the ways to God.

Afterlife Concepts

The Sufism concept of the afterlife is similar to that of Islam in general. However, some beliefs are of special interest. Your rank, power or riches in life have nothing to do with what happens in the grave (similar to Judaism and less strict Christianity). Only your actions during your life will determine what is to be expected in the grave. The Sufi Masters state that we judge ourselves and send ourselves either to paradise or hell. For example, if you die angry, you will go to hell.

Being Righteous

Similar to the viewpoints of most of the previously discussed religions, it is important for you to be righteous and especially to learn stress management methods to control negative emotions such as anger and hate. This is elaborated on in the personal concept of the afterlife (see Chapter 15).

Sikhism And The Cycle Of Birth and Death

Sikhism is related to both Islam and Hinduism. It developed in the Punjab region of India in the late 1400s and mid-1500s. In this religion, an attempt is made to reconcile iconoclastic Islam with pantheistic Hinduism. The principal forerunner of Sikhism was Kabir (1450-1518). Kabir tried to unite the orthodoxy of Islam with the philosophy and theory of Hinduism. His follower was Nanak (1469-1538), who is considered to be the Father of Sikhism. Nanak had a great problem in organizing the new religion because, although Hinduism could be tolerant of Islam, Moslems considered the Hindus to be idolaters and worshippers of many gods. Nevertheless, Nanak did not give up and spent 40 years at his special mission and in the end was successful. Sikhism repudiates Hindu idolatry in favor of a strict monotheism. The first Guru (religious teacher) was Nanak, who is adored by the Sikhs. God has many names such as *Ram, Rahim, Allah, Pritam, Yar, Makhal, Waheguru* ("wonderful enlightener and wonderful Lord"), *Nam* ("the Truth"), the Word and the Name. When God is seen throughout the universe, He is known as *Sargun* ("Quality-full"). When God is realized as being transcendent, He is known as Nirgun ("Abstract").

Sikhism emphasizes the unity of God and considers that God gave both the universe and mankind free will. God has the following qualities: love, justice, charity, mercy, peace, freedom, truth and goodness. Here, too, love is emphasized as in the NDEs. When you meditate on these qualities, you unknowingly imbibe these Godly traits.

Figure 46
Ancient engraving of Guru Nanak.

As do many other religions, Sikhism believes in reward and punishment. Sikhism asserts that the wall of your ego separates your soul from God. This leads to the cycle of birth and death (death and reincarnation). This is known as *metempsychosis*, which can only be ended through meditation or the acquisition of divine grace. In life, when your soul progresses with the performance of good deeds and remembrance of the Name, it becomes worthy of merging with God. You are made up of spirit (*shiv*) and matter (*shakti*). Your body must be taken care of because it houses your soul. Therefore, the Sikhs do not believe in asceticism which is mentioned in other religions such as Christianity, Hinduism and Buddhism. A primary goal of Sikhism is union with God. Since God dwells in the body (as well as everywhere else), the body is called the "Temple of God." This is related in the following Sikh hymn:

"Whatever is found in the Universe is found in the body,
whoever searches it shall find it."

Afterlife Concepts

Sikhism's afterlife concept is somewhat different than the previous ones that have been considered. Your life on Earth is believed to be merely a stage in the upward march of your soul. You receive birth after going through lower forms of life. (In a sense, this is true as in the development of the human embryo — ontogeny recapitulates phylogeny, which means the embryo goes through evolutionary stages such as being a one-celled animal, a fish, a reptile, a bird, etc. before changing into the human form.) Your life as a human is the final stage in your soul's progress toward divinity.

Death entails the destruction of your physical self. Your immortal soul leaves your body, and its fate depends upon the type of life you led. If you had been moral and righteous, you have no fear of death because you can merge with the Almighty. If you had been wicked, you dread death, because for you, it leads to the unending cycle of death and rebirth (reincarnation). After death, your soul goes to its next birth according to what it deserves. If you had been wicked, your soul is reborn in a lower species of animal. If you had done some good deeds, your soul will be reborn in a good family. However, the cycle of death and rebirth keeps your soul away from Divinity. Your soul can only merge with God if you led a moral and righteous life. To end the cycle of death and rebirth, you, as a virtuous person, have to meditate on the Name and then you will receive divine grace.

As with other religions such as Judaism, Christianity and Islam, your deeds and misdeeds during life are weighed against each other, and this determines whether you go to heaven or hell. For the Sikhs, hell is not a literate place; rather, it is a reincarnation into a lower species. This means that your soul will be out of the presence of God. What might be considered an intermediate realm figuratively would be rebirth into a good family. However, to achieve a figurative heaven, you have to be a virtuous person who practices repentance, prayer and love, and meditates on the Name. In that way, transmigration of your soul (death and reincarnation [*metempsychosis*]) would not occur and your soul would become one with God.

Be Righteous And Meditate

For Sikhs, in order to ensure a heavenly existence, you have to live a righteous life and practice the important stress management technique of meditation. As you can see, this is similar to most previously discussed religions and the personal afterlife concept (discussed in Chapter 15).

Bahai'sm: The Religious Synthesis

A more recent religion, founded in Iran (formerly Persia) by Mizra Ali Mohammed ibn-Radhik of Shiraz (1819-1850), was known as *Babism*. He used the theory of progressive revelation and preached that no ostensible truth was final. He forbade polygamy, concubinage, mendicancy, the use of intoxicants and drugs and slave dealing. When he died in 1850, most of his followers (the Babis) were exterminated. A leader of the Babis, Mizra Husayn Ali, became known as *Bahá'u'llah* (Glory of God), and he founded *Bahai'sm*, another and more important offshoot of Islam. *Bahai'sm* is a union of many conflicting creeds and doctrines, and many ideals and mystic philosophies. It is an attempt to establish a religious synthesis for mankind.

Afterlife Concepts

There exists a separate, rational soul for every person. In this life, your soul provides the animation for your body. Your soul is your real self, but it is undetectable by physical instruments. Your soul shows itself through character qualities such as love, compassion, faith and courage. Your soul does not die; it is everlasting. When your body dies, your soul is freed from its ties with your body and the surrounding physical world, and begins its travels through the spiritual world to a timeless and placeless extension of our own universe — not to a physically removed or remote realm. Entry to the afterlife has the potential to bring great joy. Death is similar to the process of birth as depicted in the following sayings:

> "*Bahā'u'lláh* stated: "The world beyond is as different from this world as this world is different from the child while still in the womb of its mother."

Just as the womb constitutes an important place for your initial physical development, the physical world supplies the matrix for the development of your soul. Hence, life is a kind of workshop in which you can develop and perfect those qualities that will be needed in the afterlife.

> "*Bahā'u'lláh* stated: Know thou, of a truth, that if the soul of man hath walked in the ways of God, it will assuredly return and be gathered to the glory of the Beloved.....By the righteousness of God! It shall attain a station such as no pen can depict, or tongue can describe."

In *Bahai'sm*, heaven can be considered as a state of nearness to God; hell is a state of remoteness from God. Each state results as a natural consequence of your efforts, or lack of efforts, to develop spiritually. The key to spiritual progress, therefore, is for you to follow the path described in the "Manifestations of God." This concept is similar to several of the other mystical religions previously described.

What These Religions Have In Common

After reviewing what major religions believe about the soul, an afterlife and God, several important questions arise in our spiritual journey: What are their commonalties? Are they all saying the same thing in different ways? As an introduction to answering these questions, the following is a tale I heard several years ago.

262 / SEARCHING FOR ETERNITY

The Wise Rabbi

There was a rabbi known for his Solomonic understanding and great ability to resolve conflicts. One day, arriving in separate cars, a quarreling husband and wife came to see him. First, the wife entered the synagogue and told the rabbi how her husband had mistreated her, paid her very little attention, never took her out for entertainment or dining, didn't help with the household chores, and in general, was very mean and inconsiderate. The rabbi listened patiently and when the woman was finished, he told her that he understood. The wife then asked the rabbi whether he believed that she was right in what she had said. The rabbi answered: "Yes, you were right. You were definitely right." Feeling greatly relieved, the woman thanked the rabbi and left the synagogue.

A short time later, the husband entered the house of worship. He told the rabbi that his wife had been treating him very badly. She practically never had sex with him; she never wanted to do anything that he liked, such as watching football games or going to the casinos; and she never dressed up or tried to beautify herself. In general, she was very mean and inconsiderate. The rabbi listened patiently and when the man had finished, he told him that he understood. The husband then asked the rabbi whether he believed that he was right in what he said. The rabbi answered: "Yes, you were right. You were definitely right." Feeling greatly relieved, the man thanked the rabbi and left the synagogue.

Unbeknown to the rabbi, a cleaning man had been in an adjacent room and heard what both the wife and husband had said as well as the Rabbi's reply. After the husband left, the cleaning man approached the rabbi and said: "I'm sorry to bother you, Rabbi, but I was in the adjacent room when you had been talking to the wife and her husband. Everyone was speaking so loud that I couldn't help but overhear everything."

The rabbi smiled as he listened to the cleaning man. The cleaning man continued: "Rabbi, if I may be so bold, can I tell you something."

The rabbi replied: "Certainly."

The cleaning man then said: "You were wrong when you told the wife and her husband that they were both right when they were saying such diametrically opposite things about each other."

The rabbi waited a while, smiled broadly and replied; "You know what, you're right, too." (In *Figure 47*, Marvin Herring's cartoon lets us know where the rabbi got his wisdom.)

What They Are All Saying

In a sense, even though the major religions that believe in a surviving soul, an afterlife, and God state some diametrically opposite things, each one of them is right, and together they're all right. No matter what He is called, at least in their orthodox viewpoints, an omnipotent, omniscient, omnipresent and eternal God is part of all of these religions.

God judges us all, but repentance can save us from a bitter outcome. What we do on Earth can determine our future in the afterlife. A good life leads to heaven, which can be taken literally or figuratively; a bad life leads to hell, which also can be taken literally or figuratively.

In most religions, there is an intermediate stopping off place (again taken literally or figuratively) for those of us whose lives were

Figure 47
The Secret of
the Rabbi's
Wisdom by
Marvin Herring,
December 5,
1998.

between good and bad. And if our soul repents or eliminates its negative emotions (purging and purification), it has the opportunity to go to heaven. Hence it is important during life for us to learn stress management techniques such as meditation and psychotherapy to control anger, hate, jealousy, envy, guilt, fear and anxiety. The techniques might prove helpful during those intermediate realms of the afterlife.

For most of these religions, a concept of reincarnation either presently exists or existed somewhere in their development. However, along with the concept of reincarnation is the generally held belief that righteous souls do not **have** to go through reincarnation — some can attain the Divine presence directly. For most religions, a oneness with God can be attained through prayer, contemplation and meditation (all excellent stress management techniques).

In most religions, immediately after death, the soul moves toward its ultimate union with the Divine. In some religions, there is a future resurrection of the dead (body and soul) when all mankind is judged. In almost all of these religions, God is considered as a celestial being of light, who is compassionate, forgiving and emphasizes love and learning.

What is so important in our quest to overcome death anxiety is to prove, to the greatest extent possible, the existence of a surviving soul, a positive afterlife, and God. Most of these aspects are seen in all of these religions, in NDEs, and some OBEs, past life regressions, apparitions, visions and séances and medium reports. Although a complete union with God can only be achieved in the afterlife, in most religions, a glimpse of the Celestial Presence of Light can be made through prayer, meditation and visions (often during sleep). This aspect has also been shown with NDEs, related psi phenomena and with deep meditation. So, there definitely appears to be a commonality between religious concepts and NDEs and related psi phenomena.

In the next two chapters, our spiritual journey continues as we consider the afterlife viewpoints of some Protestant religions, some religious and spiritual movements, and some modern concepts of the afterlife. All of these will then be compared with the findings of NDEs, OBEs, apparitions, visions, dreams and past life regressions.

CHAPTER THIRTEEN

RECENT CONCEPTS OF THE AFTERLIFE — PART 1
IDEAS FROM GROUPS & ORGANIZATIONS

"The world of imagination is the world of eternity. It is the divine bosom
into which we shall all go after death of the vegetative body."
(William Blake).

Most recent concepts of the soul and its afterlife travels are even more elaborate than those given in the major religions. Some of these concepts occur in branches of Christianity. Others are based on ancient traditions that have been revived. Still others reflect physics and cosmology as well as ancient religious beliefs. As we continue our spiritual journey, let us now examine some of these and see if there is any continuity among them with the previously discussed major religions, and with NDEs and related psi phenomena.

The concepts covered in this chapter are those of a wide range of groups and organizations: Seventh-Day Adventists, Jehovah's Witnesses, the Christadelphians, Unitarian Universalists, Rosicrucianism, Freemasonry, the Golden Dawn, Theosophy, Eckankar, and Urantia.

Seventh-Day Adventists: The Second Coming And The Afterlife

Seventh-Day Adventists are Christians who keep the seventh day Sabbath of the Ten Commandments (the same day as the Jews). They also look forward to the second coming of Jesus Christ (The "Adventist" part of the name). The Adventists reached their climax as a definite movement in the New World between 1840 and 1844, and they were formally established as a church in 1863. The founding fathers were Ellen White, Joseph Bates and James White. The Seventh-Day Adventists are missionaries who operate throughout the world. They uphold most of the basic Christian doctrines with the following exceptions:

• They keep the seventh day as the Sabbath — a day of rest.

• There is no human soul. After death, we rest in the ground in an unconscious state (similar to Islamic belief). When Jesus Christ reappears, the resurrected righteous and the living righteous will become glorified and ascend to meet their Lord. The second resurrection — that of the unrighteous — will occur one thousand years later and they will be consumed.

• No immediate afterlife experience occurs; the afterlife begins at the time of the coming of Jesus Christ when the righteous are physically resurrected. These are concepts without non-religious verification (as is the case with NDEs).

Jehovah's Witnesses' Spirit And Soul

Jehovah's Witnesses is an international society of Christian ministers who preach God's kingdom as the only hope for mankind. Charles T. Russel (1852-1916) founded Zion's Watch Tower — presently the Watchtower — in 1879 and Zion's Watch Tower Tract Society in 1884. In 1931, under Joseph F. Rutherford's leadership (1869-1942), the name Jehovah's Witnesses was taken. Since then, the movement has greatly enlarged. At first, the Witnesses stated that the Second Coming of Christ occurred in October 1874. Later, the Society declared that Christ returned invisibly in 1914. The prophets of old were supposed to have returned in 1925. Currently, no specific date is given for the Second Coming, but it is still considered to be imminent. Jehovah's Witnesses uphold some of the basic Christian doctrines with the exception of the following:

• There was no physical resurrection of Jesus Christ — only a spirit body arose.

• There is no Trinity. (The concept of God being composed of the Father, Son and Holy Spirit originated in 325 A.D.) God is almighty, Jesus is the son of God and is a mighty god, and the Holy Spirit is God's active force.

• God speaks through their organization and salvation is only achievable through them.

• Humans do not have an immortal soul. After death, your soul dies with your body. Your body remains unconscious in the ground (similar to Islamic belief) until the time of Jesus Christ's return and the resurrection. The resurrection is of either a physical or spiritual body.

• The spirit is not synonymous with the soul. It refers to God's active force (the Holy Spirit).

As can be seen, Jehovah's Witnesses have viewpoints similar to those of the Seventh Day Adventists with respect to the non-immortality of the human soul and the absence of an immediate afterlife experience. They are rigid in their belief that salvation is only achievable through them. Again, these are concepts without non-religious verification (as is the case with NDEs).

The Christadelphians: "Brothers Of Christ"

The Christadelphians are a community of Christians who consider the Old and New Testaments as their sole authority. After 1844, John Thomas (1805-1871), who left England and came to the United States, began the teachings that evolved into the Christadelphians (name coined in 1864). The movement was formed in Birmingham, England in the early 1860s. Since then, the Christadelphians have spread worldwide. The Christadelphians uphold basic Christian concepts with the following exceptions:

• The Jews are a special part of God's purpose.

• Life on Earth is just as important as the afterlife (similar to Judaism's viewpoint).

• After death, your soul dies along with your body; hence your soul is not immortal. Your body lies unconscious in the grave (similar to Islamic belief) until the resurrection at the time of the Second Coming of Jesus Christ.

• There is no Trinity; the one God is the Father; Jesus is not God, but the Son of God.

• The Spirit is the influence and power of God.

As can be seen, the concepts of the nature of Jesus, the absence of the Trinity, the non-immortality of the soul, and no immediate afterlife experience are similar to those of the Jehovah Witnesses. The assertion of non-immortality of the soul and no immediate afterlife experience are also similar to the viewpoints of the Seventh Day Adventists. As mentioned before, these are concepts that have no non-religious verification (as is the case with NDEs).

Unitarian Universalists' Oneness

Unitarian Universalists' roots are two-fold. First, there is Origen (about 185 A.D.) who stressed the humanity of Jesus Christ and who believed that God would allow all people (even demons) to enter heaven. Second, there is Michael Sevetus who was executed at the stake in 1553 because of his treatise "On The Errors of the Trinity." Unitarianism originated about 1600 in Transylvania and Poland where a strong liberal Protestant movement flourished. The first church was established in Transylvania in 1638. The movement first arose in the English-speaking world among English Presbyterians, and, during the 17th and 18th centuries, Universalist groups formed. Unitarian and Universalist views then moved across the Atlantic Ocean to the United States. In 1779, John Murray became the minister of the first American Universalist church. Kings Chapel in Boston, which was formed as an Anglican church in 1688, became the first Unitarian church in America in 1785. The first original American Unitarian church was established in Philadelphia in 1796 by Joseph Priestley. In 1805, Hosea Ballou in A Treatise on Atonement wrote against the Trinity, hell, and the existence of miracles. In 1825, the American Unitarian Association was formed from churches that expressed Unitarian beliefs. In 1961 the Unitarian and Universalist churches merged. Prior to their merger, they were considered to be Christian churches holding heretical beliefs about the nature of God and the afterlife. During the 19th century, a gradual change occurred and continues to the present. In 1995, the combined organization acknowledged that its sources of spirituality are: (1) Christianity: (2) Judaism; (3) other world religions; (4) Earth Centered Religions (e.g., Afro-American religions, Native American spirituality, Wicca); (5) prophets; and (6) the direct experience of mystery. Relative to God, some original Unitarian/Universalists concepts are the following:

• God is one as opposed to the Christian concept of God being a Trinity.

• The Old Testament God is not just the deity for the Israelites but is the God for all humanity.

• Jesus Christ was a human rather than being the Son of God or God incarnate (similar to Judaic and Islamic viewpoints).

• Every individual has the opportunity to go to heaven.

• In hell, one retains free will and can choose to repent. A more recent viewpoint denies the existence of hell. This is in sharp contrast with the strict Christian viewpoint that one's natural destination is torment in hell and that only those living who repent of their sins and accept Jesus Christ as Lord and Savior will go to heaven. As mentioned before, this fourth belief of the Unitarian Universalists, with regard to the chance of getting out of hell, is now being accepted by more liberal branches of Christianity.

The Unitarian Universalists can be divided into three groups: Non-Christian (the majority are in this group); Christian (about one out of four are in this group); and Other Belief Systems (the rest are either agnostic or atheistic).

You can see that the original Unitarian/Universalists concepts went well beyond the previous three Christian branches in that they considered Jesus Christ to have been human, and they allowed for every individual to have the opportunity to go to heaven. These viewpoints are incorporated in the personal afterlife viewpoint (see Chapter 15). Now, religions and movements with complicated beliefs are considered.

Rosicrucianism: The Rosy Cross

The word Rosicrucian is derived from the official emblem of the Order, which is a gold cross with a single red rose in its center. The cross symbolizes the human body, and the rose symbolizes the person's unfolding consciousness and is also considered to be the equivalent of light. (Here, too, as in so many religions and the NDE, light is important.) Rosicrucianism is not a religion. Rather, it is an international, educational, nonsectarian, fraternal Order which works on a Lodge system. The membership is open to men and women in many different fields of endeavor throughout the world. Apparently, the Order originated in Egypt around 1500 B.C. It is claimed that Pharaoh Thutmose III was the first to organize an esoteric group of initiates. It was during Pharaoh Amenhotep IV's reign that the Rosicrucians first taught the idea of a single deity. Rosicrucianism was also influenced by the Chaldean Magi, the Neo-Platonists and the Hermetists of Alexandria. A strong input was from the Jewish kabbalists and later, the Christian kabbalists. During the Middle Ages, Rosicrucianism was introduced into Western Europe.

The official founding of the Order was by the German nobleman Christian Rosenkreutz in 1425 that was detailed in a 1610 pamphlet entitled "Fama Fraternitatis." In the sixteenth and seventeenth centuries, the Rosicrucians connected with the Christian religion. In 1694 in Pennsylvania, Johannes Kelpius formed the first American Lodge. Its most recent renewal was started in 1915 by H. Spencer Lewis.

The largest and most traditional Order is the *Ancient and Mystical Order Rosae Crucis* (the Ancient and Mystical Order of the Rosy Cross, AMORC). According to the webmaster of AMORC, Sandra Huff, in 1990, AMORC had approximately 250,000 members. At that time, AMORC removed and replaced its head officer. The former head of AMORC and between 50, and 100 of its members left and formed the *Ancient Rosae Crucis* (ARC). It is not known how many members ARC has currently. Another organization is the Rosicrucian Fellowship, which was founded in 1908 by Max Heindel. At the present time, in addition to AMORC, the other major Rosicrucian organization is the Rosicrucian Fellowship. It is not unusual for members to leave AMORC and start their own organizations. AMORC has never taught magic — ritualistic or any other type — and does not include astrology in the AMORC lessons. Through its teachings, AMORC supports freedom of thought, the value of tolerance, and the value of self-responsibility. Rosicrucians' philosophy is meant to guide the development of mankind's highest potentialities. Subjects investigated by some Rosicrucian groups include: planes of consciousness, the aura, telepathy, human consciousness, cosmic consciousness, meditation, visualization, development of intuition, the structure of the soul , mystical sounds, metaphysical healing, the Universal Flame of Life and Seven Cosmic

Principles. Numerology, astrology, physical alchemy, ritual magic and other aspects of the occult are discussed in some of the groups, but not by AMORC. It is claimed that after taking courses in some of the Rosicrucian groups, one can understand the natural laws that govern all realms, which include the physical, mental, emotional, psychic and spiritual. By learning and applying natural laws over time, some of the Rosicrucian groups claim that one should be able to experience Divine or Cosmic Consciousness. However, no attempt is made to define the nature of the deity. The outcome of all the teachings should be true prosperity and peace of mind.

Afterlife Concepts

According to AMORC's Vice President and Secretary, Sandra Huff, AMORC does not describe what an afterlife could be — other than to simply state that the soul is eternal. Other aspects of the afterlife are left to the individuals' personal belief system. Aspects of the afterlife according to the Grandmaster Dr. Gerald Poesnecker of the Rosicrucian group headquartered in Quakertown, Pennsylvania, have been detailed by the noted psychic scholar and former editor of *The Journal of Religion and Psychical Research*, Dr. Claire Walker. Some of these are the following:

• You should be grown up in your thinking and avoid evil in order to expect salvation.

• The afterlife is similar in many ways to the present life. For example, sexual relations would occur, but without procreation. Immortal mothers would care for murdered babies.

• Once the Soul reaches the higher plane, it solidifies with all of the organs it had while on Earth. However, it would have more power, qualities, and sense.

• The Soul would continue to develop, and, after a number of reincarnations on that level to earn immortality, it would migrate to "a far vaster area surrounding the sun." Before that level is achieved, there are hells to endure. Right after death and rebirth on the "invisible planes," the Soul is met, given three days to visit Earth, and then goes into a sleep during its gradual adjustment to its "new spiritual organs" and the environment of its future life.

• Evolution continues in activities of the spirit that is involved in the evolution of other Heavenly Beings, or of a mineral, of Earthly inventions, and preparation for the next reincarnation, which could be on any planet and in any system.

• Plans are made in the Soul World for the next reincarnation. These plans start to be fulfilled at puberty, when the Soul starts to become autonomous. This could explain why unexpected developments manifest in teenagers (Walker, C. "Thoughts on the Objectives of Personal Immortality." In: *1995 Annual Conference Proceedings: Personal Survival of Bodily Death.* Acad. Religion. Psychical Research, Bloomfield, Connecticut, p. 34,1995).

The afterlife viewpoints of these Rosicrucian groups are complicated and difficult to understand. Their belief that you should be "grown up in your thinking and avoid evil" has been found in other religions and NDEs and related psi phenomena. Although they might be true, there is little non-religious evidence to prove the other concepts of the non-AMORC Rosicrucian groups.

The Fraternal Order Of Freemasons

Freemasonry has been defined in various ways. It has been known as "a system of morality, veiled in allegory and illustrated by symbols" (see *Figure 48*).

Freemasonry is nonsectarian, non-political and world-wide, and seeks to promote the dignity and welfare of mankind through constructive brotherhood. Freemasons are members of any of the fraternal organizations throughout the world known as "Free and Accepted Masons" or "Ancient Free and Accepted Masons." The organizational unit is the lodge. The lodges are all considered as independent units of one Masonic order.

Figure 48
"The Masonic Square and Compass." Permission granted for use of emblem by Trevor W. McKeown, Webmaster,the Grand Lodge of British Columbia.

The history of Freemasonry is vague, but it is believed to have originated from the earliest times with the common denominator of an organization that had the sole possession of knowledge of architecture and geometry. Freemasonry has purportedly been found among the ancient mystery religions that predated Christianity, in ancient Egypt, Mayan Mexico and Atlantis, and in Biblical, later Hebrew, and Classical Greek traditions. Freemasonry has been associated with the Essenes, the Druids, the Templars and the Rosicrucians. Freemasonry has been influenced by various religions such as those of ancient Egypt, Greece, Persia and Scandinavia, and Hinduism and the Kabbalah. Some Freemasons consider themselves to have a direct descent from Euclid and King Solomon. Freemasonry had a more formal organization in the Middle Ages. It was given a boost in England and Scotland when stonemasons organized into lodges. Francis Bacon has been credited by some with inventing Freemasonry. The first grand lodge was formed in England in 1717. Since then, it has spread worldwide.

It has been claimed by Anti-Masons that Freemasonry is a religion, but this is vehemently denied by Freemason organizations. As far as the afterlife is concerned, the Freemasons don't have any official position except it is stated that salvation comes from God. However, they do not address the conditions under which salvation is given. Nevertheless, from Dr. Greg Little's research into Masonic beliefs based on the 1871 masonic book by Albert Pike (reported in Little's book, *Grand Illusions*), these beliefs have been found.

• God created the universe by uttering the Word using vibrational frequencies.

• The human soul has its origin from God in heaven as a sphere of energy. It is made from the same substance as God. On Earth, the soul elongates, divides into two parts and becomes trapped prison-like in matter (the body).

• There is a spiritual world populated by numerous intelligent forms — some good and some evil.

Afterlife Concepts

Relative to the afterlife are the following sections of prayers for deceased Freemasons on the next page:

"We place you (the deceased Freemason) in the arms of our Heavenly Father, who grants his love and protection to those who put their trust in him. Because of an unshaken faith in the merits of the Lion of the Tribe of Judah (Jesus Christ), we shall gain admission into the celestial lodge above where the Supreme Architect of the Universe presides."

(*Monitor of the Grand Lodge of Texas*).

"....May we believe that death hath no power over a faithful and righteous soul! May we believe that, though, the dust returneth to the dust as it was, the spirit goeth unto thyself. As we mourn the departure of a brother beloved from the circle of our Fraternity, may we trust he hath entered into a higher brotherhood, to engage in nobler duties and in heavenly work, to find rest from earthly labor, and refreshment from earthly care....and duly prepared for a translation from the celestial Lodge, to join the Fraternity of the spirits of just men made perfect....And having faithfully discharged the great duties which we owe to God, to our neighbor, and ourselves; when at last it shall please the Grand Master of the universe to summon us into his eternal presence, may the trestle-board of our whole lives pass such inspection that it may be given unto each of us to 'eat of the hidden manna,' and to receive the 'white stone with a new name' that will insure perpetual and unspeakable happiness at his right hand."

(R. Macay, *Masonic Burial Services*).

The concept of light emphasized by the Freemason states that Light is the true knowledge of the Deity, the Eternal Good for which Freemasons have always sought. The Freemasons' adherence to the concept of light again shows how so many religions and groups with religious affiliations equate light with the celestial being of light, and as mentioned repeatedly, a celestial being of light occurs with many NDErs. The Freemasons believe that although your physical body dies, your soul lives on and can eventually unite with God. This is a concept similar to the personal viewpoint of the afterlife (see Chapter 15).

The Golden Dawn's Exploration Of The Divine

The Golden Dawn is an interrelated group of societies whose members are taught the principles of Occult Science and the Magic of

Hermes. The goal is the preservation of the knowledge known as Hermeticism or the Western Esoteric Tradition. Hermeticism is traced from the ancient Greeks. Its numerous texts contain instruction in alchemy, astrology and magic. The Golden Dawn's origin is traced to Rosicrucianism in 1614. However, its roots go back to the ancient Egyptians and Greeks, the Jewish Kabbalah and the Babylonian Chaldees. The Golden Dawn was also influenced by Theosophy (discussed next). The original Hermetic Order of the Golden Dawn was a magical fraternity founded in London in 1888 by Dr. William Wynn Westcott and Samuel Liddell MacGregor Mathers. The Golden Dawn later existed under two spin-off organizations named Stella Matutina and the Alpha et Omega. It later spread, and currently in the United States, the Golden Dawn has a strong following as "The Hermetic Order of the Golden Dawn®. (see *Figure 49*).

Although religious imagery and spiritual concepts are important components, the Golden Dawn system of magic is not a religion. The Golden Dawn was conceived as an Hermetic Society dedicated to the philosophical, psychic and spiritual evolution of humanity. In addition, it was designed as a school and a repository of knowledge about occult science and the various elements of magic and Western philosophy. Tolerance for all religions is stressed, and the symbolism used within the Golden Dawn originated from various religious sources. The curriculum includes the study of astrology, inner alchemy, Egyptian magic, Enochian magic, divination and the *Kabbalah*.

Initiation into the organization is intended to achieve

Figure 49
"The Embossed Cross and Triangle."
The illustration of the "Cross and Triangle" is reproduced by permission of the Hermetic Order of the Golden Dawn,® P.O. Box 1757, Elfers, Florida 34653.
(http:www.hermeticgoldendawn.org)

higher levels of consciousness to develop the ability to explore the Divine within yourself. Immortality can be achieved when you affiliate yourself with the immortal spiritual substance that supports all facets of the universe. Capturing that marvelous and rare essence is the ultimate goal of the Western Magical Tradition. The objective of the Golden Dawn is your purification — to extract the pure gold of spiritual completion from the outer shell of your lower personality. The introductory step is the unveiling of the Divine Light — the cultivation of the primary spark of eternal consciousness. A goal is the purification of your lower personality and the establishment of an exalted level of consciousness to allow for your ego to be able to unite with your own Higher and Divine Genius. The determination and the will to achieve union with the Divine are the only essential factors in proceeding on your path.

The germ of Light that is planted within your soul is a perpetual one that will remain intact through many different incarnations, growing stronger as you rediscover your psychic abilities with every new life cycle. A complete shift in outlook and a single-minded devotion for divine union is required for the nurturing. Self-sacrifice is required by the submission of your lower personality to the Higher and Divine Self. This results in the illumination of your soul by the inner Divine Light.

In their afterlife concepts, although the Golden Dawn considers reincarnation (as above), it follows much of the kabbalistic lore. Also, the recurrent theme of Divinity and light occurs here as is does in many previously discussed religions, other movements and the NDE. Hence, Golden Dawn's viewpoints have much importance in our quest to overcome death anxiety.

Theosophy's Quest For Life's Meaning

The word Theosophy is derived from the Greek terms *theos*, meaning "god," and *sophos*, meaning wise. Theosophy ("Ancient Religion," "Wisdom Religion") is the name given for a body of teaching that gives an explanation to the source and meaning of human life. Its scope includes the origins of the universe and mankind. Theosophy purportedly developed an orderly scheme for evolution of all of life (material and spiritual) that is governed by absolute law. The concepts of Theosophy can be traced to the writings of Plato, Plotinus, the Christian gnostics, the Jewish kabbalists and the scriptures of the major religions, especially those of Egypt, China and India. The most recent revival of Theosophy began with the establishment of The Theosophical Society in New York City on November 17, 1875, by Helena Petrovna Blatvatsky and Colonel Olcott. The principal book is Helena Blavatsky's *The Secret Doctrine*.

Afterlife Concepts

Theosophy has an intricate afterlife viewpoint that begins with the origin of the universe. The following is a synopsis:

From the causeless One Cause, the universe appears as a cosmic Ideation. From this proceeds the duality of spirit-matter and the trinity of spirit, matter and the relationship between the two, which is known as consciousness. Existing within the manifested and differentiated consciousness are the myriad units of consciousness. Each unit is known as a Divine Son or Monad. The cosmic purpose of the Monads is to evolve innate powers of conscious divinity by experiencing the limits and mastering the environments of denser matter in the mineral, vegetable and animal kingdoms of life. There is an evolution of consciousness that parallels the evolution of form. Upon reaching the human stage, the Monad's destiny can be more rapidly accomplished as intelligent cooperation is awakened. The Monad is mankind's immortal element of consciousness whose potentialities are gradually released via cycles of reincarnation.

Reincarnation is considered as an orderly, periodic withdrawal and reappearance of humanity's Higher Self into mortal states. These vehicles of mind, emotion and body allow for further opportunities for experience and growth. During the interlife periods, it is believed that your soul reviews the life just finished, evaluates its achievements, and plans its next manifestation as another human. Karma is the law of action and reaction that governs with perfect justice all events in the universe. The cyclic recurrence of mankind's spirit in material form is governed by karma.

The fruition of human experience is the illumined realization of the One Life. The recognition of this realization constitutes spiritual wisdom and gives the basis of ethics, which guarantees that the awakened powers shall be used to advance and not obstruct the evolutionary process. Beyond that stage of fulfillment, the destiny of your spirit is infinite progress in the perfection of your divine nature.

At death, the etheric double withdraws from your body, carrying with it the "higher" sheaths. Only a slender line of force, known as the silver cord, links the etheric double to your body in life. Just before dying, your life events pass over the screen of consciousness. At the moment of actual death, the silver cord is broken. Within a period of several hours, the etheric double dissolves because it cannot sustain separate existence without its body (its physical sheath) for long. You are then left with your astral body and its higher components (the astral sheath). This state is known as the pleasure or desire world (feeling-oriented world) or "Life on the Astral Plane." While on the astral plane, the desires within your surviving self work themselves out until exhausted. If you had been greatly attached to material things, you would find the astral plane to be a purgatory or hell, because you will suffer excruciating desires which will remain unmet. You might try to fulfill compulsive desires vicariously through living people.

In contrast, if you had been more aesthetic and interpersonal, you will find the astral plane more pleasurable. In this realm, you would have time to rest, grow, and delight in all that was around you. Regardless of the type of person you are, the astral plane allows for a period of purification. Without material objects, the lower emotional energies gradually run down and this allows relatively finer ones to develop.

Your time in the astral plane varies depending on the intensity of the attachment. If you are an "Earthbound" entity, you can linger for a long time on the lower astral levels in proximity to familiar haunts. Stories of ghosts could be based on clairvoyant perception of such an entity. There is no eternal punishment. Eventually, the low astral energies wear down (even if you were a hardened case), and you would rise to higher levels.

Once bondage to the physical world is released, you can realize a fresh and wonderful freedom. The astral is a realm of materially marvelous "plasticity" and subject to thought in a way that is far beyond the possibilities of real matter. The plasticity easily becomes that which you want it to be. Some of us make enslaving desired objects, but if you are a truly creative entity, you will find a mind-expanding scope to construct out of your mind and feelings. These are art and fantasy realms that are knowable only in dreams and imagination on the physical plane. This concept has been shown in the recent (October 1998) picturesque movie, *What Dreams May Come* starring Robin Williams, Cuba Gooding, Jr. and Annabella Sciorra.

Love-chords exist within the highest of astral energies. This allows for interpersonal love both within the plane and between its dwellers and those still in the world. Loved ones in the astral world visit those left behind mainly in dreams, but also in visions. When the astral energies have been exhausted, and their lessons assimilated, you then fall into a sleep, which is known as a "second death." The astral sheath falls away and dissolves. You then awaken into an even greater life in heaven.

After the physical, etheric and astral sheaths have been left behind, what remains is the divine Trinity within, plus the mental and intuitional vehicles. Life in this realm is a form of mental life on a very high level. It has two purposes: (1) rest between incarnations; and (2) assimilation of the past life on a level that can be carried over to the next life. Here your mind can create worlds based on aspirations and thoughts from your past life in order to completely understand and explore the new worlds. These shall be your highest, least-selfish ideas, because thoughts related to desire-levels shall have already fallen away. If all goes well, the mental creations provide the ultimate basis for creativity in the next real world incarnation. You create your own heaven that will be no better or worse than what was brought into it. It can either be invigorating joy, subtle happiness, ecstasy or a still peace. All of these are deeper than any fervor.

Eventually, all of the thought-seeds brought into this state will become exhausted. Rest and detachment from your last life will have run its course, and you will desire a new experience to add to what has gone before and now has been assimilated. It is the time for a new birth in a new physical, astral and lower mental encasement. The stream of karma rises and lifts you back into the course of this or another world, where you will find a prepared womb. If you are a greatly advanced soul, you might be able to help make a conscious choice with respect to your next birth. If you are not such a soul, you will simply be impelled by the karma that you have generated in lives now consciously forgotten. What you carry over are not actual memories, but a mental nature whose style, character and potentialities have shaped the long incubation of the heavenly plane. From these come a new, unique you, subtly related to the you now far in the past, who had karmic debts to pay and issues to resolve.

Theosophy suggests that there is more than a separate physical existence as we know it, and that physical existence has no meaning without that "more." Life and death repeat the same message: you are to experience — but not to hold. However, your physical body is the receptacle of the more — of all the human sheaths or principles. Full enlightenment comes to you rarely in heaven or anywhere else beyond. It occurs almost always in your physical body on Earth. Here on Earth — with day and night, good and evil — you face challenges in your fullness. Here, your complete armory is set to deal with these challenges. It is here that they must be mastered in flesh and blood reality. According to psychical scholar, Dr. Claire Walker, reincarnation is not endless. Eventually the Monad becomes an entire entity and blends with divinity, where it always retains its individual memory.

A Detailed and Complicated Afterlife

As you can see, Theosophy's afterlife concepts are well thought out but complicated and somewhat difficult to understand. The viewpoint of you being partly responsible for the type of afterlife seems to be plausible and has some non-religious verification with the variety of celestial beings seen in NDEs. In Theosophy, reincarnation is for everyone, not just the souls that have unresolved issues as is found in some other religions. Since most of the examined religions state that not everyone has to be reincarnated, it is not easy to accept the Theosophy reincarnation viewpoint. In Theosophy, there is no mention of a physical resurrection of the dead at the end-of-days. As is discussed in the personal afterlife viewpoint, (see Chapter 15), based on Judaic, Christian, and Islamic concepts, there might be a physical resurrection at the end-of-days.

Urantia's Afterlife Travels

The *Urantia Book* (see *Figure 50*) was published in 1955. The *Urantia Book* considers the possibilities in an unfinished future where there is work to be performed on greater universes that have not yet been completed. There are millennia to spend in the training for this work. Upon your death, your soul passes through the seven Mansion Worlds. The soul then travels further until it eventually reaches Paradise. This is a stationary island which is at the hub of all the other bodies that are incessantly circling it. Your soul then has the opportunity to train for jobs and stations in the formed, but still evolving minor and major universes, which are sectors within a super universe. The unrevealed but speculated work to be done after Paradise is in the four outer space levels. Your soul can even work in the present universe. Planet Earth is known as *Urantia*. The local universe is *Nebadon*, and the super universe is called *Orvonton*.

It is considered that, if you can measure up, you can participate in your own evolution, in the evolution of the Supreme God, and in the development of the great unfinished universes. If you are an ordinary person who is fully occupied with day-to-day problems of material existence, you are doomed to perish in time. Nevertheless, there are many ordinary persons who are fully occupied with day-to-day problems of material existence, who at some point in their lives can have the faintest glimmer of faith, and thus assure their survival. However, if you make wholehearted moral decisions and unqualified spiritual choices, you are progressively identified with the indwelling and divine spirit. You will then be increasingly transformed into the values of eternal survival. You will move into the unending progression of divine service. Further information on Urantia can be obtained by contacting the Urantia Foundation (see Notes and References).

This most complicated concept is, of course, highly theoretical and impossible to prove at any level. Yet, it does consider, as do many other religions and belief systems, that if you are righteous and moral, you will have the best chance for a positive afterlife experience.

Figure 50
The Three Blue Concentric Circles is a symbol for the *Urantia Book*. It is the Banner of Michael or represents the Trinity government or conveys other meanings associated with the symbol described in the *Urantia Book*. Permission granted for its use by Robert Solone of the Urantia Foundation.

Eckankar's Traveling Soul

Eckankar (ECK, The Religion of the Light and Sound of God) is an ancient wisdom that resurfaced in 1965 in the person of Paul Twitchell, a reporter and writer. In the course of his travels, he was introduced to the Vairagi ECK masters who trained him in the intricacies of Eckankar. In 1965, Twitchell became the spiritual leader of Eckankar, known as the *Mahanta*, the Living ECK Master. He served in that capacity and gave numerous lectures and wrote articles and books until his death in 1971. Darwin Gross was *Mahanta* from 1971 to 1981. The current spiritual leader of Eckankar is Sri Harold Klemp (see *Figure 51*), who has expanded the work begun by Twitchell. The Temple of ECK is located in Chanhassen, Minnesota (see *Figure 52*).

Eckankar emphasizes the value of personal experiences as the most natural way to God. According To ECK, each person is a Soul, a particle of God sent into the lower worlds (including Earth) to gain spiritual experience. The Mahanta has the special ability to act as both Inner and Outer Master for ECK students. He is Eckankar's prophet, who is given respect but not worship. He teaches the sacred name of God, HU, which lifts one spiritually into the Light and Sound of God — the ECK (the Holy Spirit). As a result of the spiritual exercises, each individual comes into contact with the Holy Spirit, which purifies him/her of karma (sin, in this definition). This makes it possible for the person to accept the full love of God in this lifetime. Personal experience with the Light and Sound of God is the cornerstone of Eckankar. The individual's goal is spiritual freedom in this lifetime, after which the person becomes a Co-worker with God, both here on Earth and in the next world.

Figure 51
Sri Harold Klemp, The *Mahanta*, the Living ECK Master. Reprinted with permission of ECKANKAR, P.O. Box 27300, Minneapolis, MN 55427. www.eckankar.org

Afterlife Concepts

The basic afterlife concept of Eckankar is Soul travel, which results from the expansion of consciousness, with the ultimate objective being the attainment of spiritual realization. Since it is believed that the Soul survives physical death, ECKists often refer to death as translation. Many ECKists prefer cremation to burial, and the memorial service honors the journey of the Soul. Karma (the spiritual law of cause and effect) and reincarnation are also part of the Eckankar belief system. You supposedly traverse many planes over 25 years of study in a type of mystery-school program. As a Spark of God, you work as an agent for the Divine Being here and in the vast worlds that lie beyond the physical realm. As a Spark of God, you carry the message of the Light and Sound to all the different worlds.

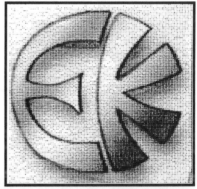

Figure 52
The ECK symbol and a photograph of *The Temple Of ECK* at Chanhassen, Minnesota. Reprinted with permission of ECKANKAR, P.O. Box 27300, Minneapolis, MN 55427. www.eckankar.org

As you can see from this brief summary, the afterlife concepts of the Eckankar religion are somewhat detailed. Nevertheless, Eckankar is similar to others in the beliefs of traversing various planes and reincarnation. As with many religions, other belief systems, and NDEs (and related psi phenomena), the concept of the light is important. Eckankar also focuses on the spiritual sound.

In the next chapter, more recent theories about the afterlife will be presented along with complex ideas presented by individuals.

CHAPTER FOURTEEN

RECENT CONCEPTS OF THE AFTERLIFE — PART 2
COMPLEX IDEAS FROM INDIVIDUALS

I was thrown out of college for cheating on the metaphysics exam;
I looked into the soul of the boy next to me.
(Woody Allen, from ben Shea, N.
Great Jewish Quotes, Ballantine Books, NY, 1993).

After that humors interlude from Woody Allen, we continue on our spiritual journey by examining some of the most important and complex afterlife ideas to evaluate their continuity with previously discussed ideas as well as with NDEs and related psi phenomena.

The afterlife concepts covered in this chapter are those that have been proposed by a wide range of individuals. In general, most of these people (with the exception of Edgar Cayce, and possibly Emmanuel Swedenborg) have not sought followers or group supporters for their theories — they have simply made their proposals in books or through other venues. Theorists in this chapter include: Emmanuel Swedenborg, William Blake, Allan Kardec (Christian Spiritism), MacDougal's Physical Soul, Ernest Holmes (Religious Science), Bô Yin Râ, Edgar Cayce, Jane Roberts (Seth), E. William Dykes, L. Ron Hubbard (Scientology), Roel van der Meulen, Bruce Moen, Fred Alan Wolf, Greg Little, Peter Novak, Simcha Paull Raphael, Ravinda Kumar, George Meek and Mansions.

A Mystical Christian Offshoot: Swedenborgianism

Emmanuel Swedenborg (1688-1772) was born in Sweden into a wealthy family (see *Figure 53*). Swedenborg was an engineer, mathematician and scientist. Later, he became a philosopher and read a great deal about religion. Between 1744 and 1745, Swedenborg began to have spiritual visions and dreams. By the time he died in 1772, the accumulations of his experiences and writings were enough to be detailed in sixteen published books. In addition, he wrote a five-volume spiritual diary. His most well-known book was *Heaven and Hell* (1758). Although Swedenborg never expected that a church denomination would be named after him or founded in his honor, fifteen years after his death (1787), a society was formed in London that interested a diverse group

of philosophers, writers and artists. It later developed into the Swedenborgian Church or The Church of the New Jerusalem. Currently, there is a General Convention of Swedenborgian Churches. There are also several other Swedenborgian denomina-

Figure 53
Emmanuel Swedenborg.
Picture used with permission
of the General Convention
of the New Jerusalem.

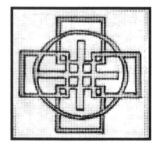

Figure 54 - Right
The logo of the Swedenborgian Church. Picture used with permission of the General Convention of the New Jerusalem.

tions. In North America, beside the General Convention, there is the General Church of the New Jerusalem with headquarters in Bryn Athyn, Pennsylvania. A small offshoot also exists there called the Nova Hierosolyma (New Jerusalem). In England, there is the General Conference of Swedenborgian Churches. Other congregations, typically started by missionary work by the General Conference or the General Convention, have become self-sustaining in Australia, Japan, and especially, in Africa. Other less organized Swedenborgian groups exist in Russia and various places in Europe.

Afterlife Concepts

As is true for Theosophy, Swedenborgianism has an intricate afterlife viewpoint. The following is a synopsis:

At death, no radical change occurs in either your lifestyle or personality. This results from the principle of correspondence, asserting that the whole natural world is linked in detail to the spiritual world. The concepts of sleeping in the grave and purgatory prior to the general resurrection are denied. Only a narrow "sea" separates the living from the dead. Your soul enters the world of spirits. Just as on Earth, free will exists in the spirit world. The spirit world serves as a middle ground between Earth and Heaven. Your soul becomes a spirit with a spiritual body. It lives in a society that consists of spirits with characters similar to those of itself. (For example, spirits from angry people would associate with each other.) Your spirit has thoughts and feelings and functions as it did in the physical world. Your spirit might not even realize that it is dead. However, your spirit cannot hide its inner nature, which shows through much clearer than it does on Earth.

Your disturbed spirit does not achieve eternal damnation or heavenly bliss immediately. First, it must be slowly educated in heavenly matters. Hence, just as on Earth, knowledge accumulation is very important. Your spirit must perfect its psychological and spiritual outlook. Once that occurs, your spirit becomes an angel. (All angels were once humans.) As an angel, you are sexual, and although you lack a physical body, you respond in the same manner you did as a human, but at a higher and more refined level. One of your angelic duties is to educate spirits in the means to discover their higher natures. For those spirits who respond properly, the heavenly path is cleared. Those spirits who cannot respond properly because of their character and refusal to cooperate go to eternal hell. Therefore, it is the spirit, and not God, that condemns itself to hell. There is no conversion after a choice is made. The heavenly realms lie in the highest section. The world of spirits is beneath the heavens, and beneath both are the hells.

If you had been righteous, following your death, heavenly life begins immediately. You do not have to be poor to be righteous; you could be rich and righteous (similar to a Judaism belief). Only a thin veil separates heaven from Earth. Heaven is considered to be a continuation and fulfillment of material existence, having a material and sensuous quality. Heaven is a realm where saints are active and joyful in a moving, dynamic environment, while still experiencing spiritual advancement. Admittance to heaven is not the end, but the journey to God continues eternally as spiritual development never ceases.

Heaven has three realms: Natural Heaven, which is very similar to Earthly existence, and where the inhabitants are male and female "natural" angels; Spiritual Heaven, which is the next higher state and is a civilized, idealized society inhabited by male and female spiritual angels; and Celestial Heaven, which is the highest state and is paradise restored. It is inhabited by male and female celestial angels.

Similar to heaven, hell also has several realms. The worst hells are those in the spiritual northwest. In them are the Roman Catholics who wished to be worshipped as gods and who consequently burned with hatred and revenge against all who refused to acknowledge their power over the souls of men and over heaven. (This applied to the Catholic hierarchy in Swedenborg's time, with its claims of divine authority, not to individual Catholics.) In other hells are found atheists, thieves, robbers, misers, the rancorous, the worldly, the greedy, the unmerciful and the hostile.

The primacy of divine love experienced in the beatific vision comes first. Then, gradually, human love between a man and woman and family and communal love follow the primacy of divine love. The love between a man and a woman, as well as other social relationships, is fundamental to heavenly life. These relationships are not seen as a conflict with divine purpose.

Swedenborg was unique in his concept that love between a man and a woman is the foundation of all other kinds of love. A husband and wife who meet in the spirit worlds only remain together if they are on the same spiritual plane. If not, they could each find other heavenly mates.

God is loved directly and indirectly through the love and charity given to others in heaven. Finally, there is no personal judgment at death and no Last Judgment at the end-of-days.

How Swedenborgianism Is Unique

You can see that Swedenborg's concepts differ from others in: (1) the lack of judgment by God after death; (2) the lack of a purgatory; (3) the lack of an end-of-days judgment; (4) the immediate ascension of a righteous soul to heaven; (5) the importance of love between husband and wife; (6) the similarity of the spirit world to Earth; and (7) the denial of reincarnation. What is similar to many other concepts, as well as NDEs, is the importance attributed to love and learning and the ascension of a righteous soul. These latter concepts are part of the personal afterlife concept (see Chapter 15).

The Afterlife According To William Blake

William Blake (see *Figure 55*) was an 18th-19th century poet and mystic who developed an afterlife concept. The following is a brief synopsis of Blake's afterlife concept:

Once you die, you leave the physical plane and your soul resides in the etheric plane for a few days. Your soul then travels to the astral plane, where it would attend spiritual classes and also enjoy the pursuit of music, art and other intellectual interests. On the as-

Figure 55
Photograph of William Blake. Permission granted for its use by Dr. Roger Bailey, Chairman, Department of English, San Antonio College, San Antonio, Texas.

tral plane, you are not changed except for the lack of a physical body. After having progressed through the astral plane, your soul enters the mental planes. These are also eventually transcended, and your soul turns within to the real self. In doing so, your soul casts off, one by one, all astral and mental layers. Your soul then goes on to higher and more subtle planes.

You can see that these concepts are similar to some of those of the Theosophists and Rosicrucians. Two of them, the presence of an astral plane and higher planes as your soul travels towards its eventual meeting with God, are components of the personal viewpoint of the afterlife (see Chapter 15).

Allan Kardec And Christian Spiritism

Christian Spiritism had two separate origins. One was in the Phillipines between 1845 and 1850 when the concept of Jesus Christ's teachings of the Holy Spirit was incorporated into the native Filipino's belief system of spirits communicating through mediums. In the Filipino version, Christian Spiritists were primarily concerned with performing healing work, using the Holy Spirit in a manner similar to that ostensibly performed by Jesus.

The other origin of Christian Spiritism occurred in the early 1850s, when the French professor, Denizard Hippolyte-Leon-Rivail (born in Lyon in 1804), who taught many subjects including astronomy, chemistry, comparative anatomy, physics, and physiology, began to investigate the extremely popular phenomenon of spirit-rapping (also known as spiritualism; see mediums in Chapter 5). Rivail stated: "I was confronted with a fact that was contrary to the laws of nature as we know them, and repugnant to my reason, but one night in May, 1855, at the home of Madame Plainemason, I myself witnessed the phenomenon of tables circling around, jumping, and even running, as it were, in such conditions that any doubts were dispelled. That was a fact: 'there must be a cause,' I thought. Something very serious is behind all this stuff that serves merely to entertain the spectators." (quoted in Harvey Martin's, *The Secret Teachings of the Espiritistas*, p. 72).

In 1856, Rivail communicated with the spirit world via the channeling of two mediums. As the result of the answers he received he wrote his first book, *The Spirit's World*. During one of the sessions, Rivail learned that in a previous life he was a Druid nomad named Allan Kardec. Liking that name, he published three more spiritual books under the name of Allan Kardec: *The Book of Mediums*, *The Gospel as Interpreted by Spiritism*, and *Spiritualist Initiation*. Kardec then dispensed with the term spiritualism, and coined the name spiritism for his new discipline. After Kardec's books were published, they influenced the Christian Spiritism movement in the Philippines. In Brazil, Kardec's Spiritist Doctrine caught on as well.

Currently, there are Kardec-related spiritism movements throughout the world. In the U.S.A., a major group is the Allan Kardec University Study Group in Austin, Texas. (See internet site: http://www.utexas.edu/students/kardec/)

Fundamental Teachings Of Spiritism

• God is the Supreme Intelligence, the first cause of everything, eternal, immutable, immaterial, omnipotent, unique, and supremely just and good.

• God created the universe, which encompasses all rational and irrational beings, both animate and inanimate, material and immaterial.

• The corporeal world is inhabited by incarnate spirits (humans); the spiritual world is inhabited by discarnate spirits.

• The universe contains other inhabited worlds with beings at different degrees of evolution: some less evolved than humans; some equal to humans; and others, more evolved than humans.

• God is the author of all the Laws of Nature (Divine Laws); they include physical and moral laws.

• A human is a spirit incarnated in a material body. The perispirit is the semi-material body which unites the spirit to the physical body.

• Spirits communicate through mediums. Good spirits offer good counsel; less evolved spirits are deceptive and show ignorance and imperfection.

• Jesus is the guide and model for all of humanity. The doctrine that he taught and exemplified is the purest expression of God's Law.

• Christ's morality is the pathway for the secure progress of all humans. Its practice is the solution for all of humanity's problems and the objective to be attained by humanity.

• Humans are granted free will but are accountable for their actions.

• Prayer improves people. Those who pray fervently and confidently can resist evil temptations, and God sends Good Spirits to assist them. Assistance is not denied when requested sincerely.

Afterlife Concepts

• The spirits are the souls of those who had lived on Earth and other worlds who, upon death, became spirits.

• Some spirits are perfected; they exist to help and uplift humanity. Other spirits are uninvolved; they continue the ignorance they had on Earth.   .

• Spirits possess free will; they can evolve and achieve perfection according to the amount of effort and determination they put out.

• A spirit's temperament is proportional to the amount of good or evil it did during its life on Earth or elsewhere. Peace and bliss characterize spirits who have arrived at supreme perfection.

• The world of spirits pre-exists and outlives everything.

• Spirits undergo incarnations and reincarnations, but they preserve their individuality before, during, and after each incarnation.

• Spirits reincarnate as many times as needed for their spiritual advancement but never regress.

As can be seen from this review, Kardec's spiritism is similar to many other religions and concepts with the belief in a Supreme Being, a spiritual world with different levels, and reincarnation. It differs in that with each incarnation, the spirit retains its individuality and spirits always evolve. Spiritism also reinforces the concept that leading a good and moral life can help insure a blessed afterlife (a components of the personal viewpoint of the afterlife; see Chapter 15).

MacDougal's Physical Soul

In the May 1907 issue of the *Journal of the American Society for Psychical Research*, a physician at Massachusetts General Hospital, Dr. Duncan MacDougall, had an article published on his research of weighing the soul to prove its existence. MacDougall had patients lying on their deathbeds that were resting on beam scales that were accurate to $2/_{10}$ths of an ounce. At the exact moment of death, the scales clanged down loudly. He examined five patients, and they lost approximately a half-ounce at the moment of death. Most religious traditions state that animals don't have a soul (at least a soul equivalent to that of a human). MacDougall then repeated his experiment on 15 dogs, but this time, he used even more accurate scales (accurate to $1/16$th of an ounce). The results showed that at the exact moment of death, the dogs weighed the same as they did before death.

About 30 years later, H. L. Twining repeated the experiment comparing mice inside of test tubes with mice outside of test tubes. The mice inside the test tubes didn't lose any weight at the exact moment of death. However, the mice outside the test tubes lost a small amount of weight at the exact moment of death. Twining attributed the latter loss as a result of the evaporation of carbon dioxide. Hence, he believed that the humans' loss of weight in MacDougall's study was also due to evaporation of carbon dioxide. Nevertheless, this is not a certainty because Twining couldn't figure out why MacDougall's dogs didn't lose weight even though they were outside (not sealed into enclosures).

Recent studies at a medical school in Virginia (reported by Little in his book, *Grand Illusions*), have also shown that at the exact moment of death, there is an inexplicable loss of weight of between $1/4$th -$1/2$ of an ounce (verifying MacDougal's findings). Whether or not the loss of weight at the exact moment of death is the escaping soul is unprovable. As is discussed later, E.W. Dykes believes the soul is energy, and Fred Alan Wolf considers that the soul has neither energy nor mass.

Religious Science

Dr. Ernest Holmes (see *Figure 56*) was a non-reincarnation minister who was an outstanding proponent of the church known as Religious Science. In 1938, in his book, *The Science of Mind* (reprinted in 1988), Dr. Holmes discussed his concepts including that we are living in a spiritual universe whose sole government is one of harmony, and that the use of right ideas is the enforcement of its law. The Science of Mind is built on the theory that there is One Infinite Mind which of necessity includes all that is, whether it be the intelligence in man, the life in the animal, or the invisible Presence which is God. In it we learn to have a spiritual sense of things. This spiritual sense of things is what is meant by the Consciousness of Christ. To be able to discern the spiritual idea back to its physical symbol is to use the mind that Jesus used.

Afterlife Concepts

Holmes' afterlife concepts are the following:

• After death, you have a subtle body formed by your present soul that operates on a different plane.

• You are, in fact, immortal now with your future subtle body already within you.

• Mentality does not depend upon your brain, but it can operate independently of your body.

• You retain your own personality and continue activities in the afterlife.

• When you reach the other side, you meet deceased friends.

• After death, passage is from one plane of life and consciousness to another. This is somewhat similar to the message of the German mystic, Bô Yin Râ (discussed next).

The concepts of surviving souls having subtle bodies, the independence of the surviving soul from the brain, the retention of the personality in the afterlife, and the meetings with deceased friends have been seen in many NDEs and related psi phenomena.

Bô Yin Râ's Afterlife Concept

Anton Schneiderfranken (1876-1943), using the spiritual name, Bô Yin Râ, first presented his afterlife concepts in a 1920 German text, *The Book on Life Beyond* (English translation, 1978). Following are some highlights from *The Book on Life Beyond* :

• To be prepared for the afterlife, you must learn the art of dying. You should be joyful, confident and serene and maintain that state of mind. To be best prepared, you should show compassion towards all living things. You should love your fellow beings as well as yourself.

• Death is painless. It occurs during a period of temporary sleep while your spiritual form frees itself from its attachment with your physical body.

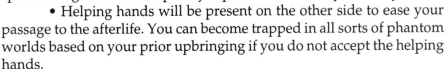

Figure 57
Bô Yin Râ, permission for use granted by
Bodo Reichengacher and the Kober Press.

- Upon awakening, you become a timeless, spiritual organism. You will have a spiritual body with spiritual senses.
- Your level of development on Earth provides the means of gaining experience in the afterlife.
- Your range of consciousness in the afterlife is infinitely wider than it is in mortal life.
- It can take time for you as a spiritual organism to completely separate itself from your body.
- Helping hands will be present on the other side to ease your passage to the afterlife. You can become trapped in all sorts of phantom worlds based on your prior upbringing if you do not accept the helping hands.
- If you are prepared, the spiritual world will be familiar. There will be mountain ranges, land and sea, snow-capped peaks, peaceful valleys, fruits, and plants, and a radiant temple, which is the source of all authentic revelations. There is much to be applauded in Bô Yin Râ's concepts. For the well-prepared, his viewpoint of the afterlife is indeed wonderful.

Edgar Cayce's Afterlife Revelations

Edgar Cayce (1877-1945), a devout Protestant Christian, was considered to be America's most documented spiritualist, clairvoyant and self-hypnotist (*Figure 58*). In 1923, Cayce met a printer, Arthur Lammers, whose hobby was metaphysical philosophy. Lammers asked Cayce to explain the mysteries of life (for example, why are we here? What is the meaning of life? What is the nature of mankind)? While under hypnosis, Cayce, who had no prior knowledge of metaphysical philosophy, gave detailed answers. This led to Cayce's 2,500 Life readings. When asked where he received the knowledge Cayce imparted, while in a trance, that his sources were: the unconscious or subconscious mind of

Figure 58
Edgar Cayce with ARE
symbol. Permission
granted for use by the
ARE, Inc.

the subject; and the universal memory of nature, which
has also been called either
Jung's Collective Uncon-
scious, the Akashic Records,
the Recording Angel, or the
Book of Life. Cayce's mind
was apparently able to tap
the mass of knowledge possessed by countless other
subconscious minds, including those who had died. The interest in
Cayce's work led to the establishment of a major foundation in his honor
in Virginia Beach, Virginia. The afterlife according to Edgar Cayce is very
detailed. The following is a synopsis:

All About Souls

All souls were present at the time of creation. Reincarnation is for
gradual evolution and purification of souls. Eventually, every soul must
return to God. Individually, when that happens, your soul becomes
aware of itself as a part of both God and of every other soul and
everything else. Each soul, including yours, is the greatest creation of
God because it is a spark from the one soul of God. Each soul consists of
two components: the spirit (the subconscious mind), which bears a
knowledge of its identity with God; and the new individual (the conscious mind), which bears a knowledge of everything it experiences. At
the moment when the desire of will is no longer different from the
thought of God, then your soul would return to God. Your subconscious
cannot be destroyed because it is a part of God. When death occurs and
your soul (subconscious mind) returns to God, your conscious mind
(ego) is destroyed. This is symbolic of the crucification of Jesus Christ.

The Christ Soul

Each of us was fostered by a soul which had completed its experience of creation and returned to God. It then became a companion and co-creator with God. This is known as the Christ soul and is the Master of the Unfallen Sons of God. The Christ soul desired to rescue the fallen, trapped souls. The Christ soul periodically took the form as a man to act as a leader of the people. First, it was as Adam, who was not the first man to have lived on earth, only the first man to receive the Christ soul. (In the Talmudic interpretation of Genesis, it is only after Adam received neshamah [the intellectual soul] that he became the first real human. As discussed before, these two concepts of Adam's humanity, could be compatible with evolution showing man-like creatures living well before the Biblical time of Adam.) Adam's received the knowledge of good and evil, and although the knowledge brought forth sin, it was necessary for spiritually evolved souls to become Christ-like. The Christ soul then reappeared in Enoch and Melchizedek, who were both born but did not die. Further incarnations of the Christ soul were in Joseph (Jacob's son), Joshua and Jeshua. According to Cayce's revelations, Jeshua was the scribe primarily responsible for forming the Hebrew Bible.

Jesus, Joseph And Mary

The belief that the Christ soul had an intermediate incarnation as Joseph is of great interest, because there is a Jewish Talmudic tradition that states that the first Messiah would come from the seed of Joseph and he would then die. A second and final Messiah would come from the seed of David, and would be the Messiah that appears at the end-of-days. Hence, if as discussed below, the Christians had misinterpreted Jesus' lineage, the second coming of Jesus for the Christians would actually be the coming of the second Messiah for the Jews, and then at the end-of-days, both Jews and Christians would be worshipping the same Messiah.

The Christ soul realized that it had to pay the karmic debt for mankind's sins; hence, it was reborn into the Virgin Mary. One thing is puzzling. There are numerous references in the Hebrew Bible stating that the Messiah would come from David's seed. Jesus Christ was traced from David's seed with Joseph [Jesus' father] shown to have descended from Jesse [David's father]:

> "And Jesse begat David the king; and David the king begat Solomon..; And Solomon begat Roboam; and Roboam begat Abia; and Abia begat Asa; And Asa begat Josaphat; and Josaphat begat.......Zorbabel begat Abiud; and Abiud begat Eliakim; and Eliakim begat Azor; And Azor begat Zadoc; and Zadoc begat Achim; and Achim begat Eliud...... Jacob begat Joseph the husband of Mary, of whom was born Jesus, who is called Christ."
>
> (Matthew 1: 6-16).

If Mary conceived Jesus as a virgin, where was Joseph's seed? It also appears that the translation from Hebrew to Greek and English should be as young woman rather than virgin. In addition, if as stated above, Jesus Christ was not of David's seed but from the seed of Joseph (Jacob's son), he would be the first Messiah of the Jews and would have been expected to die.

The Trinity

Jesus became the three dimensional manifestation of God on Earth: the Trinity (the Father, the Son and the Holy Ghost). Humanity's goal is to become as Christ's three-dimensional likeness: body (as of the Father); mind (as of the Son); and soul (as the Spirit of God). Jesus accepted the crucifixion, triumphed over death and the flesh, laid down the ego, paid back Adam's karmic debt and returned to heaven showing humanity the path back to God. Through the acceptance of Jesus (the Spirit of God and Love), all can be set free from desires and return to God.

As in strict Christian religions, this sets forth the concept that only those who accept Jesus would be saved. However, what would happen to the other two-thirds of mankind? With regard to the second coming of Jesus, Cayce's revelations stated that He would appear as He did before, and the day of the Lord is indeed at hand.

Cayce And The Kabbalah

In his revelations, Cayce also got involved with the *Kabbalah*. He stated that the ancient mystery religions of Egypt, Greece, Persia and India — all of which predated Christianity — were concerned with man's problem of freeing the soul from the world. Furthermore, Jesus said He came to fulfill the law, and part of that law was the *Kabbalah*, — the Jewish version of the ancient mysteries. With respect to fulfillment of the law, the following passage makes it difficult to believe that Jesus was planning to start a new religion:

"Think not that I am come to destroy the law (the Jewish *Torah*), or the prophets; I am not come to destroy, but to fulfil. For verily I say unto you, Till heaven and earth pass, one jot or one title shall in no way pass from the law, till all be fulfilled. Whosoever therefore shall break one of these least commandments, and shall teach men so, he shall be called the least in the kingdom of heaven: but whosoever shall do and teach them, the same shall be called great in the kingdom of heaven."

(Matthew 5: 17-19).

Stars, Planets and Souls

To Cayce the stars represent soul patterns. The twelve signs of the Zodiac are twelve patterns from which each soul chooses when entering the Earth plane. The patterns include personality traits and temperaments. The Zodiac stars influence individuals by making them either lionish, bullish, introspective or airy. The planets are old dwelling places of the soul; hence they can influence people when they come to a prominent point in the sky. Mercury affects the mind; Venus gives love; Mars gives anger; Jupiter gives strength; Saturn gives woes; Uranus affects the psyche; Neptune gives mysticism; and Pluto affects consciousness. Each of our souls can escape from the lower planes of consciousness and reach higher planes of consciousness where each soul is then free to go to higher places in the universe.

The star of Bethlehem was seen by the three Persian Magi, and it signaled the birth of Jesus. In 1600, Johannes Kepler hypothesized that the star of Bethlehem was a conjunction of Jupiter and Saturn, and it occurred at the end of Pisces, ruled by Jupiter. Jupiter is considered to be the planet of Kings. Saturn is considered to be the planet that rules the Jews. The current time (the end of the twentieth century) is at the tail-end of the Age of Pisces (the Church Age). The Age of Aquarius (The Age of the Water-Bearer, Jesus Christ) will begin around the year 2300. Christ was born as the last Lamb during the Age of Aries (the Ram) and the first Fish of sacrificial Pisces. The sign of the fish is a symbol of Christianity.

With the advent of the Age of Aquarius, after many upheavals of the land and sky (wonders will occur in the sun, moon, and stars) the true Water Bearer will rule the earth. Christ will bring Living waters that will result in eternal life.

The Soul's Other Dimensions

Cayce stated that other dimensions of our soul can be experienced in dreams, meditation and hypnosis. This has apparently been borne out by those of us who have observed past lives, visited other dimensions, seen deceased souls, angels, and heavenly creatures and have gone into outer space while under meditation, hypnosis, in dreams and during visualizations.

The Seven Chakras And Meditation

Similar to the *Kabbalah* and Eastern religions, within the body are seven chakras (spiritual centers, endocrine glands), which are somewhat representative of a miniature solar system. The plane of consciousness that we travel to upon death is usually determined by the spiritual center that had the greatest influence on us while alive. Let us consider some individual examples: If you were primarily influenced by the sex glands, your soul would be burdened with woes and would travel to Saturn. If you were mystical, you would have been influenced by the Lyden glands and head for Neptune. However, your soul could go on to higher planes of consciousness. If you were full of hatred and anger, you would have been influenced by the adrenals and would land on Mars. (Again, this emphasizes the importance of stress management techniques while alive that could control negative emotions such as hate and anger.) If you were a loving individual, you would have been influenced by the thymus gland and would have all doors opened and your soul would reach Venus. If you were into the psychic realms of consciousness, you would have been influenced by the thyroids and would travel to Uranus. If you had concentrated on the mind, you could have the mind of the soul meet the Holy Spirit and be truly awakened. Your soul would have been influenced by the pineal gland and would head for Mercury. If you had prayed and meditated fervently, you would have been influenced by the pituitary (the master gland), and your soul could eventually enter the very presence of God: your soul would land on Jupiter. (Again, this shows a major positive aspect of the stress coping technique, meditation.)

To Cayce, the seven endocrine glands serve as contact points between the Spirit and your body. These glands are the transformers of the One Force of Spirit into physical consciousness and manifestation.

Meditation is listening to God. The seven endocrine glands are activated during meditation. Spiritual energy moves upward from the sex organs. If the spiritual force can rise unhindered to the pineal and pituitary glands, you can experience an incandescence as if your entire body has been filled with light and become transparent. (Again, we have the religious and NDE significance of light.) At the pineal gland, you can become oriented to the Christ-presence and might even receive the mind of Christ. The force then flows into the pituitary and is purified. It then flows downward, strengthening and purifying your mind and body. Your conscious mind is stilled, and your subconscious mind becomes active. Images can appear from deceased souls, but you must then return to silence. As you sit in silence, you can elevate your mind by the use of the Lord's Prayer. This energy now is divine in nature. The lyden gland (control center of the soul's activity) opens its portals to this energy. This allows your subconscious (your soul's mind) to rise to the pineal gland. This energy is then transferred to the other centers of the body via the pituitary gland. The other centers are then illuminated. Meditation elicits increased vigor and health along with consciousness expansion. Your soul is now in eternity and the realization occurs that there is no death. As in dreams, with meditation you can become aware of other planes of consciousness.

Analyzing Cayce's Revelations

As with *Kabbalah*, and some other religions, all souls were present at creation. Reincarnation is for gradual evolution and purification of souls (similar to *Kabbalah* and Eastern religions but unlike formal Christianity). The seven spiritual centers inside the body are similar to those of Kabbalah and Eastern religions. The concept of souls being dispersed into planets and throughout the universe is a new concept and could allow for the origin of human-like life on other planets.

The concept of the soul having two components — the subconscious which survives death and the conscious which dies with the body — is similar to the *Kabbalah* and earlier Jewish concepts of the *nefesh* — the part of the soul staying with the body after death and other aspects of the soul going to different destinations. The adherence to a physical resurrection at the end-of-days is similar to Jewish, Christian, and Islamic tradition. The insistence that salvation is only attainable through Jesus Christ is similar to strict Christian doctrines. In the personal afterlife concept (see Chapter 15), many of Cayce's concepts are included except for the disposal of souls throughout the universe and the insistence that salvation is only attainable through Jesus Christ. The latter two concepts have not been verified by NDEs and related psi phenomena.

Seth's Afterlife Concepts

"You are in physical existence to learn and understand that your energy, translated into feelings, thoughts and emotions, causes all experience. There are no exceptions."
(Seth, *The Nature of Personal Reality*, Session 614).

In 1963, as writer Jane Roberts and her artist/writer husband Robert Butts were experimenting with an Ouija board, Seth came into their lives. By his own definition, Seth is an energy personality no longer focused in physical reality. He can be thought of as an intelligence residing outside of time and space.

After awhile, Seth no longer spoke through the Ouija board but directly through her voice. Rob translated Seth's words that amounted to almost 1,800 sessions over twenty-plus years until Jane died in 1984. There are ten published Seth books, and many more waiting to be published.

According to Seth, each of us is given the gift of creativity and literally create our individual realities through our attitudes, beliefs and thoughts. Events don't happen to people, people cause them by what they expect to see in their lives and world. In essence, every event a person encounters and participates in is a physical reflection of what he/she feels and thinks. If individuals create the reality of their existence, they certainly can change the things they do not like. There is currently a Seth Network International to keep alive the Seth material via books, tapes, and conferences.

Afterlife Concepts

The soul is connected with all aspects of the universe, and there is a continuity of consciousness. There is also a belief in reincarnation. Other aspects of the afterlife according to Seth has been detailed by the noted psychic scholar and former editor of *The Journal of Religion and Psychical Research*, Dr. Claire Walker. Some of these are the following: At death, you might or might not be greeted by relatives and friends. This would be an individual matter depending, for one thing, upon which people you had known in which other lives. On a higher level, you could not pretend to love anyone, but would reclaim the genuine relationships that had previously been established. Finally, you would participate in various dramas according to your own beliefs, in order to become free of mortal conditioning. The belief in reincarnation is similar to many other religious concepts.

Visionary Dykes' View Of The Afterlife

"No energy is ever lost. To claim that this tremendous force behind our human activities permanently disappears at the moment of death is like saying that one wave on the ocean does not produce another."
(Zen teacher, Yatautani).

E.W. Dykes is a man of multiple talents. He was an architect, economist and energy consultant, and is now an afterlife philosopher. The following is the basis of his recently published afterlife concepts ("Speculations on the Nature of the Hereafter." In: *Personal Survival of Bodily Death*), some of which was derived from the viewpoints of Frederick W.H. Myers, author of *Human Personality and its Survival of Bodily Death*:

Afterlife Concepts

As does Theosophy, Dykes' concept begins with the physical universe, which is entirely energy. As Einstein had shown, all matter can be reduced to energy. Even thought processes involve the actions of energy. Your soul is energy existing in a range of very high frequencies. If a sensitive enough instrument was available, your soul's frequency could be measured. As long as your body retains its energies at a sufficient level to remain alive, it holds your soul captive by two silver cords. Your soul directs your body, and your body is the vehicle for your soul. To enter and occupy your body, your soul's energy frequency is adjusted downward. Relative to illness, accident, or old age, your resulting weakened body loses its hold on your soul. If the breakdown continues, your soul escapes and can go through walls, other solids, visit other parts of the building, and could reach the next dimensional reality. This concept could account for NDEs and OBEs. With a NDE, when your body has strengthened sufficiently, your soul returns to the body.

After death, the silver cords rupture (similar to Theosophy), and your soul escapes. It then recognizes the invisible, unobstructed universe. The separation of soul from body can take three or four days for the adjustment of frequencies to be completed (as is discussed in *Kabbalah*).

Life and Afterlife consist of seven planes: (a) The Plane of Matter (Earth); (b) The Plane of Adjustment (Hades); (c) The Plane of Illusion (Summerland); (d) The Plane of Color; (e); The Plane of Flame; (f) (The Plane of Light; and (g) Out Yonder (Timelessness, The Supreme Degree).

The first two planes that are met following death are Hades and Summerland. The stopover in Hades is for all souls and can be long or short. Usually, it lasts three or four days. Hades is a distribution point (similar to the Jewish Gehenna and the Christian Purgatory). Your newly arrived soul reviews portions of its Earth life. Following that, depending upon your former life, your soul either descends into the pits; requires further conditioning; or moves on to Summerland.

Enlightened souls on the other side willingly accept services to incoming souls to help them in the transition. If you died violently, you are confused upon reaching the hereafter. If you are a lost soul, you are taken to a hospital-like place where trained souls bring you to your senses and the realization that you are dead.

Within the limits of their frequencies, souls group themselves according to likes and interests. Souls often gather in family groups to work on common problems. If you who died from a debilitating illness, you will have had your spiritual energy depleted. You must spend time in a resting place with trained attendants. Following return to full energy, you gravitate to the next level, known as the Plane of Illusion (Summerland). At Summerland, there is a greeting party attended by deceased family and friends. Following this is a tour of libraries, learning centers, concert halls, lakes, mountains and gardens. Here is found peace, love and beauty. Your soul (and others) have a spiritual 28-year-old face and body. There are no dangers and no money or food. In time, restlessness sets in, and your soul seek ways to go on to higher and better things.

Your religious beliefs can help or hinder your soul. For example, if you are a Muslim who believes in remaining in the ground until the time of the resurrection, then you will remain in the ground. If you were moral in life, you will be able to create your heart's desire in the afterlife. To have the best possible afterlife, while alive, you must show forgiveness and unconditional love. If you were immoral, you will suffer the pain that you had imposed on others. (Similar concepts are believed in many other religions and philosophies.)

The next plane for you as a prepared soul is The Plane of Color. In it, there is a higher frequency, and your soul receives a finer body. Following this is the Plane of Flame. Now your soul prepares to live without form. Your soul is aware of its own mind and also those of others in the group. Now your soul enters the Plane of Light. Here, form is abandoned. Pure reason reigns supreme. From this region, certain souls can take a special assignment on Earth. Most souls travel into the final plane. In Out Younder (The Supreme Degree), your soul joins with God. However, there is not a loss of individuality. Apparently, that is never lost.

Energy and Soul

You can see that Dykes' afterlife concepts are filled with energy levels and different afterlife planes. Nevertheless, aside from the energy concept, the system is similar to several other esoteric viewpoints (for example, Theosophy). Believable concepts are: (1) souls are energy in a range of very high frequencies; and (2) enlightened souls on the other side willingly accept services to newcoming souls to help them in the transition. The latter has been verified by some NDEs.

The Personal Enlightenment Of Scientology

The word Scientology is derived from the Latin term *scio*, meaning "know" and the Greek term *logos*, meaning the word or outward form by which the inward thought is expressed and made known. Hence, it means "knowing about knowing." Scientology is an applied religious philosophy that was developed by L. Ron Hubbard in the 1950s. People are not asked to believe on faith alone. Rather, Scientology works by applying its principles and observing or experiencing the results. It considers that mankind is basically good. Scientology offers mechanisms that people can use to become happier and more able to improve conditions for themselves and others. It utilizes exact principles and a practical technology for improving people's spiritual awareness, self-confidence, intelligence and ability.

Afterlife Concepts

You are an immortal spiritual being whose experience extends well beyond a single lifetime. However, this is not the Eastern religions' concept of reincarnation in which a soul is born again in different life forms. Rather, death is considered to be a transition through which you carry your past or a past for which you are accountable, to another life. Because of misdeeds and irresponsibilities in a previous life, you have to learn self-enlightened principles such as honesty, integrity, trust and concern for others to be able to face new tomorrows. Your spiritual salvation depends upon yourself and others and your attainment of brotherhood with the universe.

The Eight Dynamics

The drive for survival embraces eight dynamics. A dynamic is conceived as a series of concentric circles in which the first dynamic is the center and each new dynamic is a successive circle outside the preceding one. As you become more aware and more capable, you become more able to influence and control all of the dynamics. The goal of Scientology is to help you survive to the greatest level across all of the dynamics from the first and eventually to the eighth. The dynamics relative to the afterlife are the following:

• The seventh dynamic is the urge toward existence as a spiritual being.

• The eighth dynamic is the urge toward existence as infinity, the Supreme Being or God.

Although Scientology affirms the existence of a Supreme Being, its practice does not include the worship of God. However, it is considered that as you becomes more aware, you attain certainty of every dynamic and, as you move from the seventh dynamic to the eighth, you come to a personal awareness of infinity and God. You also understand your relationship to infinity and God. It is believed that when you are brought to a high enough state, you will be able to reach personal conclusions about the nature of God or a Supreme Being. Hence, salvation in Scientology is achieved through personal spiritual enlightenment. Scientology believes: there is a Supreme Being; the soul survives death and had past lives and will have future lives. However, it does not give specifics regarding the soul's fate in the afterlife.

Van der Meulin's
Concept Of The Afterlife

Roel van der Meulen (see *Figure 59*) was born on October 13, 1968 in Delft, the Netherlands. Van der Meulen now lives in Leiden where he is studying to be an astronomer. His avocation is having interesting ideas and concepts and then writing them as articles for the *Project Galactic Guide* on the internet. Van der Meulen has written two articles about the afterlife entitled, *The Afterlife: Dream On* and *Life After Death: Enjoy it While it Lasts.* Here is the essence from those articles:

An individual watching you die observes the decay of your bodily functions, the disappearance of your consciousness, and finally the disappearance of all of your life signs. You, in contrast, experience something entirely different. This experience is related to a change in the "internal clock" induced by death-related chemical reactions in your brain. The afterlife journey starts out, as NDErs and OBErs have affirmed, with a passage through a very large tunnel that culminates in an extremely bright light. The living have never been able to get much further than that. With you, who are actually dying, dreaming begins. Simultaneously, chemical changes occur in your brain relative to the process of dying that causes the perception of time to change. Time accelerates close to infinity causing one second in real time to last for ages. Your mind then escapes in a type of tangent to our time into a different time dimension.

As far as your dreaming is concerned, at first, it is as incoherent as ordinary dreams. This could be considered purgatory. If your mind is fortunate, it will learn to control the never-ending dream, as some living individuals can, and a kind of private heaven can be created. If your mind is unfortunate, it will never learn to control the incoherent dream, and your mind will be in purgatory forever. This could be the equivalent of hell. However, if your dream turns into a nightmare,

Figure 59
Photograph of Roel van der Meulen. Permission granted for its use by Roel van der Meulen.

that will be a real hell. So, your mind's ability to control its dreams will determine its afterlife fate.

Van der Meulin has written some caveats. During life, other people can affect your dreams. Wartime traumas are effective nightmare inducers. And the dreams that you have while alive will be the same kind of dreams you will have after death. Hence, true heaven or hell partly depends on people other than yourself. Therefore, van der Meulin advises us that we should be good to others because maybe then they will, in turn, be good to us. In that way, we can give them a chance at heaven at the same time they are giving us an opportunity for heaven. He also advises that we should enjoy ourselves as much as possible while alive, which will give us even more opportunities to have pleasant dreams and a heavenly hereafter.

Van der Meulin does not go any further in his *Project Galactic Guide* afterlife discussion, and it is probable that his reference to the mind of the deceased is equivalent to the soul. Relative to you determining your afterlife fate based on varied dreams in life, it appears from NDE research that people have some variety in their depictions depending upon their religious upbringing and the kind of life they had lived. For example, Jews might see God, Christians could see Jesus, Buddhists could envision Buddha, and atheists might just see a majestic person. And while most people describe a heavenly-like place, others have described hellish realms. In addition, time appears to have altered qualities as van der Meulin has stated about the effects of death on the brain's time clock.

Whether or not van der Meulin's afterlife presentation is, to some extent, tongue-in-cheek, it seems to be good advice, because almost all religions and organizations examined have elucidated the position that a righteous individual has a much better chance of getting to heaven than one who is self-centered, uncaring or wicked. His concept about being good to others is also a component of *Kabbalah* teaching, and has been incorporated into the personal concept of the afterlife (see Chapter 15). Hence, good advice is to use stress management techniques in order to control negative emotions.

Moen's Series Of Visions

In 1992, Bruce Moen (see *Figure 60*), an engineer, attended the Monroe Institute in Faber, Virginia and utilized the Lifeline program developed by the noted out-of-body traveler, Robert Monroe (see Chapter 4). To facilitate his experiences, Moen used the audio technology known as Hemi-Sync®. It was developed by Monroe who found that specific patterns of sound were able to shift a person's focus of attention to specific altered states of consciousness. During the Lifeline program, Moen was able to access the levels of consciousness of the Afterlife. These levels of consciousness are known as Focus 22, 23, 24, 25, 26 and 27. The numbers mean nothing specific except they are convenient labels for various areas of human consciousness. For each of these Focus levels, separate Hemi-Sync sound patterns exist. By cooperatively listening to the Hemi-Sync sound patterns for a specific Focus level, Moen was able to shift his focus of attention to that level. By learning to become aware of impressions that he received while in that specific Focus level, Moen could explore the Afterlife. He also described partnered explorations. In this technique, two or more individuals meet nonphysically and explore the afterlife together while in the same Focus level. The people don't even have to be near each other.

After the exploration of the after-life, they record their experiences in a journal and then compare notes. Moen stated that there were identical visualizations, which led him to believe that his afterlife experiences were real and not just imaginary. The impressions Moen received have been detailed in his books, *Voyages Into the Unknown: Exploring the Afterlife* (published in 1997) and *Voyage Beyond Doubt: Exploring the Afterlife Series*, Vol. 2 (published in 1998). Some of his findings are detailed as follows:

Figure 60
Photograph of Bruce Moen. Permission granted for its use by Bruce Moen.

Afterlife Concepts

Your afterlife experience depend upon: prior beliefs; habitual thinking patterns; circumstances of your death; emotional state; pain level; what nearby persons are doing or saying; diseases which affect the thinking process (for example, Alzheimer's disease); drugs taken prior to death; and where in the afterlife the "landing" takes place. However, as you "awaken" in the afterlife, the influence of physical influences can lose their effect. As you die, Helpers from the other side aid in the transition from life to death. These could be deceased family members or friends. The afterlife is a reality whether or not you choose to believe in it. A brilliant white Light (sometimes with colors) is usually seen. Love seems to come from the Light. Helpers often appear as a Light. Depending upon your religion, you might see celestial beings such as Moses and Jesus.

Death does not appear permanent. There are various places and numerous options. After death, you retains memories of your life and previous lifetimes as well. If you had committed suicide, you still retain the overwhelming feelings that you had prior to your death. Sometimes, you enter the spirit world as a ghost who tries to access live people to work out their problems.

The afterlife experience is a reflection of your former life experiences. By exploring the afterlife while alive, for example in Focus 27 of the lifeline program, you will find it easier to get into an equivalent in the afterlife. Love and learning are important in the afterlife. If you retain consciousness while dying, your conscious thoughts can be retained after death. During a living person's dreams, you in the afterlife could communicate with the living person. A living person can also communicate with you in the afterlife during prayer and meditation.

If you had committed horrendous acts without remorse, you would go to a place in the afterlife where you could continue to commit horrendous acts. However, it is possible to get out of this hellish experience if you change for the better. By the same token, if you doubt your heavenly afterlife, you can be removed from heaven. The Christian church Moen was raised in stated that, to get into heaven, you had to be baptized. If you weren't baptized, then your destination would be eternal punishment in hell. From his experiences, Moen did not find this to be the case.

The Monroe Institute

It is important to realize that you must attend the Monroe Institute course to be able to use Hemi-Sync® and not everyone will achieve the results that accrued to Bruce Moen.

Moen's visionary experiences are similar to NDEs and OBEs. These include: importance of love and learning; the brilliant bright light; meeting family and friends; and seeing a heavenly presence. Moen's visions are also quite similar to Swedenborg's visionary concepts of the afterlife. His viewpoint also stresses the importance of controlling negative emotions. The Monroe Institute's emphasis on the importance of sound is similar to Eckankar's focus on the spiritual sound.

Wolf's Quantum Soul

Fred Alan Wolf (see *Figure 61*) is a consulting physicist, lecturer, and writer. In his 1996 book, *The Spiritual Universe*, Wolf details a quantum physics model of the soul. The following are some of his conclusions:

A soul is a process without mass or energy (unlike Dykes' concept). Its action is unpredictable. It is imaginable and cannot be controlled. The soul is real and subjective, but it cannot be objectively observed. (The same is true for virtual particles in quantum mechanics.) It had been considered by some (for example, Aristotle) that the soul is confined to the body, and nothing survives beyond the body. However,

Figure 61
Photograph of
Fred Alan Wolf.
Permission
granted for its
use by Fred Alan
Wolf.

this is incorrect because the soul is in every human, animal, plant and in the entire planet. The soul is everywhere. The soul's voice travels on faster-than-light quantum waves that fill the universe. The soul has the possibility of traveling both forward and backward in time. The soul involves consciousness of knowledge, and it appears in the vacuum of space that began when the universe first appeared and will end when the universe terminates at the end of the void (according to the Big Crunch Theory, see Chapter 9).

The soul directs the body-self, but by remaining within the vacuum of space, the soul does not become the body. The universe is filled with quantum waves of possibility that travel everywhere. This could be considered the unconscious or dreaming mind of God. The soul sends signals from the future. The bodymind or self receives these messages.

Generally, the self is preoccupied with mechanical and nonconscious survival and only infrequently receives the messages. This preoccupation brings forth the duality of everything as seen by the self. The soul tries to guide the bodymind while the bodymind, in its preoccupation, tries to fulfill its material addictions. The soul tries to create self and nonself without losing itself in the battle. The soul's role is to shape the self in the world but not lose its soul character in the process, even though the self, which is embedded in matter, demands it to do so. If the soul identifies too completely with the self, it can lose its purpose. However, the soul really loves the body and the self it has created. The soul is akin to a loving parent to the childlike self.

Each of us has a soul. This is known because everyone is conscious and experiences the one same mind. Each person can communicate with the world-soul, the world, and the universe by being conscious of the surrounding world and by expanding its boundaries. The soul follows the same path as matter and energy; it appeared during the big bang (birth) and will leave at the big crunch (death). Because the soul begins when time begins and ends when time ends, the soul is immortal. It lasts for all time. The soul manifests matter and energy, and it shapes the material Earth by knowledge.

To Wolf, spirit means the vibrations of nothing. The vacuum is filled with these vibrations, and they contain the potential for anything. Soul is when the spirit becomes partially aware and partially unaware at nodes of time. A temporal node is a point in time; a spatial node is a point in space. Even though the soul is immortal, it arises from the spirit's vibrations at two temporal points: the alpha point at the beginning of the big bang, and the omega point at the end of the big crunch. Hence, the soul lasts through all time and therefore is immortal. The reflection of spirit in space is matter. The reflection of soul in matter is self. Self is a reflection of a conscious spirit, which is soul, in an unconscious that exists in a space matrix (matter). Therefore, self is a conscious reflection of the soul from an unconscious reflection of the spirit. Self, hence, is part conscious and part unconscious. The soul not having a material form and being imaginary is the basis for all reality.

People can also lose their souls by going on automatic "addictive" pilot and thereby behaving nonconsciously toward everything, including themselves. Because there is no awareness of soul, no responsibility for anything can take place. The Earth becomes lost in an illusion of uncaring mechanical action and reaction. Suffering would mount to considerable heights with the eruption of violence. A person without a soul would respond in a similar fashion.

When the voice of the Soul is heard throughout the universe as the only voice of compassion and reason that has ever existed, then humanity will be truly free and the Soul's voice will sing until the end of time.

Wolf's concept of the soul and spirit as imaginable entities that are still real has been compared to the imaginary — but real — particle concepts of quantum physics such as quarks, virtual particles and the quantum soup existing prior the big bang. Hence, although it cannot be proved objectively, this doesn't preclude the reality of the soul and the spirit.

Afterlife Concepts

Although Wolf's concepts are not given in religious terms, it appears that the soul, being eternal, would survive the death of the physical body and join the world-soul which could be considered as God's unconscious or dreaming mind or the Holy Spirit. This joining to the world-soul might be considered as a form of heaven. The fate of those who have lost their souls appears to be akin to a hell on Earth. And the time when the compassionate voice of the Soul is heard throughout the universe — with humanity becoming truly free — could be construed as the resurrection at the end-of-times judgment, when the righteous will rejoice just as the Soul's voice will sing until the end of time.

Little's Electromagnetic
Spectrum Theory

Dr. Greg Little has a diversified background (see *Figure 62*). He has advanced training and degrees in psychology, psychopharmacology and counseling. He works in criminal justice as a researcher, trainer and editor and is affiliated with Louisiana State University at Shreveport. Dr. Little has also performed research in archaeology, UFOs, UFO abductions and other psi phenomena. He has given numerous presentations and has had several hundred articles published on the topics of mental health, psychopharmacology, substance abuse treatment, antisocial personality treatments, criminal justice and various psi phenomena. Dr. Little is also an editor of *Cognitive Behavioral Treatment Review, Addictive Behaviors Treatment*, and coedits the journal, *Alternate Perceptions*. Three of his books develop his Electromagnetic Spectrum theory (*The Archetype Experience* [1984], *People of the Web* [1990] and especially, *Grand Illusions* [1994]).

Little's Electromagnetic Spectrum theory is masterful and unique in that it ties together all of these supposedly separate concepts: (1) religious beliefs of the soul, the spiritual world, heaven, hell, God, Satan, angels, demons, ghosts, persistent hauntings and communications with deceased relatives, friends, and famous personalities, Jesus, Mary, angels, demons and God (through apparitions, by prayer, meditation, hypnosis, séances, dreams, fasting and rituals); (2) apparently mythical entities such as dwarves, elves, gnomes, goblins, leprechauns, fairies, Moslem Jinn and Indian tricksters and *Maiyun*; (3) strange beasts (e.g., Mothman, the Jersey Devil, Bigfoot); (4) psi phenomena such as ESP, UFOs, crashed saucers, UFO abductions and aliens (traditional grays)

Figure 62
Photograph of Dr. Greg Little
— by permission.

and psychic surgery; (5) mind-altering drugs; (6) Carl Jung's archetypes, synchronicity and "cosmic consciousness"; (7) sacred ancient sites (e.g., Native American medicine wheels and mounds; sacred stone circles such as Stonehenge; pyramids; (8) geomagnetic fluctuations of the Earth; (9) John Keel's electromagnetic spectrum theory of UFOs; (10) neuropsychiatrist Michael Persinger's theory of interactions between the Earth's geomagnetic effects and the human nervous system producing mystical and UFO experiences; (11) apparitions (such as religious types, those occurring at bereavement and those transpiring via Dr. Raymond Moody's psychomanteum), trance channeling, near-death experiences and out-of-body experiences; (12) brilliant intuitions; (13) brain anatomy and physiology; and (14) genetic differences among people.

Basically, Little believes that a form of electromagnetic energy occasionally manifests itself into physically real forms that interact with certain humans. The process of emergence into physical reality is known as *transmutation* (changing energy into matter and vice versa). Historically, these electromagnetic forms (EMFs) have taken on many shapes including angels, demons, chariots of fire, fairies, little people, will-o-the-wisps, ghosts, apparitions, archetypes, and more recently, extraterrestials (little gray entities), UFO-like discs, triangles, globes, lights and charged plasmas. In their most solid form, the EMFs enter from the ultraviolet end of the light spectrum and appear in the middle of the visible light spectrum as an intense or luminous white light. The EMFs leave physical reality from the same end of the spectrum as they enter. In the physical realm, the EMFs are encircled by a powerful electromagnetic wave field. These energy waves are potent and can burn individuals who are too close.

The EMFs, when in their physically real stage, are under their own intelligent control. They have an underlying purpose and intelligence that appears to be intimately linked to what is occurring globally as well as individually. The EMFs adjust themselves to the particular individuals to whom they appear as well as those individuals' unconscious expectations and level of understanding. The EMFs also adjust themselves to the particular culture in which they manifest. Nevertheless, some of the EMFs exist on a "lower order" and have a decreased capability to adapt their appearance specifically for certain individuals. These EMFs have less energy and are generally involved with negative experiences.

The EMFs use the Earth's magnetic field in order to make their appearance. Geomagnetic plasmas are highly electrically charged balls of energy that form in air particles. Typically, they last less than a second, but at times, plasmas can last for hours. These plasmas have a powerful magnetic field surrounding them. They tend to emerge over time from the same places. Apparently, geomagnetic energy is required to build the sufficient energy some of these EMFs require in order to assume a physically solid shape. Certain locations on the Earth's surface represent ideal places for the EMFs to emerge and assume a shape. These locations are regions of unusual geomagnetic events and have been called "window" areas. They are often sacred sites where "special" events frequently occur. Certain rocks standing at definite angles can intensify the effects of the electromagnetic energies that are present. The angles of these rocks are quite similar to the tilt of the Earth on its axis.

At regular periodic intervals, the EMFs appear to materialize more often and with greater intensity. Ancient wheels and circles have been erected at these "window" areas. Two geomagnetic conditions tend to bring on most experiences of EMFs: (1) extremely powerful geomagnetic manifestations in the form of geomagnetic plasmas; and (2) times of geomagnetic inactivity. Most EMF appearances are associated with periods of relative geomagnetic inactivity.

When EMFs appear to individuals or small groups, profound and life-altering happenings take place. There are also frequent occurrences of synchronicity (meaningful coincidences, first discussed by Carl Jung). The life-altering occurrences can either be stressful and unbalancing or positive and beneficial. Religions have started and ended relative to the appearances of these EMFs. Certain religions have even worshipped some of these EMFs.

People can attune themselves to particular EMFs and even control them by using a variety of rites and rituals. These include meditation, hypnosis, prayer, prolonged rhythmic chanting or singing, drum beating, listening to specific musical sounds, and concentrating on specific lights. Even stressful procedures such as fasting, self-mutilation, torture and almost dying, can attune individuals to these EMFs.

A powerful alteration in the affected individuals' brain chemistry related to the magnetic field occurs as a result of any of these methods and techniques. Neurochemical alterations in the individuals' brain lead to massive internal experiences. The individual's brain chemistry is changed so that a harmony of frequencies occurs between the person and the particular EMF sought.

Little theorizes that the brain chemistry is altered as a result of naturally occurring brain magnetite that aligns itself to the field of whatever electromagnetic — or geomagnetic — force that the individual is in. This magnetite alignment slightly changes the ionic flow in the brain's cells. This increases the flow of neurotransmitters (primarily endorphins) in some brain areas while reducing their flow in other areas (as a result of inhibition). The Reticular Activating System and other brain areas in the Limbic System, mainly in the right temporal lobe, are among the richest in endorphin receptors. The pineal gland is probably also involved. According to the research of Dr. Melvin Morse, the Sylvan fissure in the right temporal lobe is the most probable site in the brain where near-death experiences occur. The ability to perceive God as a brilliant light is most likely located in the right temporal lobe. This light could be considered an EMF.

Endorphins and magnetite are most affected by a magnetic field. It has been found that magnetite can be altered through an electromagnetic field and through conscious deliberation by using one of the methods previously mentioned (e.g., prayer, meditation). It has also been observed that rituals that effect this best occur in regions of high geometric energy (vortices and window areas). The most profound results occur when the rituals are performed at night when little magnetic interference from the "solar winds" occurs. The various methods to bring forth or interact with the EMFs were learned most likely by either trial-and-error or through direct input from the EMFs themselves. Little asserts that revelations received by the ancient prophets were probably the result of direct EMF input. The effectiveness of rites at sacred sites and methods such as meditation, prayer and chanting were most likely learned by trial-and-error.

An intuition via an EMF — when the involved person is either partially awake or asleep — is probably the result of unconscious prodding by the EMF that leads to mental input from the EMF. A particular example of this phenomenon was the revelation to the German chemist, Friedrich Kekule. For years, he could not unravel the chemical configuration of the organic compound, benzene. One evening, Kekule was staring at the flames in his fireplace, again hopelessly trying to figure out the benzene ring configuration. He fell asleep, and the flames suddenly became hideous shapes that transformed themselves into writhing snakes. The snakes curled into a circle, took their tails into their mouths, rotated into a plane and had extensions sticking out from each side. All of a sudden, Kekule awoke and wrote down what he had seen in his dream. It became the benzene ring structure — a major scientific discovery.

According to Little, *archetypes* (first discovered by Carl Jung) are powerful electromagnetic forces that enter from the ultraviolet end of the light spectrum and interact with humans by altering brain chemistry. Examples of archetypes are: the Great Mother (also embodied as the Blessed Virgin Mary), Moses' burning bush, the cross in the sky of Constantine (which literally immediately transformed the entire Roman Empire into Christianity), mandalas, the shadow, angels, demons, ghosts, dwarves, elves, gnomes, goblins, leprechauns, fairies, Moslem Jinn, Indian tricksters, *Maiyun* and strange beasts (e.g., Mothman, the Jersey Devil, Bigfoot).

When archetypes first enter the physical realm, they are essentially charged geomagnetic plasmas. However, they are plasmas with intelligence and purpose. The archetypes appear to the people who observe them as a reality, and the powerful electromagnetic field that surrounds the plasmas alters the magnetite's alignment in the observer's brains. The archetypes come into physical reality by reducing their specific energy vibration. They give off powerful electromagnetic waves in a frequency that is attuned to that of the brain's magnetite. At the same time, the brain's magnetite aligns toward the suddenly appearing powerful electromagnetic field. The ionic flow in the brain's neurons change, and the brain's neurochemical dominoes reverberate in sequence taking the individual toward the direction that represents the underlying meaning of the specific archetype that appears.

Genes most likely are responsible for people's concentration of endorphin receptors, endorphin production, and magnetite concentration in various areas of the brain. It could be that people that have high concentrations of endorphins and magnetite are particularly prone to EMF interactions. These individuals are known as "electromagnetically mobile." In contrast, those individuals who have low concentrations of endorphins and magnetite rarely, if ever, encounter EMFs. They are known as "electromagnetically stable" and tend to be skeptics and disbelievers. In some of his writing, Little has stated that the genetics involved in an individual's sensitivity to EMFs can account for the religious tradition of "chosen people."

Heaven, Hell And Afterlife Concepts

Various brain structures represent gates (such as the Sylvan Fissure in the right temporal lobe). According to Dr. Paul D'Encarnacao (now deceased), the gates leading to spiritual reality are usually closed, thereby cutting off conscious awareness of spiritual reality. Under certain conditions, (e.g., intense prayer, deep meditation, deep hypnosis, vivid dreams, out-of-body-experiences and near-death experiences) the gates can open and consciousness can be released from the physical body into the "spiritual" world. During these conditions, the consciousness released by the body could be considered as the soul. It temporarily leaves the body and eventually returns as the brain's chemistry changes back to normal. At death, the gates completely open, and the soul is permanently released.

Little's concept of the soul is difficult to pin down. He has described it as energy plus some other force. Exactly what the other force is, he cannot state (personal communication, 1999). Nevertheless, Dr. Little does believe in the post-mortem existence of the soul and the possibilities of it traveling either to heaven or hell (*sheol*). Little's concept of heaven and hell is based on the electromagnetic (EM) spectrum, which is now examined more fully. In *Figure 63*, a diagrammatic representation of the entire EM spectrum is given including heaven and sheol.

Examining *Figure 63*, it can be seen that heaven and hell could **literally** exist from a scientific viewpoint. Heaven lies on the end of the electromagnetic energy spectrum starting at the ultraviolet end and extending out above cosmic rays. Heaven creates and maintains the entire spectrum from the region where energy is continually created and exuded out into all the regions of the universe. This energy is involved in the creation of stars from the innumerable "stellar nurseries" (nebulas) and in the explosion of stars. Normally, heaven cannot be seen because it lies beyond the narrow, visible light portion of the electromagnetic spectrum. Heaven is all around us and extends throughout the universe. Heaven consists of various layers that extend to the realm of "cosmic rays." However, it appears that the "uppermost" region of heaven extends above the level of cosmic rays. God resides in this uppermost region of heaven as pure light and energy and is the creator of all light and energy — the EM spectrum itself.

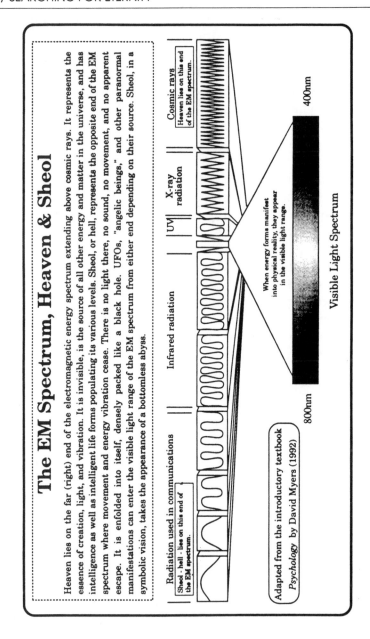

Figure 63
The EM Spectrum, Heaven & Sheol — from *Grand Illusions*.

Within heaven are EMFs that have various shapes and appearances. These EMFs serve a purpose that has often been described as God's will. They make appearances in the physical world as the need arises. Some of these EMFs still appear today by slowing their energy vibrational frequencies down to those in the visible light spectrum. The inhabitants of heaven are angels (also known as *archetypes*). Scriptures tell us that a group of angels were expelled from heaven and cast down to Earth and below because they wished to ascend to the highest heavenly parts. Their fall to Earth was lightening-like — an appropriate image for an energy form banished from the far end of the EM spectrum to the region near the visible wavelength.

Little cites Hebrew literature in asserting that the angels' "essence" is "fire" (energy). Angels can either be living creatures (e.g., *cherubim, seraphim* and *hayyot*) or wheels (*ofanium*). The "wheels" are a means of communication and transportation and serve to contain smaller, condensed energy forms. Some angels travel across the Earth collecting information and reporting the results. Little relates these "information collectors" to the biblical depictions of "the eyes of God" and "flying scrolls."

As stated in Daniel 7:10, angels emanate from the "stream of fire," which is the electromagnetic energy spectrum emanating from God. Angels were created on the second day of creation to assist God. The EM spectrum was created by God's "word," which is the initial "musical" vibrations which could also be called the big bang. Earth and its inhabitants evolved by way of the natural laws created when the EM spectrum was created and the universe was placed into its inevitable, ever-evolving motion. The angels were formed in the midst of the spectrum. Angels speak and otherwise interact with humans according to the mental vision of the involved individuals. Angels communicate and appear because of a harmonizing of their frequency with that of the involved individual.

According to tradition, the fallen angels taught mankind how to "invoke" heavenly angels in order to make them physically appear. This was performed by using a particular vibrational frequency at a specific location and time period. As soon as they fell to Earth, Satan and his helpers taught mankind how to perform these magical feats. Humans learned how to use definite chants and rituals in certain places and specific times. As mentioned before, the importance of the place and time relates to the use of the Earth's magnetic field in achieving a harmony of frequencies. Use of vibrational frequencies is the key to movement up and down the EM spectrum.

According to the Bible, Satan is one of the fallen "sons of God" who interbred with humans. He and his followers can take on the physical appearance of a human or anything else in order to deceive and manipulate people. The fallen angels can become invisible or visible at will. They have the ability to quickly change their vibrational frequency in and out of the EM spectrum.

Sheol (hell) is on the other end of the electromagnetic spectrum. It represents the far reaches of the spectrum where vibrational frequency is at a complete, or almost complete, standstill. Hell represents the farthest position from God. It is a region of darkness and shadows. Neither sound nor light is present in hell because no vibrational energy is present. Hell is a desolate place located "underneath" the Earth (below the Earth, below visible light on the EM spectrum). Hell is not vibrating and is enfolded into itself. Hell might represent what cosmologists call black holes. Black holes represent regions where matter is rolled up and enfolded densely into itself. Neither movement, sound, light or escape can take place. Hell, at the far end of the EM spectrum, is "maintained" by the "fallen angels" who collect some "evil or lost" souls and transport them to the "gates" of hell. These angels can appear to humans, delude them and lead them astray. They act as "watchers" and can usher people into the gates of hell's abyss. The fallen angels retained some powers of transmutation, but they could not alter their vibrations in order to be above the ultraviolet portion of the electromagnetic spectrum (to ascend back into heaven). Nevertheless, they **can** enter the narrow, ultraviolet band. Generally, the fallen angels reside in the infrared end of the spectrum, but some of them have the capability to transmute into the physical, visible light portion of the spectrum. These angels apparently have the desire to remove as many pieces of God (souls) into their end of the spectrum — that is, into hell. Perhaps, it is their motivation that they might eventually remove all of the created universe into their hellish domain.

According to Christian belief, about 2,000 years ago, God sent his "son" from heaven to Earth to show mankind a means to directly ascend back into heaven. These humans would have to live their lives in an appropriate manner and seek the "light" of God and reject the "darkness" of hell. These humans could attain the heavenly end of the EM spectrum by using methods such as prayer, meditation, appropriate rituals and faith in God.

Throughout the centuries, humans have interacted with God, Satan, angels and demons. They have been given methods to follow in order to avoid the demons and follow the paths of God, the prophets and angels.

Biblical references can be explained through the Electromagnetic Spectrum theory. For example, Jacob's ladder represents the entire EM spectrum shown in a vision. Jacob saw angels ascending and descending the ladder by altering their vibrational rates. The Red Sea was parted by an electromagnetic whirlwind. Pharoah's chariots were slowed down by the use of powerful electromagnetic fields that surrounded their wheels. The walls of Jericho fell down because the use of certain vibrations caused the stone to crumble. The Ark of the Covenant was a mechanical method for heavenly angels and God to communicate with the wandering tribes of Israel. The ark permitted a method of altering electromagnetic vibrational frequencies so that the ancient Israelites could always be aware of God. Certain prophets, such as Enoch and Elijah, were carried away to heaven by entering wheels which transmuted them into energy forms, permitting them to go to heaven and be with God. Jesus Christ's miraculous healing power resulted from his knowledge and adaptness in manipulating electromagnetic fields. These fields were able to change physical matter as well as alter the genetic code. Genetic manipulation occurred as the result of direct application of electromagnetic radiation fields to the DNA in critical reproductive cells. Christ taught his disciples how to heal by the use of electromagnetic forces. He did this by changing their brain chemistry. Some powerful angelic EMFs cannot be directly viewed because of the radiation they emit when in physical form. This could also be the reason why Moses couldn't directly look at the "burning bush."

A Brilliant Concept

As just shown, Dr. Greg Little's Electromagnetic Spectrum theory brilliantly integrates many disparate concepts. I believe his theory has much more validity than the ancient astronaut theory of the appearance of the Hebrews, God, angels, Ezekiel's visions of wheels, ancient monuments (such as the pyramids) and UFOs. Little's theory utilizes scientifically testable concepts such as geomagnetism, magnetite and endorphin levels in the brain and the EM spectrum itself.

In Little's viewpoint, heaven hell, angels, God, Satan and other spiritual beings are not found in a separate dimension (e.g., a fifth dimension) but are components of the EM spectrum. This is a compelling viewpoint that can include many religious, psi phenomena, and even scientific beliefs. Probably deliberately on his part, Dr. Little does not discuss the afterlife travels of the soul in depth. He does mention that good people will go to heaven and evil ones will go to hell. Dr. Little discusses the Christian belief of accepting Jesus Christ and following his concepts as a way to go to heaven. However, he does not consider that people can avoid hell without accepting Jesus Christ. For example as has been discussed in the section on Judaism in the last chapter, following the precepts of the *Torah* and *Talmud*, and being moral and righteous will pave the pathway to heaven.

The EM spectrum does not account for the later concepts of Gehenna. It is only in the early Biblical period that Gehenna is equivalent to Sheol (hell). In later Biblical periods and beyond, Gehenna is not a dark, dismal region. Rather, it is a stepping-off place where the soul is cleansed and purified so that it can travel on further toward heaven. However, Dr. Little has stated (personal consultation, 1999) that recent research by the brilliant cosmologist, Stephen Hawking, has shown that, contrary to previous belief, something can come out of black holes and become "purified" into an elemental state. So, perhaps Sheol in the electromagnetic spectrum is not completely dark, dismal and inescapable. This could go along with the later Judaic thinking about Gehenna.

As far as reincarnation, perhaps Dr. Little would agree with me that only those souls that require a great deal of purification, or have had a very brief time on Earth, would require reincarnation. Finally, according to Electromagnetic Spectrum theory, heaven, hell and the spiritual world are not in another dimension but are merely in unseen aspects of the universe's EM spectrum. Considering that cosmologists conclude that in the distant future, the universe either will expand to oblivion or self destruct with a "big crunch," (see Chapter 9) will heaven, hell and the spiritual world also come to an end? Or perhaps, God will create a new universe and take along the previous worthy inhabitants' souls? Who knows?

Aside from these minor considerations, for the concepts that it includes, Dr. Little's Electromagnetic Spectrum theory is as comprehensive as any that have previously been recorded. Certain components of it have been used in the personal afterlife concept (see Chapter 15).

Novak's Separation Of Soul And Spirit

A personal tragedy stimulated Peter Novak (an American living in LaPorte, Indiana) into a ten-year investigation into the nature of death and the afterlife (see *Figure 64*). Novak examined the fields of theology, psychology, philosophy, thanatology, comparative religion and biblical archaeology, as well as the investigations into NDEs and past-life regressions. In addition, he worked in a psychiatric hospital. The result was his concept of the division of the human psyche both during life and in the afterlife. Novak's findings are detailed in his book, *The Division of Consciousness: The Secret Afterlife of the Human Psyche.*

The Ego And The Id

As Freud discovered, the human psyche is made up of a conscious portion (the ego) and an unconscious portion (the id). The conscious portion of the mind is the part that we are aware of while awake and is, in essence, just the tip of the iceberg. It is logical and rational and involved with free will. The conscious mind is governed by the left half of the brain (in right-handed individuals), and is mainly responsible for everything that was ever accomplished in the arts and sciences. Of course, in evil individuals, it also has some responsibility for murders, wars and other acts of destruction. The unconscious portion of the mind is that part that we are not normally aware of while awake. It surfaces in dreams and intuitions; under hypnosis, meditation, mind-altering drugs and alcohol; and with psychoanalytic free association. It is the major part of the iceberg. The unconscious mind is mainly illogical and irrational, and is governed by the right half of the brain (in right-handed indi-

Figure 64
Photograph of Peter Novak. Permission granted for its use by Peter Novak.

viduals). It is the storehouse of drives, emotions, memories and desires.

A well-adjusted right-handed person uses his left brain (responsible for conscious mind) to intellectually investigate the world, but unfortunately, the emotional components from the right brain (responsible for unconscious mind) can affect decision-making which can result in poor or tragic decisions. For example, a person under the influence of alcohol can perform dangerous acts that his conscious ego would normally suppress. However, sometimes the unconscious can allow for brilliant insights as when Isaac Newton's sight of the falling apple triggered an emotional response that led to the discovery of gravity. The right brain is also responsible for much of the artistic and creative accomplishments of mankind (see *Figure 65*).

Figure 65
A Functional Representation of the Two Hemispheres of the Brain by Don Morse. In a right-handed person, the left hemisphere is primarily concerned with logic, analysis and speech, and the right hemisphere is mainly involved with holistic, spatial and emotional-type thinking. April 30, 1999.

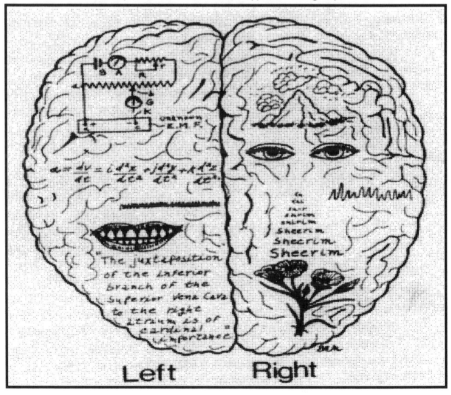

From his readings and interpretation, Novak concluded that, at some time in mankind's remote past, the two components of the mind (conscious and unconscious) were united. At that time man, had a full awareness of everything in the unconscious mind. However, because of some conflict, change or error, this full awareness was diminished and then lost. The result was a divided consciousness. Using the early Christian Gnostic model (see Chapter 12), Novak suggested that this full awareness was greater than its constituent components and was actually a state of pure will. However, after the fall, everything changed and in time an immense gulf appeared between the conscious and unconscious minds.

The Division Between Soul And Spirit

After analyzing the religious traditions of the Gnostics, ancient Egypt, Greece, Persia, China and India, as well as native tribes throughout Africa, North and South Africa, Hawaii and many other Pacific Island cultures, Novak came to the conclusion that people have two souls; a conscious soul and an unconscious soul. For example, in ancient Egypt, *ba* would be equivalent to the conscious soul, and *ka* would be comparable to the unconscious soul. Ancient Israel also thought that humans possessed two souls calling one the soul (unconscious) and the other the spirit (conscious). The early Christians, as well as many of the previous cultures, believed that the soul and spirit could separate at death. Both the conscious and unconscious portions could be savagely wrenched apart from one another at the death of the physical body as is shown here:

"For the word of God is quick, and powerful, and sharper than any two edged sword, piercing even to the dividing asunder of soul and spirit, and of the joints and marrow, and is a discerner of the thoughts and intents of the heart."
Hebrews 4: 12).

In 1945 in Nag Hammadi, Egypt, some of the writings of the early Christian sect known as the Gnostics were uncovered. Certain of their writings were relevant to the post-death separation of the soul and spirit as per the following:

"...without the soul the body does not sin, just as the soul is not saved without the spirit. But if the soul is saved when it is without evil, and the spirit is also saved, then the body becomes free from sin. For it is the spirit that quickens the soul..."
(The Apocryphon of James 11: 38-39, 12: 1-6).

Your Afterlife Travels

Your conscious and unconscious parts have different but equally crippling afterlife destinations. Your conscious portion, having no memory, loses any recollection of its former existence and wanders about in the astral planes (as has been described in some past life regressions; see Chapter 6). Inevitably, it is drawn toward matter, which means it becomes incarnated into another you. As the new you grows and develops a whole new set of memories, your reincarnated consciousness has a different unconscious affiliation. After the death of the second you, the two halves of your mind separate and the conscious portion again wanders about and loses memories of its new past self. The cycle of reincarnations continue to repeat indefinitely and each time your consciousness loses its memories of its previous incarnation. Hence, your conscious part is stuck with total amnesia. Another possible fate of the conscious portion is as a "lost soul" type of ghost that has no memories of itself.

Your unconscious portion has nothing but memories without any critical faculty of outward awareness. It, therefore, turns on itself and becomes absorbed in its own memories. Depending upon the kind of life you had lived, these memories are either pleasurable, distressful or some combination of the two. Because these memories are all your unconscious knows, in time they become its only reality. Your unconscious portion then wanders the astral planes of its own creation, which, dependent upon its former life, leads to the creation of its own heaven or hell. Your unconscious part is stuck in either realm which becomes fixed and unchanging.

Another possible fate of the unconscious portion is as a wandering ghost stuck with its own recurrent memories (as described by native cultures and the *Gilgul* of ancient Judaism; see Chapters 4 and 12).

Reunion Of Your Soul and Spirit

From his readings of the Gnostic literature and that of others, Novak concluded that, in order to end the cycles of reincarnation of your spirit (conscious part) and the fixed, unchanging realm of your soul (unconscious part) to eventually achieve a union with God, it would be necessary for your soul and spirit to be reunited before death. He illustrated this with the life and death of Jesus Christ. Jesus' descent into the underworld with the freeing of the dead can be interpreted as the liberation of the unconscious souls. Jesus' resurrection and ascension could be interpreted as a state of complete integration and awareness (reunion of soul and spirit) as per the following:

Jesus said to them, "When you make the two one, and when you make the inside like the outside, and the above like the below, and when you make the male and the female one and the same, so that the male not be male nor the female female....then you will enter the Kingdom."
(The Gospel of Thomas: 22).

Jesus said....."If one is undivided, he is filled with light, but if one is divided, he is filled with darkness."
(The Gospel of Thomas: 61).

Novak shows how the two principal groups of religions, those of the East and the West, have a great dichotomy in how they judge the fate of the soul in the afterlife. The Eastern religions (for example, Hinduism, Buddhism, Taoism) consider that, after death, the spirit wanders for a time in the interlife (Bardo) and then gets incarnated into another human being. This cycle of incarnations and reincarnations of the spirit continues for a long time. In contrast, the Western religions (for example, Judaism, Christianity, Islam) consider that, after death, the soul travels into either heaven, hell or purgatory (or some other in-between place for purification). At the end-of-days, a final judgment occurs and there is a physical resurrection and unification of the body and soul of each individual. People who had been righteous during life would be united with God in a blissful afterlife. Those who had been evil who be condemned to a tragic afterlife.

Eastern religions consider the entity that leaves the body after death to be reincarnated to be the conscious spirit. They fail to state the destiny of the unconscious soul. Western religions consider that the entity that leaves the body after death to be the unconscious soul which travels to either heaven, hell or purgatory. They fail to state the destiny of the conscious spirit. A third fate is considered by the primitive native cultures, which consider that ghosts are the result of wandering souls.

Nevertheless, Novak believes that Division Theory supports all three models of the afterlife. The Eastern religions consider the fate of the conscious mind (the spirit); the Western religions and the native cultures consider the fate of the unconscious mind (the soul).

The end-of days scenario is complicated. Consider that each conscious part (spirit) would have had been combined with innumerable unconscious parts (souls). Some of the souls would have been heavenly; some hellish. At the end-of-days, when a dark age occurs prior to the resurrection and the advent of the Messiah (Jesus Christ in the Christian version), all of the spirits and the souls would recombine along with the physical bodies (as in the orthodox Judaic, Christian and Islamic concepts). How this could ever happen is difficult to understand. Nevertheless, Novak believes that in the "dark age," first the hellish souls would be released. There would be a veritable madhouse as the numerous hellish souls would clamor with each other to combine with their spirits. In addition, the souls released from hell would be freed to enter live humans. Suddenly, the people would have all sorts of memories of previous lives overwhelming them. All kinds of mental disturbances would occur, and mankind would go insane, both individually and collectively. However, the hellish souls would have the opportunity for salvation:

> "And it shall come to pass, that whosoever shall
> call on the name of the Lord shall be delivered..."
> (Joel 2: 32).

Those souls who don't repent would either return to the unconscious hell from whence they came or be utterly destroyed. After the hellish souls had been released, the next phase in the resurrection scenario would be the return of Jesus Christ leading the heavenly souls with their Holy Spirits into the world of the living. There would then be a renewed clamor as the heavenly souls would compete with the remaining hellish souls for the spirits of both the revived deceased and the living humans. The enclosed Holy Spirits of the heavenly souls would cause the hellish souls to abandon their spirits. The outcome would be that all the hellish souls would be lost forever: either destroyed or existing in hellish unconsciousness. The formerly deceased heavenly souls with their united spirits would enter living humans. There would then be a juggling of conscious spirits and unconscious souls with living bodies, and as a result of having the Holy Spirit (from the heavenly souls), the new humans would have their imperfect human egos subordinated by the conscious remembrance of God. Each person would have memories of all his previous good lives (the bad ones would have been cast out) and would lead enjoyable lives. When their physical bodies would wear out, their combined spirit and soul (maintaining all of its previous memories) would merely have to incarnate into a new body. This then would indeed be heaven on earth.

From Division To Reunion

Peter Novak's Division Theory is a brilliant concept, and it deserves commendations. If true, it would be important for people, while alive, to practice positive stress management methods to control negative emotions in order to be righteous and have a heavenly life existence (even if only as a soul). However, there are certain aspects of the theory that are difficult to reconcile with existing beliefs.

First, almost all religions that consider reincarnation, state that the rationale of reincarnation is because in a previous life, the individual had some defects that had to be eradicated for the attainment of spiritual purity. With each rebirth, the spirit was supposed to attain a higher state of purity (see Chapters 6, 11 and 12). In addition, according to some aspects of *Kabbalah*, only a few souls need to be reincarnated, and again only for the rectification of previous defects. If the spirit has no memory at all of its previous existence, then how could it possibly purify itself to attain a higher level?

The unconscious soul supposedly has no ability to "think for itself" because of the loss of the conscious spirit. Just to use one example, according to Swedenborg, the soul becomes a spirit with a spiritual body. It lives in a society that consists of spirits with characters similar to those of itself. (For example, spirits from angry people would associate with each other.) The spirit has thoughts and feelings and functions as it did in the physical world. In some other religious concepts, the soul in its afterlife travels also is able to "think" independent thoughts.

However, the concept of the unconscious soul and the conscious spirit leaving the dead body and having independent disastrous paths in the afterlife is a viable one. Nevertheless, the belief that at the end-of-days at judgment time, it is necessary for Jesus Christ to intervene in order for the conscious spirit and the unconscious soul to unite and retain God and his spirit is a strict orthodox Christian belief. Neither Judaism nor Islam considers Jesus Christ to have been either a Son of God or God incarnate. And, it is well to remember that beyond his followers, there was no independent verification of the resurrection of Jesus Christ. Hence, there is no reason to believe that only through Jesus intervention can a conscious spirit and an unconscious soul unite and retain God and his spirit. There is just as much justification to state that at the time of the resurrection, "whosoever shall call on the name of the Lord shall be delivered." And that quotation used by Novak is from Joel, who was a Hebrew prophet, who referred to the Lord God and not to Jesus Christ.

Novak also concludes that the initial stage of the NDE (when the entity hovers over the body) is similar to the divided spirit with its memory loss (see Chapter 3); each interlife stage of a past life regression (when the entity is in a vacuum) is also similar to the spirit (see Chapter 6); and with ghostly apparitions that continue to repeat the same actions, this is reminiscent of the divided soul (see Chapter 5).

The Division of Consciousness is certainly well-thought out and has much to recommend it. Certain components of it have been used in the personal afterlife concept (see Chapter 15).

Raphael's Holistic Afterlife Concept

Simcha Paull Raphael's afterlife concept is the next of the recent viewpoints to be examined. Dr. Raphael is an ordained rabbi, a psychologist, a Jewish Chaplain and an Assistant Professor in the Department of Religion at LaSalle University (see *Figure 66*). Dr. Raphael is also the author of the acclaimed *Jewish Views of the Afterlife*. In that book, using the background of kabbalistic Judaism views of the afterlife, along with the afterlife views of Tibetan Buddhism, concepts of Elisabeth Kübler-Ross, Raymond Moody's near-death investigations and concepts of transpersonal psychology, Raphael developed his contemporary psychological model of the afterlife. This model utilizes seven transit stages which are now detailed.

Transit Stage 1: The Dying Process

For most individuals, the actual moment of death is a painless one. Certain visions usually accompany the dying process. These are: (1) the clear light (River of Light); (2) encounter with angelic spirits and

Figure 66
Photograph of Simcha Paull
Raphael. Permission granted for its
use by Dr. Raphael.

deceased relatives; (3) a life review; (4) a dissolution of the elements; and (5) passing through
the tunnel (rending the silver
cord).

The Clear Light
(The River Of Light)

A vision of a radiant light
occurs as your soul separates
from your dying physical body.
This light should be welcomed
as it helps you leave the physical
world and enter the spiritual
world. The light vision has been
corroborated in NDEs, the
Kabbalah and Tibetan Buddhism.

The Encounter With Angelic Spirits And Deceased Relatives

Your religious or cultural orientation appears to determine the
kind of celestial being you visualize. For example, a Christian would
most likely see Jesus, a Buddhist would probably see Buddha, and a Jew
might see Moses or his/her interpretation of God. An irreligious person
might see a nonspecific angelic-like being. In addition to the celestial
being, you could see deceased loved ones. Either the celestial being or the
loved one would act as a guide to assist you into the realm of post-
mortem consciousness. These type visions have also been found with
NDEs and in Talmudic and kabbalistic Judaism writings.

The Life Review

As you die, your life is reviewed either slowly or rapidly. This is
likely to prepare your soul for its departure from your body. This kind
of experiential life review has been found with NDEs, and in Talmudic
and kabbalistic Judaism writings, in the *Tibetan Book of the Dead*, and in
St. Augustine's *City of God*.

Dissolution Of The Elements

Some type of process of dissolution of the elements of life takes place. This has not been found with NDEs, because NDEs apparently occur only in the very early stage of death before any physical dissolution could have taken place. However, both Tibetan Buddhist and kabbalistic literature allude to dissolution and disconnection of the essential biological components as the dying process takes place.

Passing Through the Tunnel (Rending The Silver Cord)

Your soul now takes leave of its physical body and passes through a celestial passageway into the next world. This has been described in NDEs as a tunnel or passageway between the physical world and the world beyond. In kabbalistic writings, a tunnel is hinted at in the *Zohar*, where it states that, as the soul leaves the physical world, it enters the Cave of Makhhpelah, which acts as a corridor to Gan Eden. In Theosophy (discussed in the prior chapter), a silver cord is mentioned. It is a connective link between the body and the soul. When you die, the silver cord is snapped irreparably. The crossing of the tunnel corresponds to the final rending of the silver cord.

Transit Stage 2: Separation From The Physical Body (Hibbut Ha-Kever)

This stage is really not totally separate from Stage 1, but is part of the same process that completes all experiences relative to the physical realm. Transit Stage 2 is usually considered to be a process of giving up your attachments to your physical body and gradually accepting the reality of your death. This stage corresponds with the Jewish phenomenon known as pangs of the grave (*hibbut ha-kever*). During this stage, which can last from three-to seven days, the bioenergy aspect of your soul (*nefesh*) dissipates and eventually severs its connection with your physical body. If you had treated your body with respect and had no addictions, you might suffer little, if at all. In contrast, if you had been an addictive kind of person (for example, drugs, alcohol, nicotine, gambling, sex), you would suffer great pangs for a long time.

Your soul might refuse to give up its attachments to your physical body and the real world. Also, if you had died violently or suddenly, you might be unaware of your death. In either of those two examples, you might remain in the world of confusion (*olam ha-tohu*). As a result, your soul, which would have not accepted its death, attempts to stay close to the living and stay for a while as a ghoulish spirit (ghost). These type of souls are in the minority.

Eventually, the bioenergetic aspect of your soul dissipates and death becomes a reality. The next stage of the postmortem journey begins.

Transit Stage 3: Emotional Purification (Gehenna)

This stage corresponds with the postmortem realm of purgation, known in Jewish sources as Gehenna. Transit Stage 3 is concerned with the personal self (emotional energy field, *ruah*). This Stage is similar to a psychological catharsis, abreaction and discharge. Gehenna is comparable to prolonged, intensive psychotherapy in which negative emotions such as guilt, anger, fear, sadness, hate and shame are resolved. Following this, purification takes place and allows for the entrance into the next Transit Stage.

Transit Stage 4: Final Completion Of The Personality (Lower Gan Eden)

Transit Stage 4 (Lower Gan Eden) is a transitional stage between Gehenna and Upper Gan Eden and is based on kabbalistic teachings. In Lower Gan Eden, your soul experiences all of the positive emotions such as joy, bliss and ecstasy. Transit Stage 4 represents a place where all the acquired experiences and learning of your personal self (ruah) are given over to your transpersonal self (the neshamah). Lower Gan Eden marks the completion of the postmortem journey concerned with your individual personality. Hence, the experiences and integrated merits of your personal life are transferred to the immortal components of your soul as preparation to enter the next transcendent stage of the infinite and divine known as Upper Gan Eden. Before entering this stage, your soul again experiences the River of Light and also experiences a second life review. The meaning and consequences of the life just lived are now seen from the viewpoint of many lifetimes.

Transit Stage 5: Heavenly Repose For The Soul (Upper Gan Eden)

In Transit Stage 5, your transpersonal self (neshamah) experiences merited spiritual rewards. Upper Gan Eden is also based on kabbalistic teachings and is similar to the paradise described in various religious traditions (for example, Christianity's heaven and Tibetan Buddhism's bardo vision of the peaceful deities). In Upper Gan Eden, your soul is able to perceive everything as an integrated, unified whole. The world is observed as being inherently good, desirable, bountiful and beautiful. You receive perceptions of reverence, awe, and wonder with respect to the grand and magnificent order. In Transit Stage 5, the differences between your individual soul and the infinite divine are obscured, and, in a sense, you see God.

Nevertheless, this stage is not for everyone. If you had concentrated on the accumulation of the material things of life with no consideration for life's spirituality, then the transcendent realm of Upper Gan Eden would hardly be perceptible. In contrast, if you had led a spiritual life and experienced transpersonal states of consciousness while alive (as could occur from meditation), the transcendental bliss of Upper Gan Eden would be there to enjoy fully. Eventually your stay in Transit Stage 5 is complete and the energy level of the neshamah aspect of your soul is finished.

Transit Stage 6: Return To The Source (Tzor Ha-Hayim)

Transit Stage 6 involves the highest aspects of your soul known as universal self (*hayyah*) and transcendental field of light (*yehidah*). Tzor Ha-Hayim is the "storehouse of the souls" or the "bundle of life" and is based on kabbalistic teachings. It is where you are with God. Transit Stage 6 is the origin and terminating point for all souls in the universe. Here, your soul returns to receive its message with regard to its next incarnation.

Transit Stage 7: Preparation For Rebirth

Transit Stage 7 is the final Stage. Your soul forgets all that it has seen and learned and enters the embryo of a new mother. This is the process known as gilgul in *Kabbalah*, reincarnation in Hinduism and Buddhism and *metempsychosis* in Sikhism.

What Happened To The End-Of-Days?

Raphael's contemporary psychological model is an excellent explanation of the early stages of the afterlife, but it fails to include one belief widely held in Judaism, Christianity and Islam. That is the end-of-days scenario with the coming of the Messiah and the physical reunion of the body with the soul. Of course, the World-to-Come is considered by many rabbinic sources to be an Earthly kingdom. Nevertheless the dead are supposed to be resurrected, and, if that is to occur, the concept of gilgul could be a problem. If reincarnation occurs routinely, then we are faced with a dilemma. With a soul that has entered many bodies, which body would it unite with? Would only the righteous souls reunite? What would happen to the others? Would there be a judgment by God?

It is also believed by many religions that reincarnation is a process of purification because in a previous life, the individual had some defects that had to be eradicated for the attainment of spiritual purity. With each rebirth, the soul was supposed to a higher state of purity (see Chapters 6 and 11). Without some memory retention from a previous life, how is the soul to purify itself?

In a major Jewish concept of gilgul, not everyone gets reincarnated. Only those who failed to be purged and purified through Gehenna, or would need to return to Earth for a special purpose, would require reincarnation. The rest would go through the other stages and remain with God until the messianic era. Many of Raphael's viewpoints have been incorporated in the personal concept (see Chapter 15).

The Mansions

"In my Father's house are many mansions."
(John 14: 2).

As has already been discussed, many religions, religious organizations and societies, religious scholars, and spiritual researchers have interpreted this statement of Jesus Christ to mean that there are many planes in the afterlife voyage until the soul eventually reaches unity with God. Examples are: **(1)** Zoroastrianism's "astral world" consisting of (a) the "best existence" (equivalent of heaven); (b) the "worst existence " (equivalent of hell); and (c) "Hamistagan" (equivalent of purgatory) with subdivisions in each realm; **(2)** Tibetan Buddhism's Bardo states consisting of: (a) the first bardo, with two stages; (b) the second bardo, with two parts; and (c) the third bardo; **(3)** Judaism, which started off with Sheol (hell's equivalent) and changed to Gehenna (started off as the same as Sheol and became the equivalent of purgatory), and then moved on to heaven, which began as one heaven, became four heavens and then seven heavens (the third included hell and paradise), and finally *Kabbalah's* description of: (a) Gehenna (for purging and purification); (b) Lower Gan Eden; (c) Upper Gan Eden; and (d) Tzor ha-hayim ("storehouse of souls"); **(4)** Christianity, which started off with the Gnostic concept of seven to ten heavens and evolved into the strict Christianity concept of three regions: (a) purgatory; (b) hell and (c) heaven; **(5)** Islam's seven heavens of the firmament including: (a) an intermediate realm (equivalent of purgatory); (b) hell; (c) paradise; and (d) the abode of the Most High; **(6)** Rosicrucianism's planes of hell and spiritual planes; **(7)** Theosophy's astral plane with several levels and heaven; **(8)** Swedenborgianism's: (a) spirit world (a middle ground); (b) heaven (Natural Heaven, Spiritual Heaven and Celestial Heaven); and (c) hell (with several levels); **(9)** William Blake's: (a) etheric plane; (b) astral plane; (c) mental planes; and (d) higher and more subtle planes; **(10)** Christian Spiritism's spiritual world with different levels; **(11)** Eckankar's many planes; **(12)** Urantia's seven mansion worlds; **(13)** Edgar Cayce's lower planes of consciousness and higher planes of consciousness (that include traveling to other places in the universe); **(14)** E. W. Dykes' six planes (based on the work of Frederick W.H. Myers): (a) the Plane of Adjustment (Hades); (b) the Plane of Illusion (Summerland); (c) the Plane of Color; (d) the Plane of Flame; (e) the Plane of Light; and (f) Out Yonder (Timelessness, the Supreme Degree); **(15)** Novak's several afterlife planes; and **(16)** Raphael's: (a) Gehenna; (b) Lower Gan Eden; (c) Upper Gan Eden; and (d)Tzar Ha-Hayim.

In addition to the above, recently, two spiritual researchers (among several others) have reviewed the literature, evaluated responses from people who have had spiritual experiences and considered their own mystical encounters to arrive at their own concept of "many mansions."

Kumar's Higher Realms

Dr. Ravinda Kumar, a Hindu professor of mathematics, a trustee of the Academy of Religion and Psychical Research and author of several books on religion, psychical research and spirituality, has experienced kundalinic awakening. His afterlife concept, presented at the *Annual Conference of the Academy of Religion and Psychical Research* (1999), is the following.

The physical body is composed of solid, liquid and gas. The etheric body is composed of four kinds of subtle ethers. At death, the Soul (*Atman*) gives up the physical and etheric bodies. The etheric body hovers around the decomposing physical body for about 12 days. After death, there are six planes: Astral, Mental, Intuitional, Atmic, Monadic and Divine. Each of these six planes has several sub-planes. The astral body leaves the corpse and heads for the Astral Plane. Hardened criminals go to the Grey World, which is a state suspended between the physical and astral planes and is the abode of unrepentant criminals. The Astral Plane has seven divisions: (1) First (Lowest) Subplane, which is dark and dense and is the abode of hardened criminals with heinous records; (2) Second Subplane, which is less dark and dense and is the abode of highly materialistic individuals; (3) Third Subplane, which is the first "lighted" area, also known as Summerland; this is the abode of those who have led a good life, which was not necessarily religious; and it is similar to Earth without any evil characteristics; (4) Fourth Subplane, which is fully lighted, has finer vibrations, better physical surroundings and more beautiful components; it is a special place for children; (5) Fifth Subplane is very bright with even higher vibrations and is the most beautiful of the divisions with the most activities; it is the abode of learned people, poets, scientists, artists, important individuals and saints and of spiritual guides who communicate to Earth through mediums; (6) Sixth Subplane, which is even more well-lit with higher vibrations, more refined and advanced; it is the abode of those who were highly artistic; (7) Seventh Subplane, which is the most heavenly of the astral planes. Following spiritual advancement, one goes into a "second death" and wakens in the Mental Plane.

The Mental Plane has two divisions. The first (lower) division is Heaven (*Swarlok*); which is the heaven described in most religions. The second (higher) division is the Causal Plane (*Maharlok*). Many highly evolved souls and saints live on the mental plane; they help people on lower planes with their evolution.

The four planes beyond the Mental plane are the Intuitional, Atmic, Monadic and Divine. The Intuitional (*Buddhic*) Plane is the abode of those who were highly religious and/or intuitive. In the Atmic (*Nirvanic*) Plane are those who while alive achieved either the Hindus' Atman, the Buddhist's Light of the Void, the Sufi's Ruha, the Christian's becoming one with Jesus Christ (as well as others realizing Jung's High

Self). This plane is ultimate bliss. The next and even more advanced plane is Monadic (*Anupama*). The highest plane is Divine (*Adi*), where the soul is one with God.

In all the planes below Atmic, depending upon one's Karma, reincarnation can occur, but above Atmic, reincarnation ends.

Kumar's "mansions" are a composite of others that have been considered but vary somewhat in content and phraseology.

Meek's Spirit Worlds

In his teens, George Meek began to study the world's religions. At the age of 60, he retired from the business world to spend the rest of his life researching the basic nature of mankind. His afterlife concept, discussed in *Enjoy Your Own Funeral* (1999), is the following.

The physical body is 99% void (centers of energy in forms of atoms dispersed at tremendous distances) and uses electricity for its operation. The etheric (bioplasmic) body — usually invisible to our senses — uses the energy systems involved in acupuncture meridians and the chakras. The astral body contains the mind (conscious, subconscious, superconscious), the spirit (the nonphysical parts of the individual) and the soul (the individual spark of God that resides in each of us). (It should be noted that Meek's concept of the mind, soul and spirit differs from that of Peter Novak.)

At death, the physical body ceases to exist. The etheric body stays around for a few hours up to about three days. (Similar to Kumar's concept but with Kumar, the etheric body can stay around for 12 days.) It then dissipates into cosmic energy that activates the acupuncture and chakra systems. The astral body remains intact and escapes from the decomposing physical and etheric bodies.

The person's life style will determine which astral plane the astral body will enter. There are three groups of astral planes. The Lowest Astral Planes are dark, dismal and dangerous. They are the abode of resentful, unloving, greedy and self-centered individuals as well as drug addicts, unrecovered alcoholics, sex perverts, murderers and people who have committed suicide. The Intermediate Astral Planes are a rest and rehabilitation region. Here, the body is composed of fine material and is at a higher vibratory rate. The Third Astral Planes are the heavenly (Summerland) planes. Angels are found in this beautiful region. Here one can decide to reincarnate for further evolution or accept a second death and move higher. Once the latter occurs, the astral body is shed and rebirth occurs in the Mental-Causal Planes. On this plane the vibratory levels are high, and there is access to the accumulated wisdom of the ages. Intuitive knowledge can be passed on to receptive minds on Earth. Here also is the final opportunity for reincarnation. If the soul is evolved enough, it will be reborn into the Celestial Planes (comparable to the Biblical third heaven). On the Celestial Planes are located the great spiritual and religious leaders such as Jesus and Buddha. The levels beyond the Celestial Planes are known as the Extraterrestrial-Cosmic and contain the Galactic, Universal and Cosmic Levels. The comprehension of these is beyond our understanding while alive. It can be seen that in many ways, Meek's "mansions" are similar to those of Kumar.

The Blind Men And The Elephant

A Hindu fable by John Godfrey Saxe (from Sillar, F.C. and Meyler, R.M. *Elephants Ancient and Modern*). The original version of *The Blind Men and the Elephant* appeared in the *Udana*, a Canonical Hindu scripture.

It was six men of Indostan
To learning much inclined,
Who went to see the Elephant
(Though all of them were blind),
That each by observation
Might satisfy his mind.

The First approached the Elephant,
And happened to fall
Against his broad and sturdy side,
At once began to bawl:
"God bless me! but the Elephant
Is very like a wall!"

The Second, feeling of the tusk,
Cried,"Ho! what have we here
So very round and smooth and sharp?
To me 'tis mightly clear
This wonder of an Elephant
Is very like a spear!"

The Third approached the animal,
And happened to take
The squirming trunk within his hands,
Thus boldly up and spake:
"I see," quoth he, "the Elephant
Is very like a snake."

The Fourth reached out his eager hand,
And felt about the knee.
"What more this wondrous beast is like
Is mainly plain," quoth he;
" 'Tis clear enough the Elephant
Is very like a tree!"

The Fifth who chanced to touch the ear,
Said: "E'en the blindest man
Can tell what this resembles most:
Deny the fact who can,
This marvel of an Elephant
Is very like a fan!"

The Sixth no sooner had begun
About the beast to grope,
Than, seizing on the swinging tail
That fell within his scope,
"I see," quoth he, "the Elephant
Is very like a rope!"

And so these men of Indostan
Disputed loud and long,
Each in his own opinion

Exceeding stiff and strong
Though each was partly in the right,
And all were in the wrong!

So, oft in theologic wars,
The disputants, I ween,
Rail on in utter ignorance
Of what each other mean,
And prate about an Elephant
Not one of them has seen!

From Recent Viewpoints
To A Personal Concept

I can't say that I see the entire elephant, but I've given it a try. Considering all that has been found in our spiritual journey through NDEs, OBEs, apparitions, visions, dreams, séances, medium reports, past life regressions, immortality, God and the universe and evolution, and various religions, organizations, and individual concepts, it is possible to formulate a rational depiction of the afterlife. In the next chapter, my personal version of the afterlife is presented.

Figure 67 "The Blind Men and the Elephant" by Marvin Herring, May 18, 1999

CHAPTER FIFTEEN

A PERSONAL CONCEPT OF THE AFTERLIFE

"And the dust returneth to the earth as it was,
And the spirit returneth unto God who gave it..."
(Ecclesiastes 12: 7).

"Life is real, life is earnest, And the grave is not the goal.
Dust thou art to dust returneth, Was not spoken of the Soul."
(Longfellow, as quoted by Tribbe).

O ur spiritual journey is at its last stop. After digesting and absorbing the sources for the afterlife concepts discussed in the previous four chapters as well as the information reviewed on NDEs, OBEs, apparitions, visions, dreams, séances, medium reports, reincarnation and past life regression, and the discussion of immortality and God, there is strong, scientifically-based support for a soul that survives the deceased body, retains its memories, and travels to an afterlife where it eventually meets God. It is unimportant whether or not the soul has mass, is made up of energy, ether or some unknown substance. *What is important is that the soul exists and survives the death of the physical body.*

There have been various descriptions of the afterlife planes. In the subsequent discussion of my personal concept of the afterlife, the *Kabbalah* model has been used as the basis. However, the various stages are comparable to, for example, the model described in the last chapter by Meek (1999). The astral planes are similar. Meek's Lowest Astral Planes are comparable to the "Realm of Emotional Purification" (*Gehenna*), while his Intermediate Astral Planes are similar to the "Realm of Final Completion of the Personality" (*Lower Gans Eden*). Meek's Highest Astral

Planes are comparable to "Heavenly Repose" (*Upper Gan Eden*), while his Mental and Causal, Celestial and Extraterrestrial-Cosmic Planes are all divisions of the "Storehouse of Souls" (*Tzor Ha-Hayim*).

Even though it is currently fashionable to envision God as either Divine energy, Divine light or Divine love — without the depiction of God being some sort of an entity — I cannot totally adhere to that "fashionable" belief. I am inclined to follow the thinking of the child in the following story discussed by the eminent Rabbi David J. Wolpe in his book, *Teaching Your Children About God* (1995).

A young boy was intensely concentrating on drawing a picture. His mother said, "What are you doing?"

The child replied, "I'm drawing a picture of God."

His mother responded, "No one knows what God looks like."

The young boy answered her proudly, "Well, they will when I'm finished." (p. 47).

I certainly am not in any elevated position to tell you what God looks like, but I cannot believe that a God who has created the universe, filled in the evolutionary gaps, interceded at various times in history and instills souls could be nothing more than energy, light or love. So I can easily perceive God as a supremely purposive entity. Based on all of the previous information, let's now take an afterlife trip representing what I now consider as the most probable reality. We begin by discussing how you should prepare for it.

Your Afterlife Preparation

Preparation for your afterlife journey begins in this life — and it is never too late to start. **The life you lead is a major determinant of your afterlife experience.**

You were put on this planet **for a purpose** whether or not you understand the purpose. Everything in the universe is interconnected. Atoms that came from the instant of creation — eventually becoming stars — are what you are made from.

Whatever paths you take in life should have a goal of leading to the improvement of yourself, fellow humans, other animals, plants and the entire environmental complex — from the smallest rock to the furthermost reaches of the universe. To do this, **you should begin by doing the best possible job at home, at work and in your relationships with others.**

Since most religions preach thinking and acting righteously and morally, you should follow this theme to guide your actions and decisions. Love is also a major religious concept as well as a universal finding in NDEs. Unfortunately, many of us profess love, but all too often, we act with anger and hate and often seeth with underlying jealousies. **Hateful and angry people will not have a pleasant afterlife.** So, it behooves you to learn and practice positive stress management techniques (for example, meditation, consultations, acting calm, cool and collected), to overcome negative emotions such as hate, anger, frustration, jealousy, envy, fear and anxiety. This will help you become righteous and moral. At the same time, you should also strive to express love to all of your fellow creatures. At times, this will be an arduous task, but it should be your cardinal principle in life. Regardless of your religious orientation, you should try to follow what Jesus said 2,000 years ago:

"But I say unto you which hear, Love your enemies, do good to them which hate you, Bless them that curse you, and pray for them which despitefully use you. And unto him that smiteth thee on the one cheek offer also the other; and him that taketh away thy cloke forbid not to take thy coat also. Give to every man that asketh of thee; and of him that taketh away thy goods ask them not again. And as ye would that men should do to you, do ye also to them likewise. For if ye love them which love you, what thank have ye? for sinners also love those that love them. And if ye do good to them which do good to you, what thank have ye? for sinners also do even the same. And if ye lend to them of whom ye hope to receive, what thank have ye? for sinners also lend to sinners, to receive as much again. But love ye your enemies, and do good, and lend, hoping for nothing again; and your reward shall be great, and ye shall be the children of the Highest: for he is kind unto the unthankful and to the evil. Be ye therefore merciful, as your Father also is merciful. Judge not, and ye shall not be judged: condemn not, and ye shall not be condemned: forgive, and ye shall be forgiven: Give, and it shall be given unto you; good measure pressed down, and shaken together, and running over, shall men give into your bosom. For with the same measure that ye mete withal it shall be measured to you again."

(Luke 6: 27-38).

Remember, it is never too late to change. In addition, it is of special importance for those of us who are ardent lovers during life — and want to continue that relationship in the afterlife — to try and be on the same righteous, moral, loving, and spiritual planes.

People should never commit suicide as a way to attempt to be together forever. Both from religious concepts and NDE findings, **suicides are definitely treated differently in the afterlife** and rarely go in the same path. This was vividly displayed in the movie (October, 1998), *"What Dreams May Come"* and has been depicted in various religious literature and artwork.

To better prepare yourself for the afterlife trip, it is helpful to get a glimpse of what it would be like. However, by all means, do not attempt to induce a NDE (as was depicted in the movie, *"Flatliners"*). Rather, receive spiritual training and learn to meditate. Aside from afterlife preparation, spirituality and meditation allow for communication with your essential being and with the spark of God that is within you and everything else. These practices lead to improvement of health and feelings of well-being and connection with others. Taken together, acting righteously and morally, giving unsolicited love, being spiritual and meditating regularly should ensure that the conscious and unconscious parts of your mind are on the same level and will be a united spirit-soul in the afterlife.

Figure 68
"The Suicides" by Gustave Dore —
Dante's Divine Comedy.

What The Afterlife Might Be Like

Now that the preparation is over, the following are personal viewpoints of the probable afterlife for various types of people. As far as is known, no one has returned from the afterlife to report findings. (It should be recalled that the NDE reports typically end just prior to entering the actual afterlife. They provide us with a glimpse rather than the complete picture.) Hence, it is not known for certain if the spiritual world is in unseen parts of the electromagnetic spectrum (as proposed by Little; see Chapter 14) or is in another dimension. It actually doesn't matter **where** it is — just that it **is**. **What is really important is for each of us to have a heavenly rather than a hellish outcome to our earthly existence.** So I stress that the following descriptions are only my best speculations based on scientific evidence and religious investigations. They are presented in the form of the afterlife adventures of three radically different *fictional* individuals whom I have named Charlie Roemer, Carrie Roth and Caroline Reiss.

Charlie's Hell

Charlie's Life
Charlie Roemer was a horrible human being from any point of view. He was uncaring, ungiving, irresponsible, unloving, non-spiritual, immoral, irreligious, and unrepentant. It wasn't *all* his fault, of course. His parents were atheists and alcoholics. He had two older brothers who constantly abused him. Charlie got a naive young woman, Julie, pregnant and was forced by his parents to marry her. His first act was to take her to an old-fashioned (and very cheap) abortionist to get rid of the child. Unfortunately, Julie died from the botched abortion as well as the unborn child. Charlie was momentarily "saddened" by Julie's death, but he immediately returned to his lifestyle.

Charlie never kept a job and was in and out of jail for assorted crimes including car-jacking, robbery and rape. Charlie never went to church, didn't exercise (except when running away from the cops), and was a junk food addict. That certainly wasn't his only addiction. Charlie also became an alcoholic and went a couple of steps further. He was addicted to marijuana and crack cocaine as well as anything else that became available. During one of his addiction nightmares, he went on a killing spree and murdered three people including a young man who Charlie accused of "stealing" a former girlfriend. This time, Charlie didn't just get a prison sentence. Charlie was convicted of murder in the first degree and was sent to death row.

At age 45 — with all of his appeals exhausted — he was executed in the electric chair with a family member and several relatives of his victims serving as witnesses to his execution. Considering all of these details from Charlie's life, during his life, the conscious and unconscious parts of Charlie's mind were separate. That is, Charlie had an awareness of **what** he was doing in life, but he never considered **why** he did what he did. Charlie made his decisions quickly and he never looked back. He just followed his impulses moment-to-moment. Nor did he consider what effect he had on others — he simply didn't care.

The Early Stage Of Charlie's Afterlife

At the point of his sudden death, Charlie's exit from his body is agonizing and painful. Charlie's spirit (his consciousness) and soul (his unconscious) go on separate paths. Charlie's soul leaves his body. It maintains all of its memories but lacks the awareness of spirit. Charlie's soul travels through a dark tunnel, completely unaware of the brilliant light.

Rather than see family and friends, his soul sees visions of deceased people who had been wronged, hurt or killed by him during life. The experience is most unpleasant, especially the visions of Julie and his unborn child and the victims of his murderous spree. A celestial being of light then appears to Charlie's soul, and a life review is shown him. Considering the type of life he had led, it is a full detailing of unpleasant events. As his life unfolds before him, Charlie sees his drunken parents fighting, his brothers punching him, the forced sexual relationship with Julie, robbing the neighborhood supermarket, riding at 90 miles an hour in a stolen Cadillac, raping a beautiful blonde, the murder rampage, and the last agonizing few seconds strapped to the electric chair.

The Final Separation From The Body

Charlie's spirit hovers over his body and stays for about seven days while suffering the "pangs of the grave." It goes through an extremely painful and anguishing ordeal. Charlie's spirit tries to reenter his physical body, but its efforts are in vain. However, it becomes a ghoulish spirit and as partial payback, it haunts his older brothers for a period of time. Now, Charlie's wandering spirit is led to the stage of emotional purification, where it is joined by its soul.

Emotional Purification

Charlie's spirit rejoins his soul in a spiritual body and enters the realm of emotional purification (known as *Gehenna* in Judaism, purgatory in Catholicism or an in-between place in some other religions). Considering that, in life, Charlie had been wicked and knew nothing about how to manage his stress to purge his negative emotions (such as anger, hate, lust and revenge) this takes a relatively long time (about one year in Earth time). Even at the end of that time period, his purification isn't complete. Nevertheless, Charlie's spiritual being goes on to the next stage (known in *Kabbalah* as *Lower Gan Eden*).

Final Completion Of His Personality

Since Charlie's spirit-soul retains vestiges of its former negative personality, it is unable to enjoy positive emotions freely because it is in as astral plane with similar-type spirit-souls (facing similar negative life issues). The time spent here is limited after which Charlie's spirit-soul receives another life review. His united spirit-soul then enters the higher transcendent states.

Heavenly Repose

Charlie's united spirit-soul (with its attached spiritual body) now enters heavenly repose (known as *Upper Gan Eden* in *Kabbalah*, heaven in Christianity, and the *bardo* visions of the peaceful deities in Tibetan Buddhism) along with other similar spirit-souls. However, it still retains vestiges of its former negative personality and is "blind" to the presence of God. Therefore, it quickly moves on to the next realm.

The Storehouse Of Souls

Charlie's spirit-soul now returns to its source (known in *Kabbalah* as *tzor ha-hayyim*, "storehouse of souls" or the "bundle of life"). It is here that Charlie *could* actually be with God in all His splendor, but because Charlie's spirit-soul had such a negative previous life, it has to be reincarnated to achieve a higher state of purity.

Reincarnation

A celestial being describes for Charlie's spirit-soul the righteous path to follow in the next incarnation so that it will not be required to have repeated reincarnations. Along with the new information imparted about righteous living, Charlie's spirit-soul retains enough of the memories of its previous existence to realize the negative life it had led. An appropriate womb is then selected — a happily married woman expecting her third child. Charlie's spirit-soul enters the womb. This time it leads to a somewhat better life.

Return To The Storehouse Of Souls

It takes three reincarnations for Charlie's spirit-soul to become completely purified. It now returns to the storehouse of souls. Finally, Charlie's spirit-soul is able to "see" God and enjoy His heavenly presence.

The End-Of-Days

If there is an end-of-days with the coming of the Messiah, the resurrection of the dead and final judgment by God, Charlie's spirit with its four souls (with its memory of four previous lives) unites with its final

Figure 69
Portion of "The Garden of Earthly Delights" by Hieronymus Bosch." "Hell" is
shown here. The original is on display at Prado, Madrid, Spain.

body. Charlie receives a favorable judgment and enjoys a new life on Earth that might last for a thousand years. Charlie's spirit (with its four souls) then returns for an eternal stay in the storehouse of souls.

Although the resurrection at the end-of-days is a time-honored Judeo-Christianity-Islamic belief, it might *not* actually occur. Many spiritual leaders now speak more of a messianic era in which war is no more, peace reigns on Earth, love is rampant and the Earth is preserved in all its glory. However, that would only be for those who are alive at the time of the messianic era. Therefore, although the concept of the return of the Messiah is included in Charlie's afterlife, his afterlife journey might just as well end with an eternal stay for him in the storehouse of souls.

Although Charlie's afterlife eventually turned out to be favorable, there are truly evil people who never can be purified (Hitler would most likely be in that category). These people would most likely have a hellish eternity (see *Figure 69* on prior page).

Carrie's Paradise

Carrie's Life

Carrie was a darling, six-year old Jewish girl. She was Jim and Rebecca Roth's only child. They loved her intensely and showed it in all their words and deeds. Both of the Roths were psychologists. (Rebecca only worked in the morning while Carrie was in school and maintained the role of mother to Carrie.) The family lived in an upper middle class neighborhood.

Carrie was beautiful with hazel eyes, dark hair and a cute figure. Although only in the first grade, she loved school. Carrie was intellectually sharp and a fine athlete. She had a great potential life with everything to live for. And then it happened. It was about 5 P.M. — twilight time. Having recently learned to ride a two-wheeler, Carrie was peddling her bike on the sidewalk in front of her home. Just as she reached the driveway, the front wheel hit a slick, oily spot on the pavement. This caused the bike to skid. Carrie's hands left the bar, and the bike went out of control and landed in the street. At that moment, a car was heading toward the bike. The driver put his foot on the brake. The car skidded to a halt but not before it smashed into the bike sending Carrie caroming several feet into the air. She crashed into the pavement, smashing her skull. Resuscitation would have been useless: Carrie died instantly.

The Early Stage Of Carrie's Afterlife

Carrie's united soul (the unconscious part of her mind) and spirit (the conscious part of her mind) rapidly leave her suddenly dying body. At first, Carrie's united spirit-soul doesn't even realize that death had occurred, but soon, her spirit-soul, which is part of her spiritual body, rises up and floats.

As Carrie is rapidly thrust through a dark tunnel, she becomes somewhat apprehensive. But at the end of the tunnel, Carrie sees a magnificent light. As she approaches the light, Carrie begins to feel more calm and peaceful. Her worries melt away. Then Carrie sees a host of glowing, flying young angels — like little children with wings. Lower, and in front of them, Carrie sees lots of people. They are also surrounded by light. As they approach her, Carrie recognizes a few of them. Carrie sees her deceased Grandpop Jacob and Grandma Rachel. And there's Great Aunt Ruth. They all look wonderfully alive — just the way Carrie remembered them. Each, in turn, hugs Carrie. They relive fond memories, and collectively reassure Carrie what a wonderful place she has entered. They tell her she will be able to meet new friends, go to school, play games and have a wonderful time.

Out of the misty distance, a beautiful, heavenly woman, enveloped by a brilliant light, comes to greet her. It is the *Shekhinah*. She embraces Carrie and shows her the highlights of her short-lived life: the marvelous trip to Disney World; her fifth year birthday party with all her friends; the first day of school when she was a little nervous; seeing her first movie (*The Wizard Of Oz*); her daddy showing her how to ride the two-wheeler; and finally, the terrible crash.

The Final Separation From The Body

For Carrie, the "pangs of the grave" from separation from her dissolving body, are short-lived. In Earth time, Carrie's spiritual body remains in this state for three days.

Emotional Purification

Afterwards, Carrie's united spirit-soul travels to the realm of emotional purification. Carrie loved her parents, her grandparents, her relatives, and her friends. Carrie was honest, practically never lied (only an occasional harmless fib common in all children), was not jealous of the rich kids in the neighborhood, was only scared a few times (like when she heard screeching noises in the middle of the night), and only once had a temper tantrum. (She desperately wanted a certain doll, but when her "fit" was over, she apologized sincerely to her mother.) As a result, Carrie's stay in *Gehenna* is very short-lived (probably no more than a few days Earth time). After this time, Carrie's rejuvenated spirit-soul is emotionally purged and purified and on its way to the next stage.

Final Completion Of The Personality

Having been purified of her few emotional issues from her life, Carrie's spirit-soul is now free to complete its personality in *Lower Gan Eden*. Here, Carrie feels very happy, at peace and extremely calm. Carrie's spiritual body meets other young children and learns and plays with them — just the way it happened on Earth — but at a much higher state of awareness. Carrie meets new classmates and makes new friends. She has new teachers and a new principal. And they're all so nice to her. Carrie learns a lot of new things. After awhile, Carrie's spiritual body integrates and completes its personality. Carrie is now given a final review of her previous short life. She then leaves the small amount of negative aspects of her former personality behind and enters the higher transcendent states.

Heavenly Repose

Carrie's united spirit-soul — with its attached spiritual body — now enters her own paradise. Child-type spirit-souls who had similar minds and consciousness meet here and enjoy the beautiful and loving surroundings. Most of the children Carrie never knew in life, but she recognizes Barbie, who was a friend who had died from leukemia. Carrie also meets a former teacher who had died from a heart attack. Carrie learns wonderful things and everybody loves each other. Carrie even rejoins her grandpop, grandma and great aunt. They have a terrific time together. Carrie's paradise comes right out of the "Wonderful World of Disney." It is filled with scenes straight from Disney World with beautiful ponds, mountains, streams, waterfalls, animals of all kinds, and many Disney characters such as Mickey and Minnie Mouse, Donald and Daisy Duck, Goofy, and her favorite, Snow White.

Early in her afterlife journey, Carrie had met *Shekhinah*, but now for the first time, she "sees" a kind old man with a huge white beard and she knows that she has seen God.

The Storehouse Of Souls

Carrie's spirit-soul now returns to its source, the storehouse of souls. Carrie is here with God in all His splendor. Since during Carrie's short life she had been a wonderful child, there is no need for reincarnation for further purification. Although Carrie is having a wonderful time, she still misses her parents, her relatives, her friends, and the life she had led on Earth. She prays to God: "Can I go back?" Would it be possible?" Carrie's prayers are answered; she is given permission to return to Earth.

Carrie has one more request of God: "Can I get to choose my rebirth?" Carrie is told that because she had been such a wonderful child on Earth, that she could return to the womb of her choice.

Reincarnation

After Carrie's death, the Roths became despondent and depressed. It took them over a year to begin to get over their grief. Then one quiet evening, Jim and Rebecca made love for the first time since Carrie's tragic death. The result of their lovemaking was a success.

Nine months later, Rebecca is feeling sharp abdominal pains that are increasing in intensity and frequency. Jim rushes her to the hospital. In the delivery room, Jim is present along with the obstetrician and nurse. Finally, the last push comes and from the birth canal emerges a beautiful young girl. "Oh!," cries Jim, "she looks just like Carrie." The doctor severs the umbilical cord, washes the blood away, drapes the infant and hands her to Rebecca. Rebecca holds her new child with delight and says; "Jim, can we name her Carol? She's so much like Carrie, even the way she moves her arms." "That would be great," answers Jim.

Carrie's spirit-soul is inside her new body. Her wish came true. She has returned to her parents. Carrie, as Carol, says to herself, "I'm so happy."

Return To The Storehouse Of Souls

Carol (with Carrie's soul and her own) lived a wonderful life. She had a great career as an anthropologist. Carol got married, had four children, eight grandchildren and lived to the wonderful age of 95, at which time she died peacefully in her sleep. When Carol was 25, she went to a hypnotist who attempted a past life regression. It was successful. When Carol was awakened, she listened to the tape from her regression. She was amazed to learn that in a previous life she had been her own sister, Carrie. Carol subsequently had other regressions and was able to learn everything about Carrie's life on Earth. Carol was so pleased that she was the fulfillment of her parents' wishes and that her sister's spirit-soul was able to return to be with her. So when Carol died, she left this world knowing that she would have a wonderful afterlife with Carrie's soul as well as her own. Carrie's spirit with its two souls, with both her and Carol's memories intact, now returns to the storehouse of souls. Carrie "sees" God and enjoys His heavenly presence.

The End-Of-Days

As mentioned previously, if there is an end-of-days with the coming of the Messiah, the resurrection of the dead and a final judgment by God, Carrie's spirit — with its two souls (retaining memories of both Carrie and Carol's lives) — unites with Carol's prime-of-life body. Carrie receives a favorable judgment and enjoys a new life on Earth that might last for a thousand years. Afterwards, Carrie's spirit — with its two souls — returns to the storehouse of souls to spend an eternity with God. However, as stated before, if only a messianic era occurs in the future, Carrie's spirit (with its two souls) would remain eternally in the storehouse of souls surrounded by God's presence. Before we consider Caroline Reiss' life and afterlife, a true diversion is now presented about another little girl, who was made in Carrie's mold.

A Sandpiper To Bring You Joy

She was six years old when I first met her on the beach near where I live. I drive to this beach, a distance of three or four miles, whenever the world begins to close in on me. She was building a sand castle or something and looked up, her eyes as blue as the sea. "Hello," she said.

I answered with a nod, not really in the mood to bother with a small child. "I'm building," she said.

"I see that. What is it?" I asked, not caring.

"Oh, I don't know, I just like the feel of sand."

That sounds good, I thought, and slipped off my shoes. A sandpiper glided by.

"That's a joy," the child said.

"It's a what?"

"It's a joy. My mama says sandpipers come to bring us joy."

The bird went gliding down the beach. "Good-bye, joy," I muttered to myself, "hello, pain," and turned to walk on. I was depressed; my life seemed completely out of balance.

"What's your name?" she asked me. She wouldn't give up. "Robert," I answered. "I'm Robert Peterson."

"Mine's Wendy...I'm six."

"Hi, Wendy."

She giggled. "You're funny," she said.

In spite of my gloom, I laughed too and walked on. Her musical giggle followed me. "Come again, Mr. P," she called. "We'll have another happy day."

The days and weeks that followed belonged to others: a group of unruly Boy Scouts, PTA meetings, an ailing mother. The sun was shining one morning as I took my hands out of the dishwasher. "I need a sandpiper," I said to myself, gathering up my coat. The ever-changing balm of the seashore awaited me. The breeze was chilly, but I strode along, trying to recapture the serenity I needed. I had forgotten the child and was startled when she suddenly appeared.

"Hello, Mr. P," she said. "Do you want to play?"

"What do you have in mind?" I asked, with a twinge of annoyance.

"I don't know — you say."

"How about charades?" I asked sarcastically. The tinkling laughter burst forth again. "I don't know what that is."

"Then lets just walk," I replied. Looking at her, I noticed the delicate fairness of her face. "Where do you live?" I asked.

"Over there." She pointed toward a row of summer cottages. Strange, I thought, in winter. "Where do you go to school?"

"I don't go to school. Mommy says we're on vacation." The little girl talked as we strolled up the beach, but my mind was on other things. When she left for home, Wendy said it had been a happy day. Feeling suprisingly better, I smiled at her and agreed. Three weeks later, I rushed to the beach in a state of near panic. I was in no mood to even greet Wendy. I thought I saw her mother on the porch and felt like demanding she keep her child at home.

"Look, if you don't mind," I said crossly when Wendy caught up with me, "I'd rather be alone today." She seemed unusually pale and out of breath.

"Why?" she asked. I turned to her and shouted, "Because my mother died!" and then I thought, my God, why was I saying this to a little child?

"Oh," she said quietly, "then this is a bad day."

"Yes," I said, "and yesterday and the day before and-oh, go away!"

"Did it hurt?" she inquired.

"Did what hurt? I was exasperated with her, with myself.

"When she died, did it hurt?"

"Of course, it hurt!!!" I snapped, misunderstanding, wrapped up in myself. I strode off. A month or so after that, when I next went to the beach, she wasn't there. Feeling guilty, ashamed and admitting to myself that I missed her, I went up to the cottage after my walk and knocked at the door. A drawn-looking, young woman with honey-colored hair opened the door.

"Hello," I said. "I'm Robert Peterson. I missed your little girl today and wondered where she was."

"Oh yes, Mr. Peterson, please come in. Wendy spoke of you so much. I'm afraid I allowed her to bother you. If she was nuisance, please accept my apologies."

"Not at all — she's a delightful child," I said suddenly realizing that I meant it. "Where is she?"

"Wendy died last week, Mr. Peterson. She had leukemia. Maybe she didn't tell you."

Struck dumb, I groped for a chair. My breath caught.

"She loved this beach; so when she asked to come, we couldn't say no. She seemed so much better here and had a lot of what she called happy days. But the last few weeks, she declined rapidly." Her voice faltered: "She left something for you, if only I can find it. Could you wait a moment while I look?"

I nodded stupidly, my mind racing for something, anything to say to this lovely young woman. She handed me a smeared envelope, with MR. P printed in bold, childish letters. Inside was a drawing in bright crayon hues, a yellow beach, a blue sea, and a brown bird. Underneath was carefully printed: A SANDPIPER TO BRING YOU JOY.

Tears welled up in my eyes, and a heart that had almost forgotten to love opened wide. I took Wendy's mother in my arms. "I'm so sorry, I'm sorry, I'm so sorry," I muttered over and over, and we wept together.

Figure 70
A Sandpiper At Rest by Don Morse, November 6, 1999. A sandpiper is any one of various small wading birds of the family *Scolopacidae*. It has a long, straight bill that is very sensitive. It forages for food in sand and mud.

The precious little picture is framed now and hangs in my study. Six words — one for each year of her life — that speak to me of harmony, courage, and undemanding love. A gift from a child with sea-blue eyes and hair the color of sand — who taught me the gift of love. (*Figure 70* is an illustration of a sandpiper.)

Note: This is a true story written by Robert Petersen that was e-mailed to me by Michael Rogers from Pearl River, New York. It should serve as a reminder to all of us that we must take the time to enjoy this life and never to withhold love. On a personal basis, I pray that, like my fictional Carrie, Wendy has a second chance. Now, let us move on to Caroline.

Caroline's Heaven

Caroline's Life

Caroline Reiss was a wonderful human being. She was a special education teacher who was devoted to fulfilling the needs of mentally and physically handicapped children. Caroline was a church-going Methodist who was married to a family physician, Harvey. They had a loving relationship which culminated in three beautiful and wonderful children. The family went on many vacations, and the children were brought up to respect people of all races, religions, sexual orientations, occupations and life styles.

There were occasional family quarrels, but all were resolved in a rational, unemotional way. Caroline was always the peacemaker. She never had a harsh word for anyone and tried to see the best in all situations. Caroline took care to continually develop her mind and overall education (she went to continuing education courses whenever she could, learned and practiced stress management techniques). She carefully maintained her health and body (she ate healthy foods and worked out at a health club regularly). She also attended to her soul (she attended church and spiritual sessions frequently). After a particularly stressful day at the office, her husband Harvey came home, sat down in his favorite chair, and had a massive heart attack and died. Ironically, only a few months later, Caroline was suddenly diagnosed with leukemia. At the age of 65, she died peacefully in her sleep.

The Early Stage Of The Afterlife

Caroline's united soul and spirit leave her dying body. It is a peaceful and painless exit, although she hears a ringing or buzzing noise. Caroline retains full consciousness and memories. Her spirit-soul, which is part of her spiritual body, rises up and floats. Although it is a spiritual body, when Caroline looks at herself, she appears as she did in her early thirties. Caroline then rapidly goes through a tunnel-like darkness into an incredibly radiant, golden, all-encompassing light. Caroline sees her Uncle Eddie, Aunt Doris, Grandma Eunice, David Carpenter, the accountant, Phyllis Aaronson, the art teacher, and many other deceased relatives and friends. They all glow with an aura of light. Everyone looks just as they did in their primes. Caroline moves to greet each and every one of them and the encounters are wonderful. Just then, Jesus, glowing in a magnificent light, comes forth to greet her. (This celestial being will appear as Jesus [for Christians like Caroline], Moses or a God-like apparition [for Jews], Muhammad [for Muslims], Buddha [for Buddhists] or an angelic-like being for those of other religions or those with no organized religion.) Jesus then presents Caroline with a panoramic life review. She sees her birth, silly childhood fights with her brother Jimmy, the beautiful marriage ceremony, her magnificent honeymoon in Bermuda, the birth of her three children, the lovely homes in England's Cotswalds, the night her husband had a lethal heart attack, and the day she heard her fatal diagnosis.

The Final Separation From The Body

For Caroline, the "pangs of the grave," from separation from her dissolving body, are short-lived. In Earth time, Caroline's spiritual body remains in this state for three days.

Emotional Purification

Following the final separation from her body, Caroline's united spirit-soul travels to the realm of emotional purification. No matter how good a life Caroline had led, there were unresolved negative emotional issues — feelings of guilt, fear, shame or anger — that had been repressed or not dealt with adequately while she was alive. The catharsis involved in this emotional purification process is the equivalent of a prolonged, intensified period of psychotherapy. At the end of the emotional purification (probably no more than a month or two in Earth time because she was well-trained in stress management and was righteous during her life), her rejuvenated spirit-soul is emotionally purged and purified and moves on its way to the next stage.

Final Completion Of The Personality

Having been cleansed from her previously repressed negative emotional issues, Caroline's spirit-soul is now free to complete its personality by actively enjoying the positive emotions of fervor, joy, ecstasy, peace and tranquillity. Here, Caroline's spiritual body meets others of similar ilk, and learns and interacts, such as was done on Earth — but at a much higher state of awareness. Caroline meets former classmates, teachers, students, and co-workers, all of whom died at varying times in the past. The conversations are incredibly enlightening. After awhile, Caroline's spiritual body will have integrated and completed its personality. Caroline now receives a final review of her previous life and prepares to leave the negative aspects of her former personality behind and enter the higher transcendent states.

Heavenly Repose

Caroline's united spirit-soul (with its attached spiritual body) now enters the heavenly realm (known as *Upper Gan Eden* in *Kabbalah*, heaven in Christianity, and the *bardo* visions of the peaceful deities in Tibetan Buddhism). Spirit-souls who had similar minds and consciousness meet here and enjoy the transcendental bliss. Some of these people

Caroline never knew in life, but a few of them were former teachers and colleagues. Caroline interacts with them and learns incredible things and enjoys their love. The ultimate in happiness occurs as Caroline meets her soul mate and husband, Harvey. They remain together in heavenly bliss. The heaven they create is filled with brilliant green meadows, enchanting flowers, snow-capped mountains, azure lakes, splendid waterfalls, multicolored birds, and idyllic weather (see *Figure 71*). (As detailed in Theosophy and displayed magnificently in the recent [October 1998] movie, *"What Dreams May Come,"* people will be able to create their own version of heaven.)

Early in her afterlife journey, Caroline had met Jesus, but now for the first time, she and Harvey "see God" in all of His manifestations as depicted in the following Hasidic lyric from the 18th century (beginning of next page).

Figure 71
"The Garden of Earthly Delights" by Hieronymus Bosch — "Paradise." The original is on display at Prado, Madrid, Spain.

"Oh, Lord of the Universe
I will sing Thee a song.
Where canst Thou be found,
And where canst Thou not be found?

Where I pass—there art Thou.
Where I remain—there, too, Thou art.

Thou, Thou, and only Thou.
Doth it go well tis thanks to Thee.
Doth it go ill—ah, 'tis also thanks to Thee.

Thou art, Thou hast been, and Thou wilt be.
Thou didst reign, Thou reignest, and Thou wilt reign.

Thine is Heaven, Thine is Earth.

Thou fillest the high regions,
And Thou fillest the low regions,
Wheresoever I turn, Thou, oh Thou, art there."

(Leon Stein, Hasidic Music, *The Chicago Jewish Forum*,
Vol. II, No. 1 [Fall, 1943], p. 16).

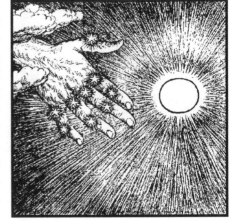

As shown previously, in many religions it is believed that the righteous person will go to heaven and the wicked person will go to hell. One of the aspects of being righteous is to be a giving person rather than a taker (as is discussed in *Kabbalah*). Hence, before continuing Caroline's journey, using the model of the give-take relationship, the following tale is a example of the difference between heaven and hell.

A Tour Of Hell And Heaven

A righteous man died and was being escorted to heaven by an angel. Before he reached the "pearly gates," he asked the messenger of God, "Would it be possible for me to have a glimpse of hell?" His request was granted, and he was transported to the "Satanic Kingdom." When he arrived there, he was astonished. There were rows and rows of beautifully garnished and embellished tables that were filled with the most appetizing and delicious looking foods that he had ever seen. Floral arrangements with the most exquisite and exotic flowers were everywhere to be observed. There were comfortable chairs and glistening light fixtures. Not only wasn't it oppressively hot, it was actually delightfully air conditioned. Then he noticed something very strange. All of the utensils — knives, forks, teaspoons and soup spoons — were about two feet long. The righteous man then took his eyes away from the tables and glanced at the inhabitants of hell. With the abundance of delicious and variegated food placed in delectable surroundings, the hellish occupants "wore" agony on their faces. They appeared anxious, grim, dejected and depressed. Everything was there to be had, but they could have nothing. [This is because each person fails in an effort to feed him- or herself with the too long utensils.]

The righteous man had seen enough of hell and asked to be taken up to heaven. The angel complied, and in a short time, he passed into the "heavenly kingdom." And he couldn't believe his eyes. Everything in heaven was the same as it had been in hell. There were the delicious foods and beautiful decorations. The same comfortable chairs were there, and just as it was in hell, the climate was perfect. What was even more amazing, was the fact that the utensils had the same hellish appearance; they were all about two feet long. Then the righteous man turned his head and looked at the heavenly inhabitants. What a contrast! They were all smiling and laughing, happy and joyous. For lo and behold, they had learned the secret of how to enter heaven, and as a result they earned the rewards of heaven. Because the two-feet long utensils were perfect for what they were doing. They were all feeding each other. The inhabitants of hell were helpless and hopeless with the same utensils because they only knew how to take; there were no givers in hell. (In *Figure 72*, Marvin Herring's cartoon illustrates a modern version of the differences between heaven and hell.)

Now that we have learned this lesson, it is time for Caroline's united spirit-soul with its attached spiritual body to leave this heavenly stay and move on to a higher realm.

The Storehouse Of Souls

Caroline's spirit-soul now returns to its source — the storehouse of souls. It is here that Caroline is actually with God in all His splendor. Since Caroline had been righteous, moral, loving and spiritual on Earth, there is no need for reincarnation for further purification.

The End-Of-Days

Caroline's united spirit-soul (with its attached spirit body) would remain in the storehouse of souls indefinitely to enjoy the splendors of God's heavenly presence until the end-of-days, when at the time of resurrection with the arrival of the Messiah, and God's final judgment, her spirit-soul reunites with its body. God judges her favorably, and Caroline enjoys a new life on Earth that might last for a thousand Earth years. If all goes well (and it should), the same fate would occur with

Figure 72
"Hell (L) and Heaven (R) on a Rainy Day" by Marvin Herring, May 6, 1999.

Caroline's soul-mate, Harvey, and they would enjoy a new life together. Afterwards, their spirit-souls would return to the storehouse of souls for an eternal stay with God.

However, as discussed before, if only a messianic era occurs in the future, Caroline's afterlife journey might just as well end with her spirit-soul having an eternal stay in the storehouse of souls, with Harvey's spirit-soul alongside hers and both spirit-souls being surrounded by God's presence.

Wishful Thinking Or Actuality?

"The results of psychical research, the deductions that we may draw, and the lessons we may learn, teach us of the continued life of the soul, of the nature of that life and of how it is influenced by our conduct here."
(Sir Arthur Conan Doyle, *The New Revelation.*
Hodder & Stoughton, London, 1918, pp. 66-67).

With the conclusion of this personal viewpoint of the afterlife, the search for eternity is over. We have reviewed all that science knows about death and the possible existence of the soul and a spiritual world as well as reviewing the masses of individual testimonies. The depictions in this chapter summarize what I conclude as the most probable sequence of events following death. Is it all wishing thinking — a fantasy? Or was this search successful?

I believe our journey through death's passages was a successful search. There is so much evidence for an afterlife that it is unreasonable to deny it or chalk it up to mere fantasies. Sir Arthur's viewpoint agrees with mine, and I believe that he was just as insightful as was his masterful creation, Sherlock Holmes.

Not only does our search conclude that an afterlife actually exists, it indicates that how you conduct your life now directly influences what you experience after death. **What you do in this life will affect your afterlife fate.** If you had died young, as in Carrie's case, most kabbalists consider the probability of a second chance for your soul (as described in the story). However, some kabbalists believe that your dying early is merely fulfilling your soul's requirements from a previous life. To me, this is an unrewarding outcome. I believe that if you were a good person whose life was terminated early, you will have the opportunity for your soul to be reincarnated in a favorable situation.

With respect to the life you lead on Earth, aside from the afterlife considerations, **it should be understood that leading a righteous life can be beneficial for you and for all those that you had contacted.** In short, your life influences everyone else in it. Being of benefit to others in life helps not just you — but all of them also. In contrast, **if you lead an immoral life, it can be harmful for you and for all those that had been around you.** This fact has major implications for your afterlife and should not be taken lightly.

In summary, the accumulated evidence for an afterlife presented in this book strongly shows that it actually exists and that our conduct on Earth directly influences what occurs in it. And while this chapter condenses this evidence into probable afterlife scenarios, we have yet to fully synthesize our findings. In the final chapter, an organized review of all of the evidence is presented concluding with answers showing why we should have a hopeful, positive outlook on life and our eventual fate.

Science Looks At The Afterlife

Scientists, including Dr. Gary Schwartz and Linda Russek, at the University of Arizona, and Dr. Charles Tart have embarked on the Susy Smith (an 87-year-old medium) Project to determine if they can scientifically prove the afterlife by examining if the dead can communicate with the living. Participants select a secret phrase known only to him/her and type it into the Project's Web site: http://www:afterlifecodes.com. The phrase is then translated into code, using an algorithm, and no one will have access to the code. After the participant dies, he/she tries in some fashion (e.g., dream, apparition, telepathy, through a medium) to communicate the phrase to any living person. If a person receives an unknown message, he/she then logs onto the Web site and gives the phrase. It is entered and scrambled to see if it matches the coded phrase of the person who died. If the phrases match, the participant will have achieved a form of "Earthly immortality" by giving the world scientific evidence of an afterlife. Among the participants are Elisabeth Kübler-Ross. To find out more information, log onto http://www:afterlifecodes.com. Time will tell if this will reveal definite evidence of the afterlife. For now, the evidence presented in this book will have to suffice.

CHAPTER SIXTEEN

A HOPEFUL OUTLOOK

"The only thing that is certain is that nothing is certain."
(Pliny The Elder, *Historia Naturalis*).

The Bible states that, in the beginning, God created Heaven and Earth — an incredibly simple yet all-encompassing statement. In the beginning of this book, our undertaking was much more humble. We examined fear, anxiety and death anxiety and considered how we can deal with death anxiety early in life and then later in life. We've evaluated how all sorts of techniques and mechanisms can be used to delay facing the inevitability of death (for example, work, play, exercise, meditation, vacations, antianxiety drugs, denial). Then, we found that as a result of aging (being in the mid-60s and higher) and stressful occurrences (such as death of loved ones and friends and serious illness in oneself), in order to overcome the overwhelming fear of death, it was essential for us to find out if there is something beyond this life. We wanted to determine if there is a surviving soul, a blissful afterlife and God. To do this, we used scientific, parapsychological, and religious principles as we took a spiritual journey through my NDE, others NDEs, OBEs, apparitions, visions, dreams, séances, medium reports, and reincarnation and past life regressions. We paused on our journey to look at the concept of immortality on Earth. We then resumed our spiritual journey with an examination of God and His relationship to the origin of the universe and the origin of life. Continuing on with our journey, we reconsidered immortality as achieved by the surviving soul as it passes through the afterlife on its way to meet God. This was evaluated as we visited various religions, traditions and individual concepts. Our spiritual journey concluded with a personal concept of the afterlife.

We've come quite a ways in our journey to overcome death anxiety. But can we now say that there is definitely a wonderful a afterlife that awaits us? All the evidence that we have uncovered seems to bear this out. Nevertheless, we cannot state that a positive afterlife is **absolutely** certain. In fact, the only conclusion that is certain is what that ancient philosopher, Pliny The Elder, said: "nothing is certain." But maybe that's the way it should be. If we knew the final score before we played the game, why would we ever bother playing? Worrying about winning the game doesn't help, so why worry? If, as is stated in the Bible, "ashes to ashes and dust to dust" is true, should we worry? It won't help no matter what the truth is. Let us not forget that "we're all in the same boat," and **"no one gets out of here alive."**

Future Calamities

Cosmology shows that in the distant future, the Earth and the entire universe will disappear. However, we might not have to wait that long. Astronomers predict that it is hypothetically possible that a comet or large asteroid might strike the Earth in the not-too-distant future and effectively destroy everything on our planet. The latest information is that an asteroid about as large as center city Philadelphia (Asteroid 1997 XF11) could have a flirtation with Earth on Thursday, October 26, 2028. It could be anywhere from 30,000 miles to 600,000 miles away from Earth. At first, some astronomers predicted that the odds of a direct hit were 1

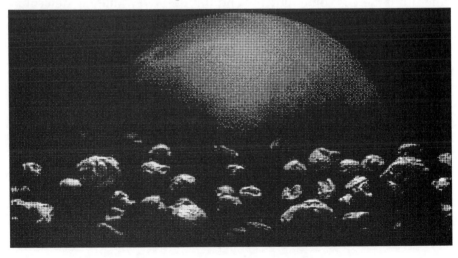

in 3,000. The next day they rescinded and said a direct hit was impossible, and the most likely outcome would be a 600,000 miles flash by from Earth. However, if a direct hit did occur at some time in the future, either cities would be leveled, a side of a continent would be destroyed, or tidal ocean waves would be churned up (as shown in the 1998 movies, *"Deep Impact"* and *"Armageddon"*).

But there are lots of other potential threats to our existence. Some scientists think that because of the burning of fossil fuels and the resultant warming of the Earth, large sections of the planet could be destroyed. Acid rain is also a worrisome occurrence. In addition, scientists are concerned that natural disasters such as volcanoes, earthquakes, tornadoes and hurricanes could increase and destroy large parts of the planet. During May, 1998, India and Pakistan conducted underground nuclear explosions, and renewed fears of a nuclear holocaust surfaced. Now these countries are constructing missiles. Japan's nuclear reactor accident in the early Fall of 1999 brought back anxiety about such accidents. And the threat of nuclear terrorism seems to loom over us to a greater extent every day.

There are even life-threatening dangers in outer space. Recently the sun released a high-energy flux of x-rays along with a cloud of charged particles. These solar flares fell into the most powerful category of electromagnetic radiation. The resulting solar "burp," known as a coronal mass ejection, had the power to disrupt power grids on Earth and kill astronauts. Fortunately, this one only glanced Earth. This event portended a "solar maximum," which is a wave of even more powerful solar flares and ejections. A solar maximum has the potential to destroy radio communication for pilots, blow out power grids and transformers and send fatal doses of radiation to astronauts and closer-to-Earth pilots as well. One of this magnitude is predicted for mid-2000 and could last for one or two years. It has been called "a billion tons of matter moving a million miles an hour." Since there are more satellites in orbit and planes flying around than ever before and many more are planned, should such a solar maximum head for Earth, the results could be disastrous. Our best hope is to pray, predict, and try to prevent.

The Millennium

When I began writing this book in 1998, the year 2000 was two years away. As I write this, it is September 1999, and the new millennium is just around the corner. Doomsday forecasters take their clues from certain Biblical sections, such as in Daniel:

> "And at that time shall Michael stand up, the great prince who standeth for the children of thy people; and there shall be a time of trouble, such as never was since there was a nation even to that same time; and at that time thy people shall be delivered, every one that shall be found written in the book. And many of them that sleep in the dust of the earth shall awake, some to everlasting life, and some to reproaches and everlasting abhorrence."
> (Daniel 12:1-2).

Other prophetic forecasts come in the complete Revelation of St. John The Divine and predictions by seers such as Nostradamus, which some interpret as an apocalypse occurring during 2000. The special significance of the year 2000 is based on these prophesies.

The early Christian scholars considered that human history would end after 6000 years. They believed that each thousand years corresponded to one day of creation. Furthermore, they believed that 2000 years had elapsed between Adam and Abraham, and another 2000 years occurred between Abraham and Jesus Christ. Finally, they considered that after another 2000 years from his birth, Jesus Christ would return and usher in a glorious reign of another 1000 years. But that return of Jesus in the year 2000 A.D. would begin with an apocalyptic war to end all wars (Armageddon). Hence, a certain part of the world's population has extreme anxiety over the ushering in of the new year. But are they correct?

First of all, is the year 2000 actually the start of a new millennium? Let's look at the evidence. According to the Institute of Standards and Technology in Greenwich, England, the year 2001 (and *not* 2000) is the beginning of the next millennium. The rationale is that Jesus Christ was born in year 1 and each millennium starts from that point. In contrast, according to the American Heritage dictionary (as well as many others), a millennium is a span of 1000 years. Hence, it would be legitimate to celebrate January 1, 2000 as the start of the new millennium. However, as far as prophetic doom is concerned, the year 2000 is nothing special. All historical evidence points to the fact that Jesus was not even born in the arbitrary year 1. In the New Testament, there is no mention of the year of Christ's birth. The Jewish leader around Jesus' time, King Herod, died soon after the lunar eclipse of March 12-13, 4 B.C. Since Jesus was alive during Herod's reign, Christ had to be born at least before March of 4 B.C. The Gospel of Luke states that Jesus was born while Cyrenius (the Grecian form of Quirinus) was governor of Syria ("And this taxing was first made when Cyrenius was governor of Syria," Luke 2:2). Historians show that Cyrenius was actually governor of Cilicia, which was a province of Syria. Nevertheless, he was still considered to be governor of Syria. There is some confusion about the dates of his reign. This is because he had two separate reigns and taxes were collected during both reigns. His first reign was around 6 B.C., which was during the reign of Herod. His second reign began in the year 6 or 7 A.D. If Luke was alluding to Cyrenius' first reign, that would reinforce the idea that Christ was born 4 B.C. or earlier. Thus, the "new" millennium may have already passed us by without much, if any, fanfare.

Not only don't we know the year of Jesus' birth, we are completely ignorant of the time of the year it was. The New Testament does not mention the date Of Jesus' birth. Many have speculated that since there were "shepherds in the field" the night Jesus was born, it had to be during Spring or Summer. Dates such as March 25th, April 19th or 20th and May 20th, have been bandied about. But no one knows.

In the early Christian church, Jesus Christ's birth was not celebrated. For the first 300 years after the writing of the New Testament, Christmas was celebrated on various dates. One of the early church fathers, Clement of Alexandria stated that Christ was born on November 17, 3 B.C. In 354 A.D., the Bishop of Rome decreed that December 25th, a pagan feast celebrating the returning Sun-god, Saturn, (known as *Saturnalia*) was to be used as the official birthdate of Jesus Christ. This custom was not followed in the East, and even today some branches of the Eastern Orthodox church celebrate January 6th as Christmas day. As far as the millennial prophecies regarding Jesus' birth are concerned, no command or example is given in the New Testament to celebrate Jesus' birth in any manner.

So how did the arbitrary year 1 start out as the new calendar? The sixth-century monk, Dionysius Exiguss (Denis le Petit) stated that the birth of Jesus was 753 years from Rome's founding. He then recalculated the date as year 1 — the purported time of Christ's birth. It is likely that Dionysius had crude data to work with and calculated Jesus' birth date by manipulating several estimates within the Roman calendar. Judging from the historical evidence, modern scholars consider that Dionysius was incorrect. The doomsday millennium has thus passed probably sometime between December 31, 1993 and December 31, 1997. But whatever the date, no one knows the actual date of Jesus' birth, and according to the New Testament, no significance should be attached to his birthdate anyway. It is also ironic that Jesus Christ and all his disciples were Jewish, and they followed the Hebrew Calendar. Many Jews around Jesus' time believed in an end-of-day's apocalypse with an ultimate triumph by the messiah. Presently, the Hebrew Calendar date is 5760. For those religious Jews and others worrying about an end-of-times event occurring at the end of 6000 years, you still have about 240 years to wait.

Quality Of Life

Being aware of all of these unknown possibilities, perhaps we ought to focus our priorities on what we **actually** experience from day-to-day. From this "present reality" perspective, it is one's *quality of life* that is most important. It is what we do — how we interact with others and conduct ourselves in every aspect of living — that produces our quality of life (good, bad, or lukewarm). Worrying about death can generate extreme anxiety and make our remaining years stressful rather than enjoyable. Death anxiety is, therefore, a waste of life — not a fulfillment of it.

As some of us age, we become more concerned with dying than with death itself. We do not want a prolonged and painful end of passage. However, for the most part — at least in hospital situations — painful deaths can be decreased greatly with the use of narcotics, intravenous (IV) sedation, antidepressants, antianxiety agents, and deep relaxation techniques (such as hypnosis, meditation and brain wave synchronizers). Victims of violent death would not have the luxury of medical assistance, but if time were available and consciousness were present, the utilization of mental relaxation techniques could help them get through the pain and suffering. At any rate, as some religions profess, since being angry at the time of death would hinder the afterlife voyage of the soul, one should try to be calm and peaceful in those last moments. Thus, being mentally prepared for one's last breath seems quite wise.

Irrespective of how one dies, you should not worry about death and dying. David Burns, in his book *The Feeling Good Handbook*, gives these excellent reasons for not worrying about death.

• For those people who worry about not fulfilling all of their aspirations, the reply could be that no one ever fulfills all of their dreams.

It is preferable to consider the good and beneficial accomplishments that one has done in life rather than suffer anguish over the unfulfilled hopes and dreams.

• Some individuals fear that there will be absolutely nothing after death (a form of obliteration into nothingness) and that it would be unpleasant. The reply could be that the closest situations that we have in life to death are having dreamless sleep and going under general anesthesia. Most people find no unpleasantness associated with going into or even being in these states. Interestingly, the Jewish *Talmud* states that sleep is $^1/_{60}$th of death. With sleep, the soul leaves the body and then returns upon awakening. In addition, before we were born, there was nothingness. Do we remember that as being unpleasant? Chances are pretty strong that you don't. If there is nothingness before life, how can one possibly become upset about nothingness following death?

• If death were impossible, think of the anguish from being in unbearable and untreatable pain from an accident, injury or disease. Would it not be preferable to die and be released from that horrendous suffering?

• Finally, if death were impossible and we would be immortals, imagine the trillions of people living on Earth, with individuals being piled on top of each other because of the lack of living space. Would that be living? We could live in outer space, but who knows what that would be like?

David Yount, in his book, *Ten Thoughts To Take Into Eternity*, gives excellent suggestions about how to conduct life as a seamless progression from the present to eternity. Yount arranged his suggestions as the following "Ten Thoughts" and devoted a chapter to each:

1. **Death doesn't hurt; life does.**
2. **You are not the first person to make this trip.**
3. **You can take it with you.**
4. **This trip is not a vacation.**
5. **You are not going somewhere, but to someone.**
6. **You are not ready, but it doesn't matter.**
7. **Be prepared for surprises.**
8. **You are leaving nothing behind.**
9. **You have been preparing all your life for this.**
10. **Enter eternity laughing.**

Worry Can Produce
The Undesired Outcome

Continually worrying about death would most likely bring it on prematurely. Studies by Haines and coworkers and Kawachi and co-workers, and a report by Abben have found that people who have high anxiety levels (individuals who worry a great deal) die much sooner from fatal coronary heart disease (heart attacks) than people who have low anxiety levels. These high-anxiety individuals are especially prone to sudden cardiac death. (The first heart attack is the last.) The conclusions one can draw from this research are simple and consistent with our ongoing theme:

    • *We should not worry about the past* (it can't be changed).

    • *We should not have fearful premonitions about the future* (it hasn't yet arrived).

    • *We should concentrate on doing the best we can with the present* (it's the only reality that we can perceive with our senses in the here-and-now).

Furthermore, we should try to be **optimistic** in our outlook on life. After all, everything presented in the first thirteen chapters of this book points to a very reasonable possibility that **God exists** and **a blissful afterlife awaits** most of us. And these conclusions have been arrived at after using scientifically-based methods. In science, we consider the laws of probability. We state that something is statistically significant if the odds are very high that it will occur.

What The Odds Tell Us

In our spiritual journey, we found overwhelming odds that the universe could not have created itself. If not self-created, God must have done it. We found major discrepancies in Darwin's theory of evolution. It was shown that even if humans descended from some ape-like creature, they have something that no form of apes — or any creature for that matter — has: the ability to think, create, write, theorize, dream and have aspirations, and to be religious, scientific, and artistic. We have an awareness of creation and our participation in it. The evidence is that these abilities didn't come to us gradually as in an evolutionary process or by chance. They came suddenly. Who gave them to us? Could it have been anyone else but God?

We found that countless millions of people have had NDEs and, with many of these, there were commonalties such as: a dark tunnel; a rapid upward movement; a brilliant light that envelops the spiritual body; a distant crossing; visits with deceased loved ones; angelic-like presences; a brilliantly lit, loving, caring God-like entity; indescribably blissful and loving feelings; the understanding that the most important things in life are love and learning; and OBEs in which objects are observed that could only be seen from an elevated position. In contrast, those individuals who were evil or who attempted suicide, frequently had hellish experiences. All of these NDEs occurred with people of all ages, both genders, and with individuals of all races, ethnic groups and religions (or even no religion at all). With all our possible scientific explanations, we could not show that the components of the NDE could be explained as physiological or psychological processes associated with the dying process. Not only that, we found that many of the NDE findings were also observed with OBEs, apparitions, visions, certain dreams, during séances and medium reports, and during past life regressions. Could all of this have been mere coincidence? Examining all of these scientifically leads one to the inescapable conclusion that the findings of all these similar occurrences could only point to the fact that they were describing the same thing. **The findings are real.**

Furthermore, we found that most of the major religions, organizations, and theorizing people had beliefs that coincided with many of the NDEs and the other psi phenomena. For example, in *Kabbalah* the soul departs the body with joy and love to meet a radiant-light-filled celestial being of love, the *Shekhinah*. As the soul departs the body, it is welcomed into the post-mortem realms by deceased family members and friends. The soul is also given a rapid life review. The soul goes through a thrusting, upward movement through the postmortem realms. The departing soul becomes enveloped by a field of light. The importance of love and learning is emphasized. If one wants to have a joyful afterlife experience, the necessity of living a good life is stressed. Evil people have a more disturbing afterlife journey. Other religions describe similar occurrences. Could the fact that religions and NDEs and related psi phenomena all display the same phenomena be a chance occurrence? Scientifically, this does not seem at all likely. There must be a common denominator, and this common denominator is the reality of the surviving soul, the afterlife, and God.

Life's Plan

We should not expect this wonderful afterlife to be handed to us on a silver platter. We should have a plan on how to live our lives. These are the rules to follow in forming and acting on your plan:

• We should live our lives with the goal to have the greatest quality and quantity of life on planet Earth while at the same time being loving, kind, considerate, righteous and spiritual.

• We should have friends, companions and lovers and try to have few, if any, enemies.

• We should use effective stress management techniques such as exercise, eating well, diversions (see *Figures 72 & 73*), consultations, and

Figure 72
Copy of a watercolor painting, "Haddonfield, NJ
First Presbyterian Church" by Don Morse, May, 1997.

relaxation therapy. Relaxation therapy, such as meditation and self-hypnosis, are especially important, because with deep states of meditation and hypnosis, not only can we become extremely relaxed (a health benefit), we can achieve planes of spirituality where we can sometimes get a glimpse of a blissful afterlife. This will help us in our own ultimate afterlife journey.

• We should try to avoid sickness and accidents so that we do not die prematurely. We want to keep the Angel of Death at bay as long as possible because, as wonderful as life after death can be, life on Earth is precious and we should enjoy every moment of it. We are here for a purpose, and premature death may well stop us in its fulfillment.

• We should control the negative emotions of anger, hate, jealousy, envy, guilt, shame, frustration, worry, fear and anxiety. This should ensure that, when we die, the pangs of the grave will be mild and

Figure 73
Copy of a watercolor painting, "Paradise Island, Bahamas"
by Don Morse, February, 1998.

short-lived, we will require little emotional purging so that our afterlife journey will be smoother and more blissful, and we will not have to be reincarnated as a different individual. However, if we die at a young age, we should rest assured that our soul will be given another chance for a full life on Earth.

• We should keep in mind all the findings of this book, so that when we are about to die, we will have no fear because of our preparation. We will know that our soul will survive, we will have a joyous afterlife, and we will meet God in all His glory.

• Finally, we should follow the advice of the characters in Woody Allen's movie, *"Everyone Says I Love You,"* who sing and dance the lyrics of that old popular song, "Enjoy yourself, it's later than you think." Or better yet, we should enjoy ourselves **now** while knowing that **the best is yet to come.**

AFTERWORD

In closing, I would like to share two wonderful stories with you. The first was from Rabbi Steven Lindemann. It appeared in "Rabbi's Message" published in *Temple Talk* (1999).

A young girl was in a religious school classroom. She was asked by the teacher to tell in her own words the story of the biblical character, Enoch. In the Bible, it states: "And Enoch walked with God, and he was not; for God took him" (Genesis 5:24).

The young girl rose from her seat and paraphrased it thusly: "Enoch used to go on long walks with God. One day they walked farther than usual and God said, 'Enoch, you are tired. Come into my house and stay and rest.' "

Isn't that a beautiful way to speak of death? The second tale is from the classic Jewish volume that discusses the concepts of death and the afterlife. The book is known as *Gesher Hachayim* ("The Bridge of Life"). The story was discussed in Rabbi David J. Wolpe's outstanding book, *Teaching Your Children About God* (1999).

Identical twins were lying next to each other in their mother's womb. The mother ate well and was in excellent health. Hence, the twins had all they needed to survive in the womb. One of the twins had the "irrational" belief that there was a world beyond the womb. The other twin was convinced that his brother's belief was utter nonsense. The first twin told his brother that there was a world where people walked upright, where there were oceans and mountains and a sky filled with stars. The other twin could hardly hold his disdain for such a foolish concept.

Suddenly, the first twin was forced through his mother's birth canal. All he had previously known was gone. The twin who was left behind viewed his brother's disappearance as a great tragedy. However, outside the womb, the parents were rejoicing.

The twin who was left behind had observed a "birth" not a death. Only he didn't know it. This is a classic viewpoint — the afterlife is a birth into a "world" that we on Earth cannot even imagine — a concept with which I heartily agree. However, there are some of us — as a result of a NDE, OBE, apparition, vision, dream or some other spiritual encounter — who have had a glimpse of that "world." And in a small way, we have "seen" what the "irrational" twin believed: **something far greater awaits us.**

The Wall

A journalist was assigned to the Jerusalem bureau of his newspaper. He got an apartment overlooking the Wailing (Western) Wall. After several weeks, he realized that whenever he looked at the wall he saw an old Jewish man praying vigorously. The journalist wondered whether there was a publishable story there. He went down to the wall, introduced himself and said, "You come every day to the wall. What are you praying for?"

The old Jewish man replied, "What am I praying for? In the morning, I pray for world peace; then I pray for the brotherhood of man. I go home, have a glass of tea, and I come back to the wall to pray for the eradication of illness and disease from the Earth."

The journalist was amazed by the old man's sincerity and persistence. "You mean you have been coming to the wall to pray every day for these things." The old man nodded. "How long have you been coming to the wall to pray for these things?"

The old Jewish man became reflective and then replied, "How long? Maybe twenty, twenty-five years."

The journalist was flabbergasted. "You mean you have been coming to the wall every day for all these years to pray for these things?" Again, the old man nodded. The astonished journalist finally asked, "How does it feel to come and pray every day for these things?"

The old Jew-ish man replied, "How does it feel? It feels like I'm talking to a wall."

• Let us be like the old man and never give up. Because, maybe, just maybe, God is on the other side of the wall and at least some of our prayers and hopes will be answered.

CHAPTER NOTES
AND REFERENCES

Introduction
The two articles I wrote about death anxiety are the following:

Morse, D.R. Confronting Existential Anxiety: The Ultimate Stressor. *Stress Med.* 1998; 14:109-119.

Morse, D.R. Stress and the Afterlife. *J. Religion and Psychical Research.* 1998; 21: 194-205.

Chapter One: Death Anxiety
The reference used for fear and anxiety are the following:

Morse, D.R. Anxiety and its Control. *Int. J. Psychosom.* 1995; 42: 54-64.

Morse, D.R. Confronting Existential Anxiety: The Ultimate Stressor. *Stress Med.* 1998; 14:109-119.

The references used for definitions of existential and death anxiety are the following:
May, R. *Existential Psychology*, 2nd ed. Random House, New York, 1969.

Morse, D.R. Confronting Existential Anxiety: The Ultimate Stressor. *Stress Med.* 1998; 14:109-119.

The references used for dealing with death anxiety early in life are the following:
Freud, S. Thoughts for the Times on War and Death. In: *Collected Papers.* Freud, S.J. Riviére, London and New York, 1959, Vol. 4, pp. 304-305.

Morse, D.R. and Furst, M.L. *Stress For Success: A Holistic Approach to Stress and its Management.* Van Nostrand Reinhold, New York, 1978.

Mindell, E. *Earl Mindell's Herb Bible.* Simon & Schuster, New York, 1992.

Morse, D.R. Anxiety and its control. *Int. J. Psychosom.* 1995; 42: 54-64.

Balch, J.F. and Balch, P.A. *Prescriptions for Natural Healing: A Practical A-Z Reference to Drug-Free Remedies Using Vitamins, Minerals, Herbs and Food Supplements,* 2nd ed. Garden City Park, New York, Avery Pub., 1997.

"Dateline" NBC TV. How O.J. Simpson can believe in his innocence: Researchers discover brain mechanisms to facilitate denial of reality. 9-10 pm (East coast, U.S.A.), February 7, 1997.

Dunamai. Religiosity, Age, Gender, and Death Anxiety. On internet Web site: http://dunamai.com/fddy.htm

Morse, D.R. Confronting Existential Anxiety: The Ultimate Stressor. *Stress Med.* 1998; 14:109-119.

Morse, D. *Electronic Pharmacy of the Mind: Use of Brain Wave Synchronizers and Other Relaxation Methods to Control Stress.* Cryptic Press, Atlanta, 1998.

The references used for dealing with death anxiety later in life are the following:

Martin, D. and Wrightsman, L.S. The Relationship Between Religious Behavior and Concern About Death. *J. Soc. Psychol.* 1965; 65: 317-323.

Bell, B. D. and Batlerson, C.T. The Death Attitude of Older Adults: A Path-Analytical Exploration. *Omega* 1975; 10(1); 59-75.

Pollak, J. Correlates of Death Anxiety: A Review of Empirical Studies. *Omega* 1980; 10(2): 97-121.

Aday, R.H. Belief in Afterlife and Death Anxiety: Correlates and Comparisons. *Omega* 1984; 15(1); 66-67.

Dunamai. Religiosity, Age, Gender, and Death Anxiety. On internet Web site: http://dunamai.com/fddy.htm

Morse, D.R. Confronting Existential Anxiety: The Ultimate Stressor. *Stress Med.* 14: 109-119, 1998.

Morse, D.R. Stress and the Afterlife. *J. Religion Psychical Res.* 1998; 21(3):194-205.

Chapter Two: My Near-Death Experience

Since this was a personal experience, there are no references.

Chapter Three: Near-Death Experiences

There have been many books and articles written about near-death experiences (NDEs), but it was Dr. Raymond Moody's investigations that led to his first book, *Life After Life,* that started the world-wide interest in this subject. There are many other excellent researchers on NDEs including: Mally Cox-Chapman, Dr. Bruce Greyson, Dr. Michael Grosso, Dr. Erlendur Haraldsson, Dr. Tom Harpur, Dr. Karlis Osis, Dr. Elisabeth Kubler-Ross, Dr. Melvin Morse, Dr. Maurice Rawlings, Dr. Kenneth Ring, Dr. Barbara Rommer, Dr. Michael Sabon, Dr. Fred Schoonmaker, the Steigers and Carol Zaleski. Dannion Brinkley, Betty Eadie, Dr. George Ritchie and the Fenwicks have written important books on NDEs. However to my knowledge, no one has done more extensive work and written more books (seven) on the subject than Dr. P.M.H. Atwater.

The version of the Hebrew Bible used is:

The Holy Scriptures According to The Masoretic Text. The Jewish Publication Society of America, Philadelphia, 1955.

The reference used for the "silver cord" and the "golden bough" is:

Steiger, B. and Steiger, S.H. *Touched by Heaven's Light.* Signet, Penguin Putnam, New York, 1999.

The information on the post-NDE sequellae of low blood pressure and electrical sensitivity can be found in:

Atwater, P.M.H. The Experience/The Experiencer: Column # 1; accessed on the internet at the following site:

http://www.cinemind.com/atwater/expers.html

The information on the post-NDE sequellae of psychic ability can be found in:
Atwater, P.M.H. *Future Memory*. Hampton Roads, Charlottesville, Virginia, 1999.
Atwater, P.M.H. The Experience/The Experiencer: Column # 2; accessed on the internet at the following site:
http://www.cinemind.com/atwater/col2.html

The information on the post-NDE sequellae of synchronicity can be found in:
Atwater, P.M.H. The Experience/The Experiencer: Column # 3; accessed on the internet at the following site:
http://www.cinemind.com/atwater/col3.html

The information on the post-NDE sequellae of religious affiliation can be found in:
Atwater, P.M.H. The Experience/The Experiencer: Column # 5; accessed on the internet at the following site:
http://www.cinemind.com/atwater/col5.html

The information on the NDE phenomena of "dark" and types of "light" can be found in:
Atwater, P.M.H. The Experience/The Experiencer: Column # 6; accessed on the internet at the following site:
http://www.cinemind.com/atwater/col6.html

The information on the four types of NDEs can be found in:
Atwater, P.M.H. The Experience/The Experiencer: Column # 7; accessed on the internet at the following site:
http://www.cinemind.com/atwater/col7.html
There is now an organization dedicated to near-death studies known as "The International Association for Near-Death Studies" (IANDS). They publish *The Journal of Near-Death Studies* and the *Vital Signs newsletter*.

The other chapter references used are the following:
Kübler-Ross, E. *On Death and Dying*. Macmillan, New York, 1969.
Moody, R.A., Jr. *Life After Life: The Investigation of a Phenomenon — Survival of Bodily Death*. Mockingbird Books, St. Simon Island, Georgia, 1975.
Atwater, P.M.W. *I Died Three Times. You Can Change Your Life*, Charlottesville, Virginia, 1977. Incredibly, Dr. Atwater had three NDEs in one year and lived to tell about it.
Moody, R.A., Jr. *Reflections on Life After Life*. Mockingbird Books, St. Simon Island, Georgia, 1977.
Osis, K. and Haraldsson, E. *At the Hour of Death*. Avon Books, New York, 1977.
Rawlings, M. *Beyond Death's Door*. Thomas Nelson, Nashville and New York, 1978.
Ritchie, G.G. *Return from Tomorrow*. Chosen Books, Waco, Texas, 1978.
Ritchie, G.G. and Sherrill, E. *My Glimpse of Eternity*. Guideposts, Carmel, New York, 1978, pp. 48-49.
Schoonmaker, F. Denver Cardiologist Discloses Findings After 18 Years of Near-Death Research. *Ambiosis I*: 1-2, 1979.
Ring, K. *Life at Death: A Scientific Investigation of the Near-Death Experience*. Coward, McCann & Geoghegan, New York, 1980.

Sabom, M. *Recollections of Death: A Medical Investigation.* Harper & Row, New York, 1982.

Greyson, B. and Flynn, C.P. (Eds.). *The Near-Death Experience.* Thomas, Springfield, Illinois, 1984.

Ring, K. *Heading Toward Omega.* Wm. Morrow, New York, 1984.

Grosso, M. *The Final Choice: Playing the Survival Game.* Stillpoint Pub., Walpole, New Hampshire, 1985.

Zaleski, C. *Otherworld Journeys.* Oxford University Press, New York and Oxford, England, 1987.

Atwater, P.M.H. *Coming Back to Life: The After-Effects of the Near-Death Experience.* Dodd Mead & Co., New York, 1988.

Moody, R.A., Jr. with Perry, P. *The Light Beyond.* Bantam Books, New York, 1988.

Sabom, S. Other World Journeys (Review). *Journal of Near Death Studies* 6(4): 258-263, 1988.

Farr, S.S. *What Tom Sawyer Learned From Dying.* Hampton Roads Publ. Co., Norfolk, Virginia, 1988, p. 33.

Harris, B. and Bascom, L. *Full Circle: The Near-Death Experience and Beyond.* Pocket Books, New York, 1990.

Morse, M. with Perry, P. *Closer to the Light: Learning From Children's Near-Death Experiences.* Villard Books, New York, 1990. Dr. Morse was the pioneer in the investigations of children's near-death experiences.

Owens, J.E., Cook, E.W. and Stevenson, I. Features of Near-Death Experience in Relation to Whether or Not Patients Were Near Death. *Lancet* 336 (8724): 1175-1177, 1990.

Ring, K. and Rosing, C. The Omega Project. *Journal of Near Death Studies* 8(4): 211-239, 1990.

Wilson, I. *The After Death Experience.* Wm. Morrow and Co., New York, 1990.

Kübler-Ross, E. *On Life After Death.* Celestial Arts, Berkeley, California, 1991.

Eadie, B.J. *Embraced by the Light.* Gold Leaf Press, Placerville, California, 1992.

Greyson, B. and Bush, N.E. Distressing Near-Death Experiences. *Psychiatry* 1992; 55: 95-110.

Harpur, T. *Life After Death.* McClelland & Stewart, Toronto, 1992. An excellent TV program based on Harpur's book was shown on the TLC channel on December 22, 1997 from 9:00-11:00 P.M. (East coast).

Morse, M. with Perry, P. *Transformed By The Light: The Powerful Effect of Near-Death Experiences on People's Lives.* Villard Books, New York, 1992.

Farr, S.S. and Sawyer, T. *What Tom Sawyer Learned From Dying.* Hampton Roads Publ. Co., Norfolk, Virginia, 1993.

Globe, D. *Through the Tunnel.* S.O.U.L. Foundation, Palm Harbor, Florida, 1993.

Rawlings, M. *To Hell and Back.* Thomas Nelson, Nashville and New York, 1993.

Atwater, P.M.H. *Beyond the Light: What Isn't Being Said About the Near-Death Experience.* Birch Lane Press, New York, 1994. This book resulted from Dr. Atwater's interviews with over 3,000 NDErs and is probably the most complete compendium yet done on NDEs, their aftereffects and implications.

Brinkley, D. *Saved By The Light.* Random House, New York, 1994.

Morse, M. *Parting Visions: Uses and Meanings of Pre-Death, Psychic and Spiritual Experiences.* Villard Books, New York, 1994.

Bascom, L.C. and Loecher, B. *By the Light.* Avon, New York, 1995.

Collins, J.J. and Fishbane, M. (Eds.) *Death, Ecstasy and Other Worldly Journeys.* State University of New York Press, Albany, New York, 1995.

Cox-Chapman, M. *The Case for Heaven: Near-Death Experiences as Evidence of the Afterlife.* Putnam's Sons, New York, 1995.

Duran, L. *The Blue Cord: A Semi-Autobiographical Novel.* Duirsoul Books, Monte Vista, Colorado, 1995.

Fenwick, P.B.C. and Fenwick, E. *The Truth In The Light: An Investigation of Over 300 Near Death Experiences.* Berkeley, New York, 1995.

Groothuis, D.R. *Deceived by the Light.* Harvest House Pub. Inc., Eugene, Oregon, 1995. This is a contrary viewpoint about near-death experiences.

Kellehear, A. *Experiences Near Death: Beyond Medicine and Religion.* Oxford University Press, New York and Oxford, England, 1995.

Kircher, P.M. *Love is the Link: A Hospice Doctor Shares Her Experience of Near Death and Dying.* Larson Publ., Burdett, New York, 1995, p. 94.

Phillips, P. *Angels, Angels, Angels: Embraced by the Light.....or Embraced by the Darkness.* Starburst Pub., Lancaster , Pennsylvania, 1995.

Robbins, D.V. *Embarrassed by the Light.* Raven House, Virginia Beach, Virginia, 1995. This is a satire.

Sharp, K.C. *After the Light.* Wm. Morrow, New York, 1995.

Steiger, B. and Steiger, S.H. *Children of the Light: The Startling and Inspiring Truth About Children's Near-Death Experiences and How They Illumine the Beyond.* Signet, New York, 1995.

Tribbe, F.G. The Breadth of Psychical Research Establishes Survival. In: *1995 Annual Conference Proceedings: Personal Survival of Bodily Death.* Acad. Religion & Psychical Research, Bloomfield, Connecticut, pp, 98-112, 1995.

Ankenberg, J. and Weldon, J. *The Facts on Near-Death Experiences.* Harvest House Publishers, Eugene, Oregon, 1996.

Biederman, J. and Biederman, M. *101 Ways to See the Light: Near Death Experiences Made Simple.* St. Martins Press, New York, 1996. This is another satire.

Brubaker, D. and Penney, M.B. *Absent From the Body: One Man's Clinical Death, A Journey Through Heaven and Hell.* Peninsula Publ., Los Altos Hills, California, 1996.

Carey, P. *Bliss.* Vintage Books, New York, 1996.

Carson, C. (Ed.) *When Ego Dies: A Compilation of Near-Death and Mystical Conversion Experiences.* Emerald Ink Publ., Houston, Texas, 1996.

Eadie, B.J. *The Awakening Heart: My Continuing Journey to Love.* Pocket Books, New York, 1996.

Fenimore, A. *Beyond the Darkness: My Near-Death Journey to the Edge of Hell.* Bantam, New York, 1996.

Ritchie, J. *Death's Door: True Stories of Near-Death Experiences.* Dell Publ. Co., New York, 1996.

Zaleski, C. *The Life of the World to Come: Near-Death Experience and Christian Hope.* Oxford University Press, New York and London, 1996.

Greene, H.L. *If I Should Wake Before I Die: The Medical and Biblical Truth About Near-Death Experiences.* Crossways Books, Wheaton, Illinois, 1997.

Hotz, R. Researchers Discover Possible "God Module" in Circuitry of Brain. *Los Angeles Times*, Oct. 28, 1997.

Lawrence, T. *Psychologist Studies "Near Death" Visions of Hell.* From the School of Health and Social Sciences, Coventry University, Coventry CVI 5FB, Great Britain, 1997.

Moody, R.A., Jr. *The Last Laugh: A New Philosophy of Near-Death Experiences, Apparitions, and the Paranormal.* William Golding Consulting, Atlanta, 1997. A major book that is must reading.

Wolf, L. *Jewish Meditation: A Kabbalistic Approach to a Balanced Life.* Presented at the Gershman YMHA, Philadelphia, June 2, 1997. Rabbi Wolf discussed the near-death experience of a blind woman who saw and described people and colors in an adjacent room during her experience.

Glynn, P. *God, The Evidence: The Reconciliation of Faith and Reason in a Postsecular World.* Prima Publishing, Rocklin, California, 1997. This book gives an excellent review about near-death experiences.

Antelme, R.S. and Rossini, S. *Becoming Osiris: The Ancient Egyptian Death Experience.* Inner Traditions Intl. Ltd, Rochester, Vermont, 1998.

Batzler, L.R. Life after Death: Part 3. *Newsletter Spiritual Frontiers Fellowship Int.* 32(1): 6-9, 1998.

Berman, P.L. *The Journey Home: What Near-Death Experiences and Mysticism Teach Us About the Gift of Life.* Pocket Books, New York, 1998.

Cook, E.W., Greyson, B. and Stevenson, I. Do Any Near-Death Experiences Provide Evidence for the Survival of Bodily Death? Relevant Features and Illustrative Case Reports. *Journal of Scientific Exploration* 12(3): 377-406, 1998.

Currie, I. *Visions of Immortality.* Element Books, Victoria, British Columbia, Canada, 1998, p. 202.

Ring, K. *Lessons From the Light.* Insight Books, New York, 1998, p. 4.

Ritchie, G.C. *Ordered to Return: My Life After Dying.* Hampton Roads Publ. Co., Norfolk, Virginia, 1998.

Rommer, B.R. The Near-Death Experience as a Divine Gift for Preparation for Living, Dying, Death and the Afterlife. In: The Academy of Religion and Psychical Research, *1999 Annual Conference Proceedings, Dying, Death and the Afterlife: Psychical and Spiritual Dimensions.* The Academy of Religion and Psychical Research, Bloomfield, Connecticut, 1999, pp. 32-42.

Atwater, P.M.W. *Brain Shift/Spirit Shift: A Theoretical Model Using Research on Near Death States to Explore the Transformation of Consciousness.* You Can Change Your Life. Charlottesville, Virginia, 1999.

Atwater, P.M.W. *Children of the New Millennium.* Three Rivers Press, New York, 1999.

Atwater, P.M.W. *The Complete Idiot's Guide to the Near-Death Experience.* Macmillan, New York, 1999.

Atwater, P.M.W. *Future Memory.* Hampton Roads Publ. Co., Charlottesville, VA, 1999.

Tribbe, F.C. (Ed.) An Arthur Ford Anthology. Blue Dolphin Publishing, Inc., Nevada City, California, 1999, pp. 128-131.

Although written as fiction, the following book describes connections between people: Redfield, J. *The Celestine Prophecy.* Warner Books, New York, 1993.

The version of the New Testament used is from the *King James Version The Holy Bible Containing the Old and New Testaments.* New York Bible Society, New York, Since 1809.

Information on many of the theories of NDE explanations can be found in Glynn's book. Glynn, P. *God, The Evidence: The Reconciliation of Faith and Reason in a Postsecular World.* Prima Publishing, Rocklin, California, 1997.

Other information on NDE theories can be found on the internet at the following sites:
http://www.iloveusa.com/Secrets/experts1.html;
http://www.iloveusa.com/Secrets/experts3.html;
http://www.lycaeum.org/drugs/synthetics/ketamine/Ketamine_near-death.html;
http://www.iloveusa.com/Secrets/experts5.html;
http://www.iloveusa.com/ Secrets/experts4.html;
http://www.chron.com/content/chronicle /nation/97/10/29/brain-god.2.0.html;
http://www.iloveusa.com/Secrets/experts7.html;
http://www.iloveusa.com/Secrets/experts6.html;
http://www.iloveusa.com/Secrets/experts2.html

Further information on NDE theories can be accessed from the internet at: http://www.iloveusa.com/Secrets/experts8.html and from the following books:
Greyson, B. and Flynn, C.P. (Eds.). *The Near-Death Experience: Problems, Prospects, Perspectives.* Thomas, Springfield, IL, 1984.
Ring, K. *Heading Toward Omega.* William Morrow, New York, 1984.
Blackmore, S. *Dying to Live: Science and the Near-Death Experience.* Prometheus, Buffalo, New York, 1993.
Blackmore, S. *In Search of the Light.* Prometheus, Amherst, New York, 1996.
Glynn, P. *God The Evidence: The Reconciliation of Faith and Reason in a Postsecular World.* Prima Publishing, Rocklin, California, 1997.

In the last section of this chapter, the fifth new case of NDE is about the experience of Frank Root, a Philadelphia artist who has produced marvelous three dimensional works about the Holocaust using a medium known as Homosote. These works have been presented at various sites and in March 1998, they were on display at the JCC in Cherry Hill, New Jersey. For information about these works, Mr. Root can be contacted at his e-mail address: juroot@aol.com.

Chapter Four: Out-Of-Body Experiences

The version of the Hebrew Bible used is:
The Holy Scriptures According to The Masoretic Text. The Jewish Publication Society of America, Philadelphia, 1955.

Excellent references used for out-of-body experiences (OBEs) are Monroe's book and the Guggenheims' book.

Monroe, R.A. *Ultimate Journey*. Doubleday, New York, 1994.

Guggenheim, B. and Guggenheim, J. *Hello From Heaven: A New Field of Research — After-Death Communication — Confirms That Life and Love are Eternal*. Bantam Books, New York, 1996.

Other references used are the following:

Tart, C.T. A Psychophysiological Study of Out-of-the-Body Experiences in a Selected Subject. *Journal of the American Society for Psychical Research* 62(1): 3-27, 1968.

Ehrenwald, J. Out-of-the Body Experiences and the Denial of Death. *Journal of Nervous and Mental Disease*. 159(4): 227-233, 1974.

Morris, R.L., Harary, S.B., Janis, J., Hartwell, J. and Roll, W.G. Studies of Communication During Out-of-Body Experiences. *Journal of the American Society for Psychical Research* 72(1) : 1-21, 1978.

Ring, K. *Life at Death: A Scientific Investigation of the Near-Death Experience*. Coward, McCann & Geoghegan, New York, 1980.

Ring, K. *Heading Toward Omega: In Search of the Meaning of the Near-Death Experience*. William Morrow, New York, 1984.

Moody, R.A., Jr. with Perry, P. *The Light Beyond: New Explorations by the Author of Life After Life*. Bantam Books, New York, 1988.

Moody, R.A. Jr. and Perry, P. *Reunions: Visionary Encounters with Departed Loved Ones*. Villard Books, New York, 1993. In this book, Dr. Moody discusses Joan Rivers' OBE.

Morse, M. *Parting Visions: Uses and Meanings of Pre-Death, Psychic and Spiritual Experiences*. Villard Books, New York, 1994.

Tribbe, F.G. The Breadth of Psychical Research Establishes Survival. In: *1995 Annual Conference Proceedings: Personal Survival of Bodily Death*. Acad. Religion. Psychical Research, Bloomfield, Connecticut, pp, 98-112,19 895.

Batzler, L.R. Life after Death: Part 3. *Newsletter Spiritual Frontiers Fellowship Int.* 32(1): 6-9, 1998.

Jedd, M. Where do You Want to Go Today? *Fate* 51(7). Issue 580: 34-39, 1998.

Batey, B. Beyond the Veil: Evidence for Life After Death. In: *The Academy of Religion and Psychical Research, 1999 Annual Conference Proceedings, Dying, Death and the Afterlife: Psychical and Spiritual Dimensions*. The Academy of Religion and Psychical Research, Bloomfield, Connecticut, 1999, pp. 5-19.

Paul, P. Out-of Body Experiences. *Journal of Religion and Psychical Research*. 23(1): in press, 2000. This is an excellent review of all the recent books on OBEs.

Although fiction, Redfield's books, show how certain individuals can have OBEs while in a deep state of meditation:

Redfield, J. *The Celestine Prophecy*. Warner Books, New York, 1993.

Redfield, J. *The Tenth Insight: Holding the Vision*. Warner Books, New York, 1996.

The Steigers give an excellent review of people having OBEs while in a state of deep meditation.

Steiger, B. and Steiger, S.H. *Touched by Heaven's Light.* Signet, Penguin Putnam, New York, 1999.

Chapter Five: Apparitions, Visions, Dreams, Séances and Medium Reports

The version of the Hebrew Bible used is:
The Holy Scriptures According to The Masoretic Text. The Jewish Publication Society of America, Philadelphia, 1955.

The version of the New Testament used is from the *King James Version The Holy Bible Containing the Old and New Testaments.* New York Bible Society, New York, Since 1809.

The dictionary used is:
Merriam-Webster, A. *Webster's Ninth New Collegiate Dictionary.* G. & C. Merriam Co., Springfield, Massachusetts, 1990.

The references used for apparitions are the following:
Moody, R.A. Jr. and Perry, P. *Reunions: Visionary Encounters with Departed Loved Ones.* Villard Books, New York, 1993.

Persinger, M.A. Average Diurnal Changes in Melatonin Levels are Associated with Hourly Incidence of Bereavement Apparitions: Support for the Hypothesis of Temporal (Limbic) Lobe Microseizuring. *Perceptual and Motor Skills* 76(1): 444-446, 1993.

Persinger, M.A. Vectoral Cerebral Hemisphericity as Differential Sources for the Sensed Presence, Mystical Experiences, and Religious Conversions. *Perceptual and Motor Skills* 76(2): 915-930, 1993.

Roney-Dougal, S.M. and Vogl, G. Some Speculations on the Effect of Geomagnetism on the Pineal Gland. *Journal of the Society for Psychical Research* 59(1): 1-15, 1993.

Haraldsson, E. Apparitions of the Dead: Analysis of a New Collection of 357 Reports. In: Delaney, D. and Cook, E.W. (Eds.). *Research in Parapsychology.* Scarecrow Press, Metuchen, New Jersey, 1994, pp. 1-6.

Irwin, H.J. The Phenomenology of Parapsychological Experiences. In: Krippner, S. (Ed.). *Advances in Parapsychological Research 7.* McFarland and Co. Inc., Jefferson, North Carolina, 1994, pp. 55-61. Here is where G.N.M. Tyrrell's 1942 discussion of wraiths and ghosts is given.

Maher, M.C. and Hansen, G.P. Quantitative Investigation of a Reported Haunting Using Several Detection Techniques. *Journal of the American Society for Psychical Research* 89(1); 19-50, 1995.

Stevenson, I. Six Modern Apparitional Experiences. *Journal of Scientific Exploration* 9(3): 351-366, 1995.

Tribbe, F.G. The Breadth of Psychical Research Establishes Survival. In: *1995 Annual Conference Proceedings: Personal Survival of Bodily Death.* Acad. Religion. Psychical Research, Bloomfield, Connecticut, pp. 98-112,1995.

Radin, D.I. and Roll, W.G. Investigations of Two Haunted Castles in Scandinavia. In: May, E.C. (Ed.). *Proceedings of the 39th Annual Convention of the Parapsychological*

Association. Parapsychological Association, Fairhaven, Massachusetts, 1996, pp. 271-278.

Osis, K. Phenomena Suggestive of Life After Death: A Spiritual Existence. In: Tart, C.T. (Ed.). *Body Mind Spirit: Exploring the Parapsychology of Spirituality.* Hampton Roads Publ., Charlottesville, Virginia, 1997, pp. 163-170.

Coghlan, A. Midnight Watch. *New Scientist* 16(2165): 42-45, December 19, 1998-January 2, 1999.

Steiger, B. and Steiger, S.H. *Touched by Heaven's Light.* Signet, Penguin Putnam, New York, 1999.

Williams, B. Can a Person Really Survive After Death: A Look at the Evidence of Three Types of Suggestive Phenomena Found in Religious Beliefs. *Journal of Religion and Psychical Research* 22(4): 209-219, 1999.

The references used for visions are the following:

Barrett, W.F. *Death-Bed Visions.* Methuen, London, 1926.

Swain, J. *On the Death of My Son: An Account of Life After Death.* Turnerstone Books, London, 1974.

Osis, K. and Haraldsson, E. Deathbed Observations by Physicians and Nurses. *Parapsychology Monograph No. 3.* Parapsychological Foundation, New York, 1981.

Kübler-Ross, E. *On Life After Death.* Celestial Arts, Berkeley, California, 1991, p. 60.

Morse, M. *Parting Visions: Uses and Meanings of Pre-Death, Psychic and Spiritual Experiences.* Villard Books, New York, 1994.

Guggenheim, B. and Guggenheim, J. *Hello From Heaven: A New Field of Research — After-Death Communication — Confirms That Life and Love are Eternal.* Bantam Books, New York, 1996.

Orloff, J. *Second Sight.* Warner Books, New York, 1996.

Tribbe, F.G. The Breadth of Psychical Research Establishes Survival. In: *1995 Annual Conference Proceedings: Personal Survival of Bodily Death.* Acad. Religion. Psychical Research, Bloomfield, Connecticut, pp, 98-112,1995.

Steiger, B. and Steiger, S.H. *Touched by Heaven's Light.* Signet, Penguin Putnam, New York, 1999.

The references used for electronic voice phenomena (communication) are the following:

Meek. G. W. *Enjoy Your Own Funeral.* Galde Press, Lakeville, Minnesota, 1999.

Steiger, B. and Steiger, S.H. *Touched by Heaven's Light.* Signet, Penguin Putnam, New York, 1999.

The references for dreams are the following:

Guggenheim, B. and Guggenheim, J. *Hello From Heaven: A New Field of Research — After-Death Communication — Confirms That Life and Love are Eternal.* Bantam Books, New York, 1996.

Weiss, M.L. *Only Love is Real.* Warner Books, New York, 1996.

Schulte, B. Brain Research Deepens the Debate About Dreams. *Phil. Inquirer*, Section C 1,4, March 2, 1998.

The references used for séances and medium reports are the following:

Lodge, O. *Raymond or Life and Death.* George H. Doranco, New York, 1916, p. 296.

Cameron, M. *The Seven Purposes.* Harper and Brothers, New York, 1918.

Doyle, A.C. *The New Revelation.* Hodder and Stoughton, London, 1918.

Darby & Joan. *Our Unseen Guest.* Harper and Brothers, New York, 1920.

White, S.E. *The Unobstructed Universe.* E.P. Dutton, New York, 1940.

Gilbert, A. *Phillip in Two Worlds.* Andrew Dakers Ltd., London, 1948.

Ford, A. *Nothing So Strange.* Harper Row, New York, 1958.

Ebon, M. *They Knew the Unknown.* World Publishing Co., Grandville, Michigan, 1971.

Taylor, R. *Witness From Beyond.* Foreward Books, South Portland, Maine, 1975, pp. 36-37.

Brandon, R. *The Spiritualists: The Passion for the Occult in the Nineteenth and Twentieth Centuries.* Knopf, New York, 1983.

Crowley, J.R. Ectoplasm: A Report From Experiences. *J. Religion Psychical Res.* 1988; 11(2): 93-109.

O'Brien, S. *Visions of Another World.* The Acquarian Press, London, 1989.

O'Brien, S. *Voices From Heaven.* The Acquarian Press, London, 1991.

Tribbe, F.G. The Breadth of Psychical Research Establishes Survival. In: *1995 Annual Conference Proceedings: Personal Survival of Bodily Death.* Acad. Religion. Psychical Research, Bloomfield, Connecticut, pp, 98-112,1995.

Gough, L. *Mediumship: A Beginner's Guide.* Headway-Holder & Stoughton, London, 1997.

Van Praagh, J. *Talking to Heaven.* Dutton, New York, 1997.

Chambers, J. (Translator). *Conversations with Eternity: The Forgotten Masterpiece of Victor Hugo.* New Paradigm Books, Boca Raton, Florida, 1998.

Haddow, A.H. Life After Death: Psi Evidence and Religious Belief *J. Religion Psychical Res.* Oct. 1998.

Steiger, B. and Steiger, S.H. *Touched by Heaven's Light.* Signet, Penguin Putnam, New York, 1999.

Tribbe, F.C. (Ed.) *An Arthur Ford Anthology.* Blue Dolphin Publishing, Inc., Nevada City, California, 1999.

Chapter Six: Reincarnation and Past Life Regressions

The version of the Hebrew Bible used is:
The Holy Scriptures According to The Masoretic Text. The Jewish Publication Society of America, Philadelphia, 1955.

The references used for reincarnation are the following:

Sheldrake, R. *A New Science of Life.* J.P. Tarcher, Los Angeles, 1981.

Cooke, E.W., Pasricha, S.K., Samararatne, G., Maung, W. and Stevenson, I. A Review of "Unsolved" Cases of the Reincarnation Type II: Comparison of Features of Solved and Unsolved Cases. *Journal of the American Society for Psychical Research* 77(2): 115-135, 1983.

Wolger, R.J. *Other Lives, Other Selves: A Jungian Psychotherapist Discovers Past Lives.* Bantam Doubleday Dell, New York, 1988.

Fisher, J. *The Case for Reincarnation.* Carrol Publishers, New York, 1992.

Holzer, H. *Life Beyond: Compelling Evidence for Past Lives and Existence After Death.* NTC/Contemporary Publ., Lincolnwood, Illinois, 1994.

Cayce, C.T. (Ed.). *Edgar Cayce You Can Remember Past Lives.* Warner Books, New York, 1996.

Van Auken, J. *Born Again & Again: How Reincarnation Occurs and What It Means To You.* A.R.E. Press, Virginia Beach, Virginia, 1997.

Parisha, S.K. Cases of the Reincarnation Type in Northern India with Birthmarks and Birth Defects. *Journal of Scientific Exploration* 12(2): 259-293, 1998.

The wiping out of memories in reincarnation is discussed in Wolf's book:

Wolf, F.A. *The Spiritual Universe: How Quantum Physics Proves the Existence of the Soul.* Simon & Schuster, New York, 1996.

The study of past life regressions was stimulated by Dr. Brian Weiss's first book, but Dr. Ian Stevenson's latest book gives physical evidence of reincarnation in the form of birthmarks and birth defects.

Weiss, B.L. *Many Lives, Many Masters.* Simon & Schuster, New York, 1988.

Stevenson, I. *Reincarnation and Biology: A Contribution to the Etiology of Birthmarks and Birth Defects.* Praeger Publishers, New York, 1997.

There is now an "Association for Past-Life Research and Therapy" and *The Journal of Regression Therapy.*

Other excellent references used for this chapter on past life regressions are the following:

Whitton, J.L. and Fisher, J. *Life Between Life: Scientific Explorations into the Void Separating One Incarnation From the Next.* Doubleday & Co., Garden City, New York, 1986.

Wolger, R.J. *Other Lives, Other Selves: A Jungian Psychotherapist Discovers Past Lives.* Bantam Doubleday Dell, New York, 1988.

Fiore, E. *You Have Been Here Before: A Psychologist Looks At Past Lives.* Ballantine Books, New York, 1991.

Moody, R.A. *Coming Book: A Psychiatrist Explores Past-Life Journeys.* Bantam Books, New York, 1991.

Weiss, B.L. *Through Time Into Healing.* Simon & Schuster, New York, 1992.

Rieder, M. *Mission to Millboro.* Blue Dolphin, Nevada City, 1993.

Cunningham, J. *A Tribe Returned.* Deep Forest Press, Crest Park, California, 1994.

Weiss, B.L. *Only Love is Real.* Warner Books, New York, 1996.

Clark, R.L. *Past Life Therapy: The State of the Art.* Rising Star Press, Austin, Texas, 1997.

Chadwick, G. *Discovering Your Past Lives: The Best Book On Reincarnation You'll Ever Read in This Lifetime.* NTC/Contemporary Publ., Lincolnwood, Illinois, 1998.

Barnes, W. *I Built the Titanic: Past Life Memories Of A Master Builder.* Edin Books, Gillette, New York, 1999.

"Super-ESP" is discussed in:

Tribbe, F.G. The Breadth of Psychical Research Establishes Survival. In: *1995 Annual Conference Proceedings: Personal Survival of Bodily Death.* Acad. Relig. Psych. Research, Bloomfield, CT, pp 98-112, 1995.

Cryptomnesia is the experience of recalling something that is deeply buried in one's memory bank. An excellent description is found in the following:

Harris, M. *Investigating the Unexplained*. Prometheus Books, Buffalo, New York, 1986.

Meditation and brain wave synchronizers are discussed in the author's recent book:

Morse, D.R. *Electronic Pharmacy of the Mind: Use of Brain Wave Synchronizers and Other Relaxation Methods to Control Stress*. Cryptic Press, Atlanta, 1998.

Personal myths of basic characters can be buried in our unconscious and could be a source of past life regressions. An excellent source of these myths is Joseph Campbell's book.

Campbell. J. *The Hero With a Thousand Faces*. MJF Books, New York, 1949.

Chapter Seven: Immortality

The references used for living eternally are the following:

Tipler, F.J. *The Physics of Immortality: Modern Cosmology, God and the Resurrection of the Dead*. Doubleday, New York, 1994.

Edwards, P. (Ed.) *Immortality*. Prometheus Books, New York, 1997.

Alford, A.F. *Gods of the New Millennium*. Eridu Books, P.O. Box 107, Walsall WS9 9YR, England, 1998.

Bowie, H. *Why Die? A Beginner's Guide to Living Forever*. PowerSurge Publ., Scottsdale, Arizona, 1998.

Cryonics and cryogenics can be accessed from the internet at:
http://tesuque.cs.sandia.gov/~bbooth/docs/cryogenics/cryogenics2.html

The references used for cloning are the following:

Flam, F. Cloning. *Phil. Inquirer*, Section C 1,4, January 5, 1998.

Editorial. Human Cloning? Not Yet. *Phil. Inquirer*, Section A 18, January 18, 1998.

The reference used for extraterrestrial migration is:

Schickentanz, A. Immortality Systems: I.S. Engineering Extra Terrestrial Migration
— Gene; Eternal Life Society: Migrating to Infinite Space-Time. It can be found on the internet at: http://www.immortalitysystems.com/

The reference used for another view of immortality is the following:

Schachter-Shalomi, Z. and Miller, R.S. *From Age-ing to Sage-ing*. Warner Books, New York, 1995.

Chapter Eight: God

The version of the Hebrew Bible used is:

The Holy Scriptures According to The Masoretic Text. The Jewish Publication Society of America, Philadelphia, 1955.

Other references used are the following:

Wise, C.C., Jr. *Thus Saith The Lord: An Autobiography of God.* Magian Press, Penn Laird, Virginia, 1984.

Schroeder, G.L. *Genesis and the Big Bang: The Discovery of Harmony Between Modern Science and the Bible.* Bantam Books, New York, 1990.

Armstrong, K. *A History of God: The 4,000-Year Quest of Judaism, Christianity, and Islam.* Knopf, New York, 1994.

Little, G. *People of the Web: What Indian Mounds, Ancient Rituals, and Stone Circles Tell Us About Modern UFO Abductions, Apparitions, and the Near Death Experience.* White Buffalo Books, Memphis, Tennessee, 1990, pp. 157-163

Little, G. *Grand Illusions: The Spectral Reality Underlying Sexual UFO Abductions, Crashed Saucers, Afterlife Experiences, Sacred Ancient Sites, and Other Enigmas.* White Buffalo Books, Memphis, Tennessee, 1994, pp. 150-157; 169.

Templeton, J.M. and Hermann, R.L. *Is God the Only Reality? Science Points to a Deeper Meaning of the Universe.* Continuum, New York, 1994.

Matt, D.C. *God & The Big Bang: Discovering Harmony Between Science & Spirituality.* Jewish Lights Publishing, Woodstock, Vermont, 1996.

Walsch, N.D. *Conversations with God: An Uncommon Dialogue. Book 1.* G.P Putnam Sons, New York, 1996.

Glynn, P. *God The Evidence: The Reconciliation of Faith and Reason in a Postsecular World.* Prima Publishing, Rocklin, California, 1997.

Schroeder, G.L. *The Science of God: The Convergence of Scientific and Biblical Wisdom.* Simon & Schuster, New York, 1997.

Walsch, N.D. *Conversations with God: An Uncommon Dialogue. Book 2.* G.P. Putnam Sons, New York, 1997.

Cahill, T. *The Gifts of the Jews: How a Tribe of Nomads Changed the Way Everyone Thinks and Feels.* Doubleday, New York, 1998.

Walsch, N.D. *Conversations with God: An Uncommon Dialogue. Book 3.* G.P. Putnam Sons, New York, 1998.

Martin, H. *The Secret Teachings of the Espiritistas.* Metamind Publications, Savannah, Georgia, 1999. This excellent book describes the development of one God (*Bathala*) by the Filipinos and the spiritist movement and the amazing concepts of psychic surgery and healing.

Weaverson, J. *About God.* Kroshka Books, a Div. of Nova Science Publishers, Inc., Commack, New York, 1999.

Chapter Nine: God and the Origin of the Universe

The version of the Hebrew Bible used is:
The Holy Scriptures According to The Masoretic Text. The Jewish Publication Society of America, Philadelphia, 1955.

The references used for God and the origin of the universe are the following:
Dr. Gerald Schroeder's books are excellent in comparing the origin of the universe with the biblical account from Genesis. Dr. Hugh Ross's books are excellent in correlating

recent discoveries from astronomy, physics, and biology with God's creation of the universe and mankind. Dr. Patrick Glynn's book gives an excellent account of the not-so-random universe. William Bramley gives the evidence for the theory that God was an extraterrestrial visitor arriving on Mount Sinai in a smoky space craft.

Shroeder, G.L. *Genesis and the Big Bang: The Discovery of Harmony Between Modern Science and the Bible.* Bantam Books, New York, 1990.

Ross, H. *The Fingerprint of God: Recent Scientific Discoveries Reveal the Unmistakable Identity of the Creator.* Promise Publishing Co., Orange, California, 1991.

Bramley, W. *The Gods of Eden.* Avon Books, New York, 1993.

Ross, H. *Creation and Time: A Biblical and Scientific Perspective on the Creation-Date Controversy.* Navpress, Colorado Springs, Colorado, 1994.

Ross, H. *The Creator and the Cosmos: How the Greatest Scientific Discoveries of the Century Reveal God.* Navpress, Colorado Springs, Colorado, 1995.

Ross, H. *Beyond the Cosmos: What Recent Discoveries in Astronomy and Physics Reveal About the Nature of God.* Navpress, Colorado Springs, Colorado, 1996.

Schroeder, G.L. *The Science of God: The Convergence of Scientific and Biblical Wisdom.* Simon & Schuster, New York, 1997.

Glynn, P. God *The Evidence: The Reconciliation of Faith and Reason in a Postsecular World.* Prima Publishing, Rocklin, California, 1997. Patrick Glynn's book gives an excellent account of the not-so-random universe.

Ross, H. *The Genesis Question: Scientific Advances and the Accuracy of Genesis.* Navpress, Colorado Springs, Colorado, 1998.

Ross, H. *Beyond the Cosmos: The Extra-Dimensionality of God: What Recent Discoveries in Astrophysics Reveal About the Glory and Love of God, 2nd Expanded Edition.* Navpress, Colorado Springs, Colorado, 1999.

Southgate, C. (Ed.) *God, Humanity and the Cosmos: A Textbook in Science and Religion.* Trinity Press International, Harrisburg, Pennsylvania, 1999. This is an excellent textbook. On page 118, a discussion of Occam's razor is given.

The references used for quantum mechanics and uncertainty are the following:

Hawking, S. *A Brief History of Time: From the Big Bang to Black Holes.* Bantam Books, New York, 1988.

Davies, P. *The Mind of God: The Scientific Basis for a Rational World.* Simon & Schuster, New York, 1992.

Schroeder, G.L. *Genesis and the Big Bang: The Discovery of Harmony Between Modern Science and the Bible.* Bantam Books, New York, 1990.

Chopra, D. *Ageless Body, Timeless Mind.* Harmony Books, New York, 1993.

Schroeder, G.L. *The Science of God: The Convergence of Scientific and Biblical Wisdom.* Simon & Schuster, New York, 1997.

The references used for the big bang theory are the following:

Hawking, S. *A Brief History of Time: From the Big Bang to Black Holes.* Bantam Books, New York, 1988.

Schroeder, G.L. *Genesis and the Big Bang: The Discovery of Harmony Between Modern Science and the Bible.* Bantam Books, New York, 1990.

Smoot, G. and Davidson, K *Wrinkles in Time*. Wm. Morrow, New York, 1993.

Templeton, J.M. and Hermann, R.L. *Is God the Only Reality? Science Points to a Deeper Meaning of the Universe*. Continuum, New York, 1994.

Matt, D.C. *God & The Big Bang: Discovering Harmony Between Science & Spirituality*. Jewish Lights Publishing, Woodstock, Vermont, 1996.

Dauber, P.M. *The Three Big Bangs: Comet Crashes, Exploding Stars, and the Creation of the Universe*. Perseus Press, San Francisco, California, 1997.

Schroeder, G.L. *The Science of God: The Convergence of Scientific and Biblical Wisdom*. Simon & Schuster, New York, 1997.

Flam, F. Scientists Say Universe is Expanding at an Ever Faster Rate. *Phil. Inquirer*, A 3, February 27, 1998.

Gleiser, M. *The Dancing Universe: From Creation Myths to the Big Bang*. Plume, New York, 1998.

The references used for how the universe began are the following:

Hawking, S. *A Brief History of Time: From the Big Bang to Black Holes*. Bantam Books, New York, 1988.

Schroeder, G.L. *Genesis and the Big Bang: The Discovery of Harmony Between Modern Science and the Bible*. Bantam Books, New York, 1990.

Hawking, S. *Black Holes and Baby Universes and Other Essays*. Bantam Books, New York, 1993.

Lemonick, M.D. *The Light at the Edge of the Universe: Leading Cosmologists on the Brink of a Scientific Revolution*. Villard Books, New York, 1993.

Morris, R. *Cosmic Questions: Galactic Halos, Cold Dark Matter and the End of Time*. Wiley, New York, 1993.

Smoot, G. and Davidson, K. *Wrinkles in Time*. Wm. Morrow, New York, 1993.

Barrow, J.D. *The Left Hand of Creation: The Origin and Evolution of the Expanding Universe*. Oxford University Press, New York and Oxford, England, 1994.

Barrow, J.D. *The Origin of the Universe*. Basic Books/HarperCollins, New York, 1994.

Silk, J. *A Short History of the Universe*. Scientific American Library, New York, 1994.

Thuan, T.X. *The Secret Melody: And Man Created the Universe*. Oxford University Press, New York and Oxford, England 1995.

Brown, W. In the Beginning: Compelling Evidence for Creation and the Flood. Center for Scientific Creation. This can be accessed on the internet at the following site: http://www.creationscience.com/

Matt, D.C. God & *The Big Bang: Discovering Harmony Between Science & Spirituality*. Jewish Lights Publishing, Woodstock, Vermont, 1996.

Dauber, P.M. *The Three Big Bangs: Comet Crashes, Exploding Stars, and the Creation of the Universe*. Perseus Press, San Francisco, California, 1997.

Glynn, P. *God The Evidence: The Reconciliation of Faith and Reason in a Postsecular World*. Prima Publishing, Rocklin, California, 1997.

Schroeder, G.L. *The Science of God: The Convergence of Scientific and Biblical Wisdom*. Simon & Schuster, New York, 1997.

Gleiser, M. *The Dancing Universe: From Creation Myths to the Big Bang*. Plume, New York, 1998.

More information on the "sponge" theory of multiple universes can be accessed at the following e-mail address: BHankeO@ aol.com

The references used for dealing with the biblical account of creation are the following:

Schroeder, G.L. *Genesis and the Big Bang: The Discovery of Harmony Between Modern Science and the Bible.* Bantam Books, New York, 1990.

Ross, H. *Creation and Time: A Biblical and Scientific Perspective on the Creation-Date Controversy.* Navpress, Colorado Springs, Colorado, 1994.

Templeton, J.M. and Hermann, R.L. *Is God the Only Reality? Science Points to a Deeper Meaning of the Universe.* Continuum, New York, 1994.

Brown, W. In the Beginning: Compelling Evidence for Creation and the Flood. Center for Scientific Creation. This can be accessed on the internet at the following site: http://www.creationscience.com/

Matt, D.C. *God & The Big Bang: Discovering Harmony Between Science & Spirituality.* Jewish Lights Publishing, Woodstock, Vermont, 1996.

Schroeder, G.L. *The Science of God: The Convergence of Scientific and Biblical Wisdom.* Simon & Schuster, New York, 1997.

Ross, H. *Beyond the Cosmos: The Extra-Dimensionality of God: What Recent Discoveries in Astrophysics Reveal About the Glory and Love of God, 2nd Expanded Edition.* Navpress, Colorado Springs, Colorado, 1999.

Chapter Ten: God And The Origin Of Life

The version of the Hebrew Bible used is:
The Holy Scriptures According to The Masoretic Text. The Jewish Publication Society of America, Philadelphia, 1955.

Dr. Gerald Schroeder's books are excellent in comparing the evolution of life with the biblical account of evolution. Dr. Patrick Glynn's book gives an excellent account of problems with Darwin's theory of evolution and gives an comprehensive account of the anthropic principle. Dr. Hugh Ross' excellent books gives evidence to show that the biblical creation matches scientific creation and reinforces the anthropic principle.

Schroeder, G.L. *Genesis and the Big Bang: The Discovery of Harmony Between Modern Science and the Bible.* Bantam Books, New York, 1990.

Ross, H. *The Fingerprint of God: Recent Scientific Discoveries Reveal the Unmistakable Identity of the Creator.* Promise Publishing Co., Orange, California, 1991.

Ross, H. *Beyond the Cosmos: What Recent Discoveries in Astronomy and Physics Reveal About the Nature of God.* Navpress, Colorado Springs, Colorado, 1996.

Schroeder, G.L. *The Science of God: The Convergence of Scientific and Biblical Wisdom.* Simon & Schuster, New York, 1997.

Glynn, P. *God The Evidence: The Reconciliation of Faith and Reason in a Postsecular World.* Prima Publishing, Rocklin, California, 1997.

Southgate, C. (Ed.) *God, Humanity and the Cosmos: A Textbook in Science and Religion.* Trinity Press International, Harrisburg, Pennsylvania, 1999. This new book offers in-depth analysis of the relationship of God to the origin of the universe and the origin of life.

It gives an outstanding description of the anthropic principle.

Chapter Eleven: The Afterlife In Major Religions - Part 1: Ancient Egyptian, Greek, Hindu, Zoroastrianism & Buddhism

An overall reference for world religions is:
Wise, C.C., Jr. *Thus Saith The Lord: An Autobiography of God.* Magian Press, Penn Laird, Virginia, 1984.

The references for the Egyptian viewpoint are the following:
Ellis, N. *Awakening Osiris: A New Translation of the Egyptian Book of the Dead.* Phanes Publishing, Grand Rapids, MI, 1988.
Bremer, J.M., Den Hout, V. and Peters, R. (Eds.). *Hidden Futures: Death and Immortality in Ancient Egypt, Anatolia, the Classical, Biblical and Arabic-Islamic World.* Amsterdam University Pr., Amsterdam, 1995.
Little, G. *Grand Illusions: The Spectral Reality Underlying Sexual UFO Abductions, Crashed Saucers, Afterlife Experiences, Sacred Ancient Sites, and Other Enigmas.* White Buffalo Books, Memphis, TN, 1994, pp. 143-157.
Wolf, F.A. *The Spiritual Universe: How Quantum Physics Proves the Existence of the Soul.* Simon & Schuster, New York, 1996.

The references for the Greek viewpoint are the following:
Bremer, J.M., Den Hout, V. and Peters, R. (Eds.). *Hidden Futures: Death and Immortality in Ancient Egypt, Anatolia, the Classical, Biblical and Arabic-Islamic World.* Amsterdam University Pr., Amsterdam, 1995.
Wolf, F.A. *The Spiritual Universe: How Quantum Physics Proves the Existence of the Soul.* Simon & Schuster, New York, 1996.

The references for the viewpoints of Hinduism are the following:
Jurji, E.J. Hinduism. In: *Collier's Encyclopedia*, Vol. 10, Couch, W.T. (Ed-in-Chief), P.F. Collier & Son, New York, 1959, pp. 67-69.
Wolf, F.A. *The Spiritual Universe: How Quantum Physics Proves the Existence of the Soul.* Simon & Schuster, New York, 1996.

A further reference for "Hinduism" can be found on the internet at:
http://www.iloveusa.com/Secrets/wisdom2.html

The references for the viewpoint of Zoroastrianism are the following:
Kraus, M. Zoroastrianism. In: *Collier's Encyclopedia*, Vol. 19, Couch, W.T. (Ed-in-Chief), P.F. Collier & Son, New York, 1959, p. 699.
A further reference for "Zoroastrianism" can be found on the internet at:
http://www.iloveusa.com/Secrets/wisdom1.html

The references for the viewpoints of Buddhism are the following:

Chan, W.-T. Buddhism. In: *Collier's Encyclopedia*, Vol. 4, Couch, W.T. (Ed-in-Chief), P.F. Collier & Son, New York, 1959, pp. 175-177.

Wolf, F.A. *The Spiritual Universe: How Quantum Physics Proves the Existence of the Soul.* Simon & Schuster, New York, 1996.

Kerrick, J. "The Tibetan Book of the Dead" can be accessed from the internet at the following five sites:

http:www.iloveusa.com/Secrets/tibet.html
http:www.iloveusa.com/Secrets/tibet1.html
http:www.iloveusa.com/Secrets/tibet2.html
http:www.iloveusa.com/Secrets/tibet3.html
http:www.iloveusa.com/Secrets/tibet4.html

Chapter Twelve: The Afterlife In Major Religions - Part 2: The Judeo-Christian & Islamic Perspectives, Sikhism and Bahai'sm

The version of the Hebrew Bible used is:

The Holy Scriptures According to The Masoretic Text. The Jewish Publication Society of America, Philadelphia, 1955.

The version of the New Testament used is from the *King James Version The Holy Bible Containing the Old and New Testaments.* New York Bible Society, New York, Since 1809.

The references for the viewpoints of Judaism are the following:

Berman, M.M. Judaism. In: *Collier's Encyclopedia*, Vol. 11, Couch, W.T. (Ed-in-Chief), P.F. Collier & Son, New York, 1959, pp. 460-468.

Little, G. *Grand Illusions: The Spectral Reality Underlying Sexual UFO Abductions, Crashed Saucers, Afterlife Experiences, Sacred Ancient Sites, and Other Enigmas.* White Buffalo Books, Memphis, TN, 1994, pp. 239-243. This book has an excellent section on the apocryphal book, *3 Enoch: The Hebrew Book of Enoch.*

Bremer, J.M., Den Hout, V. and Peters, R. (Eds.). *Hidden Futures: Death and Immortality in Ancient Egypt, Anatolia, the Classical, Biblical and Arabic-Islamic World.* Amsterdam University Pr., Amsterdam, 1995.

Labowitz, S. *Miraculous Living: A Guided Journey in Kabbalah Through the Ten Gates of the Tree of Life.* Simon & Schuster, New York, 1996. An excellent book that explores Kabbalah's ten gates of the tree of life.

Raphael. S.P. *Jewish Views of the Afterlife.* Jason Aronson, Inc., Northvale, New Jersey, 1996. This is an excellent book detailing the afterlife viewpoints of Judaism from the biblical times to Kabbalah and Hasidism and was the principal reference used in this section.

Aaron, D.A. *Endless Light: The Ancient Path of the Kabbalah to Love, Spiritual Growth, and Personal Power.* Simon & Schuster, New York, 1997. This is another excellent book on the Kabbalah.

Wolf, L. *Jewish meditation: A Kabbalistic approach to a balanced life.* Presented at the Gershman YMHA, Philadelphia, June 2, 1997.

Gillman, N. *The Death of Death: Resurrection and Immortality in Jewish Thought.* Jewish Lights, Woodstock, Vermont, 1997. This is a superb book on the evolution of the Jewish concept of the afterlife.

Croman, E.L. To Live and Live Again: Reincarnation: The Kabbalistic View. Presented at the Chabad Center, Voorhees, New Jersey, October 27, 1998.

Kerrick, J. "Kabbalah — An ancient secret tradition" can be accessed on the internet at the following site:
http://www.iloveusa.com/Secrets/kabbal.html

McMahon, J.D.S. Physiological Correlates of Religious Belief and Psychical Research: Decomposition and You. In: *1999 Annual Conference Proceedings: Dying, Death and the Afterlife: Psychical and Spiritual Dimensions.* Acad. Religion. Psychical Research, Bloomfield, Connecticut, pp, 116-122, 1999.

The references for the viewpoints of Christianity are the following:

Johnson, W.H. Christianity. In: *Collier's Encyclopedia*, Vol. 5, Couch, W.T. (Ed-in-Chief), P.F. Collier & Son, New York, 1959, pp. 227-236.

"The early Christian mystery sects" can be accessed on the internet at the following site:
http://www.iloveusa.com/Secrets/gnostic1.html
"The Apocalypse of Paul" can be accessed on the internet at the following site:
http://www.iloveusa.com/Secrets/gnostic2.html
"The Gospel of Thomas" can be accessed on the internet at the following site:
http://www.iloveusa.com/Secrets/gnostic3.html
"The Mystery teachings" can be accessed on the internet at the following site:
http://www.iloveusa.com/Secrets/gnostic4.html
"Heaven — in Jesus's own words" can be accessed on the internet at the following site:
http://www.iloveusa.com/Secrets/jesus.html
"The controversy" (with respect to Origen of Alexandria's concept of reincarnation) can be accessed on the internet at the following site: http://www.iloveusa.com/Secrets/origen1.html
"The doctrine itself" (of Origen) can be accessed on the internet at the following site:
http://www.iloveusa.com/Secrets/origen2.html
"Scriptural support for reincarnation" can be accessed at the following site:
http://www.iloveusa.com/Secrets/origen3.html
"Conclusion" (about reincarnation) can be accessed on the internet at the following site:
http://www.iloveusa.com/Secrets/origen4.html
"A comparison between early and modern Christianity" can be accessed on the internet at the following site:
http://www.iloveusa.com/Secrets/calvin1.html
"Modern Christian doctrine of absolute free will" can be accessed on the internet at the following site:
http://www.iloveusa.com/Secrets/calvin2.html

"Early Christian doctrine of slavery of the will" can be accessed on the internet at the following site:

http://www.iloveusa.com/Secrets/calvin3.html

"Proof of the slavery of the will" can be accessed on the internet at the following site: http://www.iloveusa.com/Secrets/calvin4.html

"Once you are saved — You are forever saved" can be accessed on the internet at the following site:

http://www.iloveusa.com/Secrets/calvin5.html

"Early and modern Christianity differ greatly" can be accessed on the internet at the following site:

http://www.iloveusa.com/Secrets/calvin6.html

"Universal salvation — Why it is true" can be accessed on the internet at the following site:

http://www.iloveusa.com/Secrets/calvin7.html

The references for the viewpoints of Islam are the following:

Jurji, E.J. Islam. In: *Collier's Encyclopedia*, Vol. 11, Couch, W.T. (Ed-in-Chief), P.F. Collier & Son, New York, 1959, pp. 185-187.

Bremer, J.M., Den Hout, V. and Peters, R. (Eds.). *Hidden Futures: Death and Immortality in Ancient Egypt, Anatolia, the Classical, Biblical and Arabic-Islamic World.* Amsterdam University Pr., Amsterdam, 1995.

"Islam: Allah, the Great Forgiver" can be accessed at the following site: http://www.iloveusa.com/Secrets/wisdom3.html

The references for the viewpoints of Sufism are the following:

Jurji, E.J. Sufism. In: *Collier's Encyclopedia*, Vol. 18, Couch, W.T. (Ed-in-Chief), P.F. Collier & Son, New York, 1959, p. 270.

"Sufism — The way of the heart" can be accessed on the internet at the following site: http://www.best.com/~informe/mateen/Sufi/sufi_islam.html

"What to expect in the grave: Controlling anger and passion" can be accessed on the internet at the following site: http://www.best.com/~informe/mateen/Sufi/Mercy5.html

Fine, S. "A Sufi's visit to Hell" can be accessed on the internet at the following site: http://www.best.com/~informe/mateen/Sufi/hell.html

Kabbani, S.H. "Sufism in Islam" can be accessed on the internet at the following site: http://www.best.com/~informe/mateen/Sufi/sufism_in_islam.html

The references for the viewpoints of Sikhism are the following:

Archer, J.C. Sikhs. In: *Collier's Encyclopedia*, Vol. 17, Couch, W.T. (Ed-in-Chief), P.F. Collier & Son, New York, 1959, pp. 595-597.

"Can we prove the existence of God?" "What do we know of God?" "Can we exist without a belief in God?" "Can we reconcile the existence of a merciful God with the problem of pain in the world?" "What was God's purpose in creating man?" "Is the worship of God necessary?" How was the world created according to Sikhism?" "What is the microcosmic theory in Sikhism?" "What is the concept of Truth in Sikhism?" "What happens to the individual after death?" "Is there a judgment?" "What is Hukam?" can all be accessed on the internet at the following site:

http://photon.bu.edu/~rajwi/sikhism/mansukh2.html

The references for the viewpoints of Bahai'sm are the following:
Sohrab, M.A. The Bahai' movement. In: *Collier's Encyclopedia*, Vol. 2, Couch, W.T. (Ed-in-Chief), P.F. Collier & Son, New York, 1959, p. 665.
"Not a sect, an independent religion" can be accessed on the internet at the following site:
http://oneworld.wa.com/bahai/magazine/pg10.html
"Heaven and hell: A Bahá'í view of life after death" can be accessed on the internet at the following site:
http://oneworld.wa.com/bahai/magazine/pg35.html

Chapter Thirteen: Recent Concepts of the Afterlife - Part 1: Ideas From Groups & Organizations

The version of the New Testament used is from the *King James Version The Holy Bible Containing the Old and New Testaments*. New York Bible Society, New York, Since 1809.

The references for the viewpoints of the Seventh-Day Adventists are the following:
Froom, L.E. Seventh-Day Adventists. In: *Collier's Encyclopedia*, Vol. 17, Couch, W.T. (Ed-in-Chief), P.F. Collier & Son, New York, 1959, pp. 487-488.

"More about what Seventh-day Adventists believe" can be accessed on the internet at the following site:
http://www.users.globalnet.co.uk/~advent/more.html
"The developing church" can be accessed on the internet at the following site:
http://PacUnConf.puc.edu/iom/leaders1.html

"Fundamental beliefs" can be accessed on the internet at the following site:
http://PacUnConf.puc.edu/iom/27beliefs.html

The references for the viewpoints of the Jehovah's Witnesses are the following:
Knorr, N.H.. Jehovah's Witnesses. In: *Collier's Encyclopedia*, Vol. 11, Couch, W.T. (Ed-in-Chief), P.F. Collier & Son, New York, 1959, pp. 373-374.
"Brief history of Jehovah's Witnesses" can be accessed on the internet at the following site:
http://www.serve.com/larryi/history.htm
Pappas, N. "Salvation: The Watchtower way" can be accessed on the internet at the following site:
http://www.serve.com/larryi/history.htm
"The resurrection of Jesus" can be accessed on the internet at the following site:
http://www.serve.com/larryi/arise.htm
"Trinity doctrine" can be accessed on the internet at the following site:
http://www.serve.com/larryi/trinity.htm

"Definitions and terms used by Jehovah's Witnesses" can be accessed on the internet at the following site:

http://www.serve.com/larryi/terms.htm

"Date setting" can be accessed on the internet at the following site:

http://www.serve.com/larryi/dates.htm

The references for the viewpoints of the Christadelphians are the following:

Zilmer, E.A.. Christadelphians. In: *Collier's Encyclopedia*, Vol. 5, Couch, W.T. (Ed-in-Chief), P.F. Collier & Son, New York, 1959, p. 225.

"Who are the Christadelphians? What do they believe?" can be accessed on the internet at the following site:

http://www.com/~adelphi/whoare.html

"What makes the Christadelphians special?" can be accessed on the internet at the following site:

http://www.teksupport.net.au/~chris/leaflet4.htm

"The Trinity" can be accessed on the internet at the following site:

http://www.chu.cam.ac.uk/home/aam20/notrinit.html

"Baptism and salvation" can be accessed on the internet at the following site:

http://www.chu.cam.ac.uk/home/aam20/baptism.html

"God, Jesus Christ, and the Crucifixion" can be accessed on the internet at the following site:

http://www.chu.cam.ac.uk/home/aam20/jesus.html

The references for the viewpoints of the Unitarian Universalists are the following:

Sweet, W.W. Unitarians. In: *Collier's Encyclopedia*, Vol. 19, Couch, W.T. (Ed-in-Chief), P.F. Collier & Son, New York, 1959, pp. 60-61.

Sweet, W.W. Universalism. In: *Collier's Encyclopedia*, Vol. 19, Couch, W.T. (Ed-in-Chief), P.F. Collier & Son, New York, 1959, pp. 124B-125.

"Unitarian Universalist" can be accessed on the internet at the following site:

http://www.religioustolerance.org/u-u.htm

The references for the viewpoints of Rosicrucianism are the following:

Couch, W.T. The Rosicrucian Order (Ancient Mystical Order of the Rosy Cross). In: *Collier's Encyclopedia*, Vol. 17, Couch, W.T. (Ed-in-Chief), P.F. Collier & Son, New York, 1959, p. 147.

Fogarty, H.W. Rosicrucianism. In: *The Encyclopedia of Religion*. Vol. 12, MacMillan, New York, 1987, pp. 476-477.

Walker, C. Thoughts on the Objectives of Personal Immortality. In: *1995 Annual Conference Proceedings: Personal Survival of Bodily Death*. Acad. Religion. Psychical Research, Bloomfield, Connecticut, pp, 30-43,1995.

Harrington, L. "The Rosicrucians: The secret brotherhood of the Rosy Cross" can be accessed on the internet at the following site:

http://www.newleaf-dist.com/Razamatazz/newsletter_articles/rosicrucians_secret_brotherhood_rosey_cross.htm

"Welcome: An introduction to the Rosicrucian Order" can be accessed on the internet at the following site:
http://www.rosicrucian.org/rosicruc/mastery/1-welcome.html
"Our traditional and chronological history" can be accessed on the internet at the following site:
http://www.rosicrucian.org/rosicruc/mastery/6-history.html
"Neophyte section" can be accessed on the internet at the following site:
http://www.rosicrucian.org/rosicruc/mastery/4a1-neophyte.html
"The Rosicrucian Order, AMORC" can be accessed on the internet at the following site:
http://www.amorc.org/
Wescott, W.W. "The Rosicrucians: Past and present, at home and abroad" can be accessed on the internet at the following site:
http://www.hermeticgoldendawn,org/Rosicr~1.htm

The references for the viewpoints of Freemasonry are the following:
Walker, W.K. Masons. In: *Collier's Encyclopedia*, Vol. 13, Couch, W.T. (Ed-in-Chief), P.F. Collier & Son, New York, 1959, pp. 234-236.
Leazer, G. *Fundamentalism and Freemasonry: The Southern Baptist Investigation of the Fraternal Order*. M. Evans, New York, 1995.
Little, G. *Grand Illusions: The Spectral Reality Underlying Sexual UFO Abductions, Crashed Saucers, Afterlife Experiences, Sacred Ancient Sites, and Other Enigmas.* White Buffalo Books, Memphis, TN, 1994, pp. 248-250. This book contains an excellent section on the spiritual beliefs of the masons.

"Freemasons and their beliefs" can be accessed on the internet at the following site:
http://www.frontiernet.net/~dupham/CL107799Freemasons_and_their_beliefs.html
"What Freemasons do" can be accessed on the internet at the following site:
http://www.northeastweb.com/masonic/whatdo.html
"Who Freemasons are" can be accessed on the internet at the following site:
http://www.northeastweb.com/masonic/whoare.html
The Grand Lodge of British Columbia A.F. & A.M. can be accessed on the internet at the following site:
http://freemasonry.bc.ca

The references for the viewpoints of the Golden Dawn are the following:
Wescott, W.W. "The Hermetic Order of the Golden Dawn: Historic lecture" can be accessed on the internet at the following site: http://www.hermeticgoldendawn.org/page3.htm
"The Hermetic Order of the Golden Dawn®" can be accessed on the internet at the following site:
http://www.hermeticgoldendawn.org/
"True initiation" can be accessed on the internet at the following site:
http://www.hermeticgoldendawn.org/page8.htm
Sorror, H. "The Kerubim: 'The strong ones' " can be accessed on the internet at the following site:

http://www.hermeticgoldendawn.org/kerubim.html

Zoller, R. "Why Hermeticism?" can be accessed on the internet at the following site:
http://www.hermeticgoldendawn.org/Zoller.htm

Soror, I.D. "Alchemy as a path to integration" can be accessed on the internet at the following site:
http://www.hermeticgoldendawn.org/alchemy.htm

"The Feather of Maat" can be accessed on the internet at the following site:
http://www.hermeticgoldendawn.org/maat.htm

Cicero, C. and Cicero, S.T. "Israel Regardie" can be accessed on the internet at the following site:
http://www.hermeticgoldendawn.org/page6.htm

The references for the viewpoints of Theosophy are the following:

Perkins, J.S. Theosophy. In: *Collier's Encyclopedia*, Vol. 18, Couch, W.T. (Ed-in-Chief), P.F. Collier & Son, New York, 1959, p. 539.

Walker, C. Thoughts on the Objectives of Personal Immortality. In: *1995 Annual Conference Proceedings: Personal Survival of Bodily Death.* Acad. Religion. Psychical Research, Bloomfield, Connecticut, pp, 30-43,1995.

"Theosophy: Their secrets revealed" can be accessed on the internet at the following site:
http://www.iloveusa.com/Secrets/wisdom4.html

"A Theosophist's Page" can be accessed on the internet at the following site:
http://www.ics.uci.edu/~tdo/ea/theosophy.html

The reference for the viewpoint of Urantia can be found in the following book:

Walker, C. Thoughts on the Objectives of Personal Immortality. In: *1995 Annual Conference Proceedings: Personal Survival of Bodily Death.* Acad. Religion. Psychical Research, Bloomfield, Connecticut, pp, 30-43,1995.

Another reference for Urantia can be accessed on the internet at the following site:
http://www.urantia.org/

The reference for the viewpoint of the Eckankar religion can be found in the following book:

Walker, C. Thoughts on the Objectives of Personal Immortality. In: *1995 Annual Conference Proceedings: Personal Survival of Bodily Death.* Acad. Religion. Psychical Research, Bloomfield, Connecticut, pp, 30-43,1995.

Other references for Eckanker can be accessed on the internet at the following sites:
http://www.eckankar.org/ and http://www.eckankar.org/history.html

Chapter Fourteen: Recent Concepts of the Afterlife - Part 2: Complex Ideas From Individuals

The references for the viewpoints of Swedenborgianism are the following:

Clark, E.T. Swedenborgians. In: *Collier's Encyclopedia*, Vol. 18, Couch, W.T. (Ed-in-Chief), P.F. Collier & Son, New York, 1959, p. 339.

Kirven, R.H. *A Book About Dying: Preparing for Eternal Life.* Swedenborg Foundation, West Chester, Pennsylvania, 1997.

Rhodes, L. *Tunnel to Eternity: Beyond Near-Death.* Swedenborg Foundation, West Chester, Pennsylvania, 1997. This book correlates NDEs with the Swedenborg concept of the afterlife. "Key concepts in Swedenborg's theology" can be accessed on the internet at the following site:

http://www.swedenborg.com/emanue2.html

"The New Church: Summary of Beliefs" can be accessed on the internet at the following site:

http://aztec.asu.edu/worship/newchurch/ncfaith.html

Another reference for Swedenborgianism can be accessed on the internet at the following site:

http://www.swedenborg.org/swedenb.html

The reference for the viewpoint of William Blake can be found in the following book:
Walker, C. Thoughts on the Objectives of Personal Immortality. In: *1995 Annual Conference Proceedings: Personal Survival of Bodily Death.* Acad. Religion. Psychical Research, Bloomfield, Connecticut, pp, 30-43,1995.

The references for the viewpoints of Allan Kardec and Christian Spiritism can be found in the following excellent book:
Martin, H. *The Secret Teachings of the Espiritistas.* Metamind Publications, Savannah, Georgia, 1999.

Other internet references for Allan Kardec and Christian Spiritism are:
http://www.utexas.edu/students/kardec and
http://www.bsb.nutecnet.com.br/web/cei/cei21i.htm

The reference for the viewpoint of Dr. Duncan MacDougall can be found in the following superb book, Little, G. *Grand Illusions: The Spectral Reality Underlying Sexual UFO Abductions, Crashed Saucers, Afterlife Experiences, Sacred Ancient Sites, and Other Enigmas.* White Buffalo Books, Memphis, TN, 1994, pp. 157-159.

The reference for the viewpoint of Ernest Holmes can be found in the following book:
Walker, C. Thoughts on the Objectives of Personal Immortality. In: *1995 Annual Conference Proceedings: Personal Survival of Bodily Death.* Acad. Religion. Psychical Research, Bloomfield, Connecticut, pp, 30-43,1995.

Further information on Ernest Holmes can be accessed on the internet at the following site:

http://www.religiousscience.org/whatissom1.htm

The reference for the viewpoint of Bô Yin Râ can be found in the following book:
Reichenbach. B. Personal Survival: Reflections on its Aftermath In: *1995 Annual Conference Proceedings: Personal Survival of Bodily Death.* Acad. Religion. Psychical Research, Bloomfield, Connecticut, pp, 53-61,1995.

Further information on Bô Yin Râ can be accessed on the internet at the following site: http://www.kober.holowww.com/

The reference for Edgar Cayce's concepts are the following:
Cayce, E.. The First Ten Minutes of Death In: *1995 Annual Conference Proceedings: Personal Survival of Bodily Death.* Acad. Religion. Psychical Research, Bloomfield, Connecticut, pp, 115-119, 1995.

Information on A.R.E.,®, the organization founded by Edgar Cayce, can be accessed on the internet at the following site:
http://www.are-cayce.com/index.htm

"More about Edgar Cayce" can be accessed on the internet at the following site:
http://www.calweb.com/~kevinw/cayce9.html
"Where did we come from?" can be accessed on the internet at the following site:
http://www.calweb.com/~kevinw/cayce2.html
"Who are we?" can be accessed on the internet at the following site:
http://www.calweb.com/~kevinw/cayce3.html
"How did the universe get here?" can be accessed on the internet at the following site:
http://www.calweb.com/~kevinw/cayce25.html
"Does reincarnation really happen?" can be accessed on the internet at the following site:
http://www.calweb.com/~kevinw/cayce45.html
"Who is Jesus Christ?" can be accessed on the internet at the following site:
http://www.calweb.com/~kevinw/caycejes.html
"What lies beyond?" can be accessed on the internet at the following site:
http://www.calweb.com/~kevinw/cayce5.html
"The planes of consciousness" can be accessed on the internet at the following site:
http://www.calweb.com/~kevinw/cayce55.html
"Which plane do you go to after death?" can be accessed on the internet at the following site:
http://www.calweb.com/~kevinw/cayce8.html
"Meditation — Connection with the afterlife" can be accessed on the internet at the following site:
http://www.calweb.com/~kevinw/caycemed.html
"Dreams — A gateway to the spirit world" can be accessed on the internet at the following site:
http://www.calweb.com/~kevinw/cayce7.html
"The Book of Revelations — What are its secrets?" can be accessed on the internet at the following site:
http://www.calweb.com/~kevinw/cayceel.html
"What are these religions about?" can be accessed on the internet at the following site:
http://www.calweb.com/~kevinw/cayce6.html
"Astrology — A Christian perspective" can be accessed on the internet at the following site:
http://www.calweb.com/~kevinw/cayce10.html

The reference for the afterlife concept of Seth can be found in the following book:
Walker, C. Thoughts on the Objectives of Personal Immortality. In: *1995 Annual Conference Proceedings: Personal Survival of Bodily Death.* Acad. Religion. Psychical Research, Bloomfield, Connecticut, pp, 30-43, 1995.

Other references for Seth can be accessed on the internet at the following sites:
http://www.sethnet.org/htmldocs/story.htm
http://www.sethnet.org/htmldocs/intro.htm

The reference for the viewpoint of E. William Dykes can be found in the following book:
Dykes, E.W. Speculations on the Nature of the Hereafter In: *1995 Annual Conference Proceedings: Personal Survival of Bodily Death.* Acad. Religion. Psychical Research, Bloomfield, Connecticut, pp. 44-52, 1995.

The quotation at the beginning of Dykes' article by the Zen Buddhist teacher, Yatautani, is from:
Kapleau, P. (Ed.) *The Three Pillars of Zen.* Bantam, New York, 1967, p. 43. It recently appeared in: Haddow, A.H. Life After Death: Psi Evidence and Religious Belief. *Journal of Religion and Psychical Research*, 1998; 21: 183-193.

The references for Scientology are the following:
"Introduction to the Scientology religion" can be accessed on the internet at the following site:
http://www.scientology.org/p_jpg/wis/wiseng/wis1-3/wis1_1.htm
"The religious heritage of Scientology" can be accessed on the internet at the following site:
http://www.scientology.org/p_jpg/wis/wiseng/wis1-3/wis2_1.htm
"L. Ron Hubbard: the founder of Scientology" can be accessed on the internet at the following site:
http://aboutlronhubbard.org/eng/wis3_1.htm
"What is Scientology?" can be accessed on the internet at the following site:
http://faq.scientology.org/scntlgy.htm
"Why is Scientology a religion?" can be accessed on the internet at the following site:
http://faq.scientology.org/religion.htm
"What are the dynamics?" can be accessed on the internet at the following site:
http://faq.scientology.org/dynamics.htm
"What is the Scientology concept of God?" can be accessed on the internet at the following site:
http://faq.scientology.org/god.htm
"Does Scientology believe in past lives?" can be accessed on the internet at the following site:
http://faq.scientology.org/pastlive.htm

The references for Roel van der Meulen's "Project Galactic Guide" concepts are the following:

van der Meulen, R. The Afterlife: Dream On (Unreal). It can be accessed on the internet at the following site:

http://megadodo.com/articles/2U56.html

van der Meulen, R. Life After Death: Enjoy It While It Lasts (Unreal). It can be accessed on the internet at the following site:

http://megadodo.com/articles/2U38.html

The references for Bruce Moen's visions are the following:

Moen, B.A. *Voyages Into the Unknown: Exploring the Afterlife.* Hampton Roads Publ. Co., Charlottesville, Virginia, 1997.

Moen, B.A. "Christianity" can be accessed on the internet at the following site:

http://www.afterlife-knowledge.com/chris.html

Moen, B.A. "Max's Hell" can be accessed on the internet at the following site:

http://www.afterlife-knowledge.com/maxhell.html

"Afterlife knowledge" can be accessed on the internet at the following sites:

http://www.afterlife-knowledge.com/index.html

http://www.afterlife-knowledge.com/start.html

"How do you know it's real?" can be accessed on the internet at the following site:

http://www.afterlife-knowledge.com/real.html

"What perceptual skills are required?" can be accessed on the internet at the following site:

http://www.afterlife-knowledge.com/skills.html

"Are ghosts real? Yes!" can be accessed on the internet at the following site:

http://www.afterlife-knowledge.com/ghosts.html

"Is there a heaven? a hell?" can be accessed on the internet at the following site:

http://www.afterlife-knowledge.com/hvnhl.html

"Answers to frequently asked questions" can be accessed on the internet at the following site:

http://www.afterlife-knowledge.com/answers.html

The references for Wolf's quantum physics concepts are in the following excellent and thought-provoking books:

Wolf, F.A. *The Spiritualist Universe: How Quantum Physics Proves the Existence of the Soul.* Simon & Schuster, New York, 1996.

Wolf, F.A. *The Spiritual Universe: A Physicist's Vision of Spirit, Soul, Matter and Self.* Momentpoint Press, Portsmith, Oregon, 1999.

Wolf's concepts can also be accessed on the internet at the following site:

http://www.stardrive.org/fred.shtml

The references for Little's Electromagnetic Spectrum theory are in the following superb and unique books.

Little, G. *The Archetype Experience.* Rainbow Books, Moore Haven, Florida, 1984.

Little, G. *People of the Web: What Indian Mounds, Ancient Rituals, and Stone*

Circles Tell Us About Modern UFO Abductions, Apparitions, and the Near Death Experience. White Buffalo Books, Memphis, TN 1990.

Little, G. *Grand Illusions: The Spectral Reality Underlying Sexual UFO Abductions, Crashed Saucers, Afterlife Experiences, Sacred Ancient Sites, and Other Enigmas.* White Buffalo Books, Memphis, TN, 1994. This book gives the complete presentation of Little's stimulating Electromagnetic Spectrum theory.

The references for Peter Novak's Division of consciousness section are the following:

Freud, S. *The Standard Edition of the Complete Psychological Works.* Strachey, J. (Ed.). Hogarth Press, London, 1953-1974.

Novak, P. *The Division of Consciousness: The Secret Afterlife of the Human Psyche.* Hampton Roads Publishing Co. Inc., Charlottesville, Virginia, 1997. This is an excellent, well-thought out concept that is worth considering.

Further information on Novak's Division of Consciousness theory can be accessed on the internet at the following site:

http://www.geocities.com/~divisiontheory

The reference for Simcha Paull Raphael's contemporary psychological model is the following:

Raphael, S.P. *Jewish Views of the Afterlife.* Jason Aronson, Inc, Northvale, NJ 1996. As a concept of the afterlife, I consider this to be the most comprehensive and overall the best. Of course, only the future will tell who, if anyone, is correct.

The references for Mansions are the following:

Kumar, R. Translation From Earth to Higher Realms and Back. In: *1999 Annual Conference Proceedings: Dying, Death and the Afterlife: Psychical and Spiritual Dimensions.* Acad. Religion. Psychical Research, Bloomfield, Connecticut, pp, 107-115, 1999.

Meek. G. W. *Enjoy Your Own Funeral.* Galde Press, Lakeville, Minnesota, 1999.

The "Blind Men and the Elephant" was converted to HTML by Dan Bornstein, whose e-mail address is: danfuzz@milk.com, and the fable is found on the internet at the following site:

http://www.milk.com/random-humor/elephant_fable.html

Chapter Fifteen: A Personal Concept Of The Afterlife

The version of the Hebrew Bible used is:

The Holy Scriptures According to The Masoretic Text. The Jewish Publication Society of America, Philadelphia, 1955.

The version of the New Testament used is from the *King James Version The Holy Bible Containing the Old and New Testaments.* New York Bible Society, New York, Since 1809.

Although all the previous references listed in the prior four chapter were used, those that are specifically relevant to the author's personal concept are the following:

Moody, R.A., Jr. *Life After Life: The Investigation of a Phenomenon — Survival of Bodily Death.* Mockingbird Books, St. Simon Island, Georgia, 1975.

Wilson, J. *The After Death Experience: The Physics of the Non Physical.* Wm. Morrow & Co., New York, 1987.

Wolpe, David J. *Teaching Your Children About God: A Modern Jewish Approach.* HarperCollins, 1995.

Raphael, S.P. *Jewish Views of the Afterlife.* Jason Aronson, Inc, Northvale, New Jersey, 1996.

Wolf, F.A. *The Spiritualist Universe: How Quantum Physics Proves the Existence of the Soul.* Simon & Schuster, New York, 1996.

Moody, R.A., Jr. *The Last Laugh: A New Philosophy of Near-Death Experiences, Apparitions, and the Paranormal.* William Golding Consulting, Atlanta, Georgia, 1997.

Novak, P. *The Division of Consciousness: The Secret Afterlife of the Human Psyche.* Hampton Roads Publishing Co. Inc., Charlottesville, Virginia, 1997.

Meek. G. W. *Enjoy Your Own Funeral.* Galde Press, Lakeville, Minnesota, 1999.

"Answers to the meaning of life and death" can be accessed on the internet at the following site:

http://www.iloveusa.com/Secrets/mine.html

"Diversity and generalization" can be accessed on the internet at the following site:

http://www.scientology.org/wis/wisfr/30/bw-xiii.htm

Chapter Sixteen: A Hopeful Outlook

The version of the Hebrew Bible used is:

The Holy Scriptures According to The Masoretic Text. The Jewish Publication Society of America, Philadelphia, 1955.

The reference for Henry Wadsworth Longfellow's quotation is from the following:

Tribbe, F. A Trinity of Wholeness. *Journal of Religion and Psychical Research* 1998; 21(1): 31-38.

The reference for "solar maximum" can be accessed on the internet at CNN.com under the title: Forget Y2K: Prepare for the solar maximum, September 1, 1999.

The references for the millennium can be found on the internet at the following sites: "Can the Millennium Deliver?" by Henry Grunwald at:

http://www.pathfinder.com:80/time/magazine/1998/dom/980511/the_arts.history_.can_th20.html

"Is Christmas the Birthday of Christ?" by Rod Rutherford at:

http://www.tftw.org/Tracts/christmas.html

"The Millennium Phenomenon" by R.H. at:

http://www.hillsborough.k12.nj.us/hhs/voice/2000.htm

The other references used are the following:

Haines, A.P., Imeson, J.D. and Meade, T.W. Phobic Anxiety and Ischaemic Heart Disease. *British Medical Journal* 1987; 295: 297-299.

Burns, D.D. *The Feeling Good Handbook.* Penguin Books, New York, 1990.

Kawachi, I., Colditz, G.A., Ascherio, A., Rimm, E.B., Giovannucci, E., Stampler, M.J. and Willett, W.C. Prospective Study of Phobic Anxiety and Risk of Coronary Heart Disease in Men. *Circulation* 1994; 89: 1992-1997.

Kawachi, I., Sparrow, D., Vokonas P.S. and Weiss, S.T. Symptoms of Anxiety and Risk of Coronary Heart Disease: The Normative Aging Study. *Circulation* 1994; 90: 2225-2229.

Abben, R.P. "Anxiety is Linked to Sudden Cardiac Death" can be accessed on the internet at the following site:

http://www.cardio.com/articles/anxiety.htm

Three Minutes to Impact (Chance of comets and asteroids destroying earth). *Discovery* TV channel. 9-10 P.M. (East coast), February 9, 1997.

Jaroff, L. Space: Whew! The Mile-wide Asteroid Heading for Earth Proved to be a Cosmic False Alarm, but That's no Reason not to Start Planning for the Next One. *Time* March 23, 1998; 151(11): 68-71.

Croman, E.L. Jewish View of Life After Life. Presented at the Chabad Center, Voorhees, New Jersey, October 27, 1998.

The Doomsday Asteroid. NJN PBS TV channel. 10-11 P.M. (East coast). November 1, 1998.

Yount, D. *Ten Thoughts to Take Into Eternity.* Simon & Schuster, New York, 1999.

Afterword

The version of the Hebrew Bible used is:

The Holy Scriptures According to The Masoretic Text. The Jewish Publication Society of America, Philadelphia, 1955.

Lindemann, S. Rabbi's Message: Yea, Though I Walk. *Temple Talk* 1999; 19(11): 1.

Wolpe, David J. *Teaching Your Children About God: A Modern Jewish Approach.* HarperCollins, New York, pp. 205-206.

INDEX

A

Aaron, David, ...215
Abraham, ...105, 111, 160, 216, 370
Adam, ...157, 161, 182-183, 185, 193-194, 297, 370
affect bridge, ...142
after-death communications (ADCs), ...82-83, 91, 98-123
afterlife (hereafter), 54, 158-159, 197-342, 277-280, 287-342, 343-366
    early stage, ...348, 352, 359
    planning for during life, ...376-378
    preparation, ...344-346
    unpleasant, ...345
Ahura-Mazda, ...163, 205-206
Akashic Records, ...132, 140, 296
Alford, Alan, F., ...149
Allah, ...163, 254, 256
Allen, Woody, ...285, 378
angels, ...54, 71, 83, 111, 138, 224, 246, 321, 340
    guardian, ...68, 70, 92, 105-106
    of death, ...230, 240
antihistamines (Vistaril®, Atarax®, Benadryl®), ...26
antimatter, ...174, 175
antiparticles, ...174
anthropic principle, ...177, 181
anxiety, ...13-16, (defined) 19, 146
    death, ...9, 18-34, (defined) 20, 76, 148, 184
    early in life, ...20-21
    later in life, ...26-27, 29
    overcoming, ...21-26
        normal (fear), ...18-19
anxiolytics (antianxiety agents, minor tranquilizers), ...21, 26
apocalypse, ...206-207
Apocalypse of Paul, ...246-248
apocryphal period, ...222-227
apparitions, 89-124
    defined, ...91
    methods of inducing, ...92-93

Christ, Jesus, ...38, 81, 82-83, 95, 108, 162, 233, 245-253, 266, 267, 268-269, 290, 293-294, 297-298, 323, 328, 331-332, 337, 345, 370-372
Cicero, ...127
clairaudience, clairgustation, clairolfaction, clairsentience, & clairvoyance, ...40-41,
Clark, Rabia Lynn, ...1, 138, 145
cloning, ...149
Conklin, Edward, ...189
Cooper River Park, ...33
cosmic consciousness, ...270-271
cosmology (ists),
Cox-Chapman, Mally, ...44, 55-56
creation, ...160-163, 167-170, 177
    of humans and other species, ...161-162, 165, 167-168
    of the universe, ...161, 167, 177-181
Crick, Frances, ...189
Crow (beliefs about God), ...159
cryogenics (cryonics), ...148, 150
cryptomnesia, ...133
Cunningham, J., ...140
Currie, Ian, ...35

D
daena, ...206, 208
Daniel, ...105, 215, 222, 321, 370
dark experience (with near-death), ...41
dark matter, ...176
Darwin, Charles, ...52, 191, 195, 374
David, ...162, 297
death, experiences, shared, 101, 119-123
deceased loved ones, ...93-95
deloks, ...57
deMontaigne, M., ...13
D'Encarnacao, Paul, ...319
de Rochas, Colonel, ...130
denial, ...25-26
depersonalization theory, ...51-52
devas, ...205-206, 208
dissolution of the elements, ...
diversions, ...22
division of consciousness, ...327
DNA, ...186-188

Greyson, Bruce, ...46, 54
Grosso, Michael, ...39
guf, ...232, 235
Guggenheim, B., & J., ...79, 81, 82, 98, 101, 104, 111

H
Haddow, Agnus, H., ...8, 117
hallucinations, ...48-49
Hasidism, ...243-244
Haines, A.P., ...374
Haraldsson, E., ...99, 103
Hawking, Stephen, ...171-172, 173, 178-179, 198, 201, 324
Hayyah, ...239
heaven, ...42, 84, 156, 224, 251-253, 288, 319-323, 363
Hebrews, ...160, 181-182, 215-244, 327
Heindel, Max, ...270
Heisenberg's uncertainty principle, ...169
helium, ...174, 176
hell, ...42, 58, 84, 86, 156, 208, 251-253, 269, 288, 319-323, 329-330, 363
        (also see Sheol & Gehenna)
Hemi-Sync®, ...309, 311
Hermeticism (Western Esoteric Tradition), ...270
Herring, Marvin, ...1, 87, 192, 193, 227, 262-263, 342, 364
Hinduism, ...125, 127, 138, 163, 180, 203-205, 242
Holmes, Ernest, ...293-294
Holy Spirit (Ghost), ...246-247, 267, 282, 290, 330
Hoyle, Fred, ...189
Hubbard, L. Ron, ...305
Huff, Sandra, ...270, 271
Hugo, Victor, ...8, 116
Hurst, Brian, ...118
hydrogen, ...174, 176
hypnagogic state, ...133
hypnosis, ...83, 85-86, 131-132, 139
        self-, ...22

I
I-Ching,
Ilyich, Ivan (dying vision), ...89-90
immortality, ...147-154
        interplanetary, ...149-150
        on Earth, ...151